Scott, Foresman Mathematics

L. Carey Bolster
Supervisor of Mathematics
Baltimore County Public Schools
Towson, Maryland

E. Glenadine Gibb
Professor of Mathematics Education
The University of Texas at Austin
Austin, Texas

Robert Y. Hamada
Instructional Specialist, Mathematics
Los Angeles Unified School District
Los Angeles, California

Viggo P. Hansen
Professor, Mathematics Education
California State University
Northridge, California

Joan E. Kirkpatrick
Professor, Elementary Education
University of Alberta
Edmonton, Alberta, Canada

Charles R. McNerney
Professor of Mathematics
University of Northern Colorado
Greeley, Colorado

David F. Robitaille
Professor of Mathematics Education
University of British Columbia
Vancouver, British Columbia, Canada

Harold C. Trimble
Professor of Education, Emeritus
The Ohio State University
Columbus, Ohio

Irvin E. Vance
Associate Professor of Mathematics
New Mexico State University
Las Cruces, New Mexico

Ray Walch
Teacher of Mathematics
Florida Institute of Technology
Jensen Beach, Florida

Robert J. Wisner
Professor of Mathematics
New Mexico State University
Las Cruces, New Mexico

Scott, Foresman and Company
Editorial Offices: Glenview, Illinois

Regional Offices: Palo Alto, California •
Tucker, Georgia • Glenview, Illinois •
Oakland, New Jersey • Dallas, Texas

Consultants, Grades 1–8

Linda Cox
Coordinator, Special Education
Seattle Public School
Seattle, Washington

Jane Gawronski
Director
Department of Education
San Diego County
San Diego, California

Alejandro Gonzalez
Chairman, Mathematics Department
Gay Junior High School
Harlingen, Texas

Harriet Haynes
Mathematics Staff Developer
School District 19
Brooklyn, New York

William Nibbelink
Professor of Early Childhood
and Elementary Education
University of Iowa
Iowa City, Iowa

Thomas Pagan
Executive Director
William E. Wilson Education Center
Jeffersonville, Indiana

Glenn Prigge
Professor of Mathematics
University of North Dakota
Grand Forks, North Dakota

Sidney Sharron
Supervisor in the Educational
Media and Resources Branch
Los Angeles Unified School District
Los Angeles, California

Advisors, Grade 8

Calvin Woods
Teacher
Cherry Hill, New Jersey

Glenn Allinger
Parent
Bozeman, Montana

Acknowledgments

For permission to reproduce indicated information on the following pages, acknowledgment is made to:

Information in Example A on 4 and in table on 5 from Forest Service, United States Agriculture Department, 1970. Puzzle on 159 from Puzzle 22 from THE MOSCOW PUZZLES by Boris Kordemsky, p. 8. Used by permission of Charles Scribner's Sons from THE MOSCOW PUZZLES by Boris A. Kordemsky. Copyright © 1971, 1972 by Charles Scribner's Sons. Puzzle on 183 from Problem 78 from THE MOSCOW PUZZLES by Boris A. Kordemsky. Used by permission of Charles Scribner's Sons from THE MOSCOW PUZZLES by Boris A. Kordemsky. Copyright © 1971, 1972 by Charles Scribner's Sons. Model for sketch of "Tomb of Tutankhamen" on 224 from TREASURES OF TUTANKHAMUN, edited by K. S. Gilbert with J. K. Holt and S. Hudson, drawings by P. Johnson. Published by The Metropolitan Museum of Art, 1976. Information on 225 from Mildrid Masin Pace. WRAPPED FOR ETERNITY: THE STORY OF THE EGYPTIAN MUMMY. McGraw-Hill Book Company, 1974, and THE WORLD BOOK ENCYCLOPEDIA, Vol. 19, p. 430. World Book-Childcraft International, Inc., 1979. Information in table on 247 from "Letter and Percent Frequency Chart" from p. 402 of MATHEMATICS: A HUMAN ENDEAVOR by Harold R. Jacobs. Copyright © 1970 by W. H. Freeman and Company. Reprinted by permission. Information in table on 334 from "Salaries of Athletes," THE WORLD ALMANAC & BOOK OF FACTS, 1979 edition. Copyright © Newspaper Enterprise Association, Inc., New York, N.Y., 1978. Reprinted by permission. Information in table on 336 from "Maximum Recorded Life Span of 94 Animals" from Philip L. Altman and D. S. Dittner, eds., THE BIOLOGY DATA BOOK, Federation of American Societies for Experimental Biology, 1972. Cited in *The Book of Lists* by David Wallenchinsky, Irving Wallace, and Amy Wallace, William Morrow & Company, 1977, p. 133, 134.

Acknowledgments for photographs appear on page 401.

ISBN: 0-673-20218-6

Unit 1

Unit 2

Unit 3

Unit 4

Unit 5

Unit 6

Unit 1

Chapter 1   Whole Numbers

Exponents and Expanded Form

A. An *exponent* tells how many times a number is used as a factor.

$$10^2 = 10 \times 10 = 100$$

10^2 is read "ten to the second power" or "ten squared."

■ *The first power of any whole number is that whole number.* $10^1 = 10$

■ *The zero power of any whole number, except 0, is 1.* $10^0 = 1$

B. $2^3 = 2 \times 2 \times 2 = 8$

2^3 is read "two to the third power" or "two cubed."

C. The Oakland A's total attendance for one season was 527,007 people.

You can use a place-value chart to help you write this number in *expanded form.*

billions period			millions period			thousands period			ones period		
hundred-billions 100,000,000,000	ten-billions 10,000,000,000	billions 1,000,000,000	hundred-millions 100,000,000	ten-millions 10,000,000	millions 1,000,000	hundred-thousands 100,000	ten-thousands 10,000	thousands 1000	hundreds 100	tens 10	ones 1
10^{11}	10^{10}	10^9	10^8	10^7	10^6	10^5	10^4	10^3	10^2	10^1	10^0
						5	2	7	0	0	7

527,007 *standard form*

500,000 + 20,000 + 7000 + 7 *expanded form*

$(5 \times 10^5) + (2 \times 10^4) + (7 \times 10^3) + (7 \times 10^0)$ *expanded form with exponents*

Write in standard form.

1. 10^4 2. 10^9 3. 10^3 4. 10^5 5. 10^7 6. 10^2 7. 10^6 8. 10^1

9. 7^2 10. 6^2 11. 5^3 12. 4^3 13. 6^4 14. 8^3 15. 3^4 16. 2^6

Write using exponents.

17. $10 \times 10 \times 10$ 18. $10 \times 10 \times 10 \times 10$ 19. 10×10 20. 10

21. 6×6 22. $2 \times 2 \times 2 \times 2$ 23. 3 24. $5 \times 5 \times 5$

Find each missing number.

25. $10^{\blacksquare} = 100$ 26. $10^{\blacksquare} = 10,000$ 27. $10^{\blacksquare} = 100,000$ 28. $10^{\blacksquare} = 1000$

29. $3^{\blacksquare} = 9$ 30. $7^{\blacksquare} = 49$ 31. $\blacksquare^3 = 27$ 32. $\blacksquare^3 = 125$

The total attendance for a season is given.
Write each number in expanded form with exponents.

33. Mets   1,007,328   34. Reds   2,532,497   35. Cubs   1,525,311

Write in standard form.

36. 245 million   37. 8 billion   38. 17 billion, 470 million

To the left of the billions period is the trillions period.
Write each number in standard form.

39. 345 trillion, 82 billion   40. 54 trillion, 6 billion

Rounding Whole Numbers

A. There are 3,049,500 square kilometers of forest land in the United States. Round this number to the nearest million.

3,049,500   3,049,500 is between 3,000,000 and 4,000,000. It is closer to 3,000,000 because the digit to the right of the millions place is less than 5.

3,000,000   3,049,500 rounds to 3,000,000.

B. Round 37,192 to the nearest ten-thousand.

37,192   37,192 is between 30,000 and 40,000. It is closer to 40,000 because the digit to the right of the ten-thousands place is greater than 5.

40,000   37,192 rounds to 40,000.

C. Round 17,512 to the nearest thousand.

17,512   17,512 is between 17,000 and 18,000. Since the digit to the right of the thousands place is 5, round to the higher thousand.

18,000   17,512 rounds to 18,000.

■ *When rounding, locate the digit in the place to which you are rounding. Then*
  a. increase this digit by one if the next digit to the right is 5 or greater.
  b. leave this digit the same if the next digit to the right is less than 5.

Round to the nearest ten.

1. 356   **2.** 1882   **3.** 3598   **4.** 4097   **5.** 15,470   **6.** 36,650   **7.** 57,435

Round to the nearest hundred.

8. 1476   **9.** 31,663   **10.** 74,850   **11.** 41,972   **12.** 32,964   **13.** 46,651

Round to the nearest ten-thousand.

14. 231,000   **15.** 541,675   **16.** 112,982   **17.** 597,861   **18.** 395,312

Round to the nearest million.

19. 8,231,000   **20.** 13,567,000   **21.** 329,618,161   **22.** 69,904,329

The table gives the approximate number of square kilometers of forest land in regions of the United States. Complete the table.

Region	Forest land	Round to the nearest			
		hundred-thousand	ten-thousand	thousand	hundred
New England States	135,310	**23.**	**24.**	**25.**	**26.**
Mid-Atlantic States	215,500	**27.**	**28.**	**29.**	**30.**
Lake States	218,530	**31.**	**32.**	**33.**	**34.**
Central States	186,010	**35.**	**36.**	**37.**	**38.**
Southern States	858,150	**39.**	**40.**	**41.**	**42.**
Pacific States	878,550	**43.**	**44.**	**45.**	**46.**
Mountain States	559,850	**47.**	**48.**	**49.**	**50.**

*51. What is the greatest number that you can round to 130,000 when rounding to the nearest ten-thousand? What is the least number?

Estimating Sums and Differences

A. The population of the city of Chicago is about 3,074,000. The population of the surrounding suburban area is about 3,919,100. Estimate the population of the entire metropolitan area.

3,074,000 + 3,919,100

3,000,000 + 4,000,000 = 7,000,000   Round each number so you can add mentally.

3,074,000 + 3,919,100 ≈ 7,000,000   ≈ means "is approximately equal to."

The population of the entire Chicago metropolitan area is about 7,000,000.

B. Estimate 9152 − 6804.

9152 − 6804

9000 − 7000 = 2000   Round each number so you can subtract mentally.

9152 − 6804 ≈ 2000

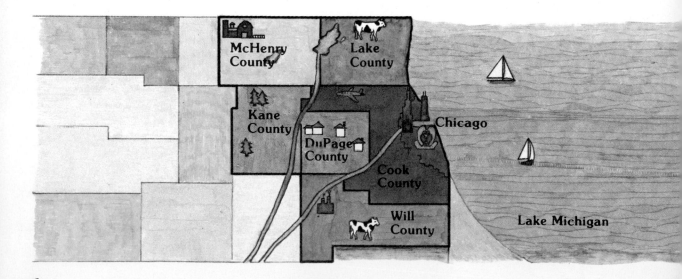

Estimate each sum or difference.

1. $145 + 781$
2. $356 + 404$
3. $711 - 232$
4. $524 - 379$
5. $326 + 475$
6. $851 + 629$
7. $958 - 407$
8. $539 - 285$
9. $710 - 230$
10. $640 - 210$
11. $7215 + 2134$
12. $5501 + 4099$
13. $8910 - 3651$
14. $6130 - 1998$
15. $6200 + 7810$
16. $8900 + 2560$
17. $17,234 + 72,541$
18. $36,215 + 52,179$
19. $23,400 - 11,095$
20. $47,800 - 23,105$
21. $308,744 + 409,321$
22. $269,112 + 852,615$
23. $714,618 - 326,502$
24. $589,214 - 251,463$
*25. $36,853 + 61,391 + 45,610$

26. The population of St. Paul is about 272,000. The population of Minneapolis is about 372,000. Estimate the total population of these twin cities.

Keeping Skillful

In one minute, write the answers to as many of these exercises as you can.

1. 9×3
2. 4×8
3. 6×7
4. 6×4
5. 7×9
6. 3×8
7. 8×7
8. 5×6
9. 6×3
10. 9×9
11. 5×8
12. 2×7
13. 9×4
14. 7×3
15. 5×5
16. 7×7
17. 9×6
18. 8×9
19. 3×9
20. 7×6
21. 6×9
22. 7×5
23. 9×8
24. 4×7
25. 8×8
26. 5×9
27. 6×6
28. 4×9
29. 9×7
30. 8×6

In one minute, write the answers to as many of these exercises as you can.

31. $64 \div 8$
32. $30 \div 6$
33. $42 \div 7$
34. $63 \div 9$
35. $48 \div 6$
36. $48 \div 8$
37. $36 \div 4$
38. $49 \div 7$
39. $72 \div 9$
40. $63 \div 7$
41. $36 \div 9$
42. $24 \div 3$
43. $28 \div 4$
44. $35 \div 7$
45. $81 \div 9$
46. $56 \div 8$
47. $54 \div 6$
48. $32 \div 8$
49. $18 \div 3$
50. $27 \div 9$
51. $42 \div 6$
52. $45 \div 9$
53. $40 \div 8$
54. $27 \div 3$
55. $56 \div 7$
56. $72 \div 8$
57. $36 \div 6$
58. $28 \div 7$
59. $54 \div 9$
60. $25 \div 5$

Adding and Subtracting Whole Numbers

The three most popular breeds of dogs registered with a kennel club are poodle, cocker spaniel, and Irish setter. The number of each breed registered with the club is given at the right.

Poodle	132,486
Cocker spaniel	86,408
Irish setter	74,276

A. What is the total number of registered poodles, cocker spaniels, and Irish setters?

Find $132,486 + 86,408 + 74,276$.

$$
\begin{array}{r}
1\;1\;\;1\;2 \\
132,486 \\
86,408 \\
+\;\;74,276 \\
\hline
293,170
\end{array}
$$

Add each column, beginning with the ones column.

The total is 293,170 dogs.

B. How many more cocker spaniels are registered than Irish setters?

Find $86,408 - 74,276$.

$$
\begin{array}{r}
3\;10 \\
86,\!408 \\
-\;74,276 \\
\hline
12,132
\end{array}
$$

Subtract each column, beginning with the ones column.

There are 12,132 more cocker spaniels registered.

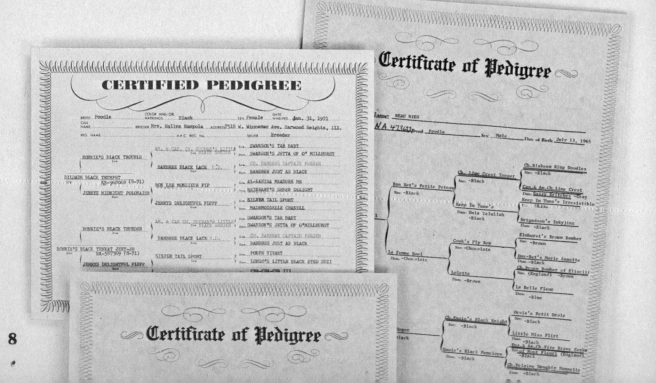

Add.

1. 218
  + 395

2. 756
  + 142

3. 3982
  + 6879

4. 8625
  + 4786

5. 21,278
  + 69,014

6. 738
  47
  + 300

7. 267
  1550
  + 60

8. 1296
  5
  + 984

9. 7
  851
  + 5177

10. 17,256
  38
  + 1,459

11. 907 + 83 + 46 + 430

12. 45 + 28 + 715 + 390

13. 153,789 + 68,214

14. 205,817 + 39,153

15. 52,345 + 837 + 7439

16. 3875 + 352 + 43,824

Subtract.

17. 745
  − 559

18. 618
  − 329

19. 2457
  − 1628

20. 6554
  − 4629

21. 2300
  − 1711

22. 4200
  − 3375

23. 4039
  − 975

24. 3205
  − 1689

25. 37,819
  − 14,301

26. 51,987
  − 26,781

27. 7235 − 5876

28. 5072 − 2438

29. 10,504 − 8219

30. 11,845 − 9243

31. 37,002 − 15,109

32. 61,005 − 26,026

33. 63,630 − 495

34. 81,930 − 756

35. 75,895 − 1774

36. The kennel club registered 15,231 Boston terriers, 32,501 Yorkshire terriers, and 989 bull terriers. Find the total number of terriers registered.

37. There are 29,681 golden retrievers registered and 7328 fewer collies registered. How many collies are registered?

More practice
Set 1, page 402

Estimating Products

A. Marie is estimating the number of entries in a telephone book. She counted 423 names on one page. There are 762 pages in the telephone book.

Estimate 762 × 423.

762 × 423 Round each number so you can multiply mentally.

800 × 400 = 320,000

762 × 423 ≈ 320,000

There are approximately 320,000 names in the telephone book.

B. Estimate 4572 × 3217.

4572 × 3217

5000 × 3000 = 15,000,000

4572 × 3217 ≈ 15,000,000

C. Estimate 385 × 2147.

385 × 2147

400 × 2000 = 800,000

385 × 2147 ≈ 800,000

Estimate each product.

1. 379×413 2. 824×563 3. 283×775 4. 310×525

5. 736×209 6. 597×166 7. 110×382 8. 679×103

9. 467×552 10. 712×803 11. 2734×4269 12. 3156×4875

13. 9043×2316 14. 2337×9281 15. 7902×2504 16. 5520×4733

17. 7603×4995 18. 3864×3917 19. 2560×6410 20. 3580×8210

Side Trip

Large Numbers

The place at the right in each period has the same name as the period. The names of the periods after billions are listed in order in the exercises. Follow the pattern to give the power of ten for the place with the same name.

billions period			millions period			thousands period			ones period		
hundred-billions	ten-billions	billions	hundred-millions	ten-millions	millions	hundred-thousands	ten-thousands	thousands	hundreds	tens	ones
10^{11}	10^{10}	10^9	10^8	10^7	10^6	10^5	10^4	10^3	10^2	10^1	10^0

1. trillions 10^{12} 2. quadrillions 10 3. quintillions

4. sextillions   5. septillions   6. octillions

7. nonillions   8. decillions   9. undecillions

10. duodecillions   11. tredecillions   12. quattuordecillions

13. quindecillions   14. sexdecillions   15. septendecillions

16. octodecillions   17. novemdecillions   18. vigintillions

19. Write 45 tredecillions in standard form.

Multiplying Whole Numbers

A. It takes 36 hours to fill a pool. Water flows into the pool at a rate of 3275 liters per hour. How many liters of water does the pool hold?

Find 36 × 3275.

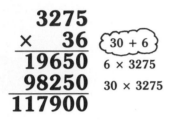

$$
\begin{array}{r}
3275 \\
\times\ \ \ \ 36 \\
\hline
19650 \\
98250 \\
\hline
117900
\end{array}
$$

30 + 6

6 × 3275

30 × 3275

The pool holds 117,900 liters of water.

B. Find 329 × 874.

$$
\begin{array}{r}
874 \\
\times 329 \\
\hline
7866 \\
17480 \\
262200 \\
\hline
287546
\end{array}
$$

9 × 874

20 × 874

300 × 874

C. Find 38 × 46 × 50.

Multiply two of the numbers. Then multiply their product by the third number.

$$
\begin{array}{r}
46 \\
\times 38 \\
\hline
368 \\
1380 \\
\hline
1748
\end{array}
\qquad
\begin{array}{r}
1748 \\
\times\ \ \ \ 50 \\
\hline
87400
\end{array}
$$

Multiply.

1. 40
   × 9

2. 70
   × 8

3. 39
   × 6

4. 57
   × 7

5. 320
   × 9

6. 540
   × 6

7. 913
   × 4

8. 731
   × 5

9. 60
   × 40

10. 90
    × 30

11. 34
    × 70

12. 48
    × 50

13. 82
    × 24

14. 63
    × 32

15. 95
    × 46

16. 48
    × 35

17. 347
    × 65

18. 696
    × 78

19. 300 × 5
20. 4 × 800
21. 50 × 410
22. 720 × 30

23. 604 × 60
24. 908 × 40
25. 125 × 60
26. 40 × 275

27. 876 × 48
28. 793 × 25
29. 432 × 800
30. 391 × 700

31. 257 × 210
32. 335 × 140
33. 342 × 279
34. 678 × 237

35. 804 × 58
36. 56 × 307
37. 3873 × 27
38. 7234 × 46

39. 23 × 49 × 56
40. 82 × 79 × 48
41. 27 × 10 × 59

42. A pump empties a pool at a rate of 180 liters of
    water per minute. How many liters can be pumped
    out of the pool in 9 hours? (1 hour = 60 minutes)

43. A large pool is filled at the rate of 66,900 liters
    per hour. It takes 30 hours to fill the pool. How
    many liters of water does the pool hold?

Multiply. When are the two products equal?

*44. 26 × 31
     62 × 13

*45. 23 × 64
     32 × 46

*46. 93 × 13
     39 × 31

*47. 25 × 74
     52 × 47

*48. 58 × 73
     85 × 37

*49. 86 × 34
     68 × 43

*50. 14 × 82
     41 × 28

*51. 45 × 21
     54 × 12

More practice
Set 2, page 402

13

Order of Operations:
Addition, Subtraction, and Multiplication

Parentheses can be used to indicate operations that are to be done first.

A. Evaluate $24 - (6 + 4)$.

$24 - (6 + 4)$

$24 - 10$ First add $6 + 4$.

14 Then subtract.

Parentheses can also be used to indicate multiplication.

6×8 can be written $6(8)$, or $(6)(8)$, or $(6)8$.

$4 \times (6 + 7)$ can be written $4(6 + 7)$.

B. Evaluate $34 - 16 - 2(4)$.

$34 - 16 - 2(4)$

$34 - 16 - 8$ First multiply $2(4)$.

$18 - 8$ Then subtract in order from left to right.

10

■ *To compute in standard order:*
  First do multiplications from left to right.
  Then do additions and subtractions from left to right.

If there are operations within parentheses, first do the operations within parentheses in standard order.
Then do the remaining operations in standard order.

C. Evaluate $27 + 5 - (19 - 6 + 8)$.

$27 + 5 - (19 - 6 + 8)$

$27 + 5 - (13 + 8)$

$27 + 5 - 21$ First do the operations within parentheses in standard order.

$32 - 21$ Do the remaining operations in standard order.

11

D. Evaluate $3(4 + 5) - 2(8 - 3)$.

$3(4 + 5) - 2(8 - 3)$

$3(9) - 2(5)$ First do the operations within the parentheses.

$27 - 10$ Do the remaining operations in standard order.

17

Evaluate.

1. $10 - (4 + 3)$ 2. $5 + (8 + 6)$ 3. $(2 + 6) + 5$

4. $(8 + 1) - 3$ 5. $15 - (9 - 6)$ 6. $12 - (5 - 2)$

7. $(72 - 48) + 36$ 8. $(69 - 32) + 27$ 9. $24 - (38 - 29)$

10. $39 - (13 + 6)$ 11. $7(11 - 9)$ 12. $6(5 + 3)$

13. $8(3 + 6)$ 14. $5(14 - 7)$ 15. $13(24) - 52$

16. $6(12) + 24$ 17. $9(16) + 12$ 18. $32(15) - 96$

19. $61 - 5(13 - 1)$ 20. $24 + 4(7 - 2)$ 21. $53 + 8(5 + 6)$

22. $67 - 3(4 + 9)$ 23. $8(7 + 3) - 46$ 24. $6(3 + 8)$

25. $(56 + 9) - (36 + 20)$ 26. $(73 + 59) + (38 - 18)$

27. $(81 - 13) - (42 + 7)$ 28. $(98 - 35) - (64 - 47)$

29. $(28 + 35) + 6(39 - 17)$ 30. $(32 - 18) + 5(24 - 8)$

31. $5(28 - 13) + 4(75 - 37)$ 32. $2(14 + 35) + 3(56 - 18)$

Insert parentheses and signs of operation to make each sentence true.

*33. $6 \quad 7 \quad 9 = 96$ *34. $9 \quad 4 \quad 4 \quad 22 = 50$

*35. $6 \quad 9 \quad 2 \quad 7 = 40$ *36. $5 \quad 18 \quad 9 \quad 42 = 3$

Time Out

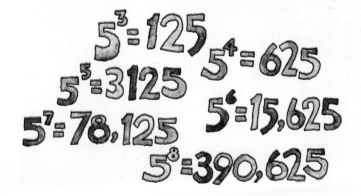

$5^3 = 125$
$5^4 = 625$
$5^5 = 3125$
$5^6 = 15,625$
$5^7 = 78,125$
$5^8 = 390,625$

What are the last three digits of 5^{347} when written in standard form?

What are the last three digits of 5^{268} when written in standard form?

15

Dividing Whole Numbers

A. A field trip to the state capital costs $32 per student. If $2350 is budgeted for the trip, how many students can go? How much money will be left over?

Find 2350 ÷ 32.

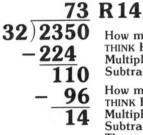

How many 32s in 235?
THINK How many 3s in 23? 7
Multiply. 7 × 32 = 224
Subtract and compare.

How many 32s in 110?
THINK How many 3s in 11? 3
Multiply. 3 × 32 = 96
Subtract and compare.
The remainder is 14.

73 students can go on the trip, and $14 will be left over.

Exact check

```
      73    Multiply the quotient
    × 32    and the divisor.
    ----
     146
    2190
    ----
    2336
  +   14    Add the remainder.
    ----     The result should be
    2350     the dividend.
```

Rough check

$$32 \times 73$$
$$\downarrow \quad \downarrow$$
$$30 \times 70 = 2100$$

Since 2100 is close to 2350, the answer 73 R14 is reasonable.

B. Find 2234 ÷ 27.

$$\begin{array}{r} 7 \\ 27\overline{)2234} \\ -189 \\ \hline 34 \end{array}$$

27 is close to 30.
THINK How many 3s in 22? *7*
34 > 27, so 7 is too small.
Try 8.

$$\begin{array}{r} 82 \text{ R}20 \\ 27\overline{)2234} \\ -216 \\ \hline 74 \\ -54 \\ \hline 20 \end{array}$$

THINK How many 3s in 7? *2*

C. Find 15,528 ÷ 33.

$$\begin{array}{r} 5 \\ 33\overline{)15528} \\ -165 \end{array}$$

THINK How many 3s in 15? *5*
165 > 155, so 5 is too big.
Try 4.

$$\begin{array}{r} 470 \text{ R}18 \\ 33\overline{)15528} \\ -132 \\ \hline 232 \\ -231 \\ \hline 18 \end{array}$$

THINK How many 3s in 23? *7*

THINK How many 3s in 1? *0*

Divide.

1. $8\overline{)427}$
2. $9\overline{)641}$
3. $5\overline{)785}$
4. $7\overline{)952}$

5. $5\overline{)2018}$
6. $8\overline{)1605}$
7. $3\overline{)2102}$
8. $4\overline{)3623}$

9. $32\overline{)679}$
10. $27\overline{)896}$
11. $63\overline{)5166}$
12. $92\overline{)5244}$

13. $91\overline{)23033}$
14. $74\overline{)17352}$
15. $37\overline{)14085}$
16. $68\overline{)51713}$

17. 8320 ÷ 49
18. 7790 ÷ 29
19. 43,968 ÷ 48

20. 33,670 ÷ 35
21. 533 ÷ 187
22. 958 ÷ 215

23. 13,894 ÷ 623
24. 19,754 ÷ 810
25. 118,663 ÷ 290

Find each missing number.

★26. $23\overline{)\rule{1.5cm}{0pt}}$ 107 R10

★27. $\rule{0.8cm}{0pt}\overline{)2450}$ 46 R12

★28. $3456\overline{)10506375}$ ▓ R ▓

29. The bus traveled 272 kilometers in 4 hours. How many kilometers per hour is this?

30. The bus rental was $1095. What was the cost for each of the 73 students?

More practice
Set 3, page 402

Problem Solving: Interpreting Remainders

Read the problem.
What facts are given?
What is the question?

READ **A.** There are 460 eighth graders enrolled in a computer course. Classes of 16 students are to be formed. How many classes are needed to include all the students?

What must you do
to solve the problem?

DECIDE Divide 460 by 16.

Do the work.

SOLVE

$$\begin{array}{r} 28 \text{ R}12 \\ 16\overline{)460} \end{array}$$

28 classes are not enough to include all the students. Another class is needed.

Read the question.
Give the answer.
Is the answer sensible?

ANSWER 29 classes are needed.

B. A carton of computer paper costs $54. How many cartons can be purchased with $900?

$$\begin{array}{r} 16 \text{ R}36 \\ 54\overline{)900} \end{array}$$

The quotient tells how many 54s in 900. Only the quotient is used in the answer.

16 cartons can be purchased.

C. How much money will be left after purchasing the paper described in example B?

$$\begin{array}{r} 16 \text{ R}36 \\ 54\overline{)900} \end{array}$$

The remainder tells how much money is left over. Only the remainder is used in the answer.

$36 will be left.

• *Discuss* Reword example A so that only the remainder is used in the answer.

18

Give each answer.

1. There are 1000 computer cards per box. How many 37-card programs can be written using one box of cards?

2. A computer prints 68 lines on a page. Marcia's program is 1596 lines long. How many lines will be printed on the last page?

3. A computer costs $8954. A school is paying for it at a rate of $175 per month. After how many months will the entire amount be paid?

4. A program the students are writing requires 48 storage locations. 4096 locations are available. How many of these programs can be written?

5. Another computer prints 54 lines on a page. Lupe's program is 1745 lines long. How many pages will be used to print it?

6. Each line on a video-display screen is 64 characters long. A display contains 19,672 characters. How many characters will be displayed on the last line?

7. An assignment requires 23 seconds of computer time. If 400 seconds are available, how many students can complete the assignment?

8. Each of the 460 students will be given a template of flow-chart symbols. The templates come in packages of 24. How many packages of templates need to be ordered?

*9. A school needs 600 boxes of computer cards. The cards are sold in cartons of 48 boxes. Each carton costs $75. Find the cost of the cards.

Order of Operations

In the standard order of operations, divisions are done before additions and subtractions. A bar can be used to indicate division.

$\dfrac{48}{6}$ means $48 \div 6$.

Evaluate $18 - \dfrac{2(7 + 5)}{3}$

$18 - \dfrac{2(7 + 5)}{3}$

$18 - \dfrac{2(12)}{3}$ Do the operation inside the parentheses.

$18 - \dfrac{24}{3}$ Then do the operation above the division bar.

$18 - 8$ Then divide.

10 Then subtract.

■ *To compute in standard order:*
First do multiplications and divisions from left to right. Then do additions and subtractions from left to right.

When parentheses and division bars are involved:

1. *Do operations within parentheses, using standard order.*
2. *Do operations above and below division bars, using standard order.*
3. *Do remaining operations, using standard order.*

Evaluate.

1. $\dfrac{36}{4}$

2. $\dfrac{54}{9}$

3. $\dfrac{8(3)}{12}$

4. $\dfrac{6(15)}{10}$

5. $\dfrac{16}{8}(7)$

6. $\dfrac{12}{4}(9)$

7. $\dfrac{11 + 9}{2}$

8. $\dfrac{15 - 3}{4}$

9. $\dfrac{64}{20 - 4}$

10. $\dfrac{45}{10 + 5}$

11. $\dfrac{75}{3(5)} - 4$

12. $\dfrac{9(8)}{12} - 1$

13. $5 + \dfrac{7(10)}{35}$

14. $9 + \dfrac{72}{6(3)}$

15. $\dfrac{8(4)}{2(8)}$

16. $\dfrac{5(9)}{3(5)}$

17. $9 + \dfrac{40 - 30}{2}$

18. $\dfrac{25 - 4}{3} - 2$

19. $\dfrac{92}{4} - \dfrac{52}{1 + 3}$

20. $\dfrac{72}{9} - \dfrac{21 + 3}{4}$

21. $\dfrac{4(9)}{3(2)} + \dfrac{10(7)}{2(5)}$

22. $\dfrac{12(5)}{3(2)} - \dfrac{4(6)}{8}$

23. $\dfrac{8(2 + 9)}{4}$

24. $\dfrac{7(9 + 3)}{6}$

25. $\dfrac{5(2 + 4 - 3)}{7 - 4}$

26. $\dfrac{6(8 - 5 + 2)}{7 + 8}$

27. $\dfrac{(7 + 8)4}{8 + 2}$

28. $\dfrac{(8 + 6)6}{9 + 3}$

Insert parentheses and signs of operations to make each sentence true.

★29. $\dfrac{5 \quad 8}{2} = 20$

★30. $\dfrac{2 \quad 5 \quad 3}{4} = 1$

★31. $\dfrac{12 \quad 3 \quad 1}{4 \quad 2} = 12$

Side Trip/Calculator

Number Patterns

Use your calculator and the rules for order of operations to compute.

1. $\dfrac{(22)(22)}{1 + 2 + 1}$

2. $\dfrac{(333)(333)}{1 + 2 + 3 + 2 + 1}$

3. $\dfrac{(4444)(4444)}{1 + 2 + 3 + 4 + 3 + 2 + 1}$

4. Use the pattern in exercises 1–3 to write the next two expressions in this pattern.

Evaluate. Use your calculator until you see a pattern.

5. $0(9) + 1$

6. $1(9) + 2$

7. $12(9) + 3$

8. $123(9) + 4$

9. $1234(9) + 5$

10. $12345(9) + 6$

11. $123456(9) + 7$

12. $1234567(9) + 8$

13. $12345678(9) + 9$

21

Bacteriologist

Bacteriologist Patricia Spooner experiments to find new ways of using good bacteria and effective ways of fighting harmful bacteria.

A bacterium is a one-celled plant. The number of bacteria increases when the single cell splits forming two one-celled plants. Thus, one bacterium splits to form two bacteria, these two split to form four, and so on. Notice that the bacteria count can be written as a power of 2.

Bacteria Count

$1 = 2^0$

$2 = 2^1$ **First split**

$4 = 2^2$ **Second split**

$8 = 2^3$ **Third split**

$16 = 2^4$ **Fourth split**

Mrs. Spooner is studying a certain bacterium that splits every hour. If one bacterium is present at time 0, how many are present after

1. 6 hours?   2. 12 hours?

3. 18 hours?   4. 24 hours?

5. If 500 bacteria are present at the beginning of an experiment, and they double every 3 hours, what will the count be after 24 hours?

6. Suppose a certain bacterium splits every 30 minutes. If one bacterium is present at time 0, after how many hours will the count be greater than 3 million?

Chapter 1 Test
Whole Numbers, pages 2–22

1. Write 3^4 in standard form.

2. Write $7 \times 7 \times 7$ using exponents.

3. Write 32,704 in expanded form with exponents.

4. Round 865 to the nearest ten.

5. Round 6872 to the nearest thousand.

6. Round 93,134 to the nearest ten-thousand.

Estimate each sum or difference.

7. $5861 + 8246$

8. $8073 - 4911$

Add.

9. $\begin{array}{r} 7856 \\ + 8279 \\ \hline \end{array}$

10. $\begin{array}{r} 384 \\ 6259 \\ + 930 \\ \hline \end{array}$

Subtract.

11. $\begin{array}{r} 3654 \\ - 2971 \\ \hline \end{array}$

12. $\begin{array}{r} 3020 \\ - 1856 \\ \hline \end{array}$

Estimate each product.

13. 821×685

14. 7218×6115

Multiply.

15. $\begin{array}{r} 43 \\ \times\ 8 \\ \hline \end{array}$

16. $\begin{array}{r} 568 \\ \times\ 20 \\ \hline \end{array}$

17. $\begin{array}{r} 457 \\ \times\ 91 \\ \hline \end{array}$

Divide.

18. $6\overline{)851}$

19. $23\overline{)4136}$

20. $37\overline{)8692}$

21. $54\overline{)7751}$

Evaluate.

22. $16 - (6 + 2)$

23. $(6 + 4)(5 + 3)$

24. $29 - 4(8 - 2)$

25. $24 - \dfrac{4 + 8}{2}$

26. $\dfrac{38 + 6}{4 + 7}$

27. Boxes of pencils are packed in cartons. Each carton holds 72 boxes. How many cartons will 2500 boxes fill?

28. Judith is purchasing paper cups for a school picnic. 1785 people will attend the picnic. There are 36 cups per package. How many packages should she buy?

Chapter 2 Decimals

Reading and Writing Decimals

Scientists give the weight of atoms in atomic weight units. A small paper clip weighs about 300 billion trillion atomic weight units. An atom of a type of carbon weighs about 12.01115 atomic weight units. Scientists say the atomic weight of this type of carbon is 12.01115.

millions	hundred-thousands	ten-thousands	thousands	hundreds	tens	ones	tenths	hundredths	thousandths	ten-thousandths	hundred-thousandths	millionths
					1	2	0	1	1	1	5	

12.01115

twelve and one thousand one hundred fifteen hundred-thousandths

The digit in the hundred-thousandths place is 5. The value of the 5 is *5 hundred-thousandths.*

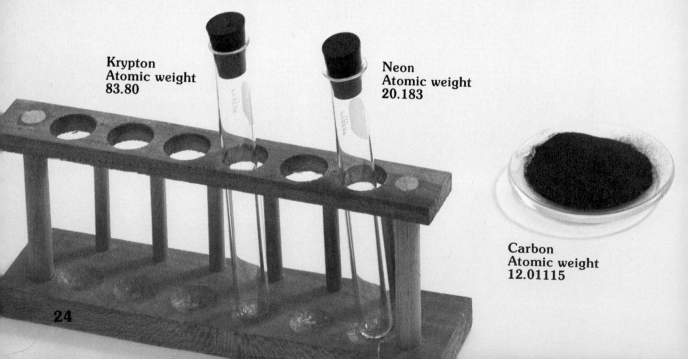

Krypton
Atomic weight
83.80

Neon
Atomic weight
20.183

Carbon
Atomic weight
12.01115

Use the information in the picture. What is the
value of the 8 in each atomic weight?

1. Manganese   2. Aluminum   3. Cobalt   4. Neon

Write a seven-digit number

5. with 0 in the ten-thousandths place.   6. with 3 in the hundredths place.

7. with 5 in the millionths place.   8. with 1 in the ones place.

Write the atomic weight of each element in words.

9. Manganese   10. Krypton   11. Cobalt   12. Aluminum

Write the decimal.

13. sixty-five hundredths   14. four and sixteen thousandths

15. ninety-seven thousandths   16. thirty-five and four hundredths

17. five thousand four hundred   18. eight and seven hundred-thousandths
    and three tenths

Sometimes very large numbers are written with digits
and words. Write these numbers with digits only.

*19. 2.6 million   *20. 300 billion trillion

*21. 4.5 billion trillion   *22. 5.7 trillion trillion

Manganese
Atomic weight
54.9380

Aluminum
Atomic weight
26.9815

Cobalt
Atomic weight
58.9332

Comparing and Ordering Decimals

A. Which space vehicle is longer, Intelsat 4A or Pioneer Venus?

Space vehicle	Length (meters)
Sakura	3.51
Fleetsatcom	1.27
ISS B	0.82
Nav Star 1	1.83
Intelsat 4A	2.82
GOES 3	2.69
Pioneer Venus	2.9

Compare 2.82 and 2.9.

2.82 ● 2.9   The ones are the same.

2.82 ● 2.9   Compare the tenths. 8 tenths is less than 9 tenths.

2.82 < 2.9   2.82 is less than 2.9.

Pioneer Venus is longer than Intelsat 4A.

B. Compare 0.7 and 0.70.

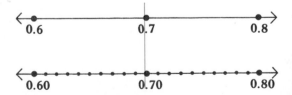

Decimals that name the same number are *equal decimals.*

0.7 = 0.70

C. Compare 0.546 and 0.54.

0.546 ● 0.54

0.546 ● 0.540 $0.54 = 0.540$

0.546 > 0.540   546 thousandths is greater than 540 thousandths.

0.546 > 0.54

D. List these numbers in order from the least to the greatest.

6.37   6.423   6.42

6.37   6.42   6.423 $6.37 < 6.42$
$6.42 < 6.423$

Write an equal decimal in hundredths.

1. 0.5   **2.** 7.4   **3.** 4.760   **4.** 1.700   **5.** 64.9   **6.** 45.8600   **7.** 16

Write an equal decimal in thousandths.

8. 5.92   **9.** 27   **10.** 4.6370   **11.** 2.84   **12.** 7320   **13.** 46.6230   **14.** 5.8

Compare these decimals. Use >, <, or =.

15. 0.43 ● 0.44   **16.** 0.6378 ● 0.63781   **17.** 0.61115 ● 0.611

18. 0.56 ● 0.560   **19.** 0.2468 ● 0.2469   **20.** 5.31 ● 5.39

21. 0.23581 ● 0.2358   **22.** 74.36 ● 74.360   **23.** 17.395 ● 17.399

List these decimals in order from the least to the greatest.

24. 5.81   9.53   5.18   **25.** 0.135   0.261   0.134

26. 0.241   0.50   0.501   0.362   **27.** 3.418   3.836   3.241   3.369

28. List the space vehicles in the table on page 26 in order from the shortest to the longest.

*29. Write the greatest number possible with five different digits and a 7 in the ten-thousandths place.

**More practice
Set 4, page 403**

Time Out

If 2 monkeys eat 2 bunches of bananas in 2 days, how many bunches of bananas will 20 monkeys eat in 20 days? (The answer is *not* 20!)

Rounding Decimals

A. One of the largest true jellyfish had tentacles that stretched about 36.57 meters. Round this number to the nearest tenth.

36.57 36.57 is between 36.5 and 36.6. It is closer to 36.6 because the digit to the right of the tenths place is greater than 5.

36.6 36.57 rounds to 36.6.

B. Round 2.36243 to the nearest thousandth.

2.36243 2.36243 is between 2.362 and 2.363. It is closer to 2.362 because the digit to the right of the thousandths place is less than 5.

2.362 2.36243 rounds to 2.362.

C. Round 14.84365 to the nearest ten-thousandth.

14.84365 14.84365 is between 14.8436 and 14.8437. Since the digit to the right of the ten-thousandths place is 5, round to the higher ten-thousandth.

14.8437 14.84365 rounds to 14.8437.

D. Round 6.095 to the nearest tenth.

6.095

6.1

E. Round 1.997 to the nearest hundredth.

1.997

2.00

Round to the nearest one.

1. 6.432   2. 4.489   3. 59.58   4. 32.67
5. 0.719   6. 0.916   7. 7.239   8. 3.119
9. 5.873   10. 2.978   11. 73.05   12. 58.04

Round to the nearest hundredth.

13. 2.155   14. 3.345   15. 9.002   16. 6.249
17. 0.728   18. 0.814   19. 0.993   20. 0.998
21. 9.061   22. 6.004   23. 2.564   24. 1.006

Round to the nearest thousandth.

25. 200.0051   26. 73.5724   27. 0.7358
28. 18.0366   29. 2.0053   30. 8.0095
31. 0.78251   32. 0.33648   33. 0.4359

Round to the nearest ten-thousandth.

34. 48.981756   35. 324.671973   36. 8.48673
37. 3.88888   38. 7.32849   39. 10.232323
40. 0.978123   41. 53.99999   42. 0.545672

Round each measure to the nearest tenth.

43. Giant squid   8.23 m long
44. Sea anemone   0.763 m wide
45. Octopus   4.85 m long
46. Freshwater turtle   0.099 m wide
47. Giant snail   0.239 m long
48. Whale shark   12.89 m long

Estimating Sums and Differences

A. The Wilsons estimated the amount of their purchases at a lawn and garden center. They rounded each price to the nearest dollar and then added the rounded prices.

Trowel: $4.50 ⟶	**$ 5**
Grass seed: $3.27 ⟶	**3**
Hose: $15.89 ⟶	**16**
Rain gauge: $10.11 ⟶	**+ 10**
Estimated sum ⟶	**$34**

B. The Wilsons estimated the difference in prices of the sprinkler nozzle and the rotating sprinkler.

Rotating sprinkler: $24.38 →	**$24**
Sprinkler nozzle: $8.78 ⟶	**− 9**
Estimated difference →	**$15**

peat moss
$5.72

fertilizer
$1.13

grass seed
$3.27

clay pot
$3.49

garden rake
$15.89

rotating sprinkler
$24.38

leaf rake
$12.92

sprinkler nozzle
$8.78

hose
$15.89

Find the estimated sum. First round to the
nearest one and then add.

1. 3.69 + 2.8 + 8.05   2. 10.3 + 6.8 + 5.4   3. 9.3 + 1.5 + 3.6
4. 7.81 + 5.35 + 8.76   5. 9.19 + 10.20 + 6.83   6. 4.17 + 6.87 + 9.99

Find the estimated difference. First round to
the nearest one and then subtract.

7. 35.8 − 31.5   8. 48.6 − 47.1   9. 50.5 − 35.6   10. 44.1 − 37.3
11. 29.3 − 15.8   12. 50.3 − 41.0   13. 10.28 − 8.73   14. 12.8 − 4.5

Use the prices in the picture. Round to the
nearest dollar and estimate the sum.

15. Trowel, gloves, rain gauge, and
clay pot

16. Fertilizer, peat moss, leaf rake,
and grass seed

17. Grass seed, deluxe gloves, hose, and
garden rake

18. Clay pot, hose, leaf rake, and
fertilizer

Use the prices in the picture. Round to the
nearest dollar and estimate the difference.

19. Garden rake and rain gauge   20. Peat moss and fertilizer

21. Deluxe gloves and gloves   22. Garden rake and leaf rake

*23. The cost of a watering can, to the nearest dollar,
is $5. What is the least possible actual cost
of the watering can? What is the greatest
possible actual cost of the watering can?

trowel
$4.50

deluxe gloves
$4.19

gloves
$2.98

rain gauge
$10.11

Adding and Subtracting Decimals

A. During Hurricane Donna, large amounts of rain fell in the Miami, Florida, area. Use the listing below to find the total rainfall at Station 1 for September 9, 10, and 11.

Rainfall for Miami, Florida

Station	Sept. 9	Sept. 10	Sept. 11
1	3.82 cm	7.37 cm	2.18 cm
2	5.99 cm	17.45 cm	2.41 cm
3	0.28 cm	27.84 cm	2.36 cm

Find 3.82 + 7.37 + 2.18.

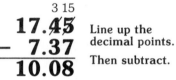

$$\begin{array}{r} \overset{1\ \ 1}{3.82} \\ 7.37 \\ +\,2.18 \\ \hline 13.37 \end{array}$$ Line up the decimal points. Then add.

The total rainfall at Station 1 was 13.37 cm.

B. How much more rain fell at Station 2 than at Station 1 on September 10?

Find 17.45 − 7.37.

$$\begin{array}{r} \overset{3\ 15}{17.4\cancel{5}} \\ -\ \ 7.37 \\ \hline 10.08 \end{array}$$ Line up the decimal points. Then subtract.

Station 2 had 10.08 cm more rain than Station 1 on September 10.

C. Find 54 − 38.27.

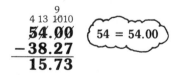

$$\begin{array}{r} \overset{\overset{9}{4\ 13\ 1010}}{5\cancel{4}.\cancel{0}\cancel{0}} \\ -\,38.27 \\ \hline 15.73 \end{array}$$ 54 = 54.00

Add or subtract.

1. 1.003
   $+ 5.379$

2. 3.31
   $- 2.697$

3. 8.3
   $+ 6.99$

4. 2.8
   $- 1.2$

5. 29.65
   $- 10.05$

6. 6.9
   $- 2.88$

7. 42.83
   $- 6.27$

8. 23.00
   $- 19.74$

9. 12.97
   $+ 28.00$

10. 11.1
    16.3
    $+ 0.2$

11. 1.008
    2.8
    $+ 4.53$

12. 3.6
    2.01
    $+ 4.73$

13. $2.00131 + 4.86 + 9 + 6.347$

14. $5.314 + 2.418 + 1.635 + 9.0001$

15. $2.9867 + 6.812 + 4 + 3.90856$

16. $25.0063 + 0.01605 + 4.0119 + 6.2$

17. $12.008 + 7.01 + 1.00639$

18. $6.1509 + 0.0051 + 0.9 + 7.48$

19. $23.79 - 13.01$

20. $5.316 - 2.211$

21. $0.89 - 0.2384$

22. $313.61 - 111.958$

23. $0.341 - 0.2709$

24. $0.3415 - 0.1762$

25. $408.29 - 219.7$

26. $0.8 - 0.6151$

27. $16 - 15.804$

Use the information on page 32 to answer these questions.

28. What was the total rainfall at Station 2 for September 9, 10, and 11?

29 What was the total rainfall at Station 3 for September 9, 10, and 11?

30. How much more rain fell at Station 3 than at Station 2 on September 10?

31. How much less rain fell at Station 1 than at Station 3 on September 11?

More practice
Set 5, page 403

Problem Solving: Too Much or Too Little Information

READ A. On Monday, Tuesday, and Wednesday, Cecilia Diaz collected $129.45, $118.30, and $146.75 in taxi fares. The total for the week was $729.45. What was the total amount of taxi fares Cecilia collected on Monday, Tuesday, and Wednesday?

DECIDE There is too much information given in the problem. To find the answer, you use only this information.

                                  Monday's fares
                           Tuesday's fares
                   Wednesday's fares

129.45 + 118.30 + 146.75

SOLVE

$$\begin{array}{r} 129.45 \\ 118.30 \\ +\ 146.75 \\ \hline 394.50 \end{array}$$

ANSWER Cecilia collected a total of $394.50 in fares on Monday, Tuesday, and Wednesday.

READ **B.** Cecilia charged a group of 5 passengers $10.50 for a trip from the airport to a hotel. How much change should she return to them?

DECIDE To find the answer, you need this information.

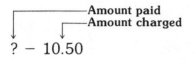

? − 10.50

The amount the passengers paid is not given in the problem. There is too little information for you to find the answer.

Find the answer to each problem that has enough information given. If there is not enough information given, write *too little information.*

1. One passenger required Cecilia to drive 52.29 km. The fare was $15.90. If the passenger paid the fare with a twenty-dollar bill, how much change should Cecilia have returned?

2. Cecilia pays $93.50 a year for license plates, $417.15 a year for insurance, and about $500 a year for mechanical maintenance of the taxi. What does she pay for license plates and insurance?

3. Cecilia paid cash for a set of 4 tires for the taxi and received $21.52 in change. What was the cost of the set of tires?

4. The taxi used 3987.6 L of fuel in June, 4261.2 L in July, and 3999.1 L in August. How many liters of fuel did the taxi use in July and August?

5. Cecilia's tips and fares for an 8-hour day totaled $153.86. How much did she earn in tips?

6. Cecilia bought a used, second taxi for $8099.97. This was $2122.51 more than the cost of her first taxi and $2500 less than the cost of a new taxi. What was the cost of her first taxi?

7. In one month, both taxis were driven 25,572.3 km. One taxi used 4008 L of fuel. How much fuel did the other taxi use?

8. In one week, Cecilia collected $237.89 in fares and $114.60 in tips. During the previous week, she collected $23.90 less in tips. How much did Cecilia collect in tips the previous week?

9. Cecilia drove 670.1 km on Monday. She drove 3216.7 km during that week and 2986.3 km the following week. How far did Cecilia drive during these two weeks?

Multiplying Decimals

A. Each of the 31 students in Ms. Futerer's woodworking class will be making a TV table. The top of each table will be a plank 0.7 m long. How much planking will the students need?

Find 31 × 0.7.

$$
\begin{array}{r}
\mathbf{0.7} \leftarrow \text{1 decimal place} \\
\underline{\times\ \mathbf{31}} \leftarrow \text{0 decimal places} \\
\mathbf{7} \\
\underline{\mathbf{21\ 0}} \\
\mathbf{21.7} \leftarrow \text{1 decimal place}
\end{array}
$$

The students will need 21.7 m of planking.

■ *To multiply decimals, multiply as with whole numbers. Then count the total number of decimal places in the factors. Show that many decimal places in the product.*

B. Find 6.1 × 0.54.

$$
\begin{array}{r}
\mathbf{0.54} \leftarrow \text{2 decimal places} \\
\underline{\times\ \ \mathbf{6.1}} \leftarrow \text{1 decimal place} \\
\mathbf{54} \\
\underline{\mathbf{3\ 240}} \\
\mathbf{3.294} \leftarrow \text{3 decimal places}
\end{array}
$$

C. Find 0.4 × 0.13.

$$
\begin{array}{r}
\mathbf{0.13} \\
\underline{\times\ \ \mathbf{0.4}} \\
\mathbf{0.052}
\end{array}
$$

Before you can show 3 decimal places in the product, you need to write an extra zero.

D. Find 7.6 × 14.25.

$$
\begin{array}{r}
\mathbf{14.25} \\
\underline{\times\ \ \ \ \mathbf{7.6}} \\
\mathbf{8\ 550} \\
\underline{\mathbf{99\ 750}} \\
\mathbf{108.300}, \text{ or } \mathbf{108.3}
\end{array}
$$

E. Study these examples.

$$3.729 \times 10 = 37.29$$ 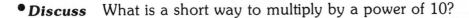 3.729

$$2.72 \times 1000 = 2720$$ 2.720

$$48 \times 100 = 4800$$ 48.00

• *Discuss*   What is a short way to multiply by a power of 10?

Multiply.

1. 41 $\times 0.02$	2. 33 $\times 0.03$	3. 59 $\times 0.06$	4. 37 $\times 0.05$	5. 0.021 $\times\ 0.06$

6. 0.033 $\times\ 0.03$	7. 0.0063 $\times 0.0005$	8. 0.041 $\times\ 0.04$	9. 0.0094 $\times 0.0008$	10. 16.42 $\times\ 0.05$

11. 6.3×0.9 12. 4.3×0.5 13. 3.2×0.06 14. 5.3×0.7

15. 9.1×0.8 16. 6.13×2.1 17. 5.17×6.4 18. 8.31×2.6

19. 0.06×4.3 20. 0.034×0.08 21. 16.2×6.03 22. 4.7×0.0006

23. 42.81×100 24. 9.02×1000 25. $5 \times 10,000$ 26. 23.6×1000

27 Find the cost of 21.7 m of planking priced at $1.05 per meter. Round your answer to the nearest cent.

Place a decimal point in the first factor to make a true number sentence.

*28. $68 \times 23.5 = 15.98$ *29. $2 \times 3 = 0.000006$ *30. $273 \times 0.4 = 1.092$

*31. $26 \times 7.3 = 18.98$ *32. $25 \times 63 = 157.5$ *33. $84 \times 6.382 = 536.088$

More practice
Set 6, page 403

Estimating Products

A. Randall Rosenquist, the manager of the school cafeteria, estimates the cost of food he purchases. If beef patties cost $0.34 each, about how much will 589 beef patties cost?

Estimate 589×0.34.

Round each factor so that only one digit is not zero. Then multiply.

$$589 \times 0.34$$

$$600 \times 0.3 = 180.0$$

$$589 \times 0.34 \approx 180$$

The cost will be about $180.

B. Estimate 0.23×4.95.

$$0.23 \times 4.95$$

$$0.2 \times 5 = 1.0$$

$$0.23 \times 4.95 \approx 1$$

C. Estimate 0.873×0.07.

$$0.873 \times 0.07$$

$$0.9 \times 0.07 = 0.063$$

$$0.873 \times 0.07 \approx 0.063$$

Select the correct answer in each row. Use estimation to help you.

1. 43 × 0.4   0.172   1.72   17.2
2. 283 × 0.8   226.4   22.64   2.264
3. 4.75 × 2.2   0.1045   10.45   104.5
4. 0.7 × 27.2   19.04   1.904   0.1904
5. 5.83 × 0.08   46.64   4.664   0.4664
6. 89.2 × 15.5   138.26   1382.6   13.826

Estimate each product.

7. 2.6 × 3.6   8. 4.4 × 5.6
9. 41 × 2.1   10. 0.738 × 7.3
11. 58 × 4.7   12. 0.521 × 2.8
13. 0.519 × 0.129   14. 721 × 0.62
15. 12.5 × 61.2   16. 0.288 × 215
17. 37.2 × 7.03   18. 0.41 × 0.46
19. 19.5 × 55.6   20. 0.38 × 0.25
21. 437.1 × 0.21   22. 1908 × 0.37
23. 0.00452 × 0.00918   24. 0.10063 × 0.285931

25. The school cafeteria uses 7.5 boxes of paper napkins each day. Each box costs $0.26. Estimate how much will be spent each day for paper napkins.

*26. Randall will order 973 cartons of milk. Each carton costs $0.083. Estimate how much the milk will cost.

Keeping Skillful

Add.

1. 496   2. 528
   + 273   + 481

3. 135   4. 742
    268   119
   + 489   + 357

Subtract.

5. 6187   6. 8147
   − 4055   − 2849

7. 6000   8. 4002
   − 4693   − 1684

Multiply.

9.   89   10. 957
   × 42   × 74

11. 385   12. 888
   × 69   × 97

13. 643   14. 278
   × 507   × 416

Divide.

15. 25,322 ÷ 58

16. 75,000 ÷ 32

39

Dividing by a Whole Number

A. A small loaf of sliced bread is about 21.6 cm long and contains 24 slices. About how thick is each slice?

Find 21.6 ÷ 24.

Place the decimal point in the quotient directly above the decimal point in the dividend.

Then divide the same way you divide whole numbers.

Each slice is about 0.9 cm thick.

B. Find 0.63 ÷ 5. Divide until the remainder is zero.

```
       0.126
  5)0.630      Write 0 in the dividend
    -5          and continue dividing.
    13
   -10
    30
   -30
     0
```

C. Find 1.12 ÷ 160. Divide until the remainder is zero.

```
        0.007     Write two zeros after
 160)1.120        the decimal point in
    -1 120        the quotient.
        0
```

D. Study these examples.

$145.89 ÷ 10 = 14.589$

$36.37 ÷ 100 = 0.3637$

$13.24 ÷ 1000 = 0.01324$

• **Discuss** What is a short way to divide by a power of 10?

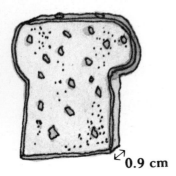

0.9 cm

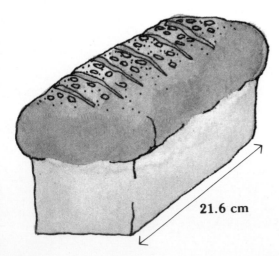

21.6 cm

Divide. Continue dividing until the remainder is zero.

1. $16\overline{)38.4}$ 2. $91\overline{)2311.4}$

3. $42\overline{)151.2}$ 4. $25\overline{)4618.75}$

5. $29\overline{)4.524}$ 6. $61\overline{)5938.96}$

7. $64\overline{)4044.8}$ 8. $15\overline{)95.28}$

9. $17.5 \div 5$ 10. $10.4 \div 4$

11. $4.26 \div 3$ 12. $11.89 \div 29$

13. $10.8 \div 15$ 14. $1.26 \div 21$

15. $33.6 \div 28$ 16. $95.71 \div 170$

17. $35.97 \div 33$ 18. $3550.5 \div 45$

19. $158.4 \div 10$ 20. $3.62 \div 100$

21. $98.65 \div 1000$ 22. $6.2 \div 1000$

23. A sausage that is about 32.6 cm long has been cut into 163 slices. About how thick is each slice?

24. A package of cheese slices is about 9.6 cm thick and contains 24 slices. About how thick is each slice?

*25. A box of 250 sheets of bakery tissue paper is about 3.7 cm high. The box is made of cardboard about 0.35 cm thick. About how thick is each sheet of tissue paper?

More practice
Set 7, page 404

Lab Activity

Dividing to Find Thickness

Measure the thickness of the following objects to the nearest millimeter. Then divide by the number of sheets to find the approximate thickness of each sheet.

1. The pages in a textbook

2. The pages in a library book

3. The pages in an unabridged dictionary

4. The pages in your notebook

5. Determine the approximate thickness of each of the covers of the above books without measuring the covers alone.

Measure the height of each of the following objects to the nearest millimeter. Then divide to find the approximate thickness of each object.

6. A stack of 10 pennies

7. A stack of 15 nickels

8. A stack of 23 dimes

Dividing Decimals

A. Electricity is measured in kilowatt-hours. A toaster uses about 39.2 kilowatt-hours of electricity per year. The cost to operate the toaster for a year is about $1.96. What is the cost of the electricity, per kilowatt-hour, needed to operate the toaster?

Find 1.96 ÷ 39.2.

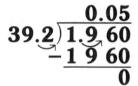

Multiply the divisor and the dividend by 10 to make the divisor a whole number. Place the decimal point in the quotient.

$$
\begin{array}{r}
0.05 \\
39.2\overline{)1.9\,60} \\
-1\,9\,60 \\
\hline
0
\end{array}
$$

Divide as with whole numbers until the remainder is zero. Write any necessary zeros in the dividend.

It costs about $0.05 per kilowatt-hour to operate the toaster.

■ *To divide a decimal by a decimal, first make the divisor a whole number by multiplying by a power of 10. Multiply the dividend by the same power of 10. Then divide.*

B. Find 9.45 ÷ 0.0035.

$$
\begin{array}{r}
2700. \\
0.0035\overline{)9.4500} \\
-7\ 0 \\
\hline
2\ 45 \\
-2\ 45 \\
\hline
000
\end{array}
$$

C. Find 6.21 ÷ 1.6. Round the quotient to the nearest tenth.

$$
\begin{array}{r}
3.88 \approx 3.9 \\
1.6\overline{)6.2\ 10} \\
-4\ 8 \\
\hline
1\ 4\ 1 \\
-1\ 2\ 8 \\
\hline
1\ 30 \\
-1\ 28 \\
\hline
2
\end{array}
$$

Divide until the quotient is in hundredths.

Then round to the nearest tenth.

Divide until the remainder is zero.

1. $0.05\overline{)4.5}$ 2. $0.06\overline{)0.84}$ 3. $2.04\overline{)7.14}$ 4. $0.71\overline{)0.568}$

5. $0.06\overline{)4.8}$ 6. $2.2\overline{)15.4}$ 7. $5.05\overline{)20.2}$ 8. $2.03\overline{)8.729}$

9. $0.001\overline{)9}$ 10. $0.13\overline{)5.2}$ 11. $8.46\overline{)42.3}$ 12. $0.26\overline{)0.0182}$

Divide. Round each quotient to the nearest tenth.

13. $3.81 \div 11$ 14. $1.46 \div 1.3$ 15. $6.47 \div 0.8$ 16. $0.3719 \div 4.17$

Divide. Round each quotient to the nearest hundredth.

17. $41.2 \div 0.3$ 18. $0.542 \div 0.07$ 19. $6.042 \div 0.8$ 20. $0.8537 \div 0.961$

21. An electric water heater costs about $209.68 to operate for one year. If one kilowatt-hour costs $0.05, how many kilowatt-hours of electricity are used by the water heater in one year? Round your answer to the nearest kilowatt-hour.

More practice
Set 8, page 404

Weather Observer

Lin Tang observes and reports weather conditions to the National Weather Service.

At each weather station, air pressure is read from a barometer and is corrected for variations in temperature, elevation, and latitude. Depending upon these factors, the corrections are added to or subtracted from the barometric reading.

Then a final correction is added to standardize all air pressure readings in terms of sea-level air pressure.

```
  25.437 ←— Barometer reading
−  0.100    Subtract temperature correction.
  25.337
−  0.012    Subtract elevation correction.
  25.325
−  0.012    Subtract latitude correction.
  25.313
+  4.90     Add sea-level correction.
  30.213 ←— Sea-level air pressure
```

Use the information in the table to compute the sea-level air pressure for each barometric reading. Subtract the corrections for temperature, elevation, and latitude; then add the sea-level correction.

	Barometer reading	Corrections			
		Temperature	Elevation	Latitude	Sea-level
1.	25.118	0.098	0.012	0.012	4.817
2.	25.437	0.094	0.012	0.012	4.837
3.	25.543	0.105	0.012	0.012	4.901
4.	25.806	0.107	0.012	0.012	4.915

Chapter 2 Test
Decimals, pages 24–44

What is the value of the 2 in each number?

1. 45.297   2. 0.67923

Write each number in words.

3. 39.831   4. 1.0004

Write the decimal for each number.

5. four and thirty-nine hundredths

6. four hundred fifty thousandths

Compare these decimals. Use > or <.

7. 0.218 ● 0.21   8. 6.77 ● 6.79

9. Round 9.8657 to the nearest tenth.

10. Round 45.37508 to the nearest hundredth.

11. Round 0.6693 to the nearest thousandth.

Round to the nearest one and then estimate each sum or difference.

12. 44.86 + 31.71

13. 6.04 + 9.51

14. 16.51 − 9.98

15. 27.41 − 16.72

Add or subtract.

16. 6.05
   + 3.001

17. 35.492
   + 7.89

18. 24.63
   − 7.4

19. 5.24
   − 3.6801

Multiply.

20. 5.9
   × 4.9

21. 6.09
   × 7.2

22. 5.814
   × 0.0002

Estimate each product.

23. 21.4 × 0.39   24. 0.573 × 0.74

Divide until the remainder is zero.

25. 6)19.2   26. 38)9.5

27. 0.09)41.4   28. 2.4)1.47

29. Find 1.153 ÷ 0.87. Round the quotient to the nearest hundredth.

If there is enough information, find the answer. If not, write *too little information*.

30. It takes about 40 minutes to fly 280.4 km from Tampa to West Palm Beach. The distance from Tampa to Miami is 60.9 km longer. How far is Tampa from Miami?

Chapter 3   Metric Measures

Overview of the Metric System

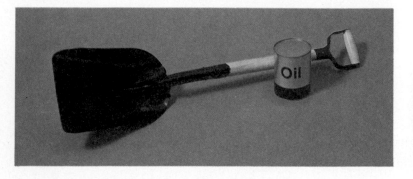 

A **meter** (m) is a metric unit of length.
The shovel is about 1 meter long.

A **liter** (L) is a metric unit of capacity.
The can contains 1 liter of motor oil.

A **gram** (g) is a metric unit of mass.
The mass of the nail is about 1 gram.

The term **mass** is used in this chapter. In common
usage, the term weight is used to mean mass. So,
weight is used in other chapters.

Prefixes are used with meter, liter, and gram
to indicate larger or smaller units. For example,
1 *kilo*meter = 1000 meters and
1 *milli*meter = 0.001 meter.

Prefix	Meaning	Metric units of length	Metric units of capacity	Metric units of mass
kilo	1000	kilometer (km)	kiloliter (kL)	kilogram (kg)
hecto	100	hectometer (hm)	hectoliter (hL)	hectogram (hg)
deka	10	dekameter (dam)	dekaliter (daL)	dekagram (dag)
		meter (m)	liter (L)	gram (g)
deci	0.1	decimeter (dm)	deciliter (dL)	decigram (dg)
centi	0.01	centimeter (cm)	centiliter (cL)	centigram (cg)
milli	0.001	millimeter (mm)	milliliter (mL)	milligram (mg)

Give or complete the unit of measure that could be used in each situation. Use *meter, liter,* or *gram.*

1. Mass of a person
   kilo▓▓▓

2. Capacity of a bucket
   ▓▓▓

3. Length of a room
   ▓▓▓

4. Height of a person
   centi▓▓▓

5. Liquid in an eyedropper
   milli▓▓▓

6. Capacity of a kettle
   ▓▓▓

7. Mass of a bowling ball
   kilo▓▓▓

8. Distance between two towns
   kilo▓▓▓

9. Mass of a dog
   kilo▓▓▓

10. Capacity of a swimming pool
    kilo▓▓▓

11. Length of a pencil
    centi▓▓▓

12. Length of a jogging track
    ▓▓▓

13. Mass of a bag of flour
    kilo▓▓▓

14. Capacity of a hot-water tank
    ▓▓▓

15. Height of a flagpole
    ▓▓▓

16. Mass of a sack of potatoes
    kilo▓▓▓

Write the word for each symbol.

17. m   18. mg   19. cm   20. g   21. mm   22. L   23. km   24. mL

Copy and complete.

25. 1 hectometer = ▓▓▓ meters

26. 1 kilogram = ▓▓▓ grams

27. 1 centimeter = ▓▓▓ meter

28. 1 milliliter = ▓▓▓ liter

29. 1 dekagram = ▓▓▓ grams

30. 1 deciliter = ▓▓▓ liter

31. 1 millimeter = ▓▓▓ meter

32. 1 kilometer = ▓▓▓ meters

33. 1 hectoliter = ▓▓▓ liters

34. 1 milligram = ▓▓▓ gram

35. 1 centigram = ▓▓▓ gram

36. 1 dekameter = ▓▓▓ meters

37. 1 kiloliter = ▓▓▓ liters

38. 1 hectogram = ▓▓▓ grams

47

Metric Units of Length

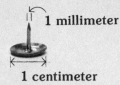

1 millimeter

1 centimeter

A. A shovel is about 1 meter long. The head of the thumbtack is about 1 **centimeter** (cm) wide. The point of the thumbtack is about 1 **millimeter** (mm) wide. The landing strip at a small airport is about 1 **kilometer** (km) long.

B. A place-value chart can help you find equal metric measures of length. When you change from one unit to another, for each step to the right, multiply by 10 to get more units that are smaller. For each step to the left, multiply by 0.1 to get fewer units that are larger.

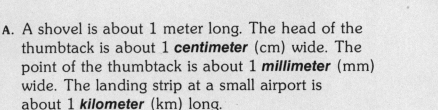

kilo	hecto	deka		deci	centi	milli
thousands	hundreds	tens	ones	tenths	hundredths	thousandths
kilometer (km)	hectometer (hm)	dekameter (dam)	meter (m)	decimeter (dm)	centimeter (cm)	millimeter (mm)
1 km = 10 hm	1 hm = 10 dam	1 dam = 10 m	1 m = 10 dm	1 dm = 10 cm	1 cm = 10 mm	
1 hm = 0.1 km	1 dam = 0.1 hm	1 m = 0.1 dam	1 dm = 0.1 m	1 cm = 0.1 dm	1 mm = 0.1 cm	

C. Find the missing number.
7 km = ▦ dam

Start at kilometers on the chart. Move 2 places to the right to get to dekameters.

$$10 \times 10$$

1 km = 100 dam
7 km = 7 × 100 dam
7 km = 700 dam

D. Find the missing number.
82.7 dm = ▦ hm

Start at decimeters. Move 3 places to the left to get to hectometers.

$$0.1 \times 0.1 \times 0.1$$

1 dm = 0.001 hm
82.7 dm = 82.7 × 0.001 hm
82.7 dm = 0.0827 hm

Find the missing number.

1. 924 cm = ▦ m
2. 48 km = ▦ m
3. 623 dam = ▦ m
4. 8643 mm = ▦ m
5. 52 m = ▦ cm
6. 4392 m = ▦ km
7. 3 m = ▦ mm
8. 82 m = ▦ dm
9. 436 m = ▦ hm
10. 32 dm = ▦ dam
11. 421 cm = ▦ km
12. 678 mm = ▦ cm
13. 153.2 cm = ▦ m
14. 84.7 hm = ▦ km
15. 0.9 m = ▦ cm
16. 211.5 cm = ▦ dm
17. 1.2 dam = ▦ cm
18. 54.8 dam = ▦ km
19. 0.32 cm = ▦ mm
20. 6391 cm = ▦ km
21. 694 mm = ▦ cm
22. 938 cm = ▦ hm
23. 68 dam = ▦ dm
24. 720 km = ▦ dam
25. 8.41 cm = ▦ mm
26. 29.6 dm = ▦ cm
27. 0.182 km = ▦ m

Choose the most sensible measure.

28. Length of a hammer
    35 mm   35 cm   35 m
29. Length of a workbench
    3 cm   3 m   3 km
30. Length of a bicycle trip
    5 mm   5 cm   5 km
31. Length of a carrot
    20 mm   20 cm   20 m
32. Length of a canoe
    4 mm   4 cm   4 m
33. Height of a bowling pin
    38 mm   38 cm   38 m
34. Length of a water ski
    2 m   6 m   12 m
35. Length of a tennis racket
    2 cm   66 cm   920 cm
36. Length of a watchband
    3 cm   20 cm   85 cm
37. Width of a desk
    1 m   4 m   10 m
38. Length of a screwdriver
    1.7 cm   17 cm   170 cm
39. Length of a broomstick
    0.5 m   1.5 m   2.5 m
40. Height of a stepladder
    10 cm   1.0 m   0.1 km
41. Length of a nail
    0.38 mm   3.8 cm   0.38 m
42. Length of a new pencil
    19 mm   1.9 mm   0.19 m
43. Width of a newspaper
    0.36 m   3.6 m   0.36 km
44. Height of a car
    16.5 cm   1.65 m   0.165 km
45. Distance from your house to school
    1.46 km   146 km   1460 km

Kilogram, Gram, and Milligram

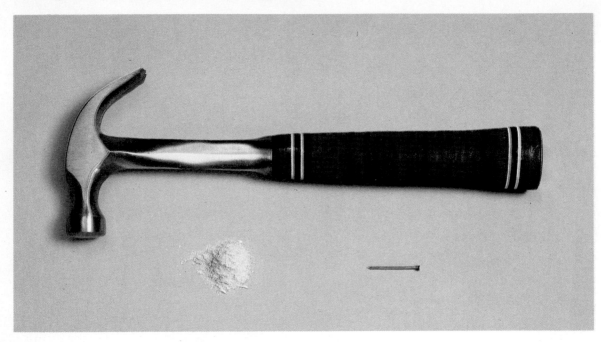

A. Of the metric units of mass given below,
kilogram (kg), gram, and ***milligram*** (mg)
are the most commonly used.

The mass of the hammer is about 1 kilogram.
The mass of the nail is about 1 gram. The
mass of a piece of sawdust is about 1 milligram.

kilogram (kg)	hectogram (hg)	dekagram (dag)	gram (g)	decigram (dg)	centigram (cg)	milligram (mg)

B. Find the missing number.
1.5 kg = ▦ mg

Start at kilograms. Move
6 places to the right to get
to milligrams.

$$1 \text{ kg} = 1{,}000{,}000 \text{ mg}$$
$$1.5 \text{ kg} = 1.5 \times 1{,}000{,}000 \text{ mg}$$
$$1.5 \text{ kg} = 1{,}500{,}000 \text{ mg}$$

C. Find the missing number.
279 mg = ▦ kg

Start at milligrams. Move
6 places to the left to get
to kilograms.

$$1 \text{ mg} = 0.000001 \text{ kg}$$
$$279 \text{ mg} = 279 \times 0.000001 \text{ kg}$$
$$279 \text{ mg} = 0.000279 \text{ kg}$$

Find the missing number.

1. 305 mg = ▦ g
2. 518 kg = ▦ g
3. 15.4 kg = ▦ g
4. 385.9 mg = ▦ g
5. 13,892 mg = ▦ kg
6. 4.3 kg = ▦ mg
7. 651 g = ▦ mg
8. 849 g = ▦ kg
9. 716.8 g = ▦ kg
10. 594.8 g = ▦ mg
11. 512 dg = ▦ dag
12. 638 dag = ▦ dg

Choose the most sensible measure.

13. Mass of a screwdriver
    46 mg   46 g   46 kg
14. Mass of a brick
    2 mg   2 g   2 kg
15. Mass of a large paper clip
    1 mg   1 g   1 kg
16. Mass of a grain of sand
    1 mg   1 g   1 kg
17. Mass of a tennis racket
    5 g   50 g   500 g
18. Mass of a hockey puck
    16.5 g   165 g   1650 g
19. Mass of a pipe wrench
    0.01 kg   0.1 kg   1 kg
20. Mass of a thumbtack
    4.75 mg   47.5 mg   475 mg
21. Mass of a person
    75 kg   7.5 kg   0.75 kg
22. Mass of a car key
    0.85 g   8.5 g   85 g
23. Mass of a pliers
    1.88 g   18.8 g   188 g
24. Mass of a dictionary
    0.2 kg   2 kg   20 kg
25. Mass of an eyelash
    95 mg   950 mg   9500 mg
26. Mass of a tennis ball
    0.56 g   56 g   560 g

Time Out

When Tim counts his collection of trading cards by 3s, there is one card left over. When he counts the cards by 5s or by 7s, there is also one card left over. What is the least number of cards Tim can have?

Liter and Milliliter

A. Of the metric units of capacity given below, liter and *milliliter* (mL) are the most commonly used.

The can of motor oil contains 1 liter. The spill of oil is about 1 milliliter.

kiloliter (kL)	hectoliter (hL)	dekaliter (daL)	liter (L)	deciliter (dL)	centiliter (cL)	milliliter (mL)

B. Find the missing number.
380 mL = ▒ L

1 mL = 0.001 L
380 mL = 380 × 0.001 L
380 mL = 0.38 L

C. Find the missing number.
68.3 L = ▒ mL

1 L = 1000 mL
68.3 L = 68.3 × 1000 mL
68.3 L = 68,300 mL

Find the missing number.

1. 768 mL = ▒ L　　2. 38 L = ▒ mL　　3. 65.3 L = ▒ mL

4. 4358 mL = ▒ L　　5. 78.15 mL = ▒ L　　6. 8.2 L = ▒ mL

7. 64.8 mL = ▒ dL　　8. 2.45 kL = ▒ daL　　9. 0.47 daL = ▒ cL

Choose the more sensible measure for the capacity of each object.

10. Paint can
4 L   4 mL

11. Drinking glass
250 L   250 mL

12. Bottle of glue
45 mL   45 L

13. Bathtub
400 mL   400 L

14. Measuring cup
5 mL   500 mL

15. Teakettle
1 L   100 L

16. Automobile fuel tank
80 L   800 L

17. Scrub pail
8 L   80 L

18. Soup spoon
1.5 mL   15 mL

*19. Swimming pool
0.6 kL   60 kL

*20. The shop teacher, Mr. Redarrow, has an 8-L can of turpentine. How many 250-mL bottles can he fill from the can?

*21. A school has 12 school buses. Each bus uses about 25 L of fuel per school day. There are an average of 20 school days per month. About how much fuel do the buses use in one month?

Keeping Skillful

Write each number in expanded form with exponents.

1. 1,456,821   2. 209,800   3. 486
4. 2,001,003   5. 80,601   6. 7192

What is the value of the 6 in each number?

7. 6023.4   8. 31.846   9. 291.56
10. 684.81   11. 841.68   12. 106.93

Round each number to the nearest one.

13. 3.892   14. 15.215   15. 6.453
16. 29.96   17. 306.72   18. 1589.62

Round each number to the nearest ten.

19. 8492   20. 3986   21. 64,843
22. 758   23. 48,347   24. 128,695

Round each number to the nearest hundredth.

25. 10.843   26. 35.968   27. 17.916
28. 15.092   29. 78.508   30. 26.995

Round each number to the nearest hundred.

31. 38,481   32. 25,512   33. 86,249
34. 17,421   35. 6243   36. 69,952

Metric Units of Area

A. *Square meter* (m^2), *square centimeter* (cm^2), and *square millimeter* (mm^2) are metric units of area.

A square centimeter is a square with sides 1 centimeter long. Other metric units of area are squares with sides that are metric units of length.

The area of the top of the card table is about 1 square meter. The area of each push button on the telephone is about 1 square centimeter.

B. Find the area of a rectangle 4 cm by 3 cm.

Area length width

$A = l \times w$

$A = 4 \times 3$

$A = 12$

Area: 12 cm^2

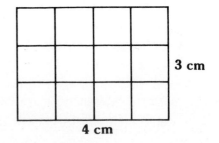

54

C. The chart shows metric units of area. Each unit is 100 times as great as the unit to the right in the chart.

| | | ×100 | ×100 | | ×0.01 | ×0.01 | |

square kilometer	square hectometer	square dekameter	square meter	square decimeter	square centimeter	square millimeter
(km²)	(hm²)	(dam²)	(m²)	(dm²)	(cm²)	(mm²)
1 km² = 100 hm²	1 hm² = 100 dam²	1 dam² = 100 m²	1 m² = 100 dm²	1 dm² = 100 cm²	1 cm² = 100 mm²	
1 hm² = 0.01 km²	1 dam² = 0.01 hm²	1 m² = 0.01 dam²	1 dm² = 0.01 m²	1 cm² = 0.01 dm²	1 mm² = 0.01 cm²	

D. Find the missing number.
18 dam² = ▦ dm²

Start at square dekameters and move 2 places to the right to get to square decimeters.

100×100

1 dam² = 10,000 dm²
18 dam² = 18 × 10,000 dm²
18 dam² = 180,000 dm²

E. Find the missing number.
324 mm² = ▦ dm²

Start at square millimeters and move 2 places to the left to get to square meters.

0.01×0.01

1 mm² = 0.0001 dm²
324 mm² = 324 × 0.0001 dm²
324 mm² = 0.0324 dm²

Find the area of each rectangle.

1. A rug, 2 m by 1 m

2. A tray, 30 cm by 50 cm

3. A mirror, 1.5 m by 1.2 m

4. A window, 120 cm by 60 cm

5. A tile, 12 cm by 12 cm

6. A card, 12.5 cm by 7.5 cm

Find the missing number.

7. 3 m² = ▦ cm²

8. 6 dm² = ▦ mm²

9. 7385 mm² = ▦ cm²

10. 829 cm² = ▦ m²

11. 1328 dm² = ▦ dam²

12. 11,824 dam² = ▦ km²

13. 4 km² = ▦ m²

14. 5 hm² = ▦ m²

15. 15,563 mm² = ▦ m²

16. 4296 mm² = ▦ dm²

*17. 3.8 hm² = ▦ dm²

*18. 6.1 dm² = ▦ mm²

Metric Units of Volume

A. **Cubic meter** (m^3), **cubic decimeter** (dm^3), and **cubic centimeter** (cm^3) are metric units of volume.

A cubic centimeter is a cube with edges 1 centimeter long. Other metric units of volume are cubes with edges that are metric units of length.

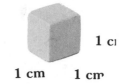

1 cm

1 cm   1 cm

The chart shows metric units of volume. Each unit is 1000 times as great as the unit to the right in the chart.

—× 1000—   —× 1000—   —× 0.001—

cubic kilometer (km³)	cubic hectometer (hm³)	cubic dekameter (dam³)	cubic meter (m³)	cubic decimeter (dm³)	cubic centimeter (cm³)	cubic millimeter (mm³)
1 km³ = 1000 hm³	1 hm³ = 1000 dam³	1 dam³ = 1000 m³	1 m³ = 1000 dm³	1 dm³ = 1000 cm³	1 cm³ = 1000 mm³	
1 hm³ = 0.001 km³	1 dam³ = 0.001 hm³	1 m³ = 0.001 dam³	1 dm³ = 0.001 m³	1 cm³ = 0.001 dm³	1 mm³ = 0.001 cm³	

B. Find the missing number.
$7.89 \ m^3 = $ ▦ cm^3

Start at cubic meters and move 2 places to the right to get to cubic centimeters.

$$\boxed{1000 \times 1000}$$

$1 \ m^3 = 1,000,000 \ cm^3$
$7.89 \ m^3 = 7.89 \times 1,000,000 \ cm^3$
$7.89 \ m^3 = 7,890,000 \ cm^3$

C. Find the missing number.
$8691 \ cm^3 = $ ▦ dm^3

Start at cubic centimeters and move 1 place to the left to get to cubic decimeters.

$1 \ cm^3 = 0.001 \ dm^3$
$8691 \ cm^3 = 8691 \times 0.001 \ dm^3$
$8691 \ cm^3 = 8.691 \ dm^3$

D. Find the volume of a box 4 cm by 3 cm by 2 cm.

Volume length width height

$$V = l \times w \times h$$

$$V = 4 \times 3 \times 2$$

$$V = 24$$

Volume: 24 cm³

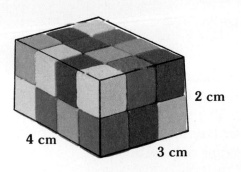

2 cm

4 cm

3 cm

Find the missing number.

1. 23 m³ = ▦ cm³

2. 5.1 m³ = ▦ mm³

3. 4,800,000 mm³ = ▦ m³

4. 3,489,000 cm³ = ▦ m³

5. 568 m³ = ▦ dam³

6. 89,000 m³ = ▦ hm³

Find the volume of each box.

7. 6 m × 5 m × 4 m

8. 8 mm × 10 mm × 6 mm

9. 3 dm × 9 dm × 8 dm

10. 4 m × 12 m × 3 m

*11. 7 cm × 8 cm × 25 mm

*12. 2.5 dm × 18 cm × 20 cm

Lab Activity

Estimating the Volume of Containers

Select five different box-shaped containers from home or your classroom. Make a chart like the one shown to record your data.

Item	Estimated volume	Actual volume
1. *Cereal box*		
2.		
3.		

1. Estimate the volume of each container, and write your estimate in the chart.

2. Measure the length, width, and height of each container, and compute its volume.

3. Subtract to find the difference of your estimate and the actual volume. Were your estimates better for smaller containers or larger containers?

Temperature

Temperature is often measured in **degrees Celsius** (°C). At sea level, water freezes at 0°C and boils at 100°C. The temperature on a hot summer day might be 33°C, and on a cold winter day −15°C.

Choose the more sensible temperature.

1. Frozen food
   −10°C   32°C

2. Soup cooking
   39°C   90°C

3. Normal body temperature of a person
   37°C   98°C

4. An icicle
   0°C   20°C

5. Steam bath
   40°C   80°C

6. Ice water
   5°C   50°C

7. Hot cider
   18°C   78°C

8. Room temperature
   20°C   70°C

9. Melting butter
   5°C   30°C

10. Melting wax
    20°C   80°C

11. Tobogganing weather
    −5°C   25°C

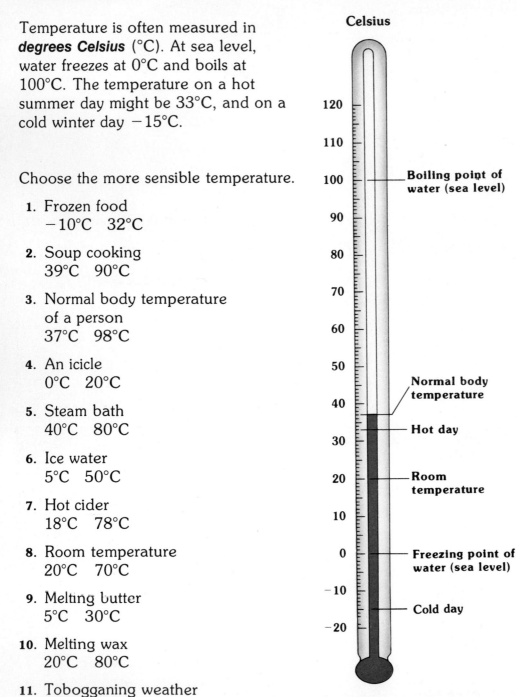

Celsius

120
110
100 — **Boiling point of water (sea level)**
90
80
70
60
50
40 — **Normal body temperature**
30 — **Hot day**
20 — **Room temperature**
10
0 — **Freezing point of water (sea level)**
−10 — **Cold day**
−20

Relationship Between Metric Units

A. The metric units of volume, mass, and capacity have a special relationship.

A cube with a volume of 1 cubic centimeter can hold 1 milliliter of water. The mass of 1 milliliter of water is 1 gram.

A cube with a volume of 1 cubic decimeter can hold 1 liter of water. The mass of 1 liter of water is 1 kilogram.

Volume	Capacity	Mass
1 cubic centimeter (1 cm³)	1 milliliter (1 mL)	1 gram (1 g)
1 cubic decimeter (1 dm³)	1 liter (1 L)	1 kilogram (1 kg)

B. Find the amount of water an aquarium 3 dm by 2 dm by 6 dm can hold, and give the mass of the water.

$V = l \times w \times h$ Find the volume of the aquarium.

$V = 3 \times 2 \times 6$

$V = 36$

The volume of the aquarium is 36 dm³, so the aquarium will hold 36 liters of water. The mass of the water is 36 kilograms.

Find the amount of water each container will hold, and give the mass of the water.

1. 8 dm by 6 dm by 3 dm

2. 4 dm by 2 dm by 10 dm

3. 5 cm by 7 cm by 9 cm

4. 10 cm by 3 cm by 6 cm

5. 36 dm by 25 dm by 13 dm

6. 15 cm by 25 cm by 12 cm

★7. 48 dm by 2.8 cm by 30 dm

★8. 56 cm by 3.2 dm by 40 cm

Precision

Sue and Jack Snowbird have a custom-made drapery business. They must measure very carefully, but they know all measurements are approximate. The **precision** of a measurement depends on the size of the unit of measure used.

A. Which measurement is more precise, 38.5 m or 46.75 m?

Measurement	Unit of measure
38.5 m	**0.1 m**
46.75 m	**0.01 m**

Since 0.01 m is a smaller unit of measure than 0.1 m, 46.75 m is the more precise measurement.

B. Which measurement is more precise, 13 cm or 128 mm?

Measurement	Unit of measure
13 cm	**1 cm**
128 mm	**1 mm**

Since millimeter is a smaller unit of measure than centimeter, 128 mm is more precise than 13 cm.

■ *The smaller the unit of measure, the more precise the measurement.*

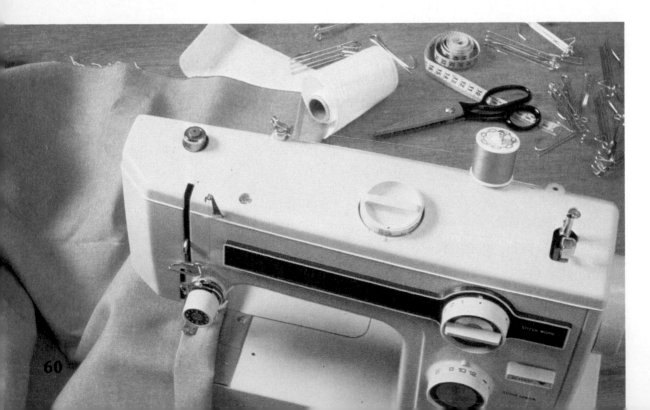

c. One drapery order requires 36.8 m of fabric. Matching chair covers require 8.55 m of fabric. How much fabric is required for the total order?

Find 36.8 m + 8.55 m.

$$\begin{array}{r} \mathbf{36.8} \\ +\ \mathbf{8.55} \\ \hline \mathbf{45.35} \end{array}$$ 36.8 m is the less precise measurement.

45.4 m Round to the nearest 0.1 m.

The total order requires 45.4 m of fabric.

■ *In computation, the answer cannot be more precise than the least precise of the measurements used.*

In each exercise, give the unit of measure.

1. 3 kg   2. 5 L   3. 3.2 cm   4. 4.5 g   5. 6.34 kg   6. 8.25 m

7. 45 mL   8. 98 mg   9. 7.38 L   10. 9.21 mm   11. 8.1 mL   12. 5.3 kg

Choose the more precise measurement.

13. 3.24 kg   24.8 kg   14. 21.6 cm   35.81 cm   15. 14.32 L   2.5 L

16. 23 g   42 kg   17. 14 L   145 mL   18. 82 m   254 km

*19. 486 mm   32.15 cm   *20. 25.6 m   12.2 cm   *21. 0.41 kg   32.4 g

Add or subtract. Round the answer to the less precise unit of measure.

22. 3.56 mg + 5.6 mg   23. 39.8 mL + 16 mL   24. 6.214 m + 32.1 m

25. 47.2 cm − 28.25 cm   26. 63.8 kg − 45 kg   27. 29.6 L − 3.831 L

28. 78.43 km   20.8 km   29. 0.76 g + 3.85 g   30. 9.5 cm + 10.8 cm

Chapter 3 Test
Metric Measures, pages 46–61

Give or complete the unit of measure that could be used in each situation. Use *meter*, *liter*, or *gram*.

1. Mass of an automobile
   kilo░░░░░░░

2. Distance from home to school
   kilo░░░░░░░

3. Capacity of a thermos bottle
   ░░░░░░░

4. Mass of a bag of peanuts
   ░░░░░░░

5. Height of a person
   centi░░░░░░░

6. Capacity of a soup bowl
   milli░░░░░░░

Write the word for each symbol.

7. kg   8. mL   9. cm   10. km

Choose the most sensible measure.

11. Temperature of a milk shake
    6°C   30°C   60°C

12. Mass of a bicycle
    2.5 kg   25 kg   250 kg

13. Length of a belt
    0.12 m   1.2 m   12 m

14. Capacity of a cream pitcher
    2.5 mL   25 mL   250 mL

15. Height of a flagpole
    10 m   100 m   1000 m

Find the missing number.

16. 2.1 km = ░░░ m

17. 347 cm = ░░░ dm

18. 2.8 g = ░░░ mg

19. 847 mL = ░░░ cL

20. 7.8 L = ░░░ daL

21. 6458 g = ░░░ kg

22. 3.4 m² = ░░░ dm²

23. 7428 cm² = ░░░ dm²

24. 2.3 hm² = ░░░ m²

25. 1347 dm³ = ░░░ m³

26. Find the area of a rectangle 32 dm by 25 dm.

27. Find the volume of a box-shaped container 54 cm by 48 cm by 10 cm.

28. Find the amount of water and the mass of the water that the container in exercise 27 can hold.

29. Which measurement is more precise, 27.4 mL or 32.85 mL?

30. A pair of drapes requires 24.25 m of trim. Slipcovers require 5.5 m of trim. How much trim is needed for 1 pair of drapes and 1 slipcover? Round your answer to the less precise unit of measure.

Problems Around Us

Find the answer to each problem that has enough information given. If there is not enough information given, write *too little information*.

1. A house and lot cost $96,250. The lot is worth $14,500. What is the cost of the house without the lot?

2. The first month that Juana played golf, she played five rounds and shot 114, 107, 109, 97, and 103. What was her average score per round?

3. Carmen used 68 liters of gas to drive 748 kilometers. How many kilometers did her car average per liter?

4. Australia has a population of 14,406,000. Tuvula has a population of 7000. Australia has how many times as many people as Tuvula?

5. Stan and Winston are brothers. Stan is 8 years older than Winston. Winston is 15 cm taller than Stan. How old is Winston?

6. Hank Aaron hit 95 more home runs than Willie Mays. If Mays hit 660 home runs, how many home runs did Aaron hit?

7. It is 863.5 kilometers from Albany to Detroit. What average speed is necessary to make this trip in 11 hours?

8. During the day, Akira sold $2459.20 worth of sports equipment. Francine sold 4 sets of golf clubs. How much more did Akira sell than Francine?

9. In 1977, Harvard University Library had 9,383,255 books. If the average width of each book was 0.03 meter, how many meters of shelf space were required to store these books?

10. In 1955, Julius Boros won $65,121 playing golf. In 1973, Jack Nicklaus won $243,241 more than that. How much did Nicklaus win in 1973?

Individualized Skills Maintenance

Diagnose

A *pages 8–9*

589 + 256

27,098 + 53,271

48 + 237 + 9210

B *pages 8–9*

954 − 287

5300 − 651

46,522 − 729

C *pages 12–13*

7 × 63

261 × 737

29 × 6728

Practice

A

1. 732
+ 197

2. 4017
+ 987

3. 6789
+ 1234

4. 37,135
+ 3,865

5. 21,157
+ 32,631

6. 400
53
+ 682

7. 1473
29
+ 321

8. 9349
652
+ 8

9. 72,512
7
+ 5,173

10. 22,609
92,437
+ 295

B

11. 637
− 249

12. 710
− 421

13. 5508
− 273

14. 40,681
− 3,743

15. 19,209
− 3,781

16. 820
− 96

17. 901
− 109

18. 1027
− 738

19. 21,095
− 8,476

20. 48,532
− 29,331

C

21. 70
× 6

22. 58
× 9

23. 65
× 30

24. 79
× 42

25. 80
× 50

26. 940
× 7

27. 347
× 28

28. 293
× 67

29. 706
× 40

30. 765
× 300

31. 825
× 391

32. 4579
× 83

Unit 1 Review

Chapter 1, pages 2-22
Add or subtract.

1. 3862
   $+\,5941$

2. 7059
   $-\,5896$

Multiply.

3. 542
   $\times\ \ 30$

4. 148
   $\times\ \ 57$

Divide.

5. $27\overline{)3925}$ **6.** $62\overline{)1983}$

Evaluate.

7. $25 - 3(8 - 2)$

8. $58 - \dfrac{6 + 12}{3}$

9. $\dfrac{(60 - 12)}{3(4)}$

Chapter 2, pages 24-44
Add or subtract.

10. 32.501
   $+\ \ 6.75$

11. 14.2
   $-\ \ 8.05$

Multiply.

12. 14.6
   $\times\ \ 2.8$

13. 4.03
   $\times\,0.93$

Divide until the remainder is zero.

14. $8\overline{)20.4}$ **15.** $47\overline{)201.63}$

16. $0.06\overline{)38.4}$ **17.** $5.9\overline{)39.53}$

18. Find $34.9 \div 0.46$. Round the quotient to the nearest tenth.

Compare these decimals. Use $>$ or $<$.

19. $0.41 \bullet 0.401$ **20.** $2.652 \bullet 2.65$

21. Round 81.275 to the nearest tenth.

Chapter 3, pages 46-61
Choose the most sensible measure.

22. Length of a jogging track
   1.5 cm   1.5 m   1.5 km

23. Mass of a textbook
   1.2 mg   1.2 g   1.2 kg

24. Capacity of a picnic jug
   4 mL   4 L   40 L

Find the missing number.

25. 1385 mL = ▦ L

26. 2.34 m = ▦ cm

27. 84 kg = ▦ mg

28. Which measurement is more precise, 3.74 L or 8.2 L?

Unit 1 Test
Chapters 1–3, pages 2–62

Add or subtract.

1.
```
   249
    72
+ 8519
```

2.
```
  43.42
+  2.051
```

3.
```
  4061
− 2918
```

4.
```
  10.509
−  3.64
```

Multiply.

5.
```
  297
×  46
```

6.
```
  5.61
×  3.2
```

Divide.

7. $46\overline{)8816}$ 8. $83\overline{)9743}$

Divide until the remainder is zero.

9. $7\overline{)32.34}$ 10. $24\overline{)65.4}$

11. $3.2\overline{)21.696}$ 12. $0.04\overline{)46.2}$

13. Find $4.87 \div 0.13$. Round the quotient to the nearest hundredth.

Compare these decimals. Use $>$ or $<$.

14. 3.06 ● 3.063   15. 3.8 ● 3.75

16. Round 3851.9269 to the nearest hundredth.

Evaluate.

17. $34 - 5(18 - 12)$

18. $46 - \dfrac{20 - 8}{4}$

19. $\dfrac{54 + 18}{3(8)}$

Choose the most sensible measure.

20. Capacity of a bottle of catsup
    5 mL   15 mL   500 mL

21. Mass of a sausage
    50 mg   50 g   50 kg

22. Height of a door
    3 cm   3 m   3 km

23. Temperature of a warm day
    5°C   25°C   90°C

Find the missing number.

24. 3485 m = ▦ km

25. 14 mL = ▦ L

26. 2.1 kg = ▦ dg

27. Which measurement is more precise, 75 cm or 123 mm?

28. Paper cups come in boxes of 36. How many boxes of cups are needed to serve 1050 drinks?

Unit 2

Chapter 4 Expressions and Equations

Evaluating Addition and Subtraction Expressions

A. Sometimes a letter is used to represent a number in a mathematical expression.

$s + 42$ $19 - v$ $m - 13$

In these expressions, the letters s, v, and m are **variables.** To *evaluate an expression*, substitute a number for the variable and compute.

B. Evaluate $s + 42$ for $s = 9$.

$s + 42$

$9 + 42$ Substitute 9 for s.

51   Add.

C. Evaluate $19 - v$ for $v = 13$.

$19 - v$

$19 - 13$ Substitute 13 for v.

6   Subtract.

D. Evaluate $m - 13$ for $m = 22$.

$m - 13$

$22 - 13$ Substitute 22 for m.

9   Subtract.

Evaluate each expression for $x = 8$.

1. $x + 18$ 2. $130 + x$

3. $47 - x$ 4. $x - 2$

Evaluate each expression for $t = 17$.

5. $t - 5$ 6. $51 - t$

7. $128 + t$ 8. $t + 96$

Evaluate $m + 16$ for

9. $m = 0.$ 10. $m = 2.$

11. $m = 4.$ 12. $m = 5.$

13. $m = 8.$ 14. $m = 13.$

Evaluate $k - 26$ for

15. $k = 37.$ 16. $k = 54.$

17. $k = 91.$ 18. $k = 102.$

Evaluate $154 - b$ for

19. $b = 9.$ 20. $b = 17.$

21. $b = 28.$ 22. $b = 0.$

23. $b = 19.$ 24. $b = 97.$

Evaluate each expression for $x = 14$ and $t = 29$. Then use the code key to solve the riddles.

						Code Key						
4	9	21	23	24	28	33	34	43	48	58	66	99
B	J	N	K	R	O	U	F	E	G	D	A	C

Here's how

$x + t - 9$

$14 + 29 - 9 = 34 \quad F$

What do you get when you wreck a recipe?

25. $x - 5$ **26.** $47 - x$ **27.** $t - 8$ **28.** $9 + x$ **29.** $x + t$ **30.** $t + t$

31. $t + 5$ **32.** $x + x$ **33.** $t - 1$ **34.** $t + x + 15$

Where do you put junked food?

35. $t + x + 5$ **36.** $t + 8 + t$ **37.** $9 + t - x$ **38.** $19 + x - t$

39. $x + t + 23$ **40.** $x + 20 + x$ **41.** $t + t - 15$

42. $t + 12 + t + t$ **43.** $t + x + t - 6$ **44.** $6 + t - x$

**More practice
Set 9, page 404**

Writing Addition and Subtraction Expressions

Many times, writing an expression helps you solve a written problem. This chart shows how to change some phrases to mathematical expressions.

Operation	Phrase	Mathematical expression
Addition	*n* plus 9 *n* increased by 9 the sum of *n* and 9 9 added to *n* 9 more than *n* the total of 9 and *n* the result of adding *n* and 9	$n + 9$

Subtraction	*n* minus 9
	n decreased by 9
	9 subtracted from *n*
	9 less than *n*
	the number remaining when
	  9 is subtracted from *n*
	the result of subtracting
	  9 from *n*
		$n - 9$

A. Write an expression for 13 less than a number *y*.

$$y - 13$$

B. Write an expression for 28 more than a number *n*.

$$n + 28$$

C. Sue is 4 years older than Ben. Ben is *y* years old. Write an expression for Sue's age.

$$y + 4$$

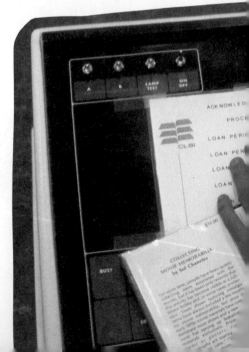

Write an expression for each exercise.

1. *m* increased by 29

2. 16 less than *b*

3. 41 subtracted from *d*

4. The total of 11 and *k*

5. A number *t* subtracted from 33

6. The result of adding a number *c* to 13

7. *s* more than 54

8. 19 decreased by a number *x*

9. The sum of 3 and a number *r*

10. 31 less than a number *h*

11. The amount remaining when the number *m* is subtracted from 8

12. The sum obtained by adding 10 to a number *n*

13. Tomas had checked out *b* books. He just checked out 3 more books. How many books has he checked out in all?

14. Susan's book is *c* centimeters long. Its width is 4 centimeters less than its length. How wide is the book?

15. Sam's book has 232 pages. Lea's book has *x* fewer pages. How many pages are in Lea's book?

16. Bill is reading page 76. There is a chart *y* pages further on. On what page is the chart?

17. Five days ago, Diana's book was *d* days late. How many days late is it now?

18. With two more cents, Dick could pay his fine of *c* cents. How much money does he have?

*19. Beth has *b* books and Dale has *d* books. Lin has 27 fewer books than Beth and Dale together. How many books does Lin have?

Solving Addition and Subtraction Equations

A. Al Oerter won the Olympic Discus Throw four times. His 1956 throw of 563.6 decimeters was 84.2 decimeters shorter than his 1968 throw. How far did he throw the discus in 1968?

$$\underset{\substack{\text{1956} \\ \text{distance}}}{563.6} = \underset{\substack{\text{1968} \\ \text{distance}}}{d} - 84.2$$

Write an equation.

$$563.6 + 84.2 = d - 84.2 + 84.2$$

84.2 is subtracted from d. To undo the subtraction and get d by itself, add 84.2 to both sides of the equation.

$$647.8 = d$$

Al's 1968 throw was 647.8 decimeters.

B. Solve $x + 27 = 45$.

$$x + 27 = 45$$
$$x + 27 - 27 = 45 - 27$$

27 is added to x. To undo the addition and get x by itself, subtract 27 from both sides of the equation.

$$x = 18$$

Solve each equation.

1. $k + 7 = 34$

2. $y - 9 = 48$

3. $61 = h - 4$

4. $109 = n - 17$

5. $93 = q + 8$

6. $216 = 63 + r$

7. $56 = 11 + s$

8. $193 = t - 81$

9. $w + 806 = 909$

10. $x - 81 = 53$

11. $117 = z - 86$

12. $231 = g + 12$

13. $m + 51.2 = 86.1$

14. $6.17 = 0.41 + p$

15. $20.13 = a + 8.16$

16. $r - 2.96 = 1.32$

17. $36.2 = x - 0.8$

18. $y - 1.07 = 2$

For each exercise, write and solve an equation.

19. 26 more than a number b is 47.

20. 19 less than a number d is 62.

21. A number y increased by 34 is 112.

22. A number n decreased by 68 is 17.

23. Mary Peters won the 1972 Olympic Women's Pentathlon with 4801 points. This was 56 points more than the score of the 1976 winner, Sigrun Siegl. How many points did Sigrun Siegl earn?

24. Robert Mathias won the Olympic Decathlon in 1948 and 1952. His 1948 score of 7139 points was 748 points less than his 1952 score. How many points did he score in 1952?

25. Al Oerter's 1960 discus throw was 56 decimeters shorter than his 1968 throw. His 1968 throw was 647.8 decimeters. How far did he throw the discus in 1960?

26. Oerter's 1964 discus throw was 46.4 decimeters longer than his 1956 throw. His 1956 throw was 563.6 decimeters. How far did he throw the discus in 1964?

**More practice
Set 10, page 404**

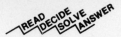

Problem Solving: Choosing the Operation

READ The Double Eagle Restaurant had 156 customers on Friday. Of these, 98 had reservations. How many customers came without a reservation?

DECIDE You can think of the problem like this.

Customers without reservations	Customers with reservations	Total number of customers
c	$+$ 98	$=$ 156

SOLVE
$$c + 98 = 156$$
$$c + 98 - 98 = 156 - 98$$
$$c = 58$$

ANSWER 58 customers came without reservations.

DECIDE You can also think of the problem like this.

Total number of customers	Customers with reservations	Customers without reservations
156	$-$ 98	$=$ c

SOLVE
$$156 - 98 = c$$
$$58 = c$$

ANSWER 58 customers came without reservations.

For each problem, write an equation. Then give the answer.

1. The Double Eagle Restaurant can seat 189 people. Its Gadsden Room holds 32 people. How many can be seated elsewhere?

2. The Maximillan Room and the Wallace Room together can seat 66 people. The Wallace Room seats 24. How many people can the Maximillan Room seat?

3. Mr. Chou paid his bill of $53.75 and now has $32.46 left. How much money did he have before he paid the bill?

4. A customer left $9.35 on the table for her lunch, including money for the tip. The bill was $7.93. How much was the tip?

5. Stacey worked 36 hours last week. This was 19.5 hours more than Melissa worked. How many hours did Melissa work last week?

6. On Tuesday, 143.5 kg of beef were served. This was 56 kg more than the amount served the previous day. How much beef was served on Monday?

7. The lamb dinner costs $7.75. The shrimp dinner costs $9.50. How much more does the shrimp dinner cost?

8. In June, the restaurant earned $17,187.92. Its expenses totaled $16,498.09. How much profit did the restaurant make?

9. In May, the restaurant made a profit of $3156.94. Its expenses totaled $15,389.68. What was the total amount the restaurant earned in May?

*10. In July, the restaurant's expenses were $12,282.46. It earned a total of $10,967.89. How much money did the restaurant lose that month?

Evaluating Multiplication and Division Expressions

A. Multiplication expressions are often written without parentheses.

$5m$ means $5(m)$ or $5 \times m$.

$7b$ means $7(b)$ or $7 \times b$.

B. Evaluate $5b$ for $b = 8$.

5b

5(8)   Substitute 8 for b.

40   Multiply.

C. Evaluate $n \div 7$ for $n = 98$.

n ÷ 7

98 ÷ 7   Substitute 98 for n.

14   Divide.

D. Evaluate $\dfrac{12}{t}$ for $t = 4$.

$$\frac{12}{t}$$

$$\frac{12}{4}$$ Substitute 4 for t.

3   Divide.

E. Evaluate $\dfrac{ab}{c}$ for $a = 12$, $b = 3$, and $c = 9$.

$$\frac{ab}{c}$$

$$\frac{12(3)}{9}$$ Substitute for each variable.

$$\frac{36}{9}$$ Then multiply.

4   Then divide.

Evaluate each expression for $r = 6$.

1. $14r$ **2.** $23r$ **3.** $84 \div r$

4. $36 \div r$ **5.** $6 \div r$ **6.** $r \div 3$

7. $r \div 6$ **8.** $r(9)$ **9.** $10r$

10. $\dfrac{r}{2}$ **11.** $\dfrac{30}{r}$ **12.** $\dfrac{3r}{3}$

13. $\dfrac{r}{r}$ **14.** $r(r)$ **15.** $\dfrac{3r}{r}$

Evaluate each expression for $a = 7$ and $b = 21$.

16. ab **17.** $b \div a$ **18.** $a(a)$

19. $\dfrac{ab}{3}$ **20** $\dfrac{ab}{u}$ **21.** $\dfrac{ab}{b}$

22. $\dfrac{4b}{a}$ **23.** $\dfrac{6a}{b}$ **24.** $\dfrac{b(b)}{a}$

Do exercises 25–45 to help
complete this poem.

Hey, Dillar Dollar,
You ten o'clock scholar,
Why do you sleep so late?

I study each night,
With all my might,
It's not the school I hate!

Then don't be so nutty,
About late night study,
And plan your time a bit better.

When my schedule is done,
Planning study and fun,

— — — — — — —.

Code Key	
1	Y
2	B
3	R
4	L
9	E
18	T
24	S
30	W
36	D
60	I
72	N

Evaluate each expression for $c = 6$ and $x = 12$.
Then use the code key to complete the poem.

Here's how

$4c$

$4(6) = 24$ S

25. $5x$ **26.** $5c$ **27.** $10c$ **28.** $\frac{x}{3}$ **29.** $\frac{2x}{c}$

30. $4c$ **31.** $\frac{3c}{2}$ **32.** $\frac{144c}{x}$ **33.** $\frac{cx}{2}$ **34.** $\frac{720}{x}$ **35.** $\frac{3x}{2}$

36. $\frac{10x}{2}$ **37.** cx **38.** $\frac{x}{c}$ **39.** $\frac{x}{2c}$

40. $\frac{cx}{18}$ **41.** $\frac{3x}{4}$ **42.** $\frac{2cx}{8}$ **43.** $\frac{cx}{4}$ **44.** $\frac{18c}{x}$ **45.** $\frac{6c}{x}$

More practice
Set 11, page 405

Writing Multiplication and Division Expressions

This chart shows how to change some phrases into mathematical expressions that involve multiplication and division.

Operation	Phrase	Mathematical expression
Multiplication	9 times n 9 multiplied by n the product of 9 and n n times 9 n multiplied by 9 the product of n and 9	$9n$ or $9(n)$
Division	n divided by 9	$n \div 9$ or $\dfrac{n}{9}$

A. Write an expression for the product of 13 and k.

$13k$

B. Write an expression for a number f divided by 23.

$\dfrac{f}{23}$

C. Write an expression for 37 divided by a number t.

$\dfrac{37}{t}$

D. Lou is 4 times as old as Jill. Jill is y years old. Write an expression for Lou's age.

$4y$

Write an expression for each exercise.

1. *w* multiplied by 18

2. *h* divided by 2

3. 14 times *x*

4. The product of *c* and 78

5. *g* divided by 4

6. A number *m* times 54

7. 32 divided by a number *v*

8. The result of multiplying 41 and *z*

9. *b* divided by 12

10. *q* divided by 7

11. The product of *r* and *s*

12. The result of dividing *a* by *b*

13. There are 24 cans of juice in each case. How many cans are there in *c* cases?

14. Each box of pepper weighs 128 grams. Find the weight of *b* boxes.

15. Milk sells at 3 cartons for *d* dollars. Find the cost of one carton of milk.

16. A liter of milk contains *c* calories. Find the number of calories in one half liter.

17. Find the weight of one loaf of bread if *n* loaves weigh 29.6 kilograms.

18. Find the time it takes to grind one kilogram of beef if *k* kilograms can be ground in 6.5 hours.

*19. How many shelves can be stacked with canned goods in *h* hours if *s* shelves can be stacked in 5 hours?

Solving Multiplication and Division Equations

A. The Apodaca School Symphony Orchestra spent $171.64 for seven new music stands. How much did each stand cost?

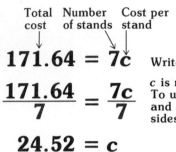

Total cost   Number of stands   Cost per stand

$$171.64 = 7c$$ Write an equation.

$$\frac{171.64}{7} = \frac{7c}{7}$$ c is multiplied by 7. To undo the multiplication and get c by itself, divide both sides of the equation by 7.

$$24.52 = c$$

Each stand cost $24.52.

B. Solve $\frac{s}{3} = 17$.

$$\frac{s}{3} = 17$$

$$(3)\frac{s}{3} = (3)17$$ s is divided by 3. To undo the division and get s by itself, multiply both sides of the equation by 3.

$$s = 51$$

Solve each equation.

1. $9t = 108$ 2. $6r = 198$ 3. $14p = 196$ 4. $51 = 3b$

5. $\frac{w}{17} = 11$ 6. $38 = \frac{a}{5}$ 7. $\frac{y}{9} = 21.2$ 8. $1.5 = \frac{h}{24}$

9. $12k = 14.4$ 10. $22.5 = 15c$ 11. $41y = 111.11$ 12. $8.74 = 19q$

13. $\frac{n}{303} = 11.11$ 14. $\frac{c}{241} = 83.18$ 15. $2.9d = 87$ 16. $5.6g = 1.68$

For each exercise, write and solve an equation.

17. 7 times a number c is 168.

18. A number j divided by 13 is 52.

19. The product of 19 and a number s is 43.7.

20. A number w divided by 12 gives a result of 15.4.

21. A number y multiplied by 53 is 10.07.

22. A number z divided by 67 is 19.73.

There are 51 orchestra members. Use this information to find each answer.

23. Musical scores for all the orchestra members cost $90.78. Find the cost for each member.

24. The conductor gave season tickets to each member. If each member received 3 tickets, how many tickets were distributed?

*25. On a recent trip, the cost of the bus for the members of the orchestra and the conductor was $1913.08. What was the cost per person?

*26. While the orchestra members and the conductor were traveling, they discovered that one fourth of them were over 13 years old. How many were older than 13?

More practice
Set 12, page 405

Problem Solving: Choosing the Operation

READ The Sole Shop is a family shoe store. Wynne is stacking shoe boxes on the shelves. Each box is 17 cm wide. How many boxes can he put side by side on a shelf that is 204 cm long?

DECIDE You can think of the problem like this.

Width per box — Number of boxes — Total width of boxes

$$17b = 204$$

SOLVE

$$17b = 204$$

$$\frac{17b}{17} = \frac{204}{17}$$

$$b = 12$$

ANSWER Wynne can put 12 boxes on the shelf.

DECIDE You can also think of the problem like this.

Total width ⟶ $\dfrac{204}{17} = b$ ⟵ Number of boxes
Width per box ⟶

SOLVE

$$\frac{204}{17} = b$$

$$12 = b$$

ANSWER Wynne can put 12 boxes on the shelf.

For each problem, write an equation. Then give the answer.

1. Last week, Wynne and Imogene helped 143 customers. Wynne helped 68 customers. How many customers did Imogene help?

2. The coach bought 36 pairs of shoelaces for $24.12. How much did the coach pay for each pair?

3. A manufacturer packs 48 pairs of shoes in each shipping carton. How many pairs are in a shipment of 9 cartons?

4. The regular cost of a pair of running shoes is $21.95. They are now on sale for $13.88. If Herb buys a pair on sale, how much will he save?

5. Along the west wall of the shoe store are a row of seats and a display cabinet. The seats take up 11.7 meters of the wall. The cabinet takes up the remaining 2.6 meters. How long is the west wall?

6. Last month, the Sole Shop was open for 26 days. Its total sales were $23,309.78. What were the average daily sales?

7. Mrs. Natsyn paid a total of $42.35 for dress shoes. This amount included $2.40 for sales tax. What was the price of the shoes?

8. In its first year of business, the Sole Shop bought 5500 m of wrapping paper. At the end of the year, 212.75 m remained. How many meters of paper were used during the year?

9. At the moment, there are 156 pairs of children's shoes on the shelves. Each shelf holds 12 pairs. How many shelves of children's shoes are there?

★10. The tennis coach spent $406.13 on tennis shoes. Each pair of shoes sells for $23.89. How many pairs did she buy?

Solving Two-Step Equations

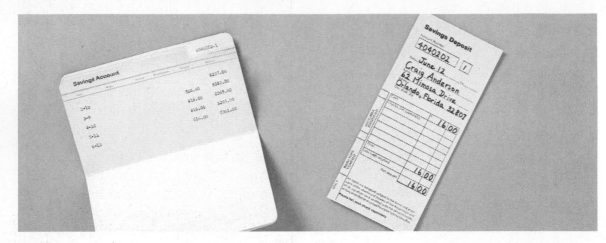

A. Craig has $237 in his savings account. If he saves $16 each month, how many months will it take him to have a total of $365 in his account?

Let m be the number of months. Then $16m$ will be the amount of his planned savings.

Planned savings	Amount already saved	Total savings

$$16m + 237 = 365$$

This equation involves both multiplication and addition. Two steps are needed to solve it.

$$16m + 237 = 365$$ 237 is added to $16m$.

$$16m + 237 - 237 = 365 - 237$$ To get $16m$ by itself, subtract 237 from both sides of the equation.

$$16m = 128$$

$$\frac{16m}{16} = \frac{128}{16}$$ To get m by itself, divide both sides of the equation by 16.

$$m = 8$$

Craig must save for 8 months.

B. Solve $3s - 3.75 = 30$.

$$3s - 3.75 = 30$$

3.75 is subtracted from 3s.

$$3s - 3.75 + 3.75 = 30 + 3.75$$

To get 3s by itself, add 3.75 to both sides of the equation.

$$3s = 33.75$$

$$\frac{3s}{3} = \frac{33.75}{3}$$

To get s by itself, divide both sides of the equation by 3.

$$s = 11.25$$

Solve each equation.

1. $4r + 13 = 41$
2. $6w - 29 = 67$
3. $28 + 13a = 171$
4. $128 = 11n - 37$
5. $7t - 2.38 = 91$
6. $154 = 29.54 + 14x$
7. $15.72 + 16h = 117$
8. $182 = 26y - 10.14$
9. $24u + 192 = 336$
10. $32b - 224 = 128$
11. $4.5p - 40.5 = 22.5$
12. $22.2 = 7.4z - 66.6$
13. $754.6 = 22f + 239.8$
14. $925.2 = 127.8 + 18k$
15. $14d + 23.5 = 153.7$

★16. $\frac{2c}{5} + 32 = 54$

★17. $\frac{4x}{7} - 89 = 91$

★18. $\frac{2.1d}{2} - 3.5 = 0.7$

19. Kimiko has $188 in her savings account. If she saves $8 each week, how long will it take for her to have $500 in her account?

★20. The Cole Investment Club is having a raffle. Raffle tickets cost $5 each and the prize cost $450. How many tickets must club members sell to make a profit of $5000?

★21. Patty earns a commission of $35.50 for each sale. Her expenses are $90.50 per week. How many sales must she make per week in order to take home $300 each week?

More practice
Set 13, page 405

Properties of Addition and Multiplication

A. Study these sums and products.

$$55 + 37 = 92$$
$$37 + 55 = 92$$

$$27.8 + 32.4 = 60.2$$
$$32.4 + 27.8 = 60.2$$

$$28(5) = 140$$
$$5(28) = 140$$

$$2.4(5.9) = 14.16$$
$$5.9(2.4) = 14.16$$

■ *Commutative Property of Addition*
The order of addends can be changed without changing their sum.

For any numbers a and b,
$a + b = b + a$.

■ *Commutative Property of Multiplication*
The order of factors can be changed without changing their product.

For any numbers a and b, $ab = ba$.

B. Study these sums and products.

$$23 + (9 + 14) = 46$$
$$(23 + 9) + 14 = 46$$

$$12 \times (3 \times 5) = 180$$
$$(12 \times 3) \times 5 = 180$$

■ *Associative Property of Addition*
The grouping of addends can be changed without changing their sum.

For any numbers a, b, and c,
$a + (b + c) = (a + b) + c$.

■ *Associative Property of Multiplication*
The grouping of factors can be changed without changing their product.

For any numbers a, b, and c,
$a(bc) = (ab)c$.

C. Study these sums and products.

$$45 + 0 = 45$$

$$0 + 243.7 = 243.7$$

$$36(1) = 36$$

$$1(855.6) = 855.6$$

■ *Addition Property of Zero*
The sum of any number and zero is that number.

For any number a, $a + 0 = a$.

■ *Multiplication Property of One*
The product of any number and one is that number.

For any number a, $a(1) = a$.

Compute. Use the properties to make your work easier. Look for pairs of numbers that are easy to add or multiply mentally.

1. $8 + 5 + 2$

2. $19 + 13 + 1 + 7$

3. $6.7 + 2.3 + 0 + 1$

4. $4.2 + 0 + 6 + 9.8$

5. $450 + 292 + 50$

6. $225 + 143 + 25$

7. $42 + 540 + 58$

8. $37 + 620 + 63$

9. $1 + 0 + 8 + 0 + 1$

10. $9 + 0 + 2 + 0 + 9$

11. $43 + 56 + 7 + 44$

12. $39 + 72 + 11 + 28$

13. $2(19)(5)$

14. $25(43)(4)$

15. $5(9)(8)$

16. $12(11)(5)$

17. $16(1)(5)(3)$

18. $50(7)(1)(2)$

19. $13(19)(0)(4)$

20. $43(59)(0)(6)$

21. $0.4(51)(10)$

22. $100(73)(0.02)$

23. $20(6)(5)(7)$

24. $5(3)(80)(4)$

★25. Is this statement *always* true?
For any numbers a and b, $a - b = b - a$.
Is it *ever* true? If so, give an example.

★26. Is this statement *ever* true? If so, give an example.
For any numbers a, b, and c,
$a - (b - c) = (a - b) - c$.

★27. Is this statement *always* true?
For any numbers a and b, $a \div b = b \div a$.
Is it *ever* true? If so, give an example.

★28. Is this statement *ever* true? If so, give an example.
For any numbers a, b, and c,
$a \div (b \div c) = (a \div b) \div c$.

Time Out

See how many different numbers you can make using *exactly* five threes.

You may use addition, subtraction, multiplication, or division.

Here's a start.

$$0 = \frac{3 - 3 + 3 - 3}{3}$$

$$1 = 3 - \frac{3}{3} - \frac{3}{3}$$

$$2 = 3 - \frac{3 + 3}{3 + 3}$$

$$3 = 3 - 3 + 3 - 3 + 3$$

See if you can do any of these in other ways.

Then see how many different numbers you can make using exactly five threes.

Distributive Property

A. Study these examples.

$$7(5 + 8) = 91$$
$$7(5) + 7(8) = 91$$

$$2.3(9 + 1.5) = 24.15$$
$$2.3(9) + 2.3(1.5) = 24.15$$

■ **Distributive Property**
For any numbers a, b, and c,
$$a(b + c) = ab + ac.$$

B. Use the distributive property to compute 15 × 23 mentally.

15 × 23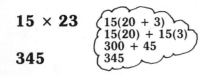

345

C. Use the distributive property to compute 26(41) + 26(59) mentally.

26(41) + 26(59)

2600

D. Write $4n + 16$ as a product.

4n + 16

4(n) + 4(4)   Write the expression as a sum of two products.

4(n + 4)   Then use the distributive property.

Compute mentally. Use the distributive property whenever it makes your work easier.

1. 6(30 + 4)

2. 9(20 + 7)

3. 13 × 32

4. 24 × 21

5. 12(91)

6. 43(82)

7. 3(14) + 3(16)

8. 12(7) + 12(3)

9. 50(37 + 3)

10. 40(27 + 23)

11. 64(73) + 36(73)

12. 73(58) + 27(58)

13. 5(13 + 4 + 3)

14. 8(17 + 9 + 4)

15. 102(75)

16. 203(63)

17. 16.2(8) + 16.2(2)

18. 29.1(12) + 29.1(8)

19. 82(56) + 18(56)

20. 29(31) + 71(31)

21. 16(17) + 17(14)

22. 63(21) + 21(37)

Use the distributive property to write each product as a sum.

Here's how

$5(n + 6)$

$5n + 5(6)$

$5n + 30$

23. $6(a + 7)$ **24.** $3(a + 3)$

25. $4(x + 5)$ **26.** $9(a + 20)$

27. $12(x + 3)$ **28.** $14(x + 5)$

29. $7(a + b)$ **30.** $9(a + b)$

31. $1.1(x + 2)$ **32.** $1.2(c + 5)$

*33. $8(2a + 3)$ *34. $0.7(3a + 8)$

Write each expression as a product.

35. $3n + 15$ **36.** $7x + 28$

37. $9a + 72$ **38.** $8b + 40$

39. $5c + 25$ **40.** $4d + 36$

41. $3x + 96$ **42.** $5x + 125$

*43. $16x + 56$ *44. $28a + 49$

*45. $72b + 45$ *46. $54x + 42$

*47. Is this statement *always* true? For any numbers a, b, c, and d, $a(b + c + d) = ab + ac + ad$. Explain your answer.

*48. Is this statement *always* true? For any numbers a, b, and c, $a \div (b + c) = (a \div b) + (a \div c)$. Explain your answer.

Keeping Skillful

Compare. Use $>$, $<$, or $=$

1. $0.6 \bullet 0.64$

2. $0.087 \bullet 0.078$

3. $0.4 \bullet 0.40$

4. $1.060 \bullet 1.600$

5. $0.007 \bullet 0.0070$

List these decimals in order from the least to the greatest.

6. $0.08 \quad 0.008 \quad 0.18$

7. $2.22 \quad 2.20 \quad 2.202$

8. $3.52 \quad 7.0 \quad 5.5$

9. $0.10 \quad 0.101 \quad 1.01$

10. $0.909 \quad 0.999 \quad 0.90$

Add or subtract.

11. $1.56 + 1.91$

12. $89.6 + 97.94$

13. $9.81 - 0.02$

14. $3.05 - 0.0064$

15. $79.008 - 11.018$

16. $6.07 - 5.98$

17. $57.9 + 28.81 + 0.0014$

18. $0.15 + 2.0001 + 16.9$

19. $4.63 + 16.9 + 18.75$

20. $0.1006 + 0.0151 + 0.0145$

Number Games

Ken said to his Aunt Martha, "Think of your age. Add 5 to that number. Multiply the result by 2. Now add 6. Divide the result by 2. What is your final answer?"

Aunt Martha told Ken that her answer was 44. Ken then said, "You are 36 years old."

To see how Ken did this, let a represent Aunt Martha's age.

Instruction	Result
1. Think of age.	a
2. Add 5.	$a + 5$
3. Multiply by 2.	$2a + 10$ $\begin{cases} 2(a+5) \\ 2a + 2(5) \end{cases}$
4. Add 6.	$2a + 16$ $\{\, 2a + 10 + 6 \,$
5. Divide by 2.	$\dfrac{2a + 16}{2}$
6. Final answer.	$a + 8$ $\begin{cases} \dfrac{2a + 2(8)}{2} \\ \dfrac{2(a + 8)}{2} \end{cases}$

Aunt Martha's final answer was 44, so $a + 8 = 44$, or $a = 36$.

To find her age, Ken just subtracted 8 from Aunt Martha's final answer.

● **Discuss** Does this always give the correct answer?

Tell the final result for each of these sets of instructions.

1. Begin with a number n.
   Add 4.
   Multiply by 6.
   Subtract 24.
   Divide by 3.

2. Begin with a number n.
   Double it.
   Add 4.
   Divide by 2.

3. Begin with a nonzero number y.
   Multiply by 4.
   Add 8.
   Divide by 2.
   Subtract 4.
   Divide by the original number.

4. Begin with a number x.
   Double it.
   Double that result.
   Add 12.
   Divide by 4.

5. Begin with a number z.
   Add 8.
   Multiply by 3.
   Subtract 24.
   Divide by 3.
   Subtract the original number.

6. Begin with a number c.
   Add 1.
   Multiply by 10.
   Add 6.
   Multiply by 2.
   Add 8.
   Divide by 4.
   Subtract 5.
   Divide by 5.

Suppose you were playing this game with a friend. If you knew the final answer of the calculations, how would you determine the number your friend started with?

7. Think of a number.
   Triple it.
   Add 3.
   Double the result.
   Divide by 6.
   Add 1.

8. Think of a number.
   Add 2.
   Multiply the result by 5.
   Add 40.
   Divide by 5.

9. Make up a number game of your own. Be sure that you can determine the correct original number from the final answer.

10. Make up a number game that has at least seven steps and always gives a final answer of 5.

Career

Moped Dealer

Louise Santiago owns a moped dealership. Her business has fixed monthly expenses of $3200. She also pays her salespeople an average commission of $30 per sale.

Ms. Santiago knows that the *break-even point* is the point at which income and expenses are equal.

If 40 mopeds are sold each month, what must the average profit per sale be for Ms. Santiago to break even?

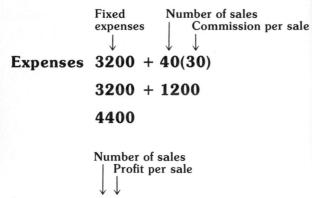

Number of sales

Fixed expenses | | Commission per sale

Expenses **3200 + 40(30)**

3200 + 1200

4400

Number of sales
| Profit per sale

Income **40p**

At the break-even point, income equals expenses.

Income   Expenses

$$40p = 4400$$

$$p = 110$$

In order to break even, Ms. Santiago must have an average profit of $110 per sale.

Find the average profit per sale needed to break even.

	Fixed expenses	Number of sales	Average commission per sale
1.	$3200	80	$30
2.	$3200	100	$30
3.	$2100	70	$25
4.	$2100	30	$25

• *Discuss*   Why do high-volume dealers often have the lowest consumer prices?

Chapter 4 Test
Expressions and Equations, pages 68–92

Evaluate each expression for $x = 12$.

1. $x + 7$
2. $20 - x$
3. $x - 6$
4. $3x$
5. $\dfrac{x}{4}$
6. $\dfrac{5x}{6}$

Write an expression for each exercise.

7. 3 less than a number n
8. The sum of a number b and 10
9. The product of 9 and a number t
10. 64 divided by w
11. The product of x and y

Solve each equation.

12. $27 + x = 53$
13. $w - 18.6 = 31$
14. $3m = 66$
15. $6x - 7 = 11$
16. $2.1 = 8a + 0.5$
17. $\dfrac{x}{7} = 14$

Compute. Use the properties to make your work easier.

18. $43 + 45 + 7 + 15$
19. $25(6)(4)(7)$
20. $13(42)$
21. $67(38) + 33(38)$

22. This month, Kirk's telephone bill was $32.15. This was $14.70 less than his bill last month. What was Kirk's phone bill last month?

23. Erin bought 3 pairs of shoes for $53.28. What was the average price per pair?

Chapter 5 Integers

Writing Integers

A. Positive and negative whole numbers, or **integers,** can be used to describe quantities such as distances above and below sea level.

The peak of Mt. Everest is about 8848 meters above sea level. The **positive integer** +8848 gives this elevation.

The lowest point in Death Valley is about 86 meters below sea level. The **negative integer** −86 gives this elevation.

B. Integers can be shown on a horizontal number line with positive integers to the right of zero. They are usually written without the positive sign. Negative integers are to the left of zero. The integer 0 is neither positive nor negative.

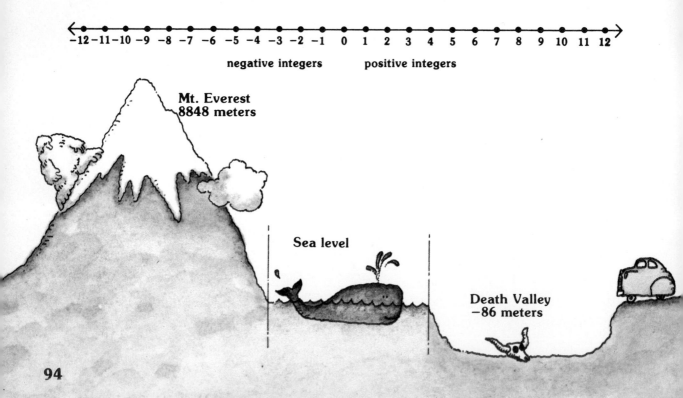

C. For each integer, there is an
opposite integer. On a number
line, an integer and its opposite
are equally distant from zero.

The opposite of 5 is −5.
The opposite of −2 is 2.
The opposite of 0 is 0.

D. Find −(−8).

Sometimes the symbol "−" means
"the opposite of." −(−8) is read
"the opposite of negative eight."

−(−8) = 8   The opposite of −8 is 8.

Give each answer.

1. If 84 represents 84 meters above sea
   level, what does −146 represent?

2. If −4 represents 4 flights
   down, what does 2 represent?

3. If −12 represents 12 kilometers west,
   what does 16 represent?

4. If 5 represents a gain of
   5 kg, what does −5 represent?

For each exercise, give an integer.

5. the opposite of 6

6. the opposite of −3

7. −(−7)

8. the opposite of −8

9. the opposite of 0.

10. −(−9)

11. the opposite of 15

12. the opposite of −28

13. −(−12)

Give the missing integer.

Here's how

8 kilometers north   8
5 kilometers south   ▦ −5

14. 8° below zero   −8
    5° above zero   ▦

15. 3 floors below ground level   −3
    15 floors above ground level   ▦

16. Increase of $28   28
    Decrease of $92   ▦

17. 9 seconds after blastoff   9
    60 seconds before blastoff   ▦

18. Withdrawal of $200   −200
    Deposit of $56   ▦

19. 5 hours before departure   −5
    3 hours after departure   ▦

Comparing and Ordering Integers

A. A number line can be used to compare integers.

$$\xleftarrow{\quad} \overset{\bullet}{-9} \ \overset{\bullet}{-8} \ \overset{\bullet}{-7} \ \overset{\bullet}{-6} \ \overset{\bullet}{-5} \ \overset{\bullet}{-4} \ \overset{\bullet}{-3} \ \overset{\bullet}{-2} \ \overset{\bullet}{-1} \ \overset{\bullet}{0} \ \overset{\bullet}{1} \ \overset{\bullet}{2} \ \overset{\bullet}{3} \ \overset{\bullet}{4} \ \overset{\bullet}{5} \ \overset{\bullet}{6} \ \overset{\bullet}{7} \ \overset{\bullet}{8} \ \overset{\bullet}{9} \xrightarrow{\quad}$$

For any two numbers on this horizontal number
line, the number farther to the right is greater.
The number farther to the left is less.

$$8 > -2 \qquad -5 < -3 \qquad -1 > -8 \qquad -7 < 0 \qquad -9 < 4$$

B. List these integers in order from the least
to the greatest.

$$5 \quad -6 \quad -12 \quad -2$$

$$-12 \quad -6 \quad -2 \quad 5 \qquad \text{\small List the integers as they appear from left to right on the number line.}$$

• Discuss   Is there a greatest integer? Is there a
least integer? Is there a greatest negative integer?
Is there a least positive integer?

Give an integer to name each labeled point.

1.   F   B   D   A   E   C   **2.**   K H J G I

   1   −15   −9

Compare these integers. Use > or <.

3. 6 ● 3	**4.** 2 ● 4	**5.** 8 ● −3	**6.** 1 ● −5
7. −4 ● 4	**8.** −19 ● 3	**9.** 0 ● −2	**10.** −4 ● −6
11. −5 ● −1	**12.** 0 ● 8	**13.** −15 ● −12	**14.** −8 ● −25
15. −10 ● 9		**16.** −19 ● −8	**17.** −24 ● −35

List these integers in order from the least to the greatest.

18. 0 −4 5

19. 8 −8 −3

20. −1 −5 0

21. 5 −2 −8 3

22. −3 3 1 −1

23. −16 13 18 −14

24. −23 6 −18 −2 0

25. 2 8 −9 −12 15

26. −6 −4 1 −18 9

This table gives the highest and lowest points of elevation for each of the six inhabited continents.

Continent	Highest point	Elevation (meters)	Lowest point	Elevation (meters)
Africa	Kilimanjaro, Tanzania	5895	Lake Assal, Djibouti	−156
Asia	Mt. Everest, Nepal-Tibet	8848	Dead Sea, Israel-Jordan	−397
Australia	Mt. Kosciusko, New South Wales	2228	Lake Eyre, South Australia	−16
Europe	Mt. El'brus, U.S.S.R.	5642	Caspian Sea, U.S.S.R.	−28
North America	Mt. McKinley, Alaska	6194	Death Valley, California	−86
South America	Mt. Aconcagua, Argentina	6960	Valdes Peninsula, Argentina	−40

27. Which continent has the point of highest elevation?

28. Which continent has the point of lowest elevation?

29. List the elevations of all twelve points in order from the least to the greatest.

★30. Which continent has the high point with the lowest elevation?

★31. Which continent has the low point with the highest elevation?

More practice
Set 14, page 406

Adding Integers

A. On the international market, the price of gold fell $3 on Monday. On Tuesday, the price rose $5. What was the net price change over these two days?

Monday's price change was −3.
Tuesday's price change was 5.

Find −3 + 5.

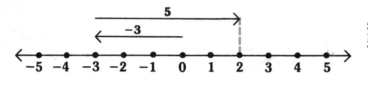

Start at zero.
Move 3 units to the left.
Then move 5 units to the right.

−3 + 5 = 2

The price rose $2.

■ *To add two integers with different signs, consider the distance each integer is from zero. Subtract the shorter distance from the longer distance. Then use the sign of the longer distance in your answer.*

B. Find 1 + (−4).

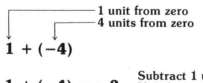

1 + (−4)

1 + (−4) = −3   Subtract 1 unit from 4 units.
Use the sign of the −4 in your answer.

● *Discuss* What is the sum of a number and its opposite?

98

c. Find −2 + (−6).

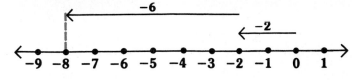

Start at zero.
Move 2 units to the left.
Then move 6 more units to the left.

−2 + (−6) = −8   The sum of two negative integers is negative.

D. You already know how to add two positive integers.
   8 + 4 = 12   The sum of two positive integers is positive.

■ *To add integers with the same sign, add without regard to
the signs. Then use the sign of the numbers in your answer.*

Find each sum.

1. −3 + (−4)	**2.** −7 + (−3)	**3.** 8 + 5	**4.** 4 + 7
5. 6 + (−8)	**6.** −4 + 5	**7.** 9 + (−1)	**8.** −7 + 4
9. −5 + 5	**10.** 0 + (−6)	**11.** −8 + 0	**12.** 6 + (−6)
13. −10 + 8	**14.** 13 + (−7)	**15.** −8 + 17	**16.** 9 + (−12)
17. 9 + 16	**18.** −8 + (−16)	**19.** −18 + 18	**20.** 13 + (−5)
21. −15 + 12	**22.** −17 + 19	**23.** −17 + 24	**24.** 19 + (−23)
25. −26 + (−25)	**26.** −23 + 28	**27.** −52 + 0	**28.** 25 + (−29)
29. −31 + 19	**30.** 20 + (−20)	**31.** −19 + 31	**32.** −19 + (−31)

★**33.** −13 + 18 + (−15)   ★**34.** 12 + (−16) + (−18)

★**35.** 15 + (−18) + (−25) + 13   ★**36.** 28 + (−57) + 39 + (−48)

★**37.** 57 + (−23) + 18 + (−9) + (−26)   ★**38.** −47 + 18 + (−54) + 14 + (−34)

39. One month, the price of gold fell $4. The
next month, the price rose $11. What was the
net price change over these two months?

More practice
Set 15, page 406

Subtracting Integers

A. Study these pairs of equations.

$$8 - 2 = 6 \qquad 11 - 7 = 4$$
$$8 + (-2) = 6 \qquad 11 + (-7) = 4$$

In each case, subtracting an integer gives the same result as adding the opposite integer.

$$4 - 3 = 1 \qquad 13 - 8 = 5$$
$$4 + (-3) = 1 \qquad 13 + (-8) = 5$$

■ *To subtract an integer, add its opposite.*

B. Find $-3 - 4$.

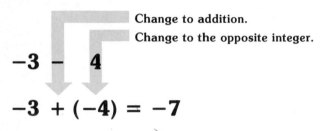

Change to addition.

Change to the opposite integer.

$$-3 - 4$$

$$-3 + (-4) = -7$$

C. Find $4 - (-5)$.

$$4 - (-5)$$

$$4 + 5 = 9$$

D. Find $-10 - (-12)$.

$$-10 - (-12)$$

$$-10 + 12 = 2$$

E. Find $14 - 18$.

$$14 - 18$$

$$14 + (-18) = -4$$

Find each difference.

1. $-4 - 3$
2. $8 - (-5)$
3. $-6 - (-1)$
4. $-4 - (-7)$
5. $8 - 4$
6. $9 - 12$
7. $-8 - (-8)$
8. $-5 - (-9)$
9. $7 - (-6)$
10. $-3 - 10$
11. $15 - 19$
12. $-12 - (-18)$
13. $18 - (-15)$
14. $-13 - 14$
15. $-17 - (-13)$
16. $19 - 12$
17. $-27 - 18$
18. $-29 - (-23)$
19. $29 - (-15)$
20. $-27 - (-27)$
21. $30 - 80$
22. $-40 - (-50)$
23. $-37 - 29$
24. $62 - (-17)$
25. $-35 - (-56)$
26. $47 - 71$
27. $-87 - (-39)$
28. $92 - 57$
29. $64 - 87$
30. $-84 - (-32)$

★31. $15 - [-6 - (-9)]$

★32. $[15 - (-6)] - (-9)$

★33. Why are the results for exercises 31 and 32 different?

Insert addition and subtraction signs to make each sentence true.

★34. $7 \blacksquare 8 \blacksquare (-9) = 24$

★35. $7 \blacksquare (-8) \blacksquare 9 = -10$

★36. $2 \blacksquare 5 \blacksquare (-11) = 8$

**More practice
Set 16, page 406**

Time Out

Find the missing numbers in these magic squares. For each magic square, the sum of the numbers in any row, column, or main diagonal must be the same.

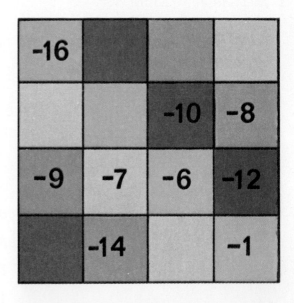

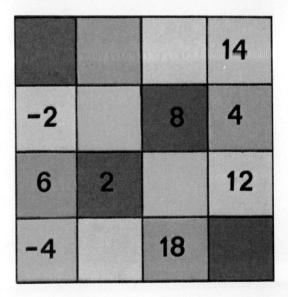

Evaluating Addition and Subtraction Expressions

Remember, when you evaluate an expression, you substitute a number for a variable.

A. Evaluate $h + 13$ for $h = -5$.

$h + 13$

$-5 + 13$ Substitute −5 for h.

8

B. Evaluate $-9 - r$ for $r = -7$.

$-9 - r$

$-9 - (-7)$ Substitute −7 for r.

$-9 + 7$

-2

C. Evaluate $-x + 5$ for $x = -3$.

$-x + 5$

$-(-3) + 5$ Substitute −3 for x.

$3 + 5$ The opposite of −3 is 3.

8

D. Evaluate $5 - (t - 3)$ for $t = 9$.

$5 - (t - 3)$

$5 - (9 - 3)$ Substitute 9 for t.

$5 - 6$ Do the operation within the parentheses first.

$5 + (-6)$ Then do the remaining operation.

-1

E. Evaluate $8 - (x + y)$ for $x = -5$ and $y = 3$.

$8 - (x + y)$

$8 - (-5 + 3)$ Substitute −5 for x and 3 for y.

$8 - (-2)$ Do the operation within the parentheses first.

$8 + 2$ Then do the remaining operation.

10

Evaluate each expression for $c = 6$.

1. $c + 5$ 2. $8 - c$ 3. $2 - c$

4. $-5 - c$ 5. $-c + 3$ 6. $-c - 9$

Evaluate each expression for $s = -5$.

7. $s - 4$ 8. $16 - s$ 9. $-15 + s$

10. $-9 - s$ 11. $-s + 8$ 12. $-s - 12$

Evaluate each expression for $d = -4$.

13. $12 - d$ 14. $-d + 18$ 15. $d - (-6)$

16. $d - 4$ 17. $-15 - d$ 18. $d + (-4)$

Evaluate each expression for $t = 4$.

19. $(8 - t) - 6$

20. $7 - (t + 3)$

21. $-8 - (6 - t)$

22. $15 - (10 - t)$

Evaluate each expression for $x = 8$ and $y = -3$.

23. $x + (y + 4)$

24. $x - (y + 3)$

25. $y - (x - 5)$

26. $11 - (y + x)$

Complete this table.

	n	$-n + 5$
27.	8	
28.	2	
29.	-6	
30.	-11	

*31. What is the greatest integer for x that will make $x + 8$ negative?

*32. What is the greatest integer for y that will make $-2 - y$ positive?

Lab Activity

Making a Slide Rule for Addition

Cut two strips of paper that are each 22 cm long and 4 cm wide. Measure and mark off 1-centimeter sections. Label as shown.

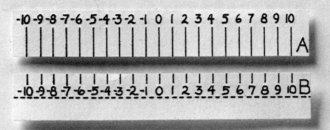

Fold the B-scale along the dotted line so that the numbers are facing out. Insert the A-scale in the folded B-scale.

To find $-3 + 7$, follow these steps.

Find the first number -3 on the A-scale. Slide the A-scale so that -3 is directly over 0 on the B-scale.

Find the second number 7 on the B-scale. Read the answer on the A-scale, directly above the second number on the B-scale.

$$-3 + 7 = 4$$

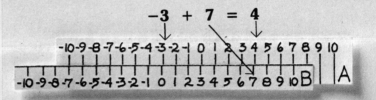

Use your slide rule to find each answer.

1. $-8 + 4$ 2. $-5 + (-2)$ 3. $6 + (-4)$

4. $3 + (-5)$ 5. $-3 + (-6)$ 6. $-7 + 2$

7. $4 + (-8)$ 8. $9 + (-10)$ 9. $-5 + (-4)$

10. How might you use your slide rule to subtract two integers?

Multiplying Integers

A. You already know how to multiply positive integers.

6 × 3 = 6(3) = 18

The product of two positive integers is positive.

B. Norm wanted to find 6 × (−3). He used this pattern to help find the answer.

6 × 3 = 18   The product decreases
6 × 2 = 12   by 6 each time.
6 × 1 = 6
6 × 0 = 0

6 × (−1) = −6   To maintain the pattern,
6 × (−2) = −12   continue to decrease by 6
6 × (−3) = −18   each time.

The product of a positive and a negative integer is negative.

C. Study this pattern.

(−5)(3) = −15   The product increases
(−5)(2) = −10   by 5 each time.
(−5)(1) = −5
(−5)(0) = 0

(−5)(−1) = 5   To maintain the pattern,
(−5)(−2) = 10   continue to increase by 5
(−5)(−3) − 15   each time.

The product of two negative integers is positive.

■ *If two integers have the same sign, their product is positive.*

■ *If two integers have different signs, their product is negative.*

Multiply.

1. 8×7
2. $2 \times (-6)$
3. $(-8) \times 4$
4. $3(-2)$
5. $9(3)$
6. $(-3)(5)$
7. $(-4)(-6)$
8. $8(-1)$
9. $(-7)(3)$
10. $(-9)(-2)$
11. $(-4)(4)$
12. $(-8)(-8)$
13. $(-5)(0)$
14. $7(-7)$
15. $8(12)$
16. $21(-3)$
17. $(-14)(-2)$
18. $(-5)(16)$
19. $(-1)(-19)$
20. $18(0)$
21. $(-16)(-3)$
22. $(-13)(6)$
23. $3(-17)$
24. $(-10)(-10)$
25. $3(-15)$
26. $(-5)(19)$
27. $(-9)(-24)$
28. $(-15)(14)$
29. $(-48)(-8)$
30. $39(-12)$
31. $(-3)^2$
32. $(-5)^3$
33. $(-2)^4$
34. $3(6)(-2)$
35. $(-3)(-5)(6)$
36. $(-5)(-7)(0)$
37. $8(-8)(5)$
38. $(-2)(-3)(-8)(4)$
39. $(-5)(2)(-6)(-3)$
40. $5(-8)(-7)(-4)(-1)$
41. $(-3)(16)(-4)(-10)(-8)$
★42. $3(-5)^3$
★43. $(-4)(-2)^4$

Give each answer.

★44. $2 - 3(4)$
★45. $(-4)(3 + 1)$
★46. $(-5)(4 - 6)$
★47. $-8 - 4(3)$
★48. $-3 - (-8)(2)$
★49. $2(-4) - 3(-4)$

Find the sign of the product when there are

★50. an odd number of negative factors.

★51. an even number of negative factors.

**More practice
Set 17, page 406**

105

Dividing Integers

A. The population of White Plains, New York, decreased by about 140 people during a 10-year span. To find the average annual change in population, you can divide 140 by 10. This gives a decrease of about 14 people each year.

You can think of a decrease of 140 people as −140 and a decrease of 14 people as −14. Then −140 ÷ 10 = −14.

B. To learn more about dividing integers, study multiplication of integers.

You know that $2(-7) = -14$, so $(-14) \div 2 = -7$.
You also know that $(-4)(-6) = 24$, so $24 \div (-4) = -6$.

■ *If two integers have different signs, their quotient is negative.*

You know that $5(3) = 15$, so $15 \div 5 = 3$.
You also know that $(-8)(4) = -32$, so $(-32) \div (-8) = 4$.

■ *If two integers have the same sign, their quotient is positive.*

C. Find $282 \div (-6)$.

$$282 \div (-6) = -47$$ The signs are different, so the quotient is negative.

D. Find $\dfrac{-125}{-5}$.

$$\frac{-125}{-5} = 25$$ The signs are the same, so the quotient is positive.

Give each missing number.

1. 5(▩) = 30
2. 30 ÷ 5 = ▩
3. 8(▩) = −72
4. (−72) ÷ 8 = ▩
5. (−9)(▩) = 63
6. 63 ÷ (−9) = ▩
7. (−7)(▩) = −42
8. (-42) ÷ (−7) = ▩
9. (−8)(▩) = 64
10. 64 ÷ (−8) = ▩
11. (−9)(▩) = −81
12. (−81) ÷ (−9) = ▩

Divide.

13. 56 ÷ 7
14. 16 ÷ (−4)
15. (−72) ÷ 9
16. (−25) ÷ (-5)
17. (−18) ÷ 2
18. 21 ÷ (−3)
19. (−36) ÷ (−4)
20. 48 ÷ 8
21. 0 ÷ (−3)
22. (−22) ÷ 11
23. 38 ÷ (−2)
24. (−42) ÷ (−3)
25. 60 ÷ (−10)
26. (−92) ÷ (−1)
27. 0 ÷ (−56)
28. (−72) ÷ 12
29. (−84) ÷ (−14)
30. 112 ÷ (−16)
31. (−102) ÷ 17
32. (−91) ÷ (−13)

33. $\frac{27}{3}$
34. $\frac{-40}{5}$
35. $\frac{30}{-3}$
36. $\frac{-45}{-5}$
37. $\frac{48}{-6}$
38. $\frac{-40}{-8}$

39. $\frac{-21}{3}$
40. $\frac{0}{-18}$
41. $\frac{-36}{-12}$
42. $\frac{63}{-21}$
43. $\frac{-51}{17}$
44. $\frac{48}{-12}$

45. $\frac{-93}{-31}$
46. $\frac{-69}{23}$
47. $\frac{-595}{35}$
48. $\frac{-882}{-21}$
49. $\frac{1071}{-17}$
50. $\frac{869}{-79}$

51. The population of Abilene, Texas, decreased by about 720 people during a 10-year span. What was the average annual change in population?

Give each answer.

★52. $\dfrac{12 - 4(-8 + 15)}{-15 + 11}$

★53. $\dfrac{(-8)(-14 + 10) - 64}{(-4)(-9 + 5)}$

★54. $\dfrac{(-3)(86) - 2(-72)}{15 - (-8)(-12 + 3)}$

★55. $\dfrac{(-5)(-12 + 8)(-7) - 16}{(-2)[-15 + 12(-3) - 5(-5)]}$

More practice Set 18, page 407

Evaluating Expressions

A. Evaluate $-3w - 7$ for $w = -2$.

$-3w - 7$

$(-3)(-2) - 7$ Substitute -2 for w.

$6 - 7$ Do the multiplication first.

$6 + (-7)$ Then do the remaining operation.

-1

B. Evaluate $\frac{n}{6} - \frac{n}{3}$ for $n = 12$.

$\dfrac{n}{6} - \dfrac{n}{3}$

$\dfrac{12}{6} - \dfrac{12}{3}$ Substitute 12 for n.

$2 - 4$ First do the divisions from left to right.

$2 + (-4)$ Then do the remaining operation.

-2

C. Evaluate $\dfrac{-5 + 3x}{4}$ for $x = -9$.

$\dfrac{-5 + 3x}{4}$

$\dfrac{-5 + 3(-9)}{4}$ Substitute -9 for x.

$\dfrac{-5 + (-27)}{4}$ Do the multiplication first.

$\dfrac{-32}{4}$ Do the operation above the division bar.

-8 Then do the remaining operation.

D. Evaluate $\dfrac{-t}{y(t + 18)}$ for $t = -20$ and $y = 5$.

$\dfrac{-t}{y(t + 18)}$

$\dfrac{-(-20)}{5(-20 + 18)}$ Substitute -20 for t and 5 for y.

$\dfrac{-(-20)}{5(-2)}$ Do the operation within the parentheses first.

$\dfrac{20}{-10}$ Above the division bar, the opposite of -20 is 20. Then do the operation below the division bar.

-2 Do the remaining operation.

Evaluate each expression for $x = -6$.

1. $5x$
2. $-8x$
3. $-6x$

4. $\dfrac{x}{2}$
5. $\dfrac{12}{x}$
6. $\dfrac{18}{-x}$

Evaluate each expression for $n = 3$.

7. $2n + 5$
8. $15 - 6n$

9. $4n - 16$
10. $-12 - 4n$

11. $5(n - 6)$
12. $-3(n + 8)$

Evaluate each expression for $y = -12$.

13. $\dfrac{y}{4} + \dfrac{y}{2}$
14. $\dfrac{y}{6} - \dfrac{y}{4}$
15. $\dfrac{y}{3} + 5$

16. $8 - \dfrac{y}{2}$
17. $\dfrac{3 - y}{5}$
18. $\dfrac{y + 8}{4}$

Evaluate each expression for $w = 2$.

19. $3w - 8$

20. $-5(w - 9)$

21. $\dfrac{4w + 2}{5}$

22. $\dfrac{3 - 6w}{-3}$

23. $\dfrac{6(w - 5)}{9}$

24. $\dfrac{-4(6 + w)}{16}$

25. $-19 + \dfrac{6w}{4}$

Evaluate each expression for $t = -20$ and $y = -4$.

26. $\dfrac{t}{10} - \dfrac{y}{4}$

27. $\dfrac{t}{2t - 5y}$

28. $\dfrac{-t(3y + 15)}{t + 5}$

★29. What is the greatest integer for x that will make $\dfrac{-x - 8}{7}$ a positive integer?

More practice
Set 19, page 407

Side Trip

Absolute Value

The **absolute value** of a number is the distance the number is from zero on a number line.

You can see from the number line that -2 is 2 units to the left of zero. The absolute value of -2 is 2. This is written $|-2| = 2$.

The number line shows that 4 is 4 units to the right of zero. The absolute value of 4 is 4. $|4| = 4$.

The number line also shows that the absolute value of 0 is 0. $|0| = 0$.

Give each answer.

1. $|4|$ **2.** $|-5|$ **3.** $|0|$ **4.** $|-16|$ **5.** $|14|$

6. $|-20|$ **7.** $-|18|$ **8.** $-|-5|$

9. $-|-(-4)|$ **10.** $|5| + |-3|$ **11.** $|5 + (-3)|$

12. $|-6| + |-8|$ **13.** $|-6 + (-8)|$

14. $|-8| - |-2|$ **15.** $|-8 - (-2)|$

Evaluate each expression for $x = 2$.

16. $|x|$ **17.** $|-x|$ **18.** $-|x|$

19. $-|-x|$ **20.** $|x - 7|$ **21.** $|x| - |7|$

Evaluate each expression for $x = -4$.

22. $|x|$ **23.** $|-x|$ **24.** $-|x|$

25. $-|-x|$ **26.** $|x - 5|$ **27.** $|x| - |5|$

28. $|5 - x|$ **29.** $|x| + |8|$ **30.** $|x + 8|$

Properties of Integers

The properties you learned for whole numbers also hold for integers.

Commutative Properties of Addition and Multiplication
The order of addends and the order of factors can be changed without changing their sum or product.

$-3 + 8 = 8 + (-3)$

$5(-9) = (-9)(5)$

Associative Properties of Addition and Multiplication
The grouping of addends and the grouping of factors can be changed without changing their sum or product.

$(13 + 8) + (-4) = 13 + [8 + (-4)]$

$[(-3)(-2)](5) = (-3)[(-2)(5)]$

Addition Property of Zero
The sum of any number and zero is that number.

$-8 + 0 = -8$

$0 + 5 = 5$

Multiplication Property of One
The product of any number and one is that number.

$8(1) = 8$

$1(-12) = -12$

Distributive Property
For any numbers a, b, and c,
$a(b + c) = ab + ac$.

$8[-5 + (-2)] = 8(-5) + 8(-2)$

Give the missing integer. Then name the property shown.

1. $8(\blacksquare) = (-15)(8)$
2. $(-5 + \blacksquare) + 6 = -5 + (4 + 6)$
3. $(\blacksquare)(-14) = -14$
4. $2[3 + (-8)] = 2(\blacksquare) + 2(-8)$
5. $-18 + 7 = (\blacksquare) + (-18)$
6. $0 + (\blacksquare) = -15$
7. $7[(-4)(-3)] = [7(-4)](\blacksquare)$
8. $8 + (-5) + (-4) = 8 + (\blacksquare) + (-5)$
9. $(-3)[4(\blacksquare)] = (-3)[(-5)(4)]$
10. $5(-3) + 3(-3) = (5 + 3)(\blacksquare)$

Give each answer. Use the properties to make your work easier.

11. $[18 + (-5)] + (-5)$
12. $-3 + 5 + (-7) + (-5)$
13. $2[50(-3)]$
14. $8(-16) + 8(6)$
15. $(-2)(18)(-50)$
16. $(-4)(16) + (-6)(16)$
17. $-57 + (-49 + 57)$

110

Chapter 5 Test
Integers, pages 94–110

Give the missing integer.

1. 6° below zero   −6
   5° above zero   ▦

2. Increase of $16   16
   Decrease of $28   ▦

Give the opposite of each integer.

3. −8   4. 19   5. 0

Compare these integers. Use > or <.

6. 4 ● −9   7. −16 ● −12

8. 0 ● −5   9. −5 ● 8

List these integers in order from the least to the greatest.

10. −8   5   −4

11. 8   −3   17   −6

Find each sum or difference.

12. −8 + (−15)

13. 14 + (−16)

14. 9 − 12

15. −6 − 10

16. 8 − (−4)

17. −15 − (−18)

Multiply or divide.

18. 5(−7)   19. (−12)(−2)

20. 9(9)   21. (−8)(11)

22. $\dfrac{54}{-9}$ 23. $\dfrac{-72}{-8}$ 24. $\dfrac{-32}{16}$

Evaluate each expression for $x = -3$.

25. $15 + x$

26. $x - 18$

27. $4 - (x + 7)$

28. $-x + 8$

29. $2x - 7$

30. $3(5 + x)$

31. $\dfrac{-3x + 5}{7}$

32. $\dfrac{x + 9}{6 + x}$

Give the missing integer.

33. $9(▦) = (-14)(9)$

34. $(8 + 7) + (-3) = 8 + [7 + (▦)]$

35. $4[(▦) + 5] = 4(-8) + 4(5)$

Locating Points with Ordered Pairs

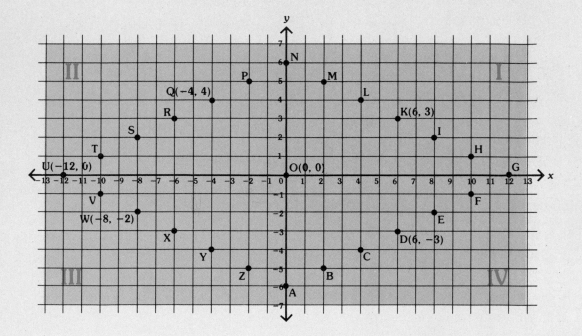

A. Any point on a plane can be located with a pair of numbers called **coordinates.** The usual coordinate system has two number lines, or **axes,** one horizontal (x) and one vertical (y). The axes intersect at the **origin,** the zero point of both number lines.

B. To find the point located by an **ordered pair** of coordinates, start at the origin. The first coordinate tells how far to move to the right (+) or left (−). The second one tells how far to move up (+) or down (−).

C. The regions of the plane that are bounded by the axes are called **quadrants.** They are labeled with Roman numerals, beginning at the upper right and going counterclockwise.

Write the letter for each ordered pair, using the
graph on page 112, to spell these words navigators use.

1. A point in the sky directly overhead
(−2, −5) (8, −2) (0, 6) (8, 2) (−10, 1) (10, 1)

2. The apparent line between the ocean and the sky
(10, 1) (0, 0) (−6, 3) (8, 2) (−2, −5) (0, 0) (0, 6)

3. An angle measured from the horizontal
(8, −2) (4, 4) (8, −2) (−10, −1) (0, −6) (−10, 1) (8, 2) (0, 0) (0, 6)

4. An instrument for measuring direction
(4, −4) (0, 0) (2, 5) (−2, 5) (0, −6) (−8, 2) (−8, 2)

5. An instrument that gives accurate time
(4, −4) (10, 1) (−6, 3) (0, 0) (0, 6) (0, 0) (2, 5) (8, −2) (−10, 1) (8, −2) (−6, 3)

Give the ordered pair and the quadrant for each point.

6. M   7. Y   8. F   9. V   10. P

Where are all the points

11. with second coordinate 0?   12. with first coordinate 0?

13. with first coordinate positive?   14. with second coordinate negative?

15. with first coordinate negative and second coordinate positive?

Reading Graphs

At age 23, Sheila Young of Detroit, Michigan, won 2 world championships for speed—one in ice skating and one in bicycling.

Sheila's winning time for the 500-meter speed-skating event was 43.56 seconds, giving her an average speed of 11.5 meters per second.

The graph at the right relates *meters per second* to *kilometers per hour*.

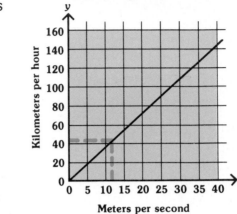

Related Speeds

Sheila's average speed was about 41 kilometers per hour.

Complete this table, using the graph to estimate the information needed.

Meters per second	Kilometers per hour
20	**1.**
40	**2.**
30	**3.**
4.	80
5.	120
6.	20
35	**7.**
8.	110

Sheila's average speed for her bicycle-racing championship was 16.3 meters per second. The graph at the right relates distance traveled and time, for that speed. Use the graph for exercises 9–16.

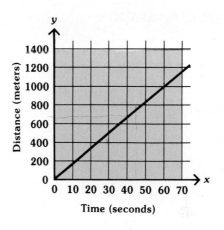

Find the approximate distance traveled for each time given.

9. 30 seconds   **10.** 60 seconds

11. 45 seconds   **12.** 10 seconds

About how long does it take to travel each given distance?

13. 400 meters   **14.** 1000 meters   **15.** 200 meters   **16.** 700 meters

A skater is doing practice laps around a rink at a constant speed. The graph below relates the skater's *distance from the starting point* (measured along the skater's path) to elapsed time.

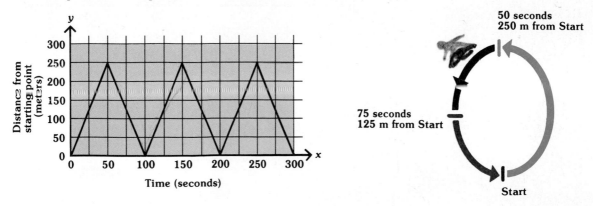

How far from the starting point is the skater at each time?

17. 25 seconds   **18.** 175 seconds   **19.** 200 seconds   **20.** 250 seconds

21. How long does each lap take?

*22. At what 2 times in the third lap is the skater about 125 meters from the starting point?

115

Making Line Graphs

Rip's beard grows 6 millimeters per week. Marlo used this equation to make a table.

$$G = 6t$$

Growth (mm) ↑   ↑ Time (weeks)

t	0	2	4	6	8	10	12	14	16
G	0	12	24	36	48	60	72	84	96

She set up a coordinate system on grid paper, using convenient numbers on the axes. Then she used the data in the table to locate points and drew a line through the points.

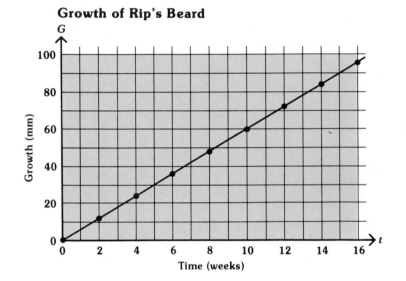

Growth of Rip's Beard

Marlo read from her graph that Rip's beard grew about 90 millimeters in 15 weeks.

When Rip went to sleep, his beard was 40 mm long. Since it grew 6 mm each week, this equation relates length of the beard to elapsed time.

$$L = 40 + 6t$$

Length ↑ ↑ Time
(mm) (weeks)

Use the equation to complete this table.

t	0	5	10	15	20
L	40	70	**1.**	**2.**	**3.**

4. Make a graph, using the data in your table. Extend your graph to include time up to 50 weeks.

Use your graph to answer these questions.

5. About how long was Rip's beard after 7.5 weeks?

6. About how long was Rip's beard after 30 weeks?

7. About how long would Rip have to sleep for the beard to reach a length of 280 mm?

*8. About how much would the beard grow from the end of the 25th week to the end of the 32nd week?

*9. About how long does it take for the beard to grow from 70 mm to 90 mm?

For exercises 10–15, use this information. Betty has $25 in her savings account. Each week she adds $5 to the account. She wrote this equation to describe her savings: $S = 25 + 5t$.

In Betty's equation, what does each of these expressions represent?

10. t 11. $5t$ 12. S

13. Make a table for Betty's equation, using these values for t: 0, 4, 8, . . ., 20.

14. Make a graph, using your table.

15. Use your graph to answer this question. About how many weeks would it take for Betty's savings to reach $100?

For exercises 16–20, use this equation: $S = 140 - 7a$.

*16. Describe a situation that fits the equation.

*17. For the situation you described, tell what each of these expressions represents: a, $7a$, S.

*18. Make a table for the equation. Use these values for a: 0, 4, 8, . . ., 20.

*19. Make a graph, using your table.

*20. Ask a question about the situation you described, and use your graph to find the answer.

Making Line Graphs for Equations

Carlos used this table to draw a graph
for the equation $y = x$.

x	−3	−2	−1	0	1	2	3
y	−3	−2	−1	0	1	2	3

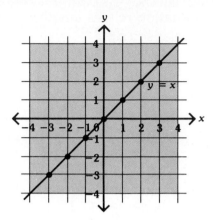

Compare the data in the table with the
equation. The equation tells how the
coordinates of a point on the graph are
related to each other. In this case, they
are equal.

Complete each table and draw the graph. Use the
same grid for all the graphs in exercises 1–6.

1. $y = x$

(Copy table and graph above.)

2. $y = x + 1$

x	−3	−2	−1	0	1	2	3
y	−2	−1	0				

3. $y = x - 1$

x	−5	−3	−1	0	1	2	3
y	−6	−4					

4. $y = x + 3$

x	−5	−4	−2	0	1	3	5
y	−2						

5. $y = x - 4$

x	−5	−4	−2	0	3	4	6
y							

6. $y = x + 5\frac{1}{2}$

x	−9	−6	−3	0	3	6	9
y							

Without making a table or graph, describe the
graph of each equation.

Here's how

$y = x + 12$ *a line parallel to the line $y = x$ and 12 units above it*

7. $y = x + 5$ **8.** $y = x + 20$ **9.** $y = x - 7$ **10.** $y = x - 50$

Complete each table and draw the graph. Use the same grid for all the graphs in exercises 11–17.

11. $y = x$ (See table on page 118.)

12. $y = 2x$

x	−3	−2	−1	0	1	2	3
y	−6	−4	−2				

13. $y = 5x$

x	−3	−2	−1	0	1	2	3
y	−15	−10					

14. $y = \frac{1}{2}x$

x	−8	−6	−4	0	2	4	8
y	−4						

15. $y = -x$

x	−3	−2	−1	0	1	2	3
y							

16. $y = -2x$

x	−4	−3	−1	0	1	3	6
y							

17. $y = -4x$

x	−3	−2	−1	0	1	2	3
y							

★18. Look over your graphs for exercises 11–17. Write the equation for each line that is rising as you move to the right.

★19. Again using your graphs for exercises 11–17, write the equation for each line that is falling as you move to the right.

Without graphing, tell whether the line for each equation is *rising* or *falling* as you move to the right.

★20. $y = -3x$ **★21.** $y = 4x$

Writing Equations for Line Graphs

Jenny wanted to find the equation for this graph. First she made a table and put in the coordinates of some points on the graph.

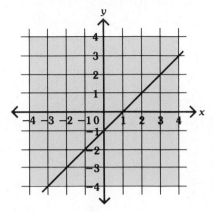

x	0	1	−1	2	3	−2
y	−1	0	−2	1	2	−3

Then she looked for a relationship between x and y that would be the same for each pair of coordinates.

She noticed that, in each pair, the y-value was 1 less than the x-value. So she wrote this equation.

$$y = x - 1$$

For each table, write the letter of the equation at the right that fits the data.

1.

x	1	0	−1	2	−2
y	4	3	2	5	1

2.

x	0	−1	−2	1	2
y	−3	−4	−5	−2	−1

3.

x	1	2	3	−1	0
y	2	1	0	4	3

4.

x	−2	−1	0	1	2
y	−6	−3	0	3	6

a. $y = x - 3$

b. $y = 3x$

c. $y = -x + 3$

d. $y = x + 3$

For each table, write an equation that fits the data.

5.

x	0	1	−1	3	−3
y	1	2	0	4	−2

6.

x	1	0	−1	−2	2
y	−3	0	3	6	−6

7.

x	−3	0	1	4	−2
y	−5	−2	−1	2	−4

★ 8.

x	1	2	3	0	−1
y	−2	−3	−4	−1	0

★9.

x	0	1	2	−1	−3
y	1	0	−1	2	4

★10.

x	2	1	0	−1	−2
y	0	1	2	3	4

Make a table for each graph, using points whose coordinates are integers. Then write an equation for the graph.

11.

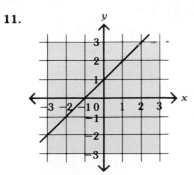

12.

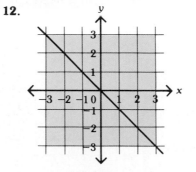

13.

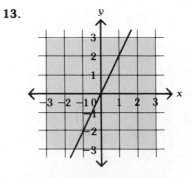

14.

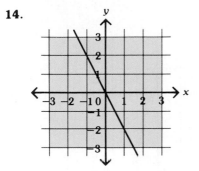

15.

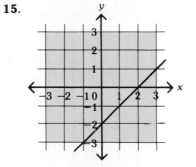

16.

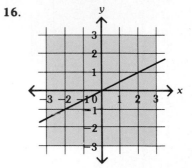

★17.

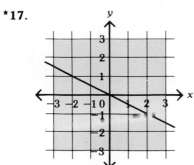

★18.

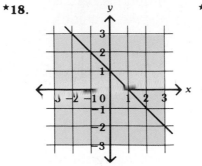

★19.

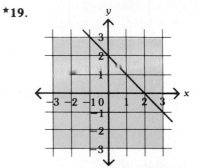

Time Out

Find the next three letters in this sequence.

![O T T F F ? ? ?]

Reading Curved Graphs

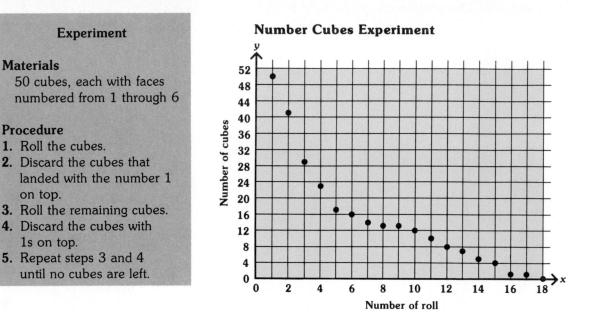

Experiment

Materials
  50 cubes, each with faces
  numbered from 1 through 6

Procedure
1. Roll the cubes.
2. Discard the cubes that
   landed with the number 1
   on top.
3. Roll the remaining cubes.
4. Discard the cubes with
   1s on top.
5. Repeat steps 3 and 4
   until no cubes are left.

Number Cubes Experiment

Pat did this experiment. He recorded his results
on a grid. His graph is *decreasing*; the y-values
decrease as you move to the right.

Use the graph to answer these questions.

How many cubes were used for the

1. second roll?   2. tenth roll?   3. eleventh roll?

On how many rolls were

4. more than 25 cubes used?   5. fewer than 25 cubes used?

★6. Why is the graph just dots instead of a continuous curve?

★7. How many 1s did Pat get on his first roll?

★8. How many 1s did he get on his second roll?

The graph below is *increasing*; the y-values increase as you move to the right.

World Population

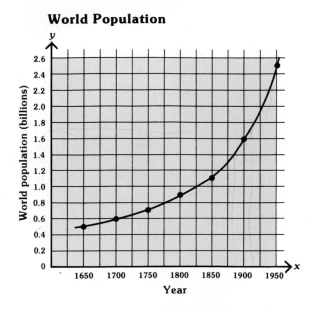

Use the graph for exercises 9–14.

9. What was the world population in 1650?

10. In about what year was the population twice what it had been in 1650?

11. About how many years did it take for the 1650 population to double? (See exercise 10.)

12. In about what year was the world population twice what it had been in 1750?

13. About how long did it take for the 1750 population to double? (See exercise 12.)

14. About how long did it take to double the population of 1850?

*15. Make a graph for the data in the table below, sketching a smooth curve through the points you mark on the grid.

Year	Population (billions)
1850	1.1
1900	1.6
1950	2.5
2000	6.8 (projected)
2050	18.3 (projected)

*16. According to the projections, about how long will it take for the 1950 population to double? (Use your graph for exercise 15.)

*17. Make a graph with these numbers along the axes.

x-axis (year):
1650, 1750, 1850, 1950

y-axis (doubling time in years):
0, 25, 50, 75, . . ., 200

For each year, mark a point to show about how long it took (or will take) for the population of that year to double. (Use your answers for exercises 11, 13, 14, and 16.)

*18. Does your graph for exercise 17 show that doubling time for world population increases or decreases as time goes on?

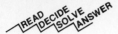

Problem Solving: Graphs

READ   At exactly 2 P.M., the *Gulliver* passes
Lost Island heading toward Nothing Atoll
at 60 kilometers per hour. At the same
moment, 550 kilometers away, the *Lilliput*
passes Nothing Atoll traveling toward
Lost Island at 40 kilometers per hour.
When will the two ships pass each other?

The *Gulliver* →
60 km per hour

Lost
Island

DECIDE   At the moment when the ships pass each
other, they will both be the same distance
from Lost Island. Make a table and a
graph for each ship, putting both graphs
on the same grid. Determine the answer
from the graphs.

SOLVE   *Gulliver*

Time	Distance from Lost Island (km)
2:00	0
3:00	60
4:00	120
5:00	180

Lilliput

Time	Distance from Lost Island (km)
2:00	550
3:00	510
4:00	470
5:00	430

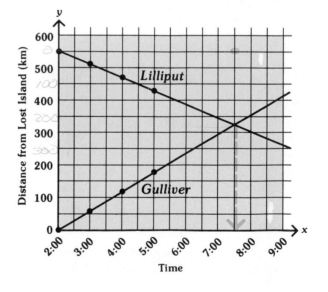

ANSWER   The ships will pass each other at
about 7:30 P.M.

124

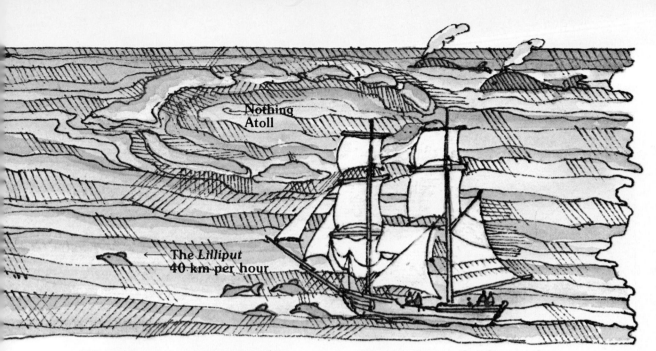

Nothing Atoll

← The *Lilliput*
40 km per hour

1. When they passed each other, about how far were the *Gulliver* and the *Lilliput* from Lost Island?

2. When the two ships passed, about how far were they from Nothing Atoll?

3. Copy the graphs for the *Gulliver* and the *Lilliput*, and extend them. Use your graph to estimate when the *Lilliput* will reach Lost Island.

4. Use your graph for exercise 3 to estimate when the *Gulliver* will reach Nothing Atoll.

5. About how far apart were the two ships at 4:30 P.M.?

For exercises 6-10, use this information. Jake and Emma plan to meet part way between their two homes, which are 17.5 km apart. They each leave home at 8:00 A.M. Every hour, Jake walks 2 km and Emma walks 3 km.

6. Make tables for Jake and Emma, showing the distance from Jake's home for each of them. Use these times: 8:00, 9:00, 10:00, 11:00.

7. Make graphs for Jake and Emma, putting both on the same grid.

8. Using your graph, estimate when Jake and Emma will meet.

9. When the two meet, about how far has Emma walked?

*10. Change the problem so that Emma leaves home at 9:00 A.M. Then repeat exercises 6-9.

Lab Activity

Making a Graph for an Experiment

Experiment

Materials

2 number cubes, each with faces numbered from 1 through 6

Procedure

1. Roll the cubes and add the 2 numbers that come up. Make a tally mark next to this sum in the table.
2. Repeat step 1 for 99 more rolls of the two cubes.
3. Complete the table.
4. Make a graph, marking a point for each ordered pair in the table. Draw a smooth curve through the points.

Sum x	Tally marks	Number of tally marks y	Ordered pairs (x,y)
2			
3			
4			
5			
6			
7			
8			
9			
10			
11			
12			

1. In this experiment, do you think that some sums would come up more often than others? Why?

2. Copy the table. Then perform the experiment, completing your table and making the graph.

3. Ask a friend to do the experiment. Are your graphs similar? Can you explain why this might be so?

Equations and Graphs

Janice made this table and graph for the equation $y = x^2 - 1$.

x	0	1	-1	2	-2	3	-3
y	-1	0	0	3	3	8	8

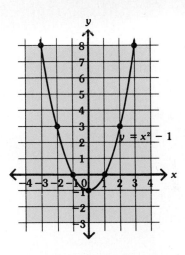

Any ordered pair that makes the equation true locates a point on the graph.

Any ordered pair that makes the equation false locates a point that is not on the graph.

Janice tested two ordered pairs to see if they located points on her graph. She used a calculator to help with the computation.

$(2.7, 6.29)$ $y = x^2 - 1$
    ↑   ↑
    x y $6.29 \stackrel{?}{=} (2.7)^2 - 1$

                 $6.29 \stackrel{?}{=} 7.29 - 1$

                 $6.29 = 6.29$ *True*

The point is on the graph.

$(1.4, 0.94)$ $y = x^2 - 1$

                 $0.94 \stackrel{?}{=} (1.4)^2 - 1$

                 $0.94 \stackrel{?}{=} 1.96 - 1$

                 $0.94 \stackrel{?}{=} 0.96$ *False*

The point is not on the graph.

1. Make a table for the equation $y = x^2 + 2$.

2. Use your table for exercise 1 to draw the graph of $y = x^2 + 2$.

Test each ordered pair to see if the point is on your graph for exercise 2. Write *yes* or *no*. Use a calculator to help with the computation.

3. $(3.8, 11.44)$ 4. $(5.1, 28.01)$

5. $(4.9, 26.01)$ 6. $(7.2, 189.72)$

7. $(0.16, 2.56)$ 8. $(14, 198)$

9. $(87, 7471)$ 10. $(145, 21{,}027)$

11. Is the point $(2.3, 10.87)$ on the graph of the equation $y = 3x^2 - 5$?

12. Is the point $(7.2, 244.28)$ on the graph of the equation $y = 4.5x^2 + 11$?

127

Chapter 6 Test
Coordinate Graphing, pages 112–127

1. In what quadrant are all the points with both coordinates negative?

2. Sound travels 0.33 kilometers per second. Use this equation to complete the table.

$$d = 0.33t$$

Distance (km) ← d Time (seconds) ← t

t	0	10	20	40	60
d	0	3.3			

3. Make a graph using the data in your table for exercise 2.

4. About how far does sound travel in 45 seconds? (Use your graph.)

5. Complete this table for the equation $y = x - 3$.

x	−2	−1	0	2	3	5
y	−5					

6. Draw the graph for the equation $y = x - 3$. Use your table.

7. Make a table for this graph. Use points with integer coordinates.

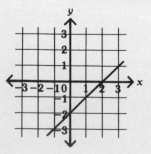

8. Write an equation that fits the data in your table for exercise 7.

9. Use the graph below. About how long did it take for the 1930 population of Roseville to double?

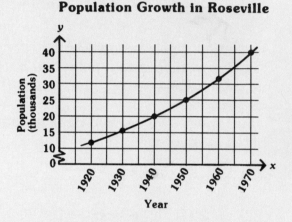

Population Growth in Roseville

10. Trains A and B are traveling toward each other. Train A was 600 km from Elm City at the time that train B left Elm City. About how far apart were trains A and B at 9:00? Use this graph.

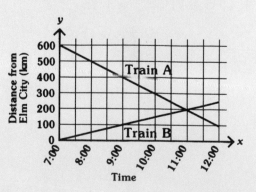

Problems Around Us

1. Mt. Bona in Alaska is 5044 meters high. Mt. Sanford, also in Alaska, is 95 meters lower than Mt. Bona. How high is Mt. Sanford?

2. In 1977, the Yale University library had 6,692,632 volumes, which was 2,690,623 fewer than the Harvard University library had. How many volumes were there in the Harvard library?

3. Mr. Trueblood is packing books in cartons. Each carton holds 48 books. How many full cartons will he have if there are 1554 books to be packed?

4. In the 1976 summer Olympic games at Montreal, the U.S. athletes won 34 gold, 35 silver, and 25 bronze medals. How many medals did they win in all?

5. Rodrigo left Iron City at 6:00 A.M., driving on Highway 24 toward Silverton at an average speed of 75 kilometers per hour. At the same moment, 412.5 kilometers away, Heidi left Silverton, driving on Highway 24 toward Iron City at an average speed of 90 kilometers per hour. About what time will they pass each other?

6. Robert bought 12 golf balls for $9.36. How much is that for each ball?

7. On January 23, 1971, a temperature of −62°C was reported in Alaska. On July 7, 1905, a record temperature of 53°C was reported in Arizona. How much higher was the Arizona temperature than the one in Alaska?

8. In 1977, the United States was the world's third largest producer of crude oil, producing an average of 33,620,000 metric tons per month. How many metric tons per year was this?

9. If 1427 eggs are to be packed in cartons holding 12 eggs each, how many cartons will be needed to hold all the eggs?

10. The Tiffany glass mosaic dome in a Chicago department store has 1,600,000 pieces of glass and covers an area of 557.5 square meters. To the nearest one, what is the average number of pieces of glass per square meter?

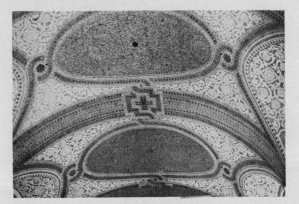

Individualized Skills Maintenance

Diagnose

A *pages 16–17*

5821 ÷ 6

2100 ÷ 32

53,421 ÷ 150

B *pages 32–33*

9.32 + 7.56

11.08 + 13.2

19.219 + 37.367

C *pages 32–33*

7.52 − 3.11

10.7 − 4.36

21.43 − 19.67

Practice

A

1. 5)485
2. 8)321
3. 6)858
4. 3)1846
5. 9)2137

6. 15)3600
7. 29)1773
8. 48)4000
9. 60)8436
10. 37)5328

11. 54)35208
12. 12)27367
13. 143)296
14. 250)1573
15. 317)12050

B

16. 9.07
    +4.39

17. 38.2
    +57.9

18. 0.736
    +0.223

19. 12.86
    + 8.5

20. 17.912
    +86.088

21. 18.09
    +26.472

22. 5.007
    +1.869

23. 20.67
    + 4.003

24. 1.001
    +4.9

25. 1.37
    +8.99

C

26. 8.74
    −5.37

27. 6.21
    −5.93

28. 10.009
    − 4.6

29. 27.000
    − 1.891

30. 10.3
    − 4.652

31. 48.91
    −28.09

32. 0.786
    −0.407

33. 0.9
    −0.123

34. 9.762
    −9.759

35. 57.217
    −29.5

Unit 2 Review

Chapter 4, pages 68–92

1. Evaluate $21 - x$ for $x = 9$.

2. Write an expression for 5 less than a number t.

Solve each equation.

3. $9 + v = 41$ 4. $\dfrac{d}{3} = 17$

5. $1 + 5a = 46$

6. Compute. Use the properties to make your work easier.

   $5.7 + 9 + 0 + 0.3$

7. Judy's phone bill last month was $35.16. This month, her bill was $4.38 less than that. How much was her bill this month?

Chapter 5, pages 94–110

8. Give the opposite of -17.

9. Compare. Use $>$, $<$, or $=$.

   $-2 \bullet -5$

10. List in order from the least to the greatest.

    $2 \quad -8 \quad -4$

Give each answer.

11. $-8 + 4$ 12. $-9 - 6$ 13. $8(-7)$

14. Evaluate $3k + 1$ for $k = -8$.

15. Give the missing integer.

    $(-7)(-4) + 5(-4) = (\text{▦} + 5)(-4)$

Chapter 6, pages 112–127

16. In which quadrant is the point with coordinates $(-2, 3)$?

17. Make a line graph for the equation $y = -x + 3$.

18. Write an equation for the line graph at the right.

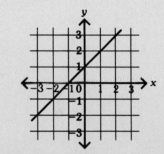

19. Using the graph below, tell about how far Alice was from Barton at 9:30.

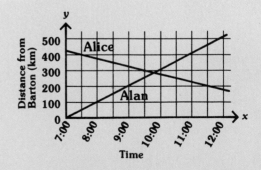

20. Use the graph above to determine about how far apart Alan and Alice were at 8:30.

Unit 2 Test
Chapters 4–6, pages 68–128

Evaluate each expression for $x = 14$.

1. $\dfrac{3x}{21}$ **2.** $-2x - 28$

Solve each equation.

3. $n - 7 = 26$ **4.** $8c = 56$

5. $4r + 7 = 43$

6. Write an expression for the product of 8 and a number y.

7. Compute. Use the properties to make your work easier.

$4 \times 9 \times 1 \times 25$

8. Give the opposite of 19.

9. Compare. Use $>$, $<$, or $=$.

$-9 \bullet -6$

10. List in order from the least to the greatest.

$-5 \quad -7 \quad -2$

Give each answer.

11. $4 - 8$ **12.** $(-6) \div (-2)$

13. $-3 + 7$

14. Give the missing integer.

$2[\blacksquare + (-1)] = 2(4) - 2(-1)$

15. In which quadrant is the point with coordinates $(8, -6)$?

16. Make a line graph for the equation $y = x - 2$.

17. Write an equation for the line graph at the right.

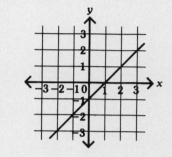

18. Using the graph below, tell about how far the *Argosy* was from Point Smith at 2:30.

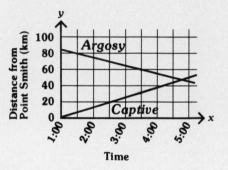

19. Use the graph above to determine about how far apart the *Argosy* and the *Captive* were at 3:30.

20. After a deposit of $15, Hal's savings account contained $47.80. How much was in the account before he made the deposit?

132

Unit 3

13

Prime and Composite Numbers

A. The number 30 can be written as the product of two whole numbers that are less than 30.

30 = 5 × 6

The numbers 5 and 6 are divisors or **factors** of 30.

Here are all the ways to write 30 as a product of two whole numbers.

30 = 1 × 30   30 = 3 × 10

30 = 2 × 15   30 = 5 × 6

Thus, the factors of 30 are 1, 2, 3, 5, 6, 10, 15, and 30.

B. Find all of the factors of 19.

19 = 19 × 1

The only factors of 19 are 19 and 1. Thus, 19 cannot be written as the product of two whole numbers that are less than 19.

C. Find all of the factors of 1.

1 = 1 × 1

The only factor of 1 is 1.

■ *A* ***composite number*** *can be written as the product of whole numbers that are less than itself. A composite number has more than two factors.*

■ *A* ***prime number*** *cannot be written as the product of whole numbers that are less than itself. A prime number has exactly two factors, 1 and the number itself.*

■ *The numbers 0 and 1 are neither prime nor composite. Every whole number greater than 1 is either prime or composite.*

1. List the first twelve prime numbers.

2. List the first twelve composite numbers.

3. Name the greatest prime number less than 100.

4. Name the greatest composite number less than 100.

If the number is a prime number, write *prime*.
If it is composite, write it as the product
of two whole numbers that are less than itself.

5. 14   6. 22   7. 31   8. 47   9. 12   10. 18   11. 72

12. 48   13. 57   14. 87   15. 49   16. 81   17. 63   18. 91

19. 121 20. 441 21. 144 22. 169 23. 225 24. 625 25. 103

List all the factors of each number.

26. 12   27. 18   28. 24   29. 54   ★30. 72   ★31. 90   ★32. 96   ★33. 80

List all the prime numbers less than 100 that have
the given ones digit. If there are none, write *none*.

34. 1   35. 2   36. 3   37. 4   38. 5   39. 6   40. 7   41. 8   42. 9

The numbers 11 and 13 are a pair of prime numbers
that differ by 2. (13 − 11 = 2) Find another pair
of prime numbers that differ by

43. 2.   44. 4.   45. 10.   46. 12.   47. 1.   48. 3.

★49. 13 and 31 are prime numbers with reversed digits.
Give all the pairs of two-digit primes with
reversed digits.

★50. Name five consecutive numbers which are composite.

Divisibility

There are rules to help decide if a whole number is divisible by a given number.

Number	Test for Divisibility
2	A number is divisible by 2 if its ones digit is 0, 2, 4, 6, or 8.
3	A number is divisible by 3 if the sum of its digits is divisible by 3.
4	A number is divisible by 4 if the number formed by its last two digits is divisible by 4.
5	A number is divisible by 5 if its ones digit is 0 or 5.
8	A number is divisible by 8 if the number formed by its last three digits is divisible by 8.
9	A number is divisible by 9 if the sum of its digits is divisible by 9.
10	A number is divisible by 10 if its ones digit is 0.

Use the divisibility tests on 531,180.

The ones digit is 0, so 531,180 is divisible by 2, 5, and 10.

The sum of the digits is 18.

$5 + 3 + 1 + 1 + 8 + 0 = 18$

Since 18 is divisible by 3 and 9, 531,180 is divisible by 3 and 9.

The number formed by the last two digits is 80. Since 80 is divisible by 4, then 531,180 is also divisible by 4.

The number formed by the last three digits is 180. Since 180 is not divisible by 8, ($180 \div 8 = 22.5$), then 531,180 is not divisible by 8.

Copy and complete the table. The check marks show that 2688 is divisible by 2, 3, 4, and 8.

	Number	Divisible by						
		2	3	4	5	8	9	10
	2688	√	√	√		√		
1.	7128							
2.	1512							
3.	4995							
4.	67,155							
5.	25,857							
6.	38,160							
7.	73,440							
8.	317,096							
9.	854,850							
10.	516,264							
11.	770,770							
12.	3,290,154							
13.	8,194,168							

If the statement is always true, write *true*. If it is not always true, give a number for which the statement is false.

14. If a number is divisible by both 2 and 3, it is divisible by 6.

15. If a number is divisible by both 3 and 5, it is divisible by 15.

16. If a number is divisible by both 2 and 6, it is divisible by 12.

Test each number for divisibility by 11. Use the test described below.

*17. 358,214

*18. 691,343

*19. 2,964,313

*20. 3,816,296

Divisibility by 11

Add the last two digits of the number to the number that remains when these digits are removed. Repeat the process. If you eventually get a number that is divisible by 11, then the original number is divisible by 11.

For example, to test 6,042,465:

```
  6042465
+      65
  60489
+    89
    693
+   93
     99
```

Since 99 is divisible by 11, so is 6,042,465.

Finding Prime Factors

A. A **factor tree** can be used to write a composite number as a product of primes.

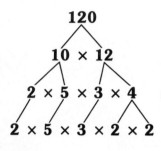

Write each composite number as a product of whole numbers. When a prime is reached, bring it down to the next line so it does not get "lost."

$120 = 2 \times 2 \times 2 \times 3 \times 5$

$120 = 2^3 \times 3 \times 5$

The **prime factorization** of 120 is $2^3 \times 3 \times 5$.

In a prime factorization, the factors are usually written in increasing order. Exponents are used for repeated factors.

B. A factor tree can begin any way. The result will always be the same prime factors.

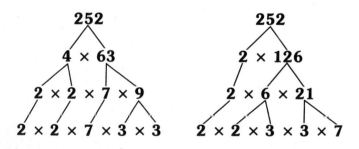

In each case, $2^2 \times 3^2 \times 7$ is the prime factorization of 252.

■*Every composite number has exactly one prime factorization.*

138

Use a factor tree to find the prime factorization of each number.

1. 24   2. 54   3. 66
4. 130   5. 144   6. 324
7. 216   8. 1000 9. 210

Construct two different factor trees for each number. Then write the prime factorization.

10. 162   11. 48   12. 240
13. 810   14. 756   15. 504
16. 132   17. 198   18. 1155
19. 6534 20. 2904 21. 4000

Write the prime factorization. Use the tests for divisibility to help you.

22. 32,400   23. 202,500
24. 165,375   25. 231,525
*26. 189,728   *27. 109,824

Write the prime factorization. Then list all of the factors of the number.

28. 8   29. 27   30. 28   31. 44
32. 60   33. 84   34. 36   *35. 1575

**More practice
Set 20, page 407**

Time Out

There are 12 roast beef sandwiches.

Seven of the sandwiches have mustard.

Five of the sandwiches have catsup.

Three of the sandwiches have both mustard and catsup.

How many sandwiches have neither mustard nor catsup?

Greatest Common Factor

A. Andrea wants to cut both pieces of material into strips of the same width. Find the widest strips that can be cut without any material being left over.

The width of the strips must divide the widths of the materials evenly.

Factors of 36: **1, 2, 3, 4, 6, 9, 12, 18, 36**

Factors of 54: **1, 2, 3, 6, 9, 18, 27, 54**

The **common factors** of 36 and 54 are 1, 2, 3, 6, 9, and 18.

The **greatest common factor** (GCF) is 18.

The widest strips that can be cut from 36-cm and 54-cm pieces of material without waste are 18 cm wide.

B. Find the GCF of 20 and 28.

Factors of 20: **1, 2, 4, 5, 10, 20**

Factors of 28: **1, 2, 4, 7, 14, 28**

The GCF of 20 and 28 is 4.

C. Find the GCF of 16 and 27.

Factors of 16: **1, 2, 4, 8, 16**

Factors of 27: **1, 3, 9, 27**

The GCF of 16 and 27 is 1.

D. You can use prime factorization to find the GCF of 48 and 60.

$$48 = 2 \times 2 \times 2 \times 2 \times 3$$
$$60 = 2 \times 2 \times 3 \times 5$$

$$2 \times 2 \times 3 = 12$$

The product of the common primes is 12.

The GCF of 48 and 60 is 12.

• **Discuss**   Can you find some examples for which the GCF of two numbers is the smaller number?

Find the common factors of each pair of numbers.

1. 8; 12   **2.** 12; 16   **3.** 24; 30   **4.** 42; 60

5. 63; 27   **6.** 90; 72   **7.** 90; 27   **8.** 72; 63

9. 45; 56   **10.** 36; 85   **11.** 9; 27   **12.** 14; 28

Find the GCF of each pair of numbers.

13. 12; 30   **14.** 30; 45   **15.** 24; 42

16. 60; 72   **17.** 51; 34   **18.** 87; 38

19. 51; 87   **20.** 34; 38   **21.** 36; 56

22. 72; 171   **23.** 726; 484   **24.** 1089; 968

Find the common factors and the GCF of each triplet of numbers.

*25. 90; 36; 126   ***26.** 52; 260; 364

More practice
Set 21, page 407

Keeping Skillful

Evaluate.

1. $\dfrac{12 + 8}{2}$

2. $\dfrac{14 - 6}{4}$

3. $\dfrac{68}{14 + 3}$

4. $\dfrac{56}{17 - 9}$

5. $\dfrac{80}{2 + 6} - 4$

6. $\dfrac{3(15)}{5} + 7$

7. $8 + \dfrac{39 - 29}{2}$

8. $\dfrac{6(3 + 7)}{2}$

9. $\dfrac{5(3) + 7 - 2}{3 + 2}$

10. $\dfrac{3(9 - 8 + 7)}{14 - 2}$

11. $\dfrac{72}{8} - \dfrac{32 + 4}{2 + 4}$

12. $\dfrac{5(8)}{4} + \dfrac{10(3 + 4)}{5(11 - 9)}$

Least Common Multiple

A. At the Western Wear Company, new shelves are to be built to store boxes of shirts. The boxes are 8 cm and 12 cm tall. A stack of 8-cm boxes must just fit between the shelves. A stack of 12-cm boxes must also just fit. Find the shortest distance between shelves that will meet these requirements.

To store the 8-cm boxes, the distance between shelves must be a multiple of 8. To store the 12-cm boxes, the distance between the shelves must be a multiple of 12.

If the distance between the shelves is a *common multiple* of 8 and 12, boxes of either size can be stored.

Multiples of 8: **8, 16, 24, 32, 40, 48, 56, 64, 72, . . .**

Multiples of 12: **12, 24, 36, 48, 60, 72, . . .**

Common multiples of 8 and 12: **24, 48, 72, . . .**

The *least common multiple* (LCM) of 8 and 12 is 24.

The shortest distance between the storage shelves is 24 cm.

B. Find the first three common multiples of 10 and 15. Then find the LCM.

Multiples of 10: **10, 20, 30, 40, 50, 60, 70, 80, 90,** . . .

Multiples of 15: **15, 30, 45, 60, 75, 90,** . . .

The first three common multiples of 10 and 15 are 30, 60, and 90.

The LCM of 10 and 15 is 30.

C. You can use prime factorization to find the LCM of 24 and 30.

$$24 = 2 \times 2 \times 2 \times 3$$

$$30 = 2 \times 3 \times 5$$

$$2 \times 2 \times 2 \times 3 \times 5 = 120$$

24 has more factors of 2 than 30 does. 24 has three 2s, so you need three 2s in the LCM.

24 and 30 each have one factor of 3. You need one 3 in the LCM.

30 has more factors of 5 than 24 does. 30 has one 5. You need one 5 in the LCM.

The LCM of 24 and 30 is 120.

• *Discuss* Can you find some examples for which the LCM of two numbers is the greater number?

List the first five multiples of each number.

1. 6 2. 9 3. 13 4. 17

5. 26 6. 34 7. 36 8. 45

For each pair of numbers, list the first three common multiples. Then find the LCM.

9. 6; 9   10. 9; 12

11. 12; 16   12. 9; 15

13. 2; 3   14. 3; 5

15. 6; 35   16. 10; 21

17. 7; 21   18. 6; 18

19. 10; 25   20. 14; 49

Use prime factorization to find the LCM of each pair of numbers.

21. 72; 48   22. 100; 40

23. 48; 50   24. 52; 54

25. 57; 58   26. 87; 88

27. 51; 87   28. 57; 81

29. 14; 15   30. 21; 22

Find the LCM of each triplet of numbers.

★31. 12; 18; 30   ★32. 15; 10; 25

★33. 45; 36; 54   ★34. 51; 57; 87

More practice
Set 22, page 407

Sequences

Each column below starts with a counting number greater than 1. Then the number is written as the sum of whole numbers greater than 1 in as many ways as possible.

2	3	4	5	6	7	8
		2 + 2	2 + 3	2 + 4	2 + 5	2 + 6
			3 + 2	3 + 3	3 + 4	3 + 5
				4 + 2	4 + 3	4 + 4
				2 + 2 + 2	5 + 2	5 + 3
					2 + 2 + 3	6 + 2
					2 + 3 + 2	2 + 3 + 3
					3 + 2 + 2	3 + 2 + 3
						3 + 3 + 2
						2 + 2 + 4
						2 + 4 + 2
						4 + 2 + 2
						2 + 2 + 2 + 2

The number of entries in each column is given below.

First column: 1   Fourth column: 3   Sixth column: 8
Second column: 1   Fifth column: 5   Seventh column: 13
Third column: 2

Here are the number of entries written as a **sequence** of numbers.

1, 1, 2, 3, 5, 8, 13, . . .

This sequence, called a Fibonacci sequence, continues without end.

1. Find the next two numbers in this sequence by listing 9 and its sums, and 10 and its sums.

Notice that each number in the sequence, after the first two numbers, is the sum of the two preceding numbers.

2. Do your lists for 9 and 10 follow this pattern?

There are many ways to construct sequences. One way is to use a rule or pattern for forming the sequence.

Consider this sequence.

3, −6, 12, −24, 48, . . .

Each number in this sequence is obtained by multiplying the preceding number by −2. The next term in this sequence would be −96.

This sequence, 1, 2, 2, 3, 3, 3, 4, 4, 4, 4, . . . , is formed by using 1 once, 2 twice, 3 three times, 4 four times, and so on. It can be continued by writing 5 for the next five numbers.

Give a rule for forming each sequence. Then use your rule to find the next three numbers.

3. 1, 4, 7, 10, 13, 16, 19, . . .

4. 3, 7, 11, 15, 19, 23, 27, . . .

5. 1, −2, 3, −4, 5, −6, 7, . . .

6. 1, 2, 4, 8, 16, 32, 64, . . .

7. 1, 22, 333, 4444, . . .

8. 1, 0, 2, 0, 0, 3, 0, 0, 0, . . .

9. Write the first six numbers in the following sequence. The first two numbers are 1 and 2. Each of the other numbers is obtained by multiplying the two numbers that precede it in the sequence.

10. Give the next three numbers in this sequence.

1, 2, 4, 7, 11, 16, 22, 29, . . .

Lab Activity

Sums of Squares

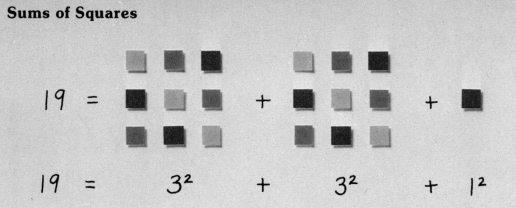

$$19 = 3^2 + 3^2 + 1^2$$

As shown, 19 objects can be grouped to show a sum of square numbers.

The numbers 1, 4, 9, 16, 25, 36, 49, 64, . . . are called **square numbers,** or **squares,** because $1 = 1^2$, $4 = 2^2$, $9 = 3^2$, $16 = 4^2$, and so on.

Try to write each counting number either as a square or as a sum of no more than four squares.

A. 19 can be represented two ways.

$$19 = 3^2 + 3^2 + 1^2$$
$$19 = 4^2 + 1^2 + 1^2 + 1^2$$

B. There are three ways to represent 25.

$$25 = 5^2$$
$$25 = 4^2 + 3^2$$
$$25 = 4^2 + 2^2 + 2^2 + 1^2$$

Separate groups of objects into square arrays to answer these questions.

1. Write each number from 1 to 50 as a square or as the sum of squares. Do not use more than four squares in the sum.

2. What is the first number in the list that has two representations?

3. What is the first number that has three representations?

4. What is the first number that requires four squares in its representation?

5. How many representations are there for the number 50?

Chapter 7 Test
Number Theory, pages 134–146

If the number is prime, write *prime*. If it is composite, write it as the product of two whole numbers that are less than itself.

1. 45

2. 123

3. 61

4. List all the factors of 28.

Is 91,020 divisible by

5. 2?

6. 3?

7. 4?

8. 5?

9. 8?

10. 9?

11. 10?

Write the prime factorization of each number.

12. 60

13. 2600

14. 376

15. List all the common factors of 24 and 56.

Find the GCF of each pair of numbers.

16. 104; 72

17. 63; 74

18. List the first three common multiples of 3 and 7.

Find the LCM of each pair of numbers.

19. 6; 21

20. 25; 14

Chapter 8   Multiplication and Division of Fractions

Finding Equal Fractions

$\frac{3}{4}$ gallon of paint

$\frac{6}{8}$ gallon of paint

Numerator ⟶ $\dfrac{3}{4}$
Denominator ⟶

$\dfrac{6}{8}$

A. The two cans contain equal amounts of paint.
$\frac{3}{4}$ and $\frac{6}{8}$ are **equal fractions.**

To find equal fractions, you can multiply both the numerator and the denominator of a fraction by the same nonzero number.

$$\overset{3 \times 4}{\frac{3}{4}} = \frac{12}{16}$$
$$\underset{4 \times 4}{}$$

Multiply both the numerator and the denominator by 4.

$$\overset{3 \times 5}{\frac{3}{4}} = \frac{15}{20}$$
$$\underset{4 \times 5}{}$$

Multiply both the numerator and the denominator by 5.

$\frac{3}{4}$, $\frac{12}{16}$, and $\frac{15}{20}$ are equal fractions.

B. Give the missing numerator.

$$\frac{2}{3} = \frac{\text{\rule{0.4em}{0.05em}}}{27}$$

$$\frac{2}{3} = \frac{\text{\rule{0.4em}{0.05em}}}{27}$$ The denominator was
$\overset{3\times9}{\longrightarrow}$ multiplied by 9.

$$\overset{2\times9}{\frac{2}{3}} = \frac{18}{27}$$ Multiply the
numerator by 9.

C. Give the missing denominator.

$$\frac{5}{7} = \frac{20}{\text{\rule{0.4em}{0.05em}}}$$

$$\overset{5\times4}{\underset{7\times4}{\frac{5}{7}}} = \frac{20}{28}$$ The numerator was
multiplied by 4.
Multiply the
denominator by 4.

• **Discuss** When is a fraction equal to zero?
When is a fraction equal to one?

Use multiplication to find four fractions equal
to the given fraction.

1. $\frac{1}{2}$ 2. $\frac{3}{5}$ 3. $\frac{1}{4}$ 4. $\frac{2}{3}$ 5. $\frac{4}{5}$ 6. $\frac{1}{8}$ 7. $\frac{4}{9}$ 8. $\frac{5}{6}$

9. $\frac{1}{9}$ 10. $\frac{6}{7}$ 11. $\frac{3}{4}$ 12. $\frac{5}{8}$ 13. $\frac{2}{5}$ 14. $\frac{1}{6}$ 15. $\frac{4}{7}$ 16. $\frac{5}{9}$

Give the missing numerator or denominator.

17. $\frac{1}{2} = \frac{\text{\rule{0.4em}{0.05em}}}{6}$ 18. $\frac{3}{5} = \frac{\text{\rule{0.4em}{0.05em}}}{20}$ 19. $\frac{2}{3} = \frac{\text{\rule{0.4em}{0.05em}}}{15}$ 20. $\frac{3}{8} = \frac{\text{\rule{0.4em}{0.05em}}}{40}$ 21. $\frac{2}{9} = \frac{\text{\rule{0.4em}{0.05em}}}{27}$

22. $\frac{7}{7} = \frac{21}{\text{\rule{0.4em}{0.05em}}}$ 23. $\frac{2}{6} = \frac{10}{\text{\rule{0.4em}{0.05em}}}$ 24. $\frac{7}{8} = \frac{28}{\text{\rule{0.4em}{0.05em}}}$ 25. $\frac{5}{6} = \frac{35}{\text{\rule{0.4em}{0.05em}}}$ 26. $\frac{3}{5} = \frac{21}{\text{\rule{0.4em}{0.05em}}}$

27. $\frac{8}{9} = \frac{96}{\text{\rule{0.4em}{0.05em}}}$ 28. $\frac{2}{13} = \frac{14}{\text{\rule{0.4em}{0.05em}}}$ 29. $\frac{2}{15} = \frac{\text{\rule{0.4em}{0.05em}}}{90}$ 30. $\frac{7}{18} = \frac{35}{\text{\rule{0.4em}{0.05em}}}$ 31. $\frac{8}{21} = \frac{24}{\text{\rule{0.4em}{0.05em}}}$

32. $\frac{5}{16} = \frac{75}{\text{\rule{0.4em}{0.05em}}}$ 33. $\frac{7}{12} = \frac{\text{\rule{0.4em}{0.05em}}}{240}$ 34. $\frac{3}{16} = \frac{\text{\rule{0.4em}{0.05em}}}{96}$ 35. $\frac{0}{8} = \frac{\text{\rule{0.4em}{0.05em}}}{24}$ 36. $\frac{7}{30} = \frac{\text{\rule{0.4em}{0.05em}}}{120}$

★**37.** $\frac{1}{3} = \frac{\text{\rule{0.4em}{0.05em}}}{51} = \frac{\text{\rule{0.4em}{0.05em}}}{108}$ ★**38.** $\frac{5}{8} = \frac{65}{\text{\rule{0.4em}{0.05em}}} = \frac{80}{\text{\rule{0.4em}{0.05em}}}$ ★**39.** $\frac{7}{16} = \frac{\text{\rule{0.4em}{0.05em}}}{128} = \frac{98}{\text{\rule{0.4em}{0.05em}}}$

40. A paint can contains $\frac{3}{5}$ gallon.
This is $\frac{\text{\rule{0.4em}{0.05em}}}{15}$ gallon

41. A trim strip is $\frac{5}{16}$ inch wide.
This is $\frac{\text{\rule{0.4em}{0.05em}}}{32}$ inch.

149

Fractions in Lowest Terms

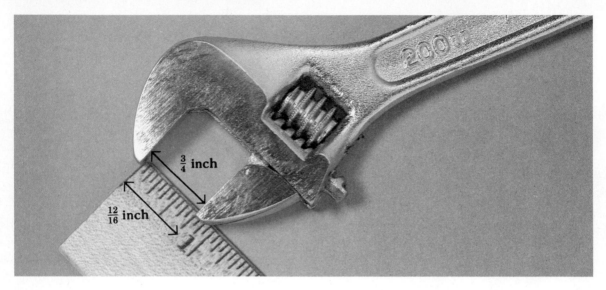

$\frac{3}{4}$ inch

$\frac{12}{16}$ inch

A. The span of the wrench is $\frac{12}{16}$ inch or $\frac{3}{4}$ inch.
$\frac{12}{16}$ and $\frac{3}{4}$ are equal fractions.

You can divide the numerator and denominator of a
fraction by a common factor to find an equal fraction.

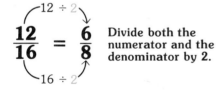
$$\frac{12}{16} = \frac{6}{8}$$
Divide both the numerator and the denominator by 2.

$$\frac{12}{16} = \frac{3}{4}$$
Divide both the numerator and the denominator by 4.

A fraction is in **lowest terms** when 1 is
the only whole number that divides both
the numerator and the denominator.

To write a fraction in lowest terms, divide
the numerator and the denominator by their
greatest common factor (GCF).

The numerator and denominator of $\frac{12}{16}$ were divided
by their GCF, 4. The result, $\frac{3}{4}$, is in lowest terms
because the GCF of 3 and 4 is 1.

B. Write $\frac{16}{24}$ in lowest terms.

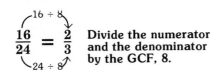

$$\frac{16}{24} = \frac{2}{3}$$

Divide the numerator and the denominator by the GCF, 8.

C. Find the missing denominator.

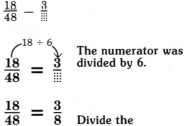

$$\frac{18}{48} = \frac{3}{\vdots}$$

The numerator was divided by 6.

$$\frac{18}{48} = \frac{3}{8}$$

Divide the denominator by 6.

Write each fraction in lowest terms.

1. $\frac{9}{12}$ **2.** $\frac{8}{20}$ **3.** $\frac{15}{25}$ **4.** $\frac{18}{27}$ **5.** $\frac{6}{7}$ **6.** $\frac{4}{9}$ **7.** $\frac{28}{35}$ **8.** $\frac{36}{48}$

9. $\frac{55}{65}$ **10.** $\frac{99}{121}$ **11.** $\frac{36}{88}$ **12.** $\frac{64}{90}$ **13.** $\frac{48}{72}$ **14.** $\frac{37}{45}$ **15.** $\frac{75}{225}$ **16.** $\frac{92}{108}$

17. $\frac{39}{104}$ **18.** $\frac{121}{143}$ **19.** $\frac{35}{105}$ **20.** $\frac{126}{216}$ **21.** $\frac{79}{86}$ **22.** $\frac{156}{196}$ **23.** $\frac{145}{210}$ **24.** $\frac{75}{385}$

Find the missing numerator or denominator.

25. $\frac{24}{36} = \frac{\vdots}{3}$ **26.** $\frac{49}{63} = \frac{\vdots}{9}$ **27.** $\frac{6}{45} = \frac{\vdots}{15}$ **28.** $\frac{36}{81} = \frac{\vdots}{9}$ **29.** $\frac{44}{110} = \frac{\vdots}{10}$

30. $\frac{35}{90} = \frac{7}{\vdots}$ **31.** $\frac{48}{76} = \frac{12}{\vdots}$ **32.** $\frac{42}{70} = \frac{3}{\vdots}$ **33.** $\frac{34}{85} = \frac{2}{\vdots}$ **34.** $\frac{33}{117} = \frac{11}{\vdots}$

★35. $\frac{56}{144} = \frac{\vdots}{18}$ **★36.** $\frac{76}{108} = \frac{19}{\vdots}$ **★37.** $\frac{136}{156} = \frac{34}{\vdots}$ **★38.** $\frac{75}{216} = \frac{\vdots}{72}$ **★39.** $\frac{44}{124} = \frac{\vdots}{31}$

Jeanne claims to have written all the fractions equal to $\frac{6}{10}$.

★40. Should Jeanne's list contain a fraction in lowest terms?

★41. Should Jeanne's list contain $\frac{30}{50}$? $\frac{90}{150}$? $\frac{120}{200}$?

★42. Do you believe that Jeanne wrote all the fractions equal to $\frac{6}{10}$? Explain your answer.

More practice
Set 23, page 408

Mixed Numbers and Improper Fractions

A. Numbers like $1\frac{3}{4}$, $3\frac{1}{4}$, and $4\frac{1}{2}$ are ***mixed numbers.*** A mixed number has a whole-number part and a fraction part.

B. A fraction that can be written as a whole number greater than zero, or as a mixed number, is called an ***improper fraction.*** Numbers like $\frac{7}{4}$, $\frac{12}{4}$, and $\frac{19}{4}$ are improper fractions.

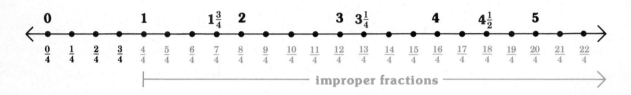

C. Write a whole number or a mixed number for $\frac{38}{3}$.

To find the mixed number or whole number for an improper fraction, divide the numerator by the denominator.

$$\begin{array}{r} 12\frac{2}{3} \longleftarrow \text{Remainder} \\ 3\overline{)38}\phantom{\frac{2}{3}} \longleftarrow \text{Divisor} \end{array}$$

$$\frac{38}{3} = 12\frac{2}{3}$$

D. Write a fraction for $3\frac{1}{4}$.

$3\frac{1}{4}$ Multiply the denominator 4 by the whole number 3, then add the numerator 1 to get 13.

$$3\frac{1}{4} = \frac{13}{4}$$ The denominator is 4.

Write a mixed number or a whole number for each fraction.

1. $\frac{7}{2}$ 2. $\frac{20}{6}$ 3. $\frac{16}{4}$ 4. $\frac{16}{5}$ 5. $\frac{13}{3}$ 6. $\frac{21}{7}$ 7. $\frac{47}{5}$ 8. $\frac{96}{8}$

9. $\frac{114}{7}$ 10. $\frac{230}{10}$ 11. $\frac{28}{9}$ 12. $\frac{34}{5}$ 13. $\frac{64}{4}$ 14. $\frac{57}{5}$ 15. $\frac{87}{8}$ 16. $\frac{138}{9}$

17. $\frac{200}{7}$ 18. $\frac{49}{12}$ 19. $\frac{50}{15}$ 20. $\frac{84}{24}$ 21. $\frac{92}{36}$ 22. $\frac{79}{25}$ 23. $\frac{125}{50}$ 24. $\frac{341}{1}$

Write a fraction for each mixed number.

25. $3\frac{1}{2}$ 26. $4\frac{3}{4}$ 27. $5\frac{1}{8}$ 28. $7\frac{5}{6}$ 29. $2\frac{7}{9}$ 30. $1\frac{3}{5}$ 31. $6\frac{2}{9}$

32. $3\frac{2}{3}$ 33. $8\frac{3}{5}$ 34. $6\frac{1}{6}$ 35. $4\frac{7}{8}$ 36. $7\frac{1}{2}$ 37. $2\frac{3}{7}$ 38. $11\frac{2}{5}$

39. $9\frac{5}{8}$ 40. $10\frac{3}{8}$ 41. $4\frac{1}{3}$ 42. $7\frac{3}{7}$ 43. $4\frac{5}{12}$ 44. $5\frac{7}{16}$ 45. $4\frac{4}{15}$

46. $3\frac{11}{12}$ 47. $6\frac{3}{16}$ 48. $2\frac{7}{15}$ 49. $1\frac{19}{24}$ 50. $1\frac{23}{36}$ 51. $2\frac{7}{36}$ 52. $2\frac{5}{24}$

For the fraction $\frac{a}{b}$, what can you say about a and b if

★53. $\frac{a}{b} = 1$?   ★54. $\frac{a}{b} = 0$?

★55. $\frac{a}{b} < 1$?   ★56. $\frac{a}{b} > 1$?

★57. $\frac{a}{b}$ can be written as a whole number greater than 1?

More practice
Set 24, page 408

Fractions and Terminating Decimals

Every fraction can be written as a decimal. To write a decimal for a fraction, divide the numerator by the denominator. If the division eventually results in a remainder of zero, the decimal is a **terminating decimal.**

A. Write a decimal for $\frac{5}{8}$.

$$\begin{array}{r} 0.625 \\ 8\overline{)5.000} \\ -48 \\ \hline 20 \\ -16 \\ \hline 40 \\ -40 \\ \hline 0 \end{array}$$

Divide until the remainder is zero.

$\frac{5}{8} = 0.625$

• **Discuss** How would you write a decimal for $267\frac{5}{8}$?

B. Write a fraction for 0.59.

0.59 is 59 hundredths.

$0.59 = \frac{59}{100}$

• **Discuss** How would you write a mixed number for 38.59?

Write a decimal for each fraction.

1. $\frac{1}{2}$	2. $\frac{1}{4}$	3. $\frac{1}{8}$
4. $\frac{1}{5}$	5. $\frac{3}{4}$	6. $\frac{3}{8}$
7. $\frac{9}{10}$	8. $\frac{7}{10}$	9. $\frac{3}{20}$
10. $\frac{11}{20}$	11. $\frac{4}{25}$	12. $\frac{7}{25}$
13. $\frac{13}{50}$	14. $\frac{27}{50}$	15. $\frac{4}{100}$
16. $\frac{7}{1000}$	17. $\frac{85}{1000}$	18. $\frac{3}{100}$
19. $\frac{33}{500}$	20. $\frac{77}{250}$	21. $\frac{45}{12}$
22. $\frac{39}{12}$	23. $\frac{52}{8}$	24. $\frac{75}{8}$
★25. $43\frac{11}{32}$	★26. $25\frac{17}{32}$	★27. $34\frac{13}{64}$
★28. $58\frac{27}{64}$	★29. $62\frac{41}{125}$	★30. $29\frac{8}{125}$

Write a fraction for each decimal.

31. 0.6	32. 0.9
33. 0.34	34. 0.82
35. 0.04	36. 0.07
37. 0.089	38. 0.047
★39. 24.178	★40. 86.326

Fractions and Repeating Decimals

For some fractions, dividing the numerator by the denominator results in a quotient that has a repeating digit or group of digits. This quotient is called a **repeating decimal**.

A. Write a decimal for $\frac{5}{6}$.

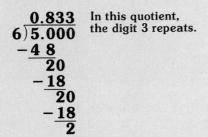

In this quotient, the digit 3 repeats.

$\frac{5}{6} = 0.833...$

The repeating digit, or group of digits, is called the **repetend.** A bar is used to indicate the repetend. $0.833... = 0.8\overline{3}$

$\frac{5}{6} = 0.8\overline{3}$

B. Write a decimal for $\frac{15}{22}$.

$$\begin{array}{r} 0.68181 \\ 22\overline{)15.00000} \\ -13\,2 \\ \hline 1\,80 \\ -1\,76 \\ \hline 40 \\ -22 \\ \hline 180 \\ -176 \\ \hline 40 \\ -22 \\ \hline 18 \end{array}$$

$\frac{15}{22} = 0.6\overline{81}$

● **Discuss** How many different remainders are possible in a division exercise in which the divisor is 7? in which the divisor is 12?

Write a decimal for each number.

1. $\frac{1}{3}$ 2. $\frac{1}{6}$ 3. $\frac{4}{9}$ 4. $\frac{2}{9}$ 5. $\frac{5}{11}$ 6. $\frac{7}{11}$ 7. $\frac{11}{12}$

8. $\frac{5}{12}$ 9. $\frac{7}{15}$ 10. $\frac{4}{15}$ 11. $\frac{74}{30}$ 12. $\frac{97}{30}$ 13. $\frac{1}{7}$ 14. $\frac{2}{7}$

15. $\frac{3}{7}$ 16. $\frac{4}{7}$ 17. $\frac{5}{74}$ 18. $\frac{11}{27}$ 19. $\frac{8}{37}$ 20. $\frac{13}{54}$ 21. $\frac{73}{101}$

22. $\frac{100}{333}$ 23. $\frac{40}{111}$ 24. $\frac{8}{41}$ 25. $\frac{57}{123}$ ★26. $18\frac{7}{33}$ ★27. $21\frac{17}{82}$ ★28. $47\frac{19}{505}$

Multiplying Fractions and Whole Numbers

A. The stone base has been spread on $\frac{3}{5}$ of the road.

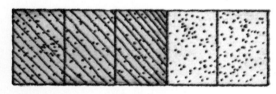

Concrete has been poured over $\frac{1}{2}$ of the stone base.

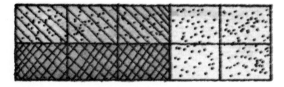

What part of the road has both the stone base and the concrete?

You can see that $\frac{1}{2}$ of $\frac{3}{5}$ is $\frac{3}{10}$. $\frac{3}{10}$ of the road has both a stone base and the concrete.

You can find the answer by multiplying.

$$\frac{1}{2} \times \frac{3}{5} = \frac{3}{10} \quad \begin{array}{l} \longleftarrow (1 \times 3) \\ \longleftarrow (2 \times 5) \end{array}$$

■ *To multiply fractions, multiply the numerators and multiply the denominators.*

If possible, first divide a numerator and a denominator by a common factor.

B. Find $\frac{1}{6} \times \frac{4}{5}$.

$$\frac{1}{\overset{}{\underset{3}{6}}} \times \frac{\overset{2}{4}}{5} = \frac{2}{15} \quad \begin{array}{l}\text{The denominator 6 and} \\ \text{the numerator 4 were} \\ \text{each divided by 2.}\end{array}$$

c. Find $\frac{3}{4} \times 32$.

$$\frac{3}{4} \times \mathbf{32}$$

$$\frac{3}{\underset{1}{4}} \times \frac{\overset{8}{\cancel{32}}}{1} = 24 \quad \textbf{First write 32 as a fraction.}$$

D. Find $\frac{1}{5} \times \frac{3}{4} \times 10$.

$$\frac{1}{5} \times \frac{3}{4} \times \mathbf{10}$$

$$\frac{1}{\underset{1}{5}} \times \frac{3}{\underset{2}{4}} \times \frac{\overset{\overset{1}{2}}{\cancel{10}}}{1} = \frac{3}{2} = 1\frac{1}{2}$$

Multiply.

1. $\frac{1}{4} \times \frac{2}{3}$ **2.** $\frac{3}{5} \times \frac{1}{6}$ **3.** $\frac{1}{3} \times \frac{7}{8}$ **4.** $\frac{3}{7} \times \frac{1}{3}$ **5.** $\frac{3}{5} \times \frac{5}{8}$

6. $\frac{2}{5} \times \frac{7}{12}$ **7.** $\frac{7}{8} \times \frac{3}{7}$ **8.** $\frac{4}{9} \times \frac{3}{10}$ **9.** $\frac{3}{4} \times \frac{2}{3}$ **10.** $\frac{2}{9} \times \frac{1}{2}$

11. $\frac{1}{2} \times \frac{1}{2}$ **12.** $\frac{1}{3} \times \frac{1}{3}$ **13.** $\frac{1}{4} \times \frac{1}{4}$ **14.** $\frac{2}{3} \times \frac{2}{3}$ **15.** $\frac{3}{4} \times \frac{3}{4}$

16. $\frac{4}{5} \times \frac{5}{6}$ **17.** $\frac{2}{3} \times \frac{3}{10}$ **18.** $\frac{4}{7} \times \frac{3}{8}$ **19.** $\frac{2}{5} \times \frac{5}{6}$ **20.** $\frac{6}{7} \times \frac{7}{9}$

21. $\frac{1}{2} \times 10$ **22.** $\frac{1}{3} \times 9$ **23.** $\frac{2}{5} \times 25$ **24.** $\frac{3}{4} \times 12$ **25.** $\frac{1}{2} \times 5$

26. $7 \times \frac{1}{4}$ **27.** $6 \times \frac{5}{8}$ **28.** $10 \times \frac{3}{4}$ **29.** $3 \times \frac{5}{12}$ **30.** $8 \times \frac{3}{10}$

31. $4 \times \frac{3}{14}$ **32.** $5 \times \frac{4}{15}$ **33.** $6 \times \frac{5}{9}$ **34.** $9 \times \frac{5}{6}$ **35.** $8 \times \frac{9}{10}$

36. $\frac{1}{2} \times \frac{2}{3} \times \frac{5}{6}$ **37.** $\frac{2}{3} \times \frac{3}{4} \times \frac{1}{5}$ **38.** $\frac{3}{8} \times \frac{4}{5} \times \frac{1}{2}$ **39.** $\frac{3}{7} \times \frac{7}{10} \times \frac{2}{3}$

40. $\frac{5}{8} \times \frac{1}{3} \times 6$ **41.** $\frac{7}{9} \times \frac{3}{4} \times 7$ **42.** $5 \times \frac{2}{3} \times \frac{5}{12}$ **43.** $4 \times \frac{3}{8} \times \frac{1}{5}$

★44. A concrete layer is on $\frac{7}{8}$ of a 14-mile highway. The asphalt topping is on $\frac{1}{4}$ of the concrete. How many miles of the road have both concrete and asphalt?

★45. A paver uses about 300 tons of concrete per hour. How many tons are used in $\frac{1}{2}$ minute?

**More practice
Set 25, page 408**

Multiplying Mixed Numbers

A. For a party, the Zientys are making $2\frac{1}{2}$ times this recipe. How much chicken do they need?

Find $2\frac{1}{2} \times 2\frac{3}{4}$

$$2\frac{1}{2} \times 2\frac{3}{4}$$

$\frac{5}{2} \times \frac{11}{4} = \frac{55}{8} = 6\frac{7}{8}$ Write $2\frac{1}{2}$ and $2\frac{3}{4}$ as fractions.

They need $6\frac{7}{8}$ cups of chicken.

B. How much bacon do they need?

Find $2\frac{1}{2} \times 6$.

$$2\frac{1}{2} \times 6$$

$\frac{5}{2} \times \frac{\overset{3}{\cancel{6}}}{1} = 15$

They need 15 slices of bacon.

Multiply.

1. $5 \times 3\frac{2}{5}$
2. $8 \times 1\frac{1}{4}$
3. $14 \times 2\frac{3}{7}$
4. $3\frac{5}{7} \times 21$
5. $7\frac{2}{3} \times 12$

6. $20 \times 6\frac{1}{5}$
7. $4\frac{1}{3} \times 15$
8. $9\frac{1}{2} \times 16$
9. $5\frac{1}{2} \times 13$
10. $3\frac{3}{4} \times 11$

11. $6\frac{1}{2} \times \frac{2}{3}$
12. $8\frac{1}{4} \times \frac{1}{6}$
13. $3\frac{3}{5} \times \frac{1}{2}$
14. $2\frac{3}{8} \times \frac{4}{5}$
15. $5\frac{1}{4} \times \frac{3}{7}$

16. $1\frac{2}{3} \times \frac{3}{5}$
17. $7\frac{3}{4} \times \frac{4}{9}$
18. $4\frac{4}{5} \times \frac{5}{6}$
19. $\frac{1}{3} \times 2\frac{5}{8}$
20. $\frac{3}{10} \times 6\frac{2}{3}$

21. $5\frac{1}{3} \times 3\frac{1}{2}$
22. $1\frac{1}{4} \times 4\frac{1}{2}$
23. $2\frac{1}{3} \times 2\frac{1}{7}$
24. $1\frac{3}{4} \times 1\frac{3}{4}$
25. $2\frac{1}{2} \times 2\frac{1}{2}$

26. $1\frac{1}{3} \times 1\frac{7}{8}$
27. $3\frac{1}{8} \times 4\frac{4}{5}$
28. $2\frac{5}{8} \times 3\frac{1}{7}$
29. $6\frac{3}{4} \times 5\frac{1}{3}$
30. $5\frac{5}{8} \times 8\frac{4}{9}$

31. $\frac{7}{10} \times 2\frac{1}{2} \times 1\frac{3}{7}$
32. $2\frac{1}{2} \times \frac{3}{5} \times 2\frac{1}{3}$
33. $1\frac{4}{5} \times 3\frac{2}{3} \times \frac{5}{8}$

34. $1\frac{3}{5} \times 4\frac{1}{8} \times 2\frac{1}{2}$
35. $1\frac{1}{5} \times 4\frac{1}{2} \times 3\frac{1}{3}$
36. $5\frac{5}{7} \times 2\frac{1}{3} \times 1\frac{7}{8}$

37. How much sugar is needed for $2\frac{1}{2}$ times the recipe?

38. How much flour is needed for $2\frac{1}{2}$ times the recipe?

*39. The party guests ate $\frac{2}{8}$ of $2\frac{1}{2}$ times the recipe. How much of the original recipe was eaten?

**More practice
Set 26, page 408**

More practice
Set 26, page 408

Time Out

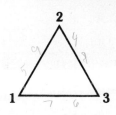

The numbers 1, 2, and 3 are placed at the vertices of the triangle. Arrange the numbers 4, 5, 6, 7, 8, and 9 along the sides of the triangle so that the sum of the numbers along each side is 17.

Florist

Bill Moylan is a florist. One of the items he sells is Japanese flower arrangements. An arrangement in a shallow dish is called a *moribana* arrangement. The three main stems represent heaven, people, and earth. The lengths H, P, and E of these stems depend on the length L and the depth D of the dish.

$H = 1\frac{1}{2}L + D$

$P = \frac{2}{3}H$

$E = \frac{1}{2}P$

Find the lengths of the stems for these bowls.

Dish length l.	Dish depth D	Length of the heaven stem (H) $H = 1\frac{1}{2}L + D$	Length of the people stem (P) $P = \frac{2}{3}H$	Length of the earth stem (E) $E = \frac{1}{2}P$
8 in.	3 in.	1.	2.	3.
10 in.	6 in.	4.	5.	6.
8 in.	2 in.	7.	8.	9.
6 in.	3 in.	10.	11.	12.
10 in.	4 in.	13.	14.	15.

Reciprocals

A. Two numbers whose product is 1 are **reciprocals.**

$$\frac{2}{3} \times \frac{3}{2} = \frac{6}{6} = 1$$

$\frac{3}{2}$ is the reciprocal of $\frac{2}{3}$ and $\frac{2}{3}$ is the reciprocal of $\frac{3}{2}$.

If you interchange the numerator and the denominator of a nonzero fraction, you form the reciprocal of the fraction.

B. Find the reciprocal of $\frac{4}{5}$.

$$\frac{4}{5}$$

$\frac{5}{4}$ Interchange the numerator and the denominator.

Check

$$\frac{4}{5} \times \frac{5}{4} = \frac{20}{20} = 1$$

The reciprocal of $\frac{4}{5}$ is $\frac{5}{4}$.

C. Find the reciprocal of 8.

$$8 = \frac{8}{1} \quad \text{Write 8 as a fraction.}$$

$\frac{1}{8}$ is the reciprocal of 8.

D. Find the reciprocal of $3\frac{1}{4}$.

$$3\frac{1}{4} = \frac{13}{4} \quad \text{Write } 3\frac{1}{4} \text{ as a fraction.}$$

$\frac{4}{13}$ is the reciprocal of $3\frac{1}{4}$.

Give the reciprocal of each number.

1. $\frac{5}{8}$ 2. $\frac{9}{16}$ 3. $\frac{7}{12}$ 4. $\frac{3}{4}$

5. $\frac{25}{32}$ 6. $\frac{11}{50}$ 7. $\frac{1}{7}$ 8. $\frac{1}{10}$

9. $\frac{1}{16}$ 10. $\frac{1}{32}$ 11. 5   12. 9

13. 12   14. 16   15. $\frac{8}{3}$ 16. $\frac{15}{4}$

17. $5\frac{1}{2}$ 18. $10\frac{1}{3}$ 19. $2\frac{3}{8}$ 20. $8\frac{2}{9}$

21. $7\frac{1}{10}$ 22. $6\frac{7}{8}$ 23. $4\frac{3}{16}$ 24. $12\frac{2}{3}$

Give the missing number.

25. $\frac{7}{8} \times \blacksquare = 1$

26. $\blacksquare \times 4 = 1$

27. $5\frac{1}{4} \times \blacksquare = 1$

28. $7 \times \frac{1}{7} = \blacksquare$

29. $\blacksquare \times 3\frac{4}{5} = 1$

30. $\frac{1}{3} \times \blacksquare = 1$

★31. Give a number that does not have a reciprocal.

Dividing by a Fraction

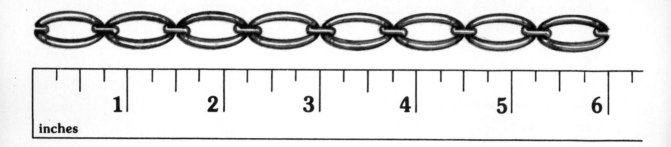

A. Karen is making a chain belt. Each link is $\frac{3}{4}$ inch long. How many links does she need for a 6-inch section of the belt?

Find $6 \div \frac{3}{4}$.

You can find the answer by counting the number of $\frac{3}{4}$-inch links that fit in 6 inches.

$6 \div \frac{3}{4} = 8$

You can also find the answer by multiplying by the reciprocal of the divisor.

$6 \div \frac{3}{4}$

$\frac{6}{1} \times \frac{4}{3}$ Write 6 as a fraction.
Multiply by the reciprocal of $\frac{3}{4}$.

$\overset{2}{\cancel{6}}{1} \times \frac{4}{\underset{1}{\cancel{3}}} = \frac{8}{1} = 8$

Karen needs 8 links.

B. How many links does Karen need to make the belt $22\frac{1}{2}$ inches long?

Find $22\frac{1}{2} \div \frac{3}{4}$.

$22\frac{1}{2} \div \frac{3}{4}$ Write $22\frac{1}{2}$ as a fraction.
Multiply by the reciprocal of $\frac{3}{4}$.

$\overset{15}{\underset{1}{\cancel{\frac{45}{2}}}} \times \overset{2}{\underset{1}{\cancel{\frac{4}{3}}}} = \frac{30}{1} = 30$

She needs 30 links.

■ *Dividing by a number is the same as multiplying by its reciprocal.*

C. Find $\frac{3}{8} \div \frac{2}{3}$.

$\frac{3}{8} \div \frac{2}{3}$

$\frac{3}{8} \times \frac{3}{2} = \frac{9}{16}$

Divide.

1. $7 \div \frac{1}{2}$ 2. $8 \div \frac{1}{3}$ 3. $5 \div \frac{3}{5}$ 4. $12 \div \frac{3}{4}$ 5. $10 \div \frac{5}{6}$

6. $16 \div \frac{4}{7}$ 7. $14 \div \frac{7}{10}$ 8. $15 \div \frac{5}{9}$ 9. $18 \div \frac{2}{5}$ 10. $20 \div \frac{4}{5}$

11. $\frac{2}{3} \div \frac{5}{6}$ 12. $\frac{3}{4} \div \frac{7}{8}$ 13. $\frac{3}{8} \div \frac{6}{7}$ 14. $\frac{2}{9} \div \frac{4}{5}$ 15. $\frac{5}{12} \div \frac{5}{6}$

16. $\frac{3}{7} \div \frac{3}{5}$ 17. $\frac{9}{10} \div \frac{2}{5}$ 18. $\frac{7}{12} \div \frac{7}{8}$ 19. $\frac{5}{8} \div \frac{15}{16}$ 20. $\frac{8}{9} \div \frac{11}{21}$

21. $\frac{4}{9} \div \frac{2}{3}$ 22. $\frac{2}{3} \div \frac{4}{9}$ 23. $\frac{7}{8} \div \frac{1}{2}$ 24. $\frac{1}{2} \div \frac{7}{8}$ 25. $\frac{3}{5} \div \frac{3}{5}$

26. $\frac{3}{8} \div \frac{7}{16}$ 27. $\frac{7}{16} \div \frac{3}{8}$ 28. $\frac{9}{10} \div \frac{4}{9}$ 29. $\frac{7}{12} \div \frac{14}{15}$ 30. $\frac{11}{12} \div \frac{5}{7}$

31. $1\frac{5}{8} \div \frac{1}{4}$ 32. $3\frac{3}{4} \div \frac{1}{6}$ 33. $2\frac{5}{6} \div \frac{1}{3}$ 34. $4\frac{2}{3} \div \frac{1}{2}$ 35. $5\frac{1}{4} \div \frac{3}{8}$

36. $2\frac{1}{2} \div \frac{1}{5}$ 37. $3\frac{1}{3} \div \frac{1}{10}$ 38. $4\frac{4}{5} \div \frac{5}{6}$ 39. $5\frac{2}{5} \div \frac{9}{10}$ 40. $6\frac{1}{8} \div \frac{7}{8}$

41. $3\frac{3}{8} \div \frac{2}{5}$ 42. $5\frac{2}{3} \div \frac{2}{3}$ 43. $7\frac{5}{9} \div \frac{5}{6}$ 44. $9\frac{1}{8} \div \frac{3}{5}$ 45. $11\frac{1}{5} \div \frac{7}{9}$

46. $4\frac{5}{12} \div \frac{3}{8}$ 47. $6\frac{4}{7} \div \frac{4}{21}$ 48. $8\frac{7}{11} \div \frac{5}{22}$ 49. $10\frac{5}{8} \div \frac{15}{16}$ 50. $8\frac{3}{4} \div \frac{7}{12}$

51. Karen has an order for a 5-inch bracelet. How many $\frac{1}{4}$-inch links does she need for the bracelet?

52. How many $\frac{3}{8}$-inch flowers does Karen need to make a belt that is $23\frac{1}{4}$ inches long?

*53. Use this example to explain why dividing by a fraction is the same as multiplying by the reciprocal of the divisor.

$$\frac{3}{4} \div \frac{7}{8} = \frac{\frac{3}{4}}{\frac{7}{8}} \times \frac{\frac{8}{7}}{\frac{8}{7}} = \frac{\frac{3}{4} \times \frac{8}{7}}{1} = \frac{3}{4} \times \frac{8}{7}$$

More practice
Set 27, page 409

Dividing by a Mixed Number or a Whole Number

A remora fish adheres to the back of a shark by suction. When the shark finds food, the remora eats the leftovers. The remora is not a parasite. It just likes to take a free ride.

A nurse shark is $9\frac{3}{4}$ feet long, and the remora fish is $1\frac{1}{2}$ feet long. How many times as long as the remora fish is the shark?

Find $9\frac{3}{4} \div 1\frac{1}{2}$.

$$9\frac{3}{4} \div 1\frac{1}{2}$$

$$\frac{39}{4} \div \frac{3}{2} \quad \text{Write each number as a fraction.}$$

$$\overset{13}{\underset{2}{\cancel{\frac{39}{4}}}} \times \overset{1}{\underset{1}{\cancel{\frac{2}{3}}}} = \frac{13}{2} = 6\frac{1}{2}$$

The shark is $6\frac{1}{2}$ times as long as the remora fish.

Divide.

1. $6 \div 1\frac{2}{3}$

2. $9 \div 6\frac{3}{4}$

3. $4\frac{2}{3} \div 1\frac{1}{6}$

4. $3\frac{1}{8} \div 1\frac{1}{3}$

5. $7 \div 5$

6. $8 \div 3$

7. $2\frac{1}{4} \div 9$

8. $6\frac{3}{4} \div 3$

9. $2\frac{5}{8} \div 7\frac{1}{2}$

10. $6\frac{1}{4} \div 2\frac{1}{2}$

11. $6\frac{3}{8} \div 2\frac{1}{8}$ 12. $5\frac{4}{5} \div 2\frac{3}{10}$ 13. $\frac{5}{6} \div 2\frac{1}{2}$

14. $\frac{3}{8} \div 1\frac{3}{4}$ 15. $10\frac{1}{2} \div 2\frac{1}{3}$ 16. $13\frac{3}{4} \div 1\frac{2}{3}$

17. $9 \div 4\frac{3}{8}$ 18. $16 \div 3\frac{2}{3}$ 19. $4\frac{1}{4} \div 7\frac{7}{8}$

20. $3 \div 5\frac{1}{7}$ 21. $4 \div 8\frac{2}{3}$ 22. $15\frac{4}{5} \div 5\frac{2}{3}$

23. $16\frac{1}{3} \div 6\frac{3}{5}$ 24. $22\frac{1}{2} \div 6\frac{7}{8}$ 25. $24\frac{3}{4} \div 8\frac{1}{4}$

26. $12\frac{3}{5} \div 7\frac{1}{3}$ 27. $10\frac{1}{4} \div 6\frac{2}{5}$ 28. $13\frac{1}{3} \div 8\frac{3}{4}$

Here are some interesting facts about animals.
Divide, and complete the sentence with the answer.

29. $162 : 3\frac{3}{5}$

White sharks reach a length of ▓▓ feet.

30. $7\frac{1}{8} \div 7\frac{1}{8}$

The hiccup fish's hiccup can be heard ▓▓ mile away.

31. $82\frac{1}{2} \div 16\frac{1}{2}$

An ant has ▓▓ noses.

32. $58\frac{1}{2} \div 3\frac{1}{4}$

Bee hummingbirds are so small that ▓▓ of them weigh one ounce.

*33. $24 \div 3\frac{3}{8} \div 1\frac{7}{9}$

The Archer fish shoots a stream of water that can hit an insect ▓▓ feet away.

More practice
Set 28, page 409

Keeping Skillful

Solve each equation.

1. $n + 1.31 = 3.85$

2. $x - 8.6 = 10.9$

3. $6.85 = y - 3.46$

4. $7.9 = 6.2 + n$

5. $6.2 = 5.81 + z$

6. $7.5 = p - 3.24$

7. $q - 8.5 = 2.31$

8. $r + 7.1 = 9.63$

9. $0.5s = 7$

10. $0.2t = 16$

11. $64 = 3.2t$

12. $111 = 3.7x$

13. $0.75y = 1.2$

14. $0.52z = 10.4$

15. $\frac{n}{0.5} = 12$

16. $\frac{p}{0.8} = 15$

17. $3.4 = \frac{r}{6}$

18. $4.8 = \frac{s}{9}$

19. $\frac{t}{1.2} = 8.7$

Using Reciprocals to Solve Equations

A. Ed Harvey is making a model from an 1899 photograph. The images in the photograph are $\frac{1}{4}$ the height they will be in the model. The image of a person in the photograph is $\frac{5}{16}$ inch tall. How tall should the model of a person be?

Size of model
Size in photograph

$$\frac{1}{4}n = \frac{5}{16}$$ Write an equation.

$$\left(\frac{4}{1}\right)\frac{1}{4}n = \left(\frac{4}{1}\right)\frac{5}{16}$$ Multiply both sides of the equation by the reciprocal of $\frac{1}{4}$.

$$1n = \left(\frac{4}{1}\right)\frac{5}{16}$$

$$n = 1\frac{1}{4}$$

The model of a person should be $1\frac{1}{4}$ inches tall.

B. Solve $\frac{x}{5} = 7\frac{1}{3}$.

$$\frac{x}{5} = 7\frac{1}{3}$$

$$\frac{1}{5}x = \frac{22}{3} \qquad \frac{x}{5} = \frac{1}{5}x$$

$$\left(\frac{5}{1}\right)\frac{1}{5}x = \left(\frac{5}{1}\right)\frac{22}{3}$$

Multiply both sides of the equation by the reciprocal of $\frac{1}{5}$.

$$1x = \left(\frac{5}{1}\right)\frac{22}{3}$$

$$x = 36\frac{2}{3}$$

C. Solve $3\frac{1}{4} = 2\frac{1}{2}y$.

$$3\frac{1}{4} = 2\frac{1}{2}y$$

$$\frac{13}{4} = \frac{5}{2}y$$

Write $3\frac{1}{4}$ and $2\frac{1}{2}$ as fractions.

$$\left(\frac{2}{5}\right)\frac{13}{4} = \left(\frac{2}{5}\right)\frac{5}{2}y$$

Multiply both sides of the equation by the reciprocal of $\frac{5}{2}$.

$$1\frac{3}{10} = y$$

Solve each equation.

1. $\frac{1}{3}s = 18$ **2.** $\frac{1}{5}x = 20$ **3.** $\frac{3}{4}z = 24$ **4.** $\frac{5}{6}q = 30$

5. $\frac{2}{5}w = \frac{3}{8}$ **6.** $\frac{3}{7}n = \frac{2}{3}$ **7.** $\frac{7}{8}u = \frac{3}{4}$ **8.** $\frac{5}{9}j = \frac{2}{3}$

9. $\frac{x}{7} = 3\frac{2}{3}$ **10.** $\frac{a}{6} = 5\frac{3}{5}$ **11.** $\frac{r}{9} = 6\frac{5}{6}$ **12.** $\frac{s}{8} = 4\frac{7}{10}$

13. $3a = 4\frac{1}{3}$ **14.** $5b = 2\frac{3}{4}$ **15.** $7c = 4\frac{3}{5}$ **16.** $6k = 5\frac{1}{4}$

17. $\frac{5}{8}r = 5\frac{3}{5}$ **18.** $\frac{1}{6}t = 3\frac{2}{3}$ **19.** $\frac{3}{4}y = 6\frac{2}{3}$ **20.** $\frac{4}{7}z = 8\frac{1}{4}$

21. $2\frac{5}{6} = 2\frac{5}{6}t$ **22.** $3\frac{2}{3} = 3\frac{2}{3}x$ **23.** $1\frac{3}{4} = 2\frac{1}{2}b$ **24.** $5\frac{3}{4} = 1\frac{4}{5}n$

25. In the photograph, the height of the image of a streetcar is $\frac{3}{5}$ inch. This is $\frac{1}{4}$ the height of a streetcar in the model. What is the height of a streetcar in the model?

★26. In the photograph, the height of an image is $\frac{1}{240}$ of actual size. Find the actual height of a streetcar.

Problem Solving: Choosing the Operation

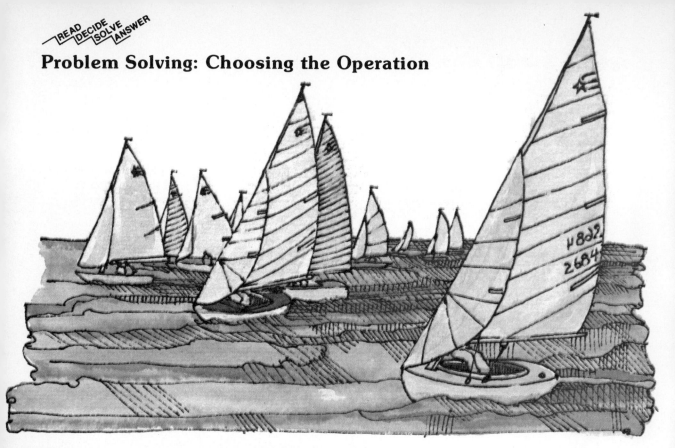

READ **A.** A nautical mile is slightly longer than a land mile. A sailboat traveled at an average rate of $3\frac{3}{4}$ nautical miles per hour for $2\frac{1}{3}$ hours. How far did it travel?

DECIDE Use the distance formula to write an equation.

Distance Rate Time

$$d \;=\; r\,t$$

$$d \;=\; 3\tfrac{3}{4}\left(2\tfrac{1}{3}\right)$$

SOLVE

$$d = 3\tfrac{3}{4}\left(2\tfrac{1}{3}\right)$$

$$d = 8\tfrac{3}{4}$$

ANSWER The sailboat traveled $8\frac{3}{4}$ nautical miles.

READ   **B.** At $4\frac{1}{2}$ nautical miles per hour, how long does it take to sail $3\frac{3}{5}$ nautical miles?

DECIDE   Use the distance formula to write an equation.

$$d = rt$$

$$3\tfrac{3}{5} = 4\tfrac{1}{2}t$$

SOLVE $3\tfrac{3}{5} = 4\tfrac{1}{2}t$

$$\frac{18}{5} = \frac{9}{2}t$$

$$\left(\frac{2}{9}\right)\frac{18}{5} = \left(\frac{2}{9}\right)\frac{9}{2}t$$

$$\frac{4}{5} = t$$

ANSWER   It takes $\frac{4}{5}$ hour.

For each problem, write an equation. Then give the answer.

1. A motorboat travels at a rate of 12 nautical miles per hour for $2\frac{1}{2}$ hours. How far does it travel?

2. A pleasure boat travels 7 hours at an average speed of $10\frac{1}{2}$ nautical miles per hour. How far does it travel?

3. A boat travels $12\frac{1}{2}$ nautical miles in $3\frac{1}{3}$ hours. At what rate does the boat travel?

4. How long does it take to go the $4\frac{1}{4}$ nautical miles from North Point to Hawkins Point in a speedboat at an average rate of 17 nautical miles per hour?

5. A speedboat traveled at a rate of $19\frac{1}{2}$ nautical miles per hour. How long did it take to reach a marina 26 nautical miles away?

6. Eric Shun plans to cruise $13\frac{1}{2}$ nautical miles in 3 hours. At what rate will the boat travel?

7. A sailboat running with the wind travels at a rate of $5\frac{1}{4}$ nautical miles per hour for $1\frac{1}{6}$ hours. How far does the sailboat travel?

8. When the wind is reduced, a sailboat travels at a rate of $2\frac{3}{4}$ nautical miles per hour. At this rate, how far does the sailboat travel in $2\frac{1}{2}$ hours?

9. An oyster boat travels 13 nautical miles to the oyster beds at a rate of $6\frac{1}{2}$ nautical miles per hour. How long does it take to get to the oyster beds?

Fractions as Decimals

José tried to use his calculator to decide if the decimal for a fraction is terminating or repeating.

A. He divided 5 by 64 to find the decimal for $\frac{5}{64}$. His calculator display can show 8 digits but stopped at 7. So the decimal for $\frac{5}{64}$ terminates.

B. He divided to find the decimal for $\frac{1}{5120}$. 8 digits were shown. Since his calculator cannot show more than 8 digits, he cannot tell whether the decimal terminates or repeats.

Look at the prime factorization of 5120.

$$5120 = 2 \times 2 \times 2 \times 2 \times 2 \times 2 \times 2 \times 2 \times 2 \times 2 \times 5$$

If the only prime factors of the denominator are 2s and 5s, the decimal terminates. Otherwise, the decimal repeats. The decimal for $\frac{1}{5120}$ terminates.

Note: To use this procedure, first be sure the fraction is in lowest terms.

These fractions are in lowest terms. Tell whether the decimal for each fraction terminates or repeats. First divide with your calculator. If your calculator shows as many digits as it can possibly display, check the prime factorization of the denominator.

1. $\frac{38}{125}$
2. $\frac{107}{293}$
3. $\frac{25}{512}$
4. $\frac{32}{387}$
5. $\frac{87}{1024}$
6. $\frac{23}{256}$
7. $\frac{73}{250}$
8. $\frac{5}{216}$

9. $\frac{29}{410}$
10. $\frac{17}{390}$
11. $\frac{19}{255}$
12. $\frac{25}{294}$
13. $\frac{53}{128}$
14. $\frac{35}{186}$
15. $\frac{175}{624}$
16. $\frac{19}{832}$

Chapter 8 Test
Multiplication and Division of Fractions, pages 148–170

1. Use multiplication to find four fractions equal to $\frac{3}{8}$.

Give the missing numerator or denominator.

2. $\frac{\text{\small|||}}{3} = \frac{8}{12}$ 3. $\frac{3}{4} = \frac{\text{\small|||}}{28}$

4. $\frac{3}{5} = \frac{15}{\text{\small|||}}$ 5. $\frac{7}{\text{\small|||}} = \frac{35}{40}$

Write each fraction in lowest terms.

6. $\frac{14}{21}$ 7. $\frac{24}{28}$ 8. $\frac{40}{72}$

Write a mixed number or a whole number for each fraction.

9. $\frac{7}{3}$ 10. $\frac{24}{5}$ 11. $\frac{21}{3}$

Write a fraction for each number.

12. $2\frac{1}{6}$ 13. $4\frac{3}{8}$ 14. 0.147

Write a decimal for each number.

15. $\frac{1}{5}$ 16. $\frac{2}{3}$ 17. $\frac{13}{4}$

18. $\frac{1}{9}$ 19. $\frac{3}{4}$ 20. $\frac{19}{3}$

Multiply.

21. $\frac{1}{2} \times 16$ 22. $\frac{5}{8} \times \frac{2}{3}$

23. $4 \times 2\frac{3}{8}$ 24. $4\frac{1}{2} \times 5\frac{1}{3}$

Give the reciprocal of each number.

25. $\frac{2}{3}$ 26. $2\frac{1}{4}$ 27. 3

Divide.

28. $5 \div \frac{1}{3}$ 29. $\frac{5}{8} \div \frac{3}{4}$

30. $1\frac{3}{4} \div \frac{4}{5}$ 31. $3\frac{1}{3} \div 1\frac{1}{2}$

Solve each equation.

32. $\frac{5}{6}x = \frac{2}{3}$ 33. $\frac{a}{4} = 1\frac{7}{8}$

34. A boat sails at a rate of $4\frac{1}{2}$ nautical miles per hour for 8 hours. Find the distance it travels.

35. A recipe requires $1\frac{3}{4}$ cups of milk. Colette is making $3\frac{1}{2}$ times the recipe. How much milk does she need?

Chapter 9 Addition and Subtraction of Fractions

Finding Common Denominators

Two or more fractions with the same denominator
have a **common denominator.**

A. Find a common denominator for $\frac{3}{8}$ and $\frac{7}{10}$.

A common denominator for $\frac{3}{8}$ and $\frac{7}{10}$ is a common
multiple of the denominators, 8 and 10.

List multiples of the larger denominator, 10,
until you find one that is also a multiple of 8.

Multiples of 10: **10, 20, 30, 40, . . .**   Is 10 a multiple of 8? *No*
Is 20 a multiple of 8? *No*
Is 30 a multiple of 8? *No*
Is 40 a multiple of 8? *Yes*

The least common multiple of 8 and 10 is 40,

so the **least common denominator** of $\frac{3}{8}$ and $\frac{7}{10}$ is 40.

B. Write $\frac{2}{3}$ and $\frac{3}{4}$ with a common denominator.

The product of the denominators is always a
common denominator.

$3 \times 4 = 12$ A common denominator of $\frac{2}{3}$ and $\frac{3}{4}$ is 12.

Write $\frac{2}{3}$ and $\frac{3}{4}$ with a denominator of 12.

$$\frac{2}{3} = \frac{}{12} \qquad \frac{3}{4} = \frac{}{12}$$

$$\frac{2}{3} = \frac{8}{12} \qquad \frac{3}{4} = \frac{9}{12}$$

● **Discuss**   Is the product of the denominators always
the least common denominator? Try $\frac{5}{6}$ and $\frac{4}{9}$.

Give the least common denominator.

1. $\frac{1}{2}$ $\frac{3}{4}$ 2. $\frac{1}{4}$ $\frac{3}{8}$ 3. $\frac{5}{12}$ $\frac{1}{3}$

4. $\frac{1}{2}$ $\frac{2}{3}$ 5. $\frac{3}{5}$ $\frac{3}{4}$ 6. $\frac{3}{4}$ $\frac{5}{6}$

7. $\frac{4}{9}$ $\frac{3}{4}$ 8. $\frac{3}{10}$ $\frac{4}{5}$ 9. $\frac{5}{6}$ $\frac{7}{18}$

10. $\frac{7}{25}$ $\frac{3}{5}$ 11. $\frac{11}{18}$ $\frac{5}{8}$ 12. $\frac{7}{12}$ $\frac{4}{9}$

Write these fractions with a common denominator.

13. $\frac{2}{3}$ $\frac{3}{5}$ 14. $\frac{3}{5}$ $\frac{7}{10}$ 15. $\frac{5}{8}$ $\frac{2}{3}$

16. $\frac{2}{3}$ $\frac{8}{9}$ 17. $\frac{5}{6}$ $\frac{7}{8}$ 18. $\frac{4}{9}$ $\frac{3}{5}$

19. $\frac{3}{4}$ $\frac{1}{6}$ 20. $\frac{3}{5}$ $\frac{5}{8}$ 21. $\frac{3}{8}$ $\frac{7}{12}$

22. $\frac{5}{6}$ $\frac{4}{9}$ 23. $\frac{7}{10}$ $\frac{5}{6}$ 24. $\frac{3}{4}$ $\frac{7}{18}$

25. $\frac{3}{10}$ $\frac{5}{12}$ 26. $\frac{7}{10}$ $\frac{5}{16}$ 27. $\frac{7}{12}$ $\frac{3}{16}$

28. $\frac{5}{18}$ $\frac{7}{24}$ 29. $\frac{9}{16}$ $\frac{11}{24}$ 30. $\frac{11}{15}$ $\frac{8}{25}$

31. $\frac{3}{4}$ $\frac{5}{8}$ $\frac{1}{2}$ 32. $\frac{2}{3}$ $\frac{1}{2}$ $\frac{5}{6}$

33. $\frac{1}{3}$ $\frac{3}{5}$ $\frac{3}{4}$ 34. $\frac{3}{8}$ $\frac{1}{2}$ $\frac{2}{3}$

★35. $\frac{5}{9}$ $\frac{3}{4}$ $\frac{9}{10}$ $\frac{4}{5}$ ★36. $\frac{5}{12}$ $\frac{7}{9}$ $\frac{5}{8}$ $\frac{7}{10}$

★37. $\frac{3}{8}$ $\frac{5}{6}$ $\frac{1}{4}$ $\frac{2}{3}$ ★38. $\frac{4}{5}$ $\frac{3}{16}$ $\frac{9}{10}$ $\frac{5}{8}$

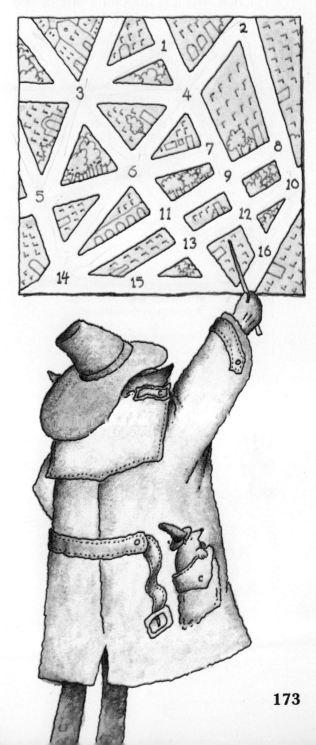

Comparing and Ordering Fractions and Mixed Numbers

A. The chart shows the lengths of some animals. Which is smaller, the centipede or the cricket?

Animal	Length (inches)
Spider	$\frac{3}{8}$
Wasp	$\frac{3}{4}$
Ladybug	$\frac{3}{10}$
Centipede	$1\frac{1}{4}$
Cricket	$1\frac{3}{4}$
Katydid	$1\frac{3}{10}$

Compare $1\frac{1}{4}$ and $1\frac{3}{4}$.

$1\frac{1}{4}$ ● $1\frac{3}{4}$ The whole numbers are the same. Compare the fractions.

$1\frac{1}{4} < 1\frac{3}{4}$ The denominators are the same. Compare the numerators. $1 < 3$

The centipede is smaller.

B. Compare $\frac{5}{6}$ and $\frac{3}{4}$.

$\frac{5}{6}$ ● $\frac{3}{4}$

$\frac{10}{12}$ ● $\frac{9}{12}$ Write the fractions with a common denominator.

$\frac{10}{12} > \frac{9}{12}$ Compare the numerators.

$\frac{5}{6} > \frac{3}{4}$

C. Write $\frac{5}{6}$, $\frac{7}{12}$, and $\frac{2}{3}$ in order from the least to the greatest.

$\frac{5}{6} = \frac{10}{12}$ Write the fractions with a common denominator.

$\frac{7}{12} = \frac{7}{12}$

$\frac{2}{3} = \frac{8}{12}$

$\frac{7}{12} \quad \frac{8}{12} \quad \frac{10}{12}$ Write the fractions in order.
$\downarrow \qquad \downarrow \qquad \downarrow$
$\frac{7}{12} \quad \frac{2}{3} \quad \frac{5}{6}$

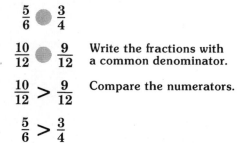

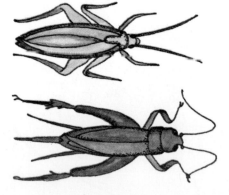

Compare. Use >, <, or =.

1. $\frac{5}{8}$ ● $\frac{3}{8}$ 2. $\frac{5}{12}$ ● $\frac{7}{12}$ 3. $\frac{8}{9}$ ● $\frac{6}{9}$

4. $\frac{9}{10}$ ● $\frac{4}{5}$ 5. $\frac{8}{12}$ ● $\frac{2}{3}$ 6. $\frac{2}{3}$ ● $\frac{4}{5}$

7. $2\frac{5}{6}$ ● $2\frac{3}{4}$ 8. $5\frac{1}{2}$ ● $3\frac{5}{8}$ 9. $6\frac{6}{10}$ ● $6\frac{9}{15}$

10. $8\frac{4}{15}$ ● $8\frac{4}{5}$ 11. $7\frac{12}{24}$ ● $7\frac{8}{16}$ 12. $9\frac{4}{5}$ ● $9\frac{3}{8}$

List in order from the least to the greatest.

13. $\frac{3}{4}$ $\frac{5}{6}$ $\frac{2}{3}$ 14. $\frac{1}{2}$ $\frac{7}{10}$ $\frac{4}{5}$ 15. $\frac{2}{5}$ $\frac{2}{3}$ $\frac{1}{2}$

16. $\frac{5}{8}$ $\frac{2}{3}$ $\frac{3}{4}$ 17. $\frac{7}{8}$ $\frac{9}{10}$ $\frac{7}{12}$ 18. $\frac{5}{16}$ $\frac{7}{12}$ $\frac{7}{8}$

19. $4\frac{5}{6}$ $4\frac{4}{5}$ $4\frac{7}{10}$ 20. $3\frac{2}{3}$ $3\frac{5}{6}$ $3\frac{4}{9}$

Use the chart on page 174. Which is smaller?

21. Spider or wasp   22. Cricket or katydid

23. Wasp or ladybug   24. Centipede or katydid

Use the expression $3\frac{1}{2} \times$ ▦ for exercises 25–27. What must be true about the second factor if the product is

*25. less than $3\frac{1}{2}$?

*26. more than $3\frac{1}{2}$?

*27. equal to $3\frac{1}{2}$?

More practice
Set 29, page 409

Cross-Products

You can check if two fractions are equal by finding cross-products with your calculator.

Find 18 × 12.
Find 27 × 8.

Compare the products.

216 = 216

Since the products are the same, the fractions are equal.

$\frac{18}{27} = \frac{8}{12}$

Use your calculator. Are the fractions in each row equal to the one in the box? Write *yes* or *no*.

$\frac{2}{3}$	1. $\frac{30}{45}$	2. $\frac{24}{36}$
$\frac{5}{6}$	3. $\frac{36}{40}$	4. $\frac{40}{48}$
$\frac{4}{7}$	5. $\frac{28}{49}$	6. $\frac{36}{63}$
$\frac{7}{8}$	7. $\frac{42}{48}$	8. $\frac{63}{72}$
$\frac{7}{12}$	9. $\frac{56}{94}$	10. $\frac{77}{132}$

Adding and Subtracting Fractions

A. During ballet class, $\frac{3}{4}$ hour is spent doing stretching exercises at the barre. The remaining $\frac{1}{2}$ hour of class is spent doing floor exercises. How long is ballet class?

Find $\frac{3}{4} + \frac{1}{2}$.

$$\frac{3}{4} = \frac{3}{4}$$ Write the fractions with a common denominator.

$$+\frac{1}{2} = +\frac{2}{4}$$ Add the numerators.

$$\frac{5}{4} = 1\frac{1}{4}$$ Rename $\frac{5}{4}$.

Ballet class is $1\frac{1}{4}$ hours long.

B. Find $\frac{11}{12} - \frac{3}{4}$.

$$\frac{11}{12} = \frac{11}{12}$$ Write the fractions with a common denominator.

$$-\frac{3}{4} = -\frac{9}{12}$$ Subtract the numerators.

$$\frac{2}{12} = \frac{1}{6}$$ Write $\frac{2}{12}$ in lowest terms.

Add.

1. $\frac{1}{2}$
   $+\frac{3}{4}$

2. $\frac{3}{4}$
   $+\frac{1}{8}$

3. $\frac{1}{2}$
   $+\frac{3}{5}$

4. $\frac{5}{6}$
   $+\frac{3}{7}$

5. $\frac{1}{5}$
   $+\frac{2}{3}$

6. $\frac{5}{8}$
   $+\frac{4}{9}$

7. $\frac{1}{4}$
   $+\frac{5}{6}$

8. $\frac{5}{9} + \frac{1}{2}$

9. $\frac{3}{4} + \frac{2}{3}$

10. $\frac{5}{6} + \frac{3}{8}$

11. $\frac{7}{8} + \frac{1}{2}$

12. $\frac{3}{4} + \frac{4}{7}$

13. $\frac{3}{8} + \frac{9}{10}$

14. $\frac{5}{6} + \frac{3}{10}$

15. $\frac{1}{4} + \frac{5}{12} + \frac{5}{6}$

16. $\frac{2}{3} + \frac{4}{9} + \frac{3}{5}$

17. $\frac{3}{8} + \frac{2}{3} + \frac{7}{12}$

Subtract.

18. $\frac{1}{2}$
    $-\frac{1}{6}$

19. $\frac{2}{3}$
    $-\frac{1}{2}$

20. $\frac{1}{2}$
    $-\frac{2}{5}$

21. $\frac{2}{5}$
    $-\frac{1}{4}$

22. $\frac{3}{4}$
    $-\frac{5}{8}$

23. $\frac{5}{6}$
    $-\frac{2}{3}$

24. $\frac{4}{5}$
    $-\frac{2}{3}$

25. $\frac{7}{8} - \frac{2}{3}$

26. $\frac{2}{3} - \frac{5}{9}$

27. $\frac{3}{4} - \frac{1}{6}$

28. $\frac{5}{6} - \frac{3}{5}$

29. $\frac{5}{6} - \frac{4}{9}$

30. $\frac{7}{10} - \frac{3}{8}$

31. $\frac{2}{3} - \frac{5}{12}$

32. $\frac{9}{10} - \frac{5}{6}$

33. $\frac{11}{12} - \frac{1}{8}$

34. $\frac{7}{12} - \frac{7}{15}$

35. The class does two types of floor exercises. Adagio exercises develop balance and control. Allegro exercises are fast steps to increase speed and precision. During $\frac{1}{2}$ hour of floor exercises, $\frac{1}{3}$ hour is spent doing adagio exercises. How much time is spent doing allegro exercises?

36. During one week, the class did barre exercises for $\frac{2}{3}$ hour on Monday, $\frac{1}{2}$ hour on Wednesday, and $\frac{3}{4}$ hour on Friday. How long did the class do barre exercises that week?

More practice
Set 30, page 409

Adding Mixed Numbers

A. Matsubo and Lily went on a fishing trip. Matsubo caught a $3\frac{7}{8}$-pound trout, and Lily caught a $4\frac{1}{2}$-pound trout. What was the total weight of these fish?

Find $3\frac{7}{8} + 4\frac{1}{2}$.

$$3\frac{7}{8} = \quad 3\frac{7}{8}$$
$$+\, 4\frac{1}{2} = \; +\, 4\frac{4}{8}$$
$$\overline{\qquad\qquad\quad 7\frac{11}{8} = 8\frac{3}{8}}$$

Write the fractions with a common denominator.
Add the fractions.
Add the whole numbers.

Rename $7\frac{11}{8}$.

$7 + \frac{11}{8}$

$7 + 1\frac{3}{8} = 8\frac{3}{8}$

Together, the fish weighed $8\frac{3}{8}$ pounds.

B. Find $12\frac{1}{6} + 5\frac{3}{8} + 2\frac{11}{24}$.

$$12\frac{1}{6} = \quad 12\frac{4}{24}$$
$$5\frac{3}{8} = \quad 5\frac{9}{24}$$
$$+\; 2\frac{11}{24} = \; +\; 2\frac{11}{24}$$
$$\overline{\qquad\qquad\quad 19\frac{24}{24} = 20}$$

Rename $19\frac{24}{24}$.

$19 + \frac{24}{24}$

$19 + 1 = 20$

Add.

1. $4\frac{1}{6}$
$+3\frac{1}{2}$

2. $7\frac{2}{3}$
$+8\frac{1}{4}$

3. $12\frac{5}{6}$
$+\ 7\frac{1}{6}$

4. $8\frac{1}{2}$
$+\ \frac{4}{5}$

5. $12\frac{3}{8}$
$+\ 9\frac{7}{16}$

6. $8\frac{7}{8}$
$+9\frac{1}{2}$

7. $\frac{5}{6}$
$+17\frac{5}{8}$

8. $20\frac{3}{4}$
$+14\frac{1}{6}$

9. $4\frac{3}{4}$
$+18\frac{3}{4}$

10. $9\frac{2}{5}$
$+11$

11. $9\frac{3}{5}$
$+12\frac{1}{2}$

12. $7\frac{3}{8}$
$+17\frac{3}{4}$

13. 15
$+13\frac{1}{2}$

14. $5\frac{7}{8}$
$+29\frac{4}{5}$

15. $16\frac{1}{4}$
$+\ 8\frac{5}{6}$

16. $7\frac{5}{6}$
$+24\frac{5}{9}$

17. $18\frac{3}{8}$
$+\ \frac{2}{3}$

18. $14\frac{1}{2}$
$+\ 7\frac{3}{7}$

19. $8\frac{2}{3} + 19$

20. $9\frac{5}{9} + 16\frac{2}{5}$

21. $32\frac{2}{3} + \frac{4}{7}$

22. $11 + 22\frac{3}{7}$

23. $2\frac{5}{6} + 3\frac{1}{2} + 9\frac{2}{3}$

24. $6\frac{1}{2} + 4\frac{3}{8} + 9\frac{1}{4}$

25. $3\frac{2}{3} + 5\frac{3}{4} + 8\frac{1}{5}$

26. $7\frac{1}{2} + 9\frac{2}{3} + \frac{4}{5}$

27. $7\frac{2}{3} + 3\frac{5}{8} + \frac{5}{6}$

28. $2\frac{1}{2} + \frac{5}{6} + 8\frac{2}{5}$

29. $8\frac{2}{3} + 5\frac{4}{9} + 3\frac{5}{6}$

30. $1\frac{3}{4} + 6\frac{5}{8} + 2\frac{5}{6}$

★31. $3\frac{9}{10} + 2\frac{7}{12} + 5\frac{3}{16}$ ★32. $4\frac{11}{18} + 5\frac{1}{12} + \frac{7}{20}$ ★33. $8\frac{5}{16} + 1\frac{7}{24} + 5\frac{3}{20}$

34. Becky caught three perch weighing $1\frac{3}{4}$ pounds, $2\frac{1}{8}$ pounds, and $1\frac{2}{3}$ pounds. How many pounds of perch did she catch altogether?

35. Cindy caught a trout weighing $4\frac{3}{4}$ pounds and two perch weighing $2\frac{3}{8}$ pounds and $1\frac{5}{6}$ pounds. How many pounds of fish did she catch altogether?

★36. Doug caught $4\frac{1}{3}$ pounds more fish than Gloria. She caught 3 pounds more than Stan, who caught $2\frac{5}{8}$ pounds. How many pounds of fish did Doug catch?

More practice
Set 31, page 410

Subtracting Mixed Numbers

A. A white pine cone is $4\frac{1}{4}$ inches long. An Austrian pine cone is $2\frac{3}{4}$ inches long. How much longer is a white pine cone than an Austrian pine cone?

Find $4\frac{1}{4} - 2\frac{3}{4}$.

$$
\begin{aligned}
4\frac{1}{4} &= 3\frac{5}{4} \\
-2\frac{3}{4} &= -2\frac{3}{4} \\
\hline
&\;\;1\frac{2}{4} = 1\frac{1}{2}
\end{aligned}
$$

Rename $4\frac{1}{4}$.
$4\frac{1}{4} = 4 + \frac{1}{4}$
$= 3\frac{4}{4} + \frac{1}{4}$
$= 3\frac{5}{4}$

A white pine cone is $1\frac{1}{2}$ inches longer.

B. Find $52 - 41\frac{2}{3}$.

$$
\begin{aligned}
52 &= 51\frac{3}{3} \\
-41\frac{2}{3} &= -41\frac{2}{3} \\
\hline
&\;\;10\frac{1}{3}
\end{aligned}
$$

Rename 52.
$52 = 51 + 1$
$= 51 + \frac{3}{3}$
$= 51\frac{3}{3}$

180

c. Find $71\frac{1}{2} - 69\frac{4}{5}$.

$$71\frac{1}{2} = \qquad 71\frac{5}{10} = \qquad 70\frac{15}{10}$$
$$-\ 69\frac{4}{5} = \qquad -\ 69\frac{8}{10} = \qquad -\ 69\frac{8}{10}$$
$$\rule{6cm}{0pt} 1\frac{7}{10}$$

First write the fractions with a common denominator.

Then rename $71\frac{5}{10}$.

Subtract.

1. $14\frac{5}{6}$
$-\ 7\frac{1}{3}$

2. $12\frac{2}{3}$
$-\ 1\frac{1}{4}$

3. 8
$-2\frac{4}{9}$

4. 26
$-\ 5\frac{1}{7}$

5. $9\frac{1}{2}$
$-2\frac{5}{6}$

6. $6\frac{5}{8}$
$-3\frac{2}{3}$

7. $10\frac{2}{5}$
$-\ \ \frac{2}{3}$

8. $7\frac{1}{5}$
$-3\frac{1}{6}$

9. $18\frac{3}{8}$
$-\ 6\frac{5}{8}$

10. $27\frac{2}{3}$
$-\ 6\frac{5}{6}$

11. $10\frac{5}{7}$
$-\ 3$

12. 12
$-11\frac{3}{8}$

13. $54\frac{8}{9} - 31\frac{1}{2}$

14. $48\frac{1}{2} - 48\frac{1}{6}$

15. $42\frac{1}{3} - 13\frac{2}{5}$

16. $36\frac{1}{4} - 15$

17. $20 - \frac{3}{7}$

18. $1\frac{5}{8} - \frac{3}{4}$

19. $22\frac{2}{5} - 11\frac{1}{2}$

20. $45\frac{1}{6} - 24\frac{3}{5}$

21. $54\frac{1}{4} - 13\frac{4}{9}$

22. $37\frac{3}{5} - 35\frac{1}{2}$

23. $68 - 17\frac{5}{9}$

24. $76\frac{5}{8} - 5\frac{2}{3}$

Cone	Length (inches)
Norway spruce	$4\frac{1}{8}$
Loblolly	$4\frac{3}{16}$
Scotch pine	$1\frac{1}{4}$
Hemlock	$\frac{7}{8}$

Find the difference in the lengths of each pair of cones.

25. Norway spruce and loblolly

26. Norway spruce and Scotch pine

27. Loblolly and hemlock

28. Scotch pine and hemlock

More practice
Set 32, page 410

Evaluating Expressions

A. Evaluate $n + \frac{3}{4}$ for $n = 2\frac{3}{8}$.

$n + \frac{3}{4}$

$2\frac{3}{8} + \frac{3}{4}$ Substitute $2\frac{3}{8}$ for n.

$3\frac{1}{8}$

B. Evaluate $y - 2\frac{1}{2}$ for $y = 3\frac{1}{3}$.

$y - 2\frac{1}{2}$

$3\frac{1}{3} - 2\frac{1}{2}$ Substitute $3\frac{1}{3}$ for y.

$\frac{5}{6}$

C. Evaluate $5 - \left(z - \frac{2}{5}\right)$ for $z = 1\frac{1}{2}$.

$5 - \left(z - \frac{2}{5}\right)$

$5 - \left(1\frac{1}{2} - \frac{2}{5}\right)$

$5 - 1\frac{1}{10}$

$3\frac{9}{10}$

D. Evaluate $a + b + 2$ for $a = 1\frac{5}{6}$ and $b = \frac{7}{8}$.

$a + b + 2$

$1\frac{5}{6} + \frac{7}{8} + 2$

$4\frac{17}{24}$

Evaluate each expression for $n = \frac{2}{3}$.

1. $n + 1\frac{1}{3}$ 2. $n - \frac{1}{8}$ 3. $5\frac{1}{6} - n$ 4. $n + 3\frac{4}{5}$

Evaluate each expression for $d = 2\frac{5}{8}$.

5. $d + \frac{3}{8}$ 6. $2\frac{3}{4} - d$ 7. $2\frac{3}{5} + d$ 8. $6 - d$

Evaluate each expression for $x = 1\frac{3}{4}$.

9. $\left(9\frac{5}{6} - x\right) - \frac{2}{3}$ 10. $4\frac{1}{2} - \left(x - \frac{5}{8}\right)$ 11. $\left(x - \frac{2}{5}\right) - \frac{1}{2}$ 12. $x - \left(1\frac{5}{6} - 1\frac{1}{2}\right)$

Evaluate each expression for $a = 2\frac{3}{4}$ and $b = \frac{7}{8}$.

13. $a + b + 3\frac{1}{2}$ 14. $a - b + \frac{2}{3}$ 15. $a - \left(2\frac{1}{3} - b\right)$ 16. $2 - (a - b)$

More practice
Set 33, page 410

Fraction Dominoes

From a box of dominoes, remove the dominoes that are doubles (tiles with the same number at both ends) and the dominoes that have a blank. You can use the remaining fifteen dominoes to represent fractions.

 $\frac{3}{4}$

 $\frac{5}{2}$

1. Arrange the dominoes to match the pattern below. Place the extra three dominoes, one in each row, so the sum in each row is $2\frac{1}{2}$.

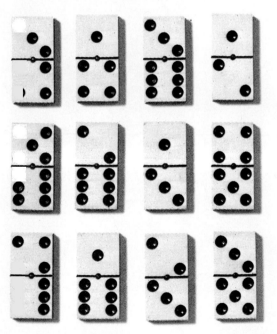

2. Arrange the fifteen dominoes in three rows of five so the sum of the fractions shown in each row is 10.

Solving Addition and Subtraction Equations

A. The Hardisty Bicycle Club went on a tour. They rode $4\frac{3}{4}$ miles after supper to get to their overnight camp, which was $27\frac{1}{2}$ miles from home. How far had they ridden before supper?

Miles before supper   Miles after supper   Total miles

$$n + 4\frac{3}{4} = 27\frac{1}{2}$$ Write an equation.

$$n + 4\frac{3}{4} - 4\frac{3}{4} = 27\frac{1}{2} - 4\frac{3}{4}$$ To get n by itself, subtract $4\frac{3}{4}$ from both sides of the equation.

$$n = 22\frac{3}{4}$$

They rode $22\frac{3}{4}$ miles before supper.

B. Solve $b - 2\frac{1}{3} = 25\frac{3}{4}$.

$$b - 2\frac{1}{3} = 25\frac{3}{4}$$

$$b - 2\frac{1}{3} + 2\frac{1}{3} = 25\frac{3}{4} + 2\frac{1}{3}$$ To get b by itself, add $2\frac{1}{3}$ to both sides of the equation.

$$b = 28\frac{1}{12}$$

Solve each equation.

1. $k + \frac{2}{5} = \frac{9}{10}$

2. $b - \frac{3}{4} = \frac{11}{12}$

3. $r - \frac{3}{5} = 7$

4. $b - \frac{7}{8} = 3\frac{1}{4}$

5. $2\frac{3}{4} + n = 4\frac{3}{8}$

6. $5\frac{2}{3} + 4\frac{3}{5} = n$

7. $4\frac{3}{4} = n - 1\frac{2}{3}$

8. $1\frac{5}{8} + n = 3\frac{7}{12}$

9. $a + 1\frac{3}{5} = 4$

10. $2\frac{1}{3} = d - \frac{4}{5}$

11. $8 - 2\frac{2}{3} = b$

12. $3\frac{2}{3} = c + 1\frac{1}{2}$

13. $h + 4\frac{3}{10} = 5\frac{3}{5}$

14. $b - \frac{7}{8} = 3\frac{1}{4}$

15. $4\frac{3}{7} + r = 8$

16. $c - 5\frac{5}{6} = 7\frac{5}{12}$

17. $8\frac{3}{4} = u - 4\frac{2}{5}$

18. $3\frac{4}{5} + 5\frac{2}{3} = e$

19. $7\frac{1}{8} + n = 8\frac{3}{4}$

20. $n - 9\frac{2}{3} = 6\frac{3}{5}$

21. $12\frac{1}{2} = 8\frac{2}{3} + r$

22. $s + 26\frac{2}{3} = 38$

23. $2\frac{5}{6} + w = 45\frac{1}{3}$

24. $x + 8\frac{1}{2} = 45\frac{1}{3}$

★25. $\frac{3}{4}x - 2\frac{1}{2} = 3\frac{1}{2}$

★26. $\frac{3}{5}a - 2\frac{1}{2} = 1\frac{7}{10}$

★27. $\frac{3}{4}n + 1\frac{1}{2} = 7\frac{3}{4}$

★28. $\frac{2}{3}b + 3\frac{5}{6} = 8\frac{1}{3}$

29. Wendy's pack weighed $2\frac{3}{4}$ pounds more than Michelle's pack. Wendy's pack weighed $18\frac{5}{6}$ pounds. How much did Michelle's pack weigh?

30. The group rode $51\frac{5}{12}$ miles in two days. They rode $27\frac{1}{2}$ miles the first day. How far did they ride on the second day?

More practice
Set 34, page 410

Problem Solving: Choosing the Operation

READ June 21 is the longest day of the year in the Northern Hemisphere. Edmonton, Alberta, Canada, has $17\frac{1}{20}$ hours of daylight during the 24 hours. How many hours of darkness does the city have?

DECIDE You can write this equation.

Daylight   Dark   Total
hours   hours hours

$$17\frac{1}{20} + n = 24$$

SOLVE
$$17\frac{1}{20} + n = 24$$

$$17\frac{1}{20} - 17\frac{1}{20} + n = 24 - 17\frac{1}{20}$$

$$n = 6\frac{19}{20}$$

ANSWER Edmonton has $6\frac{19}{20}$ hours of darkness on June 21.

•Discuss Give another equation for this example.

Write an equation. Then give the answer.

1. On December 21, Yellowknife, Northwest Territories, Canada, has $4\frac{19}{20}$ hours of daylight. How many hours of darkness does it have?

2. On June 21, Hilo, Hawaii, has $13\frac{1}{5}$ hours of daylight. Yellowknife has 20 hours. How many fewer hours of daylight does Hilo have?

3. On September 21, Calgary, Alberta, has $11\frac{3}{5}$ hours of darkness. How many hours of daylight does it have?

4. On October 14, Alert, Northwest Territories, has $1\frac{7}{10}$ hours of daylight. On that day the sun sets and does not rise again until February. On October 14, Calgary has $6\frac{1}{3}$ times as much daylight as Alert. How much daylight does Calgary have?

5. On June 21, Columbus, Ohio, has $14\frac{1}{2}$ hours of daylight. On December 21, it has $9\frac{1}{6}$ hours of daylight. How many more hours of daylight does it have on June 21?

6. Mexico City, Mexico, has $2\frac{9}{20}$ hours more daylight on June 21 than on December 21, when it has $10\frac{3}{4}$ hours of daylight. How many hours of daylight does it have on June 21?

7. Leningrad, U.S.S.R., has $3\frac{3}{8}$ times as many hours of daylight on June 21 as on December 21, when there are $5\frac{1}{2}$ hours of daylight. How many hours of daylight does Leningrad have on June 21?

Chapter 9 Test
Addition and Subtraction of Fractions, pages 172–187

Write these fractions with a common denominator.

1. $\frac{5}{6}$ $\frac{7}{12}$ **2.** $\frac{4}{5}$ $\frac{2}{3}$

3. $\frac{4}{9}$ $\frac{5}{6}$ **4.** $\frac{5}{6}$ $\frac{7}{8}$

Compare. Use $>$, $<$, or $=$.

5. $\frac{3}{4}$ ● $\frac{4}{5}$ **6.** $\frac{2}{3}$ ● $\frac{5}{9}$

7. $2\frac{3}{5}$ ● $2\frac{6}{10}$ **8.** $7\frac{2}{5}$ ● $7\frac{5}{8}$

Write in order from the least to the greatest.

9. $\frac{3}{4}$ $\frac{5}{8}$ $\frac{1}{2}$ **10.** $7\frac{5}{6}$ $7\frac{2}{3}$ $7\frac{4}{9}$

Add.

11. $\begin{array}{r} \frac{2}{3} \\ +\frac{3}{5} \\ \hline \end{array}$ **12.** $\begin{array}{r} \frac{5}{6} \\ +\frac{5}{8} \\ \hline \end{array}$ **13.** $\begin{array}{r} \frac{3}{4} \\ +\frac{1}{6} \\ \hline \end{array}$

14. $\begin{array}{r} 7\frac{1}{2} \\ +8\frac{3}{5} \\ \hline \end{array}$ **15.** $\begin{array}{r} 4\frac{5}{6} \\ +7\frac{1}{8} \\ \hline \end{array}$ **16.** $\begin{array}{r} 6\frac{2}{3} \\ +11 \\ \hline \end{array}$

17. $13\frac{2}{3} + \frac{3}{8}$ **18.** $3\frac{5}{6} + 2\frac{1}{3} + 8\frac{1}{2}$

Subtract.

19. $\begin{array}{r} \frac{3}{4} \\ -\frac{1}{6} \\ \hline \end{array}$ **20.** $\begin{array}{r} \frac{7}{10} \\ -\frac{1}{6} \\ \hline \end{array}$ **21.** $\begin{array}{r} \frac{6}{7} \\ -\frac{1}{3} \\ \hline \end{array}$

22. $7\frac{5}{6} - 4\frac{1}{3}$ **23.** $7 - 3\frac{1}{4}$

24. $8\frac{1}{6} - 5\frac{3}{8}$ **25.** $9\frac{2}{5} - 1\frac{3}{4}$

Evaluate each expression for $n = 2\frac{1}{4}$.

26. $n + 3\frac{4}{5}$ **27.** $n - 1\frac{7}{8}$

28. $\left(n - \frac{5}{6}\right) - 1\frac{1}{3}$ **29.** $7\frac{1}{2} - \left(5\frac{1}{8} - n\right)$

Solve.

30. $a + \frac{3}{5} = \frac{7}{10}$ **31.** $b - \frac{5}{8} = \frac{3}{4}$

32. $3\frac{2}{3} + y = 5\frac{3}{8}$ **33.** $m - 4\frac{3}{5} = 7\frac{2}{3}$

34. After Pam cut $4\frac{7}{8}$ feet from a board, there was a $5\frac{3}{4}$-foot piece left. How long was the board before she cut it?

35. Ana's dog weighed $7\frac{1}{4}$ pounds in July. Now it weighs $10\frac{3}{4}$ pounds. How much weight has the dog gained since July?

Problems Around Us

1. Parícutin, a volcano in Mexico, is 2271 m high. Mt. Wrangell in Alaska is about 2046 m higher. How high is Mt. Wrangell?

2. The elevation of Montgomery, Alabama, is 67.4 m. The elevation of Flagstaff, Arizona, is 2135.4 m. To the nearest tenth, how many times the elevation of Montgomery is this?

3. Greenland Ranch, California, was 56.7°C on July 10, 1913. It was 118.8° colder than this in Prospect Creek Camp, Alaska, on January 23, 1971. How cold did it get in Prospect Creek Camp?

4. One year in Winslow, Arizona, there were 73 days with temperatures of 32°C or above and 140 days with temperatures of 0°C or below. How many of the 365 days were between 0°C and 32°C?

5. Mike wants the same number of shirts and jogging shorts for his sports store. The shirts come in boxes of 9. The jogging shorts come in boxes of 15. What is the smallest number of each that he should buy?

6. The Panama Canal is 81.62 km long. The Suez Canal is 162.15 km long. How much longer is the Suez Canal?

7. The distance from Hister to Toomay is $15\frac{3}{4}$ miles. Jeri walks at a rate of $3\frac{1}{2}$ miles per hour. How long will it take her to walk from Hister to Toomay?

8. Faeroe Island is $\frac{20}{21}$ as large as Shetland Island, which is 1469 km². To the nearest square kilometer, how large is Faeroe Island?

9. On Wednesday, BCD closed at $28\frac{5}{8}$ points, after a gain of $1\frac{1}{8}$ points. What was BCD when it opened that day?

10. In 1979, the low for FGX was $6\frac{3}{4}$ points. The high was $14\frac{3}{8}$ points. What was the difference between the high and the low?

Individualized Skills Maintenance

Diagnose

A *pages 36–37*

0.03 × 46

5.98 × 2.7

3.71 × 1000

B *pages 40–43*

48.6 ÷ 15

38.07 ÷ 4.7

9.97 ÷ 1000

Practice

A

1.   27
   × 0.05

2.   35
   × 0.07

3.   64
   × 0.08

4.   76
   × 0.06

5.   82
   × 0.09

6.   0.063
   ×   0.9

7.   4.2
   × 0.08

8.   7.8
   × 0.7

9.   0.0053
   ×   0.04

10.   43.6
   × 0.03

11. 8.5 × 2.7

12. 48 × 0.23

13. 0.063 × 0.059

14. 17.8 × 3.6

15. 43.3 × 10

16. 9.56 × 1000

17. 0.2 × 10,000

18. 8.473 × 1000

19. 0.21 × 1000

20. 2.5 × 10,000

21. 0.011 × 10

22. 0.123 × 100

B

23. 7)39.2

24. 6)26.04

25. 18)127.8

26. 75)667.5

27. 22)68.42

28. 38)74.10

29. 29)2242.28

30. 102)250.308

31. 0.2)1.94

32. 0.9)0.468

33. 3.5)65.45

34. 0.07)3.577

35. 2.9)0.7859

36. 0.01)46.1

37. 0.72)21.6

38. 4.06)60.9

39. 72 ÷ 10

40. 9.1 ÷ 100

41. 45.4 ÷ 1000

42. 8840 ÷ 10,000

43. 0.63 ÷ 10

44. 0.6 ÷ 100

45. 0.17 ÷ 1000

46. 10.1 ÷ 10,000

Unit 3 Review

Chapter 7, pages 134–146

1. List all the factors of 30.

2. Is 418,342 divisible by 8? Write *yes* or *no*.

3. Write the prime factorization of 160.

4. Find the greatest common factor of 30 and 45.

5. Find the least common multiple of 15 and 25.

Chapter 8, pages 148–170

6. Write $\frac{32}{40}$ in lowest terms.

7. Write a whole number or a mixed number for $\frac{39}{8}$.

8. Write a decimal for $\frac{7}{5}$.

9. Give the reciprocal of 7.

Multiply or divide.

10. $\frac{3}{8} \times \frac{4}{5}$ 11. $3\frac{2}{3} \times 4\frac{1}{2}$

12. $\frac{2}{5} \div \frac{4}{9}$ 13. $6 \div 1\frac{1}{5}$

14. Solve $\frac{x}{3} = 3\frac{5}{6}$.

15. Norm has $6\frac{2}{3}$ feet of rope. He cuts it into 10 equal pieces. How long is each piece of rope?

Chapter 9, pages 172–187

Write these fractions with a common denominator.

16. $\frac{7}{8}$ $\frac{1}{12}$ 17. $\frac{3}{5}$ $\frac{1}{6}$

18. Write in order from the least to the greatest.

$5\frac{1}{6}$ $5\frac{5}{12}$ $5\frac{1}{9}$

Add or subtract.

19. $\frac{5}{6}$ 20. $2\frac{1}{8}$ 21. $\frac{7}{10}$
$+\frac{1}{4}$ $+7\frac{3}{4}$ $-\frac{3}{5}$

22. $14 + 1\frac{4}{9}$ 23. $4\frac{1}{3} + 6 + 3\frac{7}{8}$

24. $2\frac{1}{4} - 1\frac{8}{9}$ 25. $6 - \frac{4}{5}$

26. Evaluate $n - 1\frac{1}{2}$ for $n = 3\frac{1}{3}$.

27. Solve $2\frac{7}{8} + x = 5\frac{1}{4}$.

28. Mr. Myer's apple tree was $14\frac{3}{4}$ feet tall when he planted it. Since then it has grown $4\frac{1}{2}$ feet. How tall is it now?

Unit 3 Test
Chapters 7-9, pages 134-188

1. Is 51 prime? Write *yes* or *no*.

2. Is 531,072 divisible by 9? Write *yes* or *no*.

3. Write the prime factorization of 140.

4. Find the greatest common factor of 27 and 63.

5. Find the least common multiple of 8 and 22.

6. Write $\frac{35}{42}$ in lowest terms.

7. Write a fraction for $7\frac{2}{3}$.

8. Write a fraction for 0.219.

9. Give the reciprocal of $\frac{7}{8}$.

Multiply or divide.

10. $\frac{6}{7} \times \frac{3}{10}$ 11. $6 \times 4\frac{2}{3}$

12. $\frac{3}{4} \div \frac{15}{16}$ 13. $1\frac{4}{5} \div 2\frac{1}{4}$

14. Solve $\frac{3}{4}x = \frac{2}{3}$.

Write these fractions with a common denominator.

15. $\frac{5}{6}$ $\frac{1}{10}$ 16. $\frac{3}{8}$ $\frac{9}{16}$

Compare. Use >, <, or =.

17. $\frac{4}{5}$ ● $\frac{3}{4}$ 18. $6\frac{1}{3}$ ● $6\frac{3}{9}$

Add or subtract.

19. $\frac{7}{12}$ $+ \frac{1}{8}$ 20. $\frac{3}{4}$ $- \frac{2}{5}$ 21. $4\frac{1}{6}$ $- 1\frac{1}{9}$

22. $16 + 3\frac{3}{5}$ 23. $4\frac{1}{2} + 3\frac{1}{6} + \frac{3}{4}$

24. $8\frac{1}{4} - 5\frac{3}{10}$ 25. $8 - 1\frac{2}{3}$

26. Evaluate $\frac{7}{10} + n$ for $n = \frac{1}{6}$.

27. Solve $b + \frac{4}{9} = \frac{7}{12}$.

28. A recipe requires $1\frac{1}{3}$ cups of raisins. Josie is making $\frac{1}{2}$ the recipe. What amount of raisins does she need?

29. Linc bought $4\frac{1}{4}$ pounds of cherries. He ate $\frac{1}{2}$ pound. How many pounds of cherries were left?

Unit 4

Chapter 10 Exponents and Scientific Notation

Exponents and Powers of 10

A. A positive exponent tells how many times a number is used as a factor.

$$10^2 = 10 \times 10 = 100$$

You can also use a negative number as an exponent.

$$10^{-2} = \frac{1}{10^2} = \frac{1}{100} = 0.01$$

Powers of 10	
With exponent	In standard form
10^4	10,000
10^3	1000
10^2	100
10^1	10
10^0	1
10^{-1}	0.1
10^{-2}	0.01
10^{-3}	0.001
10^{-4}	0.0001

•**Discuss** How many *zeros* are there in the standard form for 10^4? for 10^3? for 10^5?

•**Discuss** How many *decimal places* are there in the standard form for 10^{-1}? for 10^{-3}? for 10^{-5}?

B. An electron microscope can enlarge a cell 100,000 times. Write this number as a power of 10.

$$\underbrace{100,000}_{\text{5 zeros}} = 10^5$$

C. The thickness of some cells is only 0.00001 cm. Write this number as a power of 10.

$$\underbrace{0.00001}_{\text{5 places}} = 10^{-5}$$

Write each number as a power of 10.

1. 100 2. 10,000 3. 1 4. 0.01 5. 1,000,000

6. 0.1 7. 1000 8. 0.000001 9. 0.00000001 10. 10,000,000

Write each number in standard form.

11. 10^3 12. 10^6 13. 10^{-2} 14. 10^{15} 15. 10^0

16. 10^{10} 17. 10^{-7} 18. 10^8 19. 10^9 20. 10^{-12}

21. A germ culture for an experiment contained 10^6 bacteria. Write this number in standard form.

22. Very small measurements, like the width of a virus, are sometimes given in *microns*. One micron is equal to 0.000001 meter. Write this number as a power of 10.

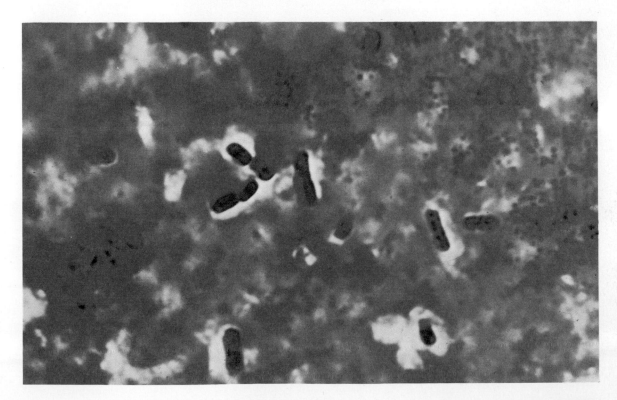

Multiplying by Powers of 10 Using Exponents

A. Seawater weighs 1.025 grams per cubic centimeter. Find the weight of 10^8 cubic centimeters of seawater.

Find 1.025×10^8.

Multiplying a number by 10 yields a larger number; you move the decimal point 1 place to the right.

$$10^8 = 10 \times 10 \times 10 \times 10 \times 10 \times 10 \times 10 \times 10$$

When you multiply by 10^8, you are multiplying by eight 10s. So you move the point 8 places to the right.

$$1.025 \times 10^8 = \underbrace{102{,}500{,}000}_{\text{8 places}}$$

The weight of 10^8 cubic centimeters of seawater is 102,500,000 grams.

B. Find 85.04×10^{-3}.

$$85.04 \times 10^{-3}$$

$$85.04 \times \frac{1}{10^3}$$

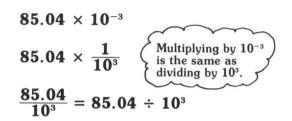

Multiplying by 10^{-3} is the same as dividing by 10^3.

$$\frac{85.04}{10^3} = 85.04 \div 10^3$$

Dividing a number by 10 yields a smaller number; you move the decimal point 1 place to the left.

$$10^3 = 10 \times 10 \times 10$$

When you multiply by 10^{-3}, you are dividing by three 10s. So you move the point 3 places to the left.

$$85.04 \times 10^{-3} = \underbrace{0.08504}_{\text{3 places}}$$

■*To multiply by a power of 10 that has a positive exponent, move the decimal point to the right. The exponent tells how many places to move the point.*

■*To multiply by a power of 10 that has a negative exponent, move the decimal point to the left. The exponent tells how many places to move the point.*

c. Find 0.932×10^5.   **D.** Find 4135×10^{-6}.   **E.** Find $10^{-3} \times 9$.

$$0.932 \times 10^5$$

$$\underline{93,200}$$
5 places

$$4135 \times 10^{-6}$$

$$\underline{0.004135}$$
6 places

$$10^{-3} \times 9$$

$$\underline{0.009}$$
3 places

Find each product.

1. 8.7956×10^2 2. 78.3×10^1 3. $10^2 \times 94.6$

4. $10^5 \times 8.234$ 5. 4.384×10^{-2} 6. 23.764×10^{-3}

7. 3.4569×10^4 8. $10^{-5} \times 0.01$ 9. $10^{-1} \times 895.23$

10. 72.56×10^{10} 11. 234.25×10^{-8} 12. 87.976×10^7

13. 178×10^{-1} 14. 0.714×10^{-4} ★15. 70.8×10^0

Complete this table.

	Substance	Weight per cubic centimeter (grams)	Number of cubic centimeters	Total weight (grams)
16.	Gasoline	0.68	10^6	
17.	Steel	7.87	10^3	
18.	Charcoal	0.4	10^8	
19.	Wool	1.32	10^2	
20.	Milk	1.0032	10^4	
21.	Sand (dry)	1.5	10^{10}	
22.	Clay (porcelain)	2.2	10^7	

Find each answer. Use the data in the table above.

★23. Which weighs more: 10^2 cubic centimeters of milk or 10^2 cubic centimeters of wool?

★24. Which weighs less: 10^5 cubic centimeters of gasoline or 10^4 cubic centimeters of steel?

More practice
Set 35, page 411

Scientific Notation for Large Numbers

You can write large numbers more compactly with *scientific notation.*

A. Scientists think that dinosaurs lived on earth about 190,000,000 years ago. Write this number in scientific notation.

190,000,000
8 places

Imagine a decimal point after the first nonzero digit. Count the number of places from there to the actual decimal point.

1.9×10^8

Write the number as a product of 1.9 and 10^8.

Standard form ⟶ $190{,}000{,}000 = 1.9 \times 10^8$ ⟵ Scientific notation

Check Does $1.9 \times 10^8 = 190{,}000{,}000$? Yes, because multiplying by 10^8 moves the decimal point 8 places to the right.

■ To put a number in scientific notation, write it as a product so that
- (a) the first factor is greater than or equal to 1 and less than 10, and
- (b) the second factor is a power of 10.

198

B. Write 14,000,000 in scientific notation.

14,000,000
7 places

1.4×10^7

C. Write 893.5 in scientific notation.

893.5
2 places

8.935×10^2

Tell whether each number is written in scientific notation. Write *yes* or *no*.

1. 758
2. 8.12×10^3
3. 23.46×10^5
4. 4.698×10^6
5. 3.005×10^4
6. 5×10^4
7. 23×10^6
8. 1×10^2

Give each missing exponent.

9. $832 = 8.32 \times 10^{\text{▦}}$
10. $75 = 7.5 \times 10^{\text{▦}}$
11. $325.67 = 3.2567 \times 10^{\text{▦}}$
12. $7856.2 = 7.8562 \times 10^{\text{▦}}$

Write each number in scientific notation.

13. 150
14. 3900
15. 836,000
16. 579,200
17. 3,200,000
18. 67,100,000
19. 875.2
20. 937.56
21. 70,600
22. 19
23. 6,000,000
24. 17,010
25. 925
26. 8
27. 48.2
28. 1001
29. 278,000
30. 6.83
31. 10
32. 1300

33. Mammals may have become dominant on earth about 35,000,000 years ago. Write this number in scientific notation.

34. The sun is estimated to be 4,500,000,000 years old. Write this number in scientific notation.

More practice
Set 36, page 411

Scientific Notation for Small Numbers

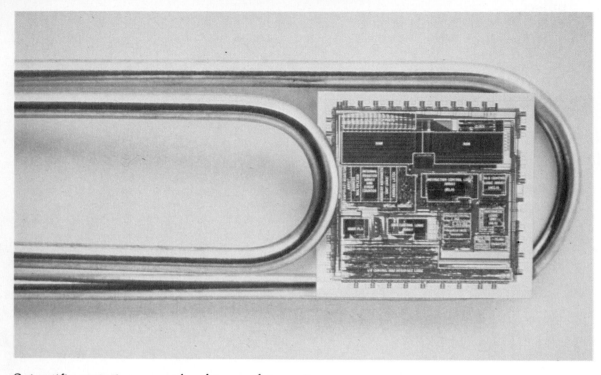

Scientific notation can also be used to write
very small numbers more compactly.

A. A certain computer can recall a piece of data
from its memory in 0.00000065 second. Write
this number in scientific notation.

0.00000065   Imagine a decimal point after
the first nonzero digit. Count
7 places   the number of places from there
to the actual decimal point.

6.5×10^{-7} Use a negative exponent with 10
when the original number is less than 1.

Standard
form → **0.00000065 = 6.5×10^{-7}** ← Scientific
notation

Check   Does $6.5 \times 10^{-7} = 0.00000065$?
Yes, because multiplying by 10^{-7} moves
the decimal point 7 places to the left.

B. Write 0.00055 in scientific notation.

0.00055

⎣_4 places_⎦

5.5×10^{-4}

C. Write 0.0891 in scientific notation.

0.0891

⎣_2 places_⎦

8.91×10^{-2}

Tell whether each number is written in scientific notation. Write *yes* or *no*.

1. 0.37
2. 3.46×10^{-2}
3. 57.234×10^{-4}
4. 4.276×10^{-5}
5. 796.4×10^{-3}
6. 0.0345
7. 4.7952×10^{-8}
8. 0.1×10^{-1}

Give each missing exponent.

9. $0.043 = 4.3 \times 10^{\square}$
10. $0.00587 = 5.87 \times 10^{\square}$
11. $0.0234 = 2.34 \times 10^{\square}$
12. $0.111 = 1.11 \times 10^{\square}$
13. $0.000056 = 5.6 \times 10^{\square}$
14. $0.000000001 = 1 \times 10^{\square}$

Write each number in scientific notation.

15. 0.369
16. 0.0079
17. 0.0001497
18. 0.0000009
19. 0.047
20. 0.00403
21. 0.00000005
22. 0.0000861
23. 0.000061
24. 0.011
25. 0.000001
26. 0.000201

27. It takes 0.000036 meter of magnetic tape to store a 5-digit number. Write this measure in scientific notation.

A *microsecond* is 0.000001 second. Write each time below in seconds, using scientific notation.

*28. 3 microseconds
*29. 35 microseconds
*30. 4.8 microseconds
*31. 0.078 microseconds

More practice
Set 37, page 411

Multiplying Powers of 10

A. Find $10^3 \times 10^2$.

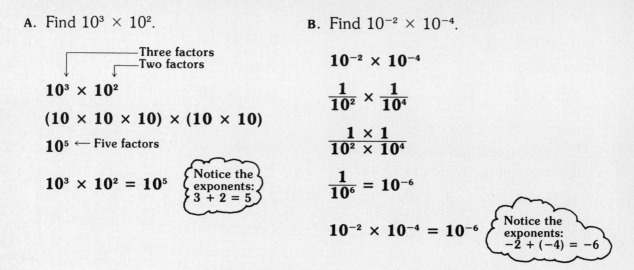

┌── Three factors
│ ┌── Two factors
↓ ↓
$10^3 \times 10^2$

$(10 \times 10 \times 10) \times (10 \times 10)$

10^5 ← Five factors

$10^3 \times 10^2 = 10^5$ *Notice the exponents: $3 + 2 = 5$*

B. Find $10^{-2} \times 10^{-4}$.

$10^{-2} \times 10^{-4}$

$\dfrac{1}{10^2} \times \dfrac{1}{10^4}$

$\dfrac{1 \times 1}{10^2 \times 10^4}$

$\dfrac{1}{10^6} = 10^{-6}$

$10^{-2} \times 10^{-4} = 10^{-6}$ *Notice the exponents: $-2 + (-4) = -6$*

■ *You can multiply powers of 10 by adding the exponents.*

C. Find $10^2 \times 10^6$.

$10^2 \times 10^6$

10^{2+6}

10^8

D. Find $10^{-4} \times 10^{-1}$.

$10^{-4} \times 10^{-1}$

$10^{-4+(-1)}$

10^{-5}

E. Find 10×10^{-3}.

10×10^{-3}

$10^{1+(-3)}$

10^{-2}

F. Find $1000 \times 10,000$ using exponents.

$1000 \times 10,000$

$10^3 \times 10^4$

10^{3+4}

10^7

$10,000,000$

G. Find 0.0001×100 using exponents.

0.0001×100

$10^{-4} \times 10^2$

10^{-4+2}

10^{-2}

0.01

Write each product as a power of 10.

1. $10^4 \times 10^3$
2. $10^5 \times 10^8$
3. $10^{-3} \times 10^{-5}$
4. $10^{-2} \times 10^{-11}$
5. $10^3 \times 10^{-1}$
6. $10^8 \times 10^{-6}$
7. $10^{-7} \times 10$
8. $10^{-4} \times 10^{-4}$
9. $10^{-5} \times 10^5$
10. $10^{-6} \times 10^0$
11. $10^4 \times (10^6 \times 10^{-3})$
12. $(10^4 \times 10^6) \times 10^{-3}$
13. $10^0 \times 10^4 \times 10^{-5}$

Find each product, using exponents. Give answers in standard form.

14. 1000×100
15. $10 \times 10{,}000$
16. 0.1×0.01
17. 1000×0.01
18. 0.001×10
19. 100×0.01
20. 0.001×0.001
21. $0.001 \times 10{,}000$
22. 0.00001×0.001
23. $100 \times 10 \times 0.01$
24. $0.1 \times 0.01 \times 0.0001$

Use the method of example B to show that

★25. $10^{-1} \times 10^{-1} = 10^{-2}$.

★26. $10^{-5} \times 10^{-2} = 10^{-7}$.

★27. $10^{-4} \times 10^{-3} = 10^{-7}$.

More practice
Set 38, page 111

Keeping Skillful

Solve.

1. $4x + 1 = 33$
2. $2c + 7 = 19$
3. $5n + 12 = 77$
4. $8a + 2 = 74$
5. $3t - 5 = 37$
6. $7d - 24 = 18$
7. $6g - 9 = 21$
8. $9s - 37 = 26$
9. $96 = 6x + 36$
10. $32 = 6h - 4$
11. $36 = 6a + 6$
12. $49 = 9c - 23$
13. $3v + 42 = 150$
14. $15y - 21 = 84$
15. $7m + 37 = 93$
16. $23 + 6r = 107$
17. $125 = 17 + 9x$
18. $103 = 28 + 5t$
19. $12r - 75 = 81$
20. $167 = 24 + 13k$

Multiplying Numbers in Scientific Notation

A. In its orbit about the sun, the earth travels about 2,560,000 kilometers each day. It completes one orbit in 365 days. Find the length of the earth's orbit.

Find $2,560,000 \times 365$.

$(2.56 \times 10^6) \times (3.65 \times 10^2)$ Use scientific notation.

$(2.56 \times 3.65) \times (10^6 \times 10^2)$ You can rearrange factors without changing their product.

9.344×10^8   Multiply.

$934,400,000$ Write the standard form.

The length of the earth's orbit is about 934,400,000 kilometers.

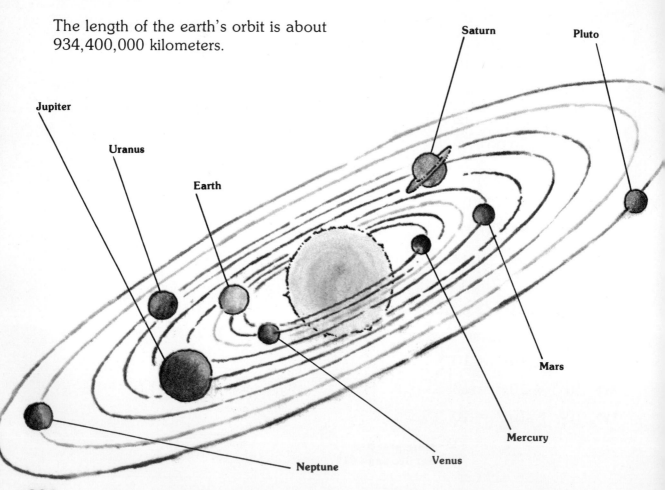

204

B. Multiply 0.013×0.0055 using scientific notation.

0.013 × 0.0055

$(1.3 \times 10^{-2}) \times (5.5 \times 10^{-3})$

$(1.3 \times 5.5) \times (10^{-2} \times 10^{-3})$

7.15×10^{-5}

0.0000715

C. Multiply $400,000 \times 0.00000098$ using scientific notation.

400,000 × 0.00000098

$(4 \times 10^{5}) \times (9.8 \times 10^{-7})$

$(4 \times 9.8) \times (10^{5} \times 10^{-7})$

39.2×10^{-2}

0.392

Multiply, using scientific notation. Then give the answer in standard form.

1. $(3.5 \times 10^{4}) \times (2.7 \times 10^{3})$

2. $(1.6 \times 10^{-2}) \times (4.8 \times 10^{5})$

3. 1900×170

4. 0.000302×0.029

5. $50,000 \times 1200$

6. $67,000 \times 110,000$

7. 0.000518×0.00027

8. 0.0058×63

9. $65,000 \times 0.0000033$

★10. $2100 \times 0.000195 \times 1800$

★11. $0.68 \times 346,000 \times 0.000024$

Find the length of orbit for each planet in this table. Give the answers in standard form.

	Planet	Distance per day (kilometers)	Number of days
12.	Mercury	4.11×10^{6}	8.80×10^{1}
13.	Venus	3.01×10^{6}	2.25×10^{2}
14.	Mars	2.08×10^{6}	6.87×10^{2}
15.	Jupiter	1.12×10^{6}	4.33×10^{3}
16.	Saturn	8.29×10^{5}	1.08×10^{4}
17.	Uranus	5.84×10^{5}	3.07×10^{4}
18.	Neptune	4.67×10^{5}	5.99×10^{4}
19.	Pluto	4.08×10^{5}	9.08×10^{4}

More practice
Set 39, page 411

Dividing Powers of 10

A. Find $\dfrac{10^5}{10^3}$.

$\dfrac{10^5}{10^3}$ ← Five factors
← Three factors

$\dfrac{\overset{1}{\cancel{10}} \times \overset{1}{\cancel{10}} \times \overset{1}{\cancel{10}} \times 10 \times 10}{\underset{1}{\cancel{10}} \times \underset{1}{\cancel{10}} \times \underset{1}{\cancel{10}}}$

$\dfrac{10^2}{1} = 10^2$

$\dfrac{10^5}{10^3} = 10^2$ (Notice the exponents: $5 - 3 = 2$)

B. Find $\dfrac{10^2}{10^4}$.

$\dfrac{10^2}{10^4}$

$\dfrac{\overset{1}{\cancel{10}} \times \overset{1}{\cancel{10}}}{\underset{1}{\cancel{10}} \times \underset{1}{\cancel{10}} \times 10 \times 10}$

$\dfrac{1}{10^2} = 10^{-2}$

$\dfrac{10^2}{10^4} = 10^{-2}$ (Notice the exponents: $2 - 4 = 2 + (-4) = -2$)

■ *You can divide powers of 10 by subtracting the exponents.*

C. Find $\dfrac{10^8}{10^3}$.

$\dfrac{10^8}{10^3}$

10^{8-3}

10^5

D. Find $\dfrac{10^2}{10^6}$.

$\dfrac{10^2}{10^6}$

10^{2-6}

10^{-4}

E. Find $\dfrac{1,000,000}{10,000}$.

$\dfrac{1,000,000}{10,000}$

$\dfrac{10^6}{10^4}$

10^{6-4}

10^2

100

F. Find $\dfrac{0.001}{0.1}$.

$\dfrac{0.001}{0.1}$

$\dfrac{10^{-3}}{10^{-1}}$

$10^{-3-(-1)}$

10^{-2}

0.01

Write each quotient as a power of 10.

1. $\dfrac{10^5}{10^2}$ 2. $\dfrac{10^6}{10^5}$ 3. $\dfrac{10^2}{10^7}$

4. $\dfrac{10^1}{10^3}$ 5. $\dfrac{10^9}{10^4}$ 6. $\dfrac{10^4}{10^9}$

7. $\dfrac{10^5}{10^8}$ 8. $\dfrac{10^8}{10^5}$ 9. $\dfrac{10^6}{10^{-3}}$

10. $\dfrac{10^8}{10^{-6}}$ 11. $\dfrac{10^{10}}{10^{-2}}$ 12. $\dfrac{10^7}{10^{-3}}$

13. $\dfrac{10^{-4}}{10^{-3}}$ 14. $\dfrac{10^{-5}}{10^{-6}}$ 15. $\dfrac{10^{-2}}{10^4}$

16. $\dfrac{10^{-3}}{10^{-3}}$ 17. $\dfrac{10^2}{10^2}$ 18. $\dfrac{10^8}{10^{-8}}$

Find each quotient, using exponents.
Give the answers in standard form.

19. $\dfrac{1000}{100}$ 20. $\dfrac{100}{100}$ 21. $\dfrac{100}{10,000}$

22. $\dfrac{10,000}{10}$ 23. $\dfrac{10}{100}$ 24. $\dfrac{10}{0.1}$

25. $\dfrac{0.1}{0.001}$ 26. $\dfrac{0.01}{0.1}$ 27. $\dfrac{0.001}{0.001}$

28. $\dfrac{0.0001}{0.01}$ 29. $\dfrac{0.1}{0.01}$ 30. $\dfrac{0.001}{0.01}$

31. $\dfrac{100}{0.01}$ 32. $\dfrac{0.01}{100}$ 33. $\dfrac{10,000}{0.001}$

More practice
Set 10, page 412

Time Out

There are three houses in a row: a log cabin, a cottage, and a ranch house. Each house is a different color, and a different animal lives in each.

The red house is next door to the green house.

The gerbil lives in the cottage.

The ranch house is not green.

The dog's house is red.

The rabbit lives in the middle house.

One of the houses is blue.

Which animal lives in the log cabin?

Dividing Numbers in Scientific Notation

U.S.A.

Population: 218,000,000

Area: 9,400,000 km²

Find the average number of people per square kilometer in the U.S.

Find $\dfrac{218,000,000}{9,400,000}$.

$\dfrac{2.18 \times 10^8}{9.4 \times 10^6}$ Use scientific notation.

$\dfrac{2.18}{9.4} \times \dfrac{10^8}{10^6}$ Separate into 2 divisions.

0.2×10^2 Divide. Round the quotient of the decimals to the nearest tenth.

20 Write the standard form.

The average number of people per square kilometer in the U.S. is about 20.

Divide, using scientific notation. Round the quotient
of the decimals to the nearest tenth. Give the
answer in standard form.

1. $\dfrac{7.3 \times 10^5}{3.2 \times 10^2}$ 2. $\dfrac{6.4 \times 10^6}{4 \times 10^3}$ 3. $\dfrac{4.09 \times 10^7}{5.3 \times 10^2}$

4. $\dfrac{645,000,000}{930}$ 5. $\dfrac{610}{230,000}$ 6. $\dfrac{0.0032}{0.00074}$

7. $\dfrac{8,000,000}{0.042}$ 8. $\dfrac{0.0079}{50,000}$ 9. $\dfrac{630,000}{0.18}$

10. $\dfrac{43,000}{27.9}$ 11. $\dfrac{57,600,000}{3490}$ 12. $\dfrac{0.716}{0.00845}$

Find the average number of people per square
kilometer in each country listed. Use scientific
notation, rounding the quotient of the decimals to
the nearest tenth. Give the answers in standard
form.

	Country	Population	Area (km²)
13.	Australia	14,000,000	7,700,000
14.	Bangladesh	85,000,000	140,000
15.	Barbados	265,000	430
16.	Canada	23,000,000	9,200,000
17.	China	950,000,000	9,600,000
18.	India	635,000,000	3,200,000
19.	Monaco	30,000	2.4
20.	Singapore	2,300,000	590
21.	Taiwan	17,000,000	35,000
22.	U.S.S.R.	259,000,000	22,000,000

More practice
Set 41, page 412

209

Using Scientific Notation

Legend has it that the inventor of the game of chess was asked by the king to name a reward.

The inventor chose wheat: 1 grain for the first square of the chessboard, 2 grains for the second square, 4 for the third, and so on. Each square was to have twice as many grains as the square before.

Find the number of wheat grains for each of these squares. Use your calculator to help.

1. The 4th square
2. The 5th square
3. The 6th square
4. The 8th square
5. The 10th square
6. The 12th square
7. The 14th square
8. The 16th square
9. The 18th square
10. The 20th square
11. The 22nd square
12. The 25th square

13. The number of grains needed for the last, or 64th, square is 9,223,372,036,854,775,808. Write this number in scientific notation, with the decimal factor rounded to the nearest tenth.

14. A large railroad grain hopper can hold a hundred tons of wheat, or about 2.8×10^{10} grains. How many of these hoppers would it take to hold the wheat for the 64th square? (Use your answer to exercise 13.) Use scientific notation, rounding the quotient of the decimals to the nearest tenth. Give the answer in standard form.

15. The number of grains needed to fill all the squares is 18,446,744,073,709,551,615. Write this number in scientific notation, with the decimal factor rounded to the nearest tenth.

16. In a recent year, the total U.S. wheat production was about 1.8×10^{16} grains. At that rate, how long would it take the U.S. to produce enough wheat to fill the inventor's request? (Use your answer to exercise 15.) Use scientific notation. Give the answer in standard form.

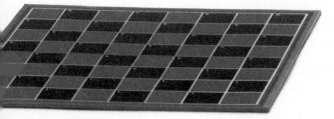

Side Trip

Significant Digits

The measure 0.072 g is accurate to thousandths of a gram. The **significant digits,** 7 and 2, show that there are 72 thousandths of a gram.

Ordinarily, the significant digits in a number begin with the first nonzero digit on the left, and end with the last digit on the right.

Number	Number of significant digits
80.5 km	3
0.014 mm	2
920 people	3
5.0 L	2
0.003010 g	4

Tell how many significant digits there are in each number.

1. 3049.5 2. 17.06

3. 2.0 4. 13.10

5. 0.0003 6. 0.0102

7. 0.40 8. 0.0520

In a number that is known to be rounded, ending zeros are not significant. If the number 600,000,000 has been rounded to the nearest million, it has 3 significant digits.

Each of the numbers below is rounded to the nearest hundred. Tell how many significant digits there are in each number.

9. 2700 10. 900

11. 55,000 12. 8000

13. 60,000 14. 100,000

Scientists often use significant digits in their calculations.

When they multiply or divide two numbers, they first determine which one has fewer significant digits. The product or quotient is rounded to have as many significant digits as that number has.

17.1 ← 3 significant digits
× 2.8 ← 2 significant digits
47.88 ≈ **48**   Round to 2 significant digits.

Find each product or quotient. Round your answers using the method described above.

15. 2.6 × 1.2

16. 24.5 × 2.8

17. 0.73 × 0.58

18. 39 ÷ 8

19. 375 ÷ 26

20. 167.3 ÷ 14.2

Chapter 10 Test
Exponents and Scientific Notation, pages 194–212

1. Write 100,000 as a power of 10.

2. Write 10^{-4} in standard form.

Give each product in standard form.

3. 7.8×10^5

4. 6.09×10^{-3}

5. 0.001543×10^{10}

6. 0.0002×10^{-4}

Write each product or quotient as a power of 10.

7. $10^2 \times 10^5$ 8. $10^{-4} \times 10^{-3}$

9. $10^{-8} \times 10^3$ 10. $\dfrac{10^6}{10^4}$

11. $\dfrac{10^{-3}}{10^{-2}}$ 12. $\dfrac{10^2}{10^{-2}}$

Find each product or quotient using exponents. Give the answers in standard form.

13. $100 \times 10,000$ 14. 1000×0.01

15. 0.00001×0.0001

16. $\dfrac{100,000}{100}$ 17. $\dfrac{100}{10,000}$

18. $\dfrac{0.001}{0.1}$ 19. $\dfrac{1000}{0.01}$

Write each number in scientific notation.

20. 4081   21. 3,500,000

22. 0.77   23. 0.0000062

Multiply, using scientific notation. Give the answers in standard form.

24. $3,800,000 \times 410,000$

25. 0.00025×0.0073

Divide, using scientific notation. Round the quotient of the decimals to the nearest tenth. Give the answer in standard form.

26. $\dfrac{3,300,000,000}{120,000}$

27. Loose snow weighs about 0.125 grams per cubic centimeter. About how much does 10^6 cubic centimeters of loose snow weigh? Give the answer in standard form.

Chapter 11   Ratio and Proportion

Ratios and Equal Ratios

A. If 4 L of seawater evaporates, about 140 g of salt will remain. The **ratio** of grams of salt to liters of seawater is 140 to 4.

Grams of salt $\longrightarrow$ $\dfrac{\mathbf{140}}{\mathbf{4}}$
Liters of seawater $\longrightarrow$

B. You can use multiplication or division to find equal ratios.

$\dfrac{140}{4} = \dfrac{280}{8}$ Multiply both 140 and 4 by 2.

$\dfrac{140}{4} = \dfrac{35}{1}$ Divide both 140 and 4 by 4.

280 to 8 and 35 to 1 also give the ratio of grams of salt to liters of seawater.

C. If two ratios are equal, they form a **proportion** and the **cross-products** are equal.

You can use cross-products to check if two ratios form a proportion.

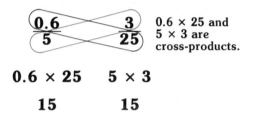 0.6 × 25 and 5 × 3 are cross-products.

0.6×25 5×3

15   15

The cross-products are equal, so the ratios form a proportion.

$\dfrac{0.6}{5} = \dfrac{3}{25}$

■*If two ratios form a proportion, then the cross-products are equal. If the cross-products are equal, then the ratios form a proportion.*

For each exercise, write two equal ratios for grams of salt to liters of seawater.

1. Great Salt Lake: 600 g of salt in 3 L of water

2. Arctic Ocean: 50 g of salt in 5 L of water

3. Dead Sea: 540 g of salt in 2 L of water

4. Northern section, Caspian Sea: 1.5 g of salt in 1 L of water

5. Western section, Caspian Sea: 320 g of salt in 1 L of water

Do the ratios form a proportion? Write *yes* or *no*.

6. $\dfrac{3}{4}$ $\dfrac{24}{32}$ 7. $\dfrac{16}{28}$ $\dfrac{4}{7}$ 8. $\dfrac{49}{55}$ $\dfrac{7}{8}$ 9. $\dfrac{5}{9}$ $\dfrac{30}{56}$

10. $\dfrac{4}{10}$ $\dfrac{10}{25}$ 11. $\dfrac{8}{6}$ $\dfrac{36}{28}$ 12. $\dfrac{33}{11}$ $\dfrac{9}{3}$ 13. $\dfrac{22}{55}$ $\dfrac{4}{10}$

14. $\dfrac{13}{18}$ $\dfrac{78}{108}$ 15. $\dfrac{196}{200}$ $\dfrac{23}{24}$ 16. $\dfrac{0.3}{5}$ $\dfrac{2.4}{4}$ 17. $\dfrac{2}{0.7}$ $\dfrac{16}{5.6}$

18. $\dfrac{0.4}{12}$ $\dfrac{0.6}{20}$ 19. $\dfrac{1.5}{3}$ $\dfrac{4.5}{10}$ 20. $\dfrac{0.2}{0.9}$ $\dfrac{0.6}{2.7}$ 21. $\dfrac{0.4}{0.5}$ $\dfrac{1.6}{2}$

22. A small desalting plant produces 40 million liters of fresh water every 5 days. How many liters are produced per day?

23. A large desalting plant produces 20 million liters of fresh water a day. How many liters are produced in 5 days?

24. If it costs $0.25 to produce 1000 L of fresh water from seawater, how much does it cost to produce 10,000 L of fresh water?

*25. A human can safely drink water that contains less than 5 g of salt per liter. For each of exercises 1–5, tell whether a human can safely drink the water.

Solving Proportions

A. Golf balls are on sale at 6 for $9. At this price, how much should Kimiko pay for 14 golf balls?

Golf balls $\longrightarrow$ $\dfrac{6}{9} = \dfrac{14}{n}$ Dollars $\longrightarrow$

Write a proportion.

$$6 \times n = 9 \times 14$$ Write the cross-products.

$$6n = 126$$ Multiply.

$$\dfrac{6n}{6} = \dfrac{126}{6}$$ Divide both sides of the equation by 6 to find n.

$$n = 21$$

Kimiko should pay $21 for the golf balls.

B. Find a in $\dfrac{a}{4.9} = \dfrac{8}{14}$.

$$\dfrac{a}{4.9} = \dfrac{8}{14}$$

$$a \times 14 = 4.9 \times 8$$

$$14a = 39.2$$

$$a = 2.8$$

Solve each proportion.

1. $\frac{2}{5} = \frac{r}{20}$ 2. $\frac{3}{4} = \frac{t}{24}$ 3. $\frac{d}{7} = \frac{5}{35}$

4. $\frac{12}{15} = \frac{8}{x}$ 5. $\frac{6}{27} = \frac{4}{m}$ 6. $\frac{n}{8} = \frac{7}{56}$

7. $\frac{5}{h} = \frac{50}{30}$ 8. $\frac{4}{r} = \frac{44}{99}$ 9. $\frac{6}{19} = \frac{y}{38}$

10. $\frac{c}{2} = \frac{63}{18}$ 11. $\frac{15}{n} = \frac{6}{14}$ 12. $\frac{d}{8} = \frac{70}{80}$

13. $\frac{14}{z} = \frac{8}{12}$ 14. $\frac{45}{81} = \frac{10}{s}$ 15. $\frac{w}{64} = \frac{18}{32}$

16. $\frac{27}{63} = \frac{12}{n}$ 17. $\frac{8}{21} = \frac{a}{42}$ 18. $\frac{15}{25} = \frac{f}{40}$

19. $\frac{0.5}{1.5} = \frac{3}{k}$ 20. $\frac{1.2}{0.8} = \frac{6}{t}$ 21. $\frac{h}{0.7} = \frac{9}{2.1}$

22. $\frac{4.5}{5} = \frac{9.0}{q}$ 23. $\frac{0.3}{2.4} = \frac{x}{7.2}$ 24. $\frac{8.1}{3.6} = \frac{2.7}{m}$

25. If 6 table-tennis balls cost $1.98, how much would 15 balls cost?

26. If 12 arrows cost $42, how much would 5 arrows cost?

27. If 4 tennis balls cost $3.50, how many tennis balls can you buy for $5.25?

*28. At one store, 4 badminton rackets cost $21. At another store, 3 rackets cost $16. Which store offers the better price?

More practice
Set 42, page 412

Keeping Skillful

Compare the integers.
Use > or <.

1. 17 ⬤ 28
2. 6 ⬤ 3
3. 7 ⬤ −7
4. 0 ⬤ −1
5. −8 ⬤ 0
6. −25 ⬤ 25
7. −3 ⬤ −17
8. 9 ⬤ −37
9. −4 ⬤ −9
10. −8 ⬤ −3
11. −14 ⬤ −20
12. −82 ⬤ −3

List the integers in order from the least to the greatest.

13. 6 −4 3 −1
14. −8 0 −9 9 8
15. −2 −10 −7 −1
16. 6 −6 1 −1
17. 0 −4 3 −5 2
18. −21 −38 14 −16
19. −10 8 6 −4 −5
20. −9 −5 −17 −3 0

217

Problem Solving: Scale Models

Models are usually made to scale. A scale of 2 to 25 means that 2 units on the model represents 25 units on the actual object. For example, 2 cm represents 25 cm, and 2 m represents 25 m.

READ   The Wright Brothers' *Flyer* was the first successful airplane. Suppose a model of this airplane is built to a scale of 3 to 80. If the wingspan of the model is 45 cm, what was the actual wingspan?

DECIDE   Write a proportion.

Model wingspan (cm) $\longrightarrow$ $\dfrac{3}{80} = \dfrac{45}{n}$
Actual wingspan (cm) $\longrightarrow$

SOLVE

$$\frac{3}{80} = \frac{45}{n}$$

$$3 \times n = 80 \times 45$$

$$3n = 3600$$

$$n = 1200$$

ANSWER   The actual wingspan was 1200 cm.

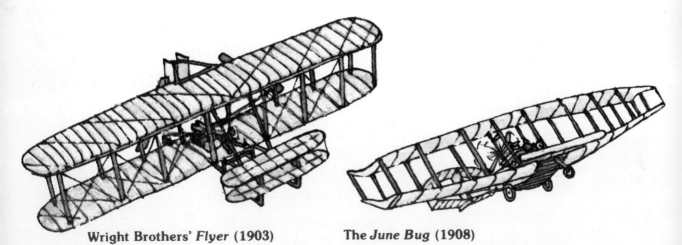

Wright Brothers' *Flyer* **(1903)**   **The** *June Bug* **(1908)**

218

For exercises 1–10, write a proportion. Then give the answer. If necessary, round to the nearest one.

A model of the *Grand* was built to a scale of 2 to 75.

1. The model has a 75 cm wingspan. Find the wingspan of the airplane.

2. The airplane was 2000 cm long. Find the length of the model.

A model of the *June Bug* was built to a scale of 1 to 20.

3. The model is 45.5 cm long. Find the length of the airplane.

4. The airplane had a 1390 cm wingspan. Find the wingspan of the model.

A model of the *Demoiselle* was built to a scale of 3 to 50.

5. The model has a wingspan of 33 cm. Find the wingspan of the airplane.

6. The airplane was 610 cm long. Find the length of the model.

A model of a modern jumbo jet was built to a scale of 5 to 72.

7. The model is 4.9 m long. Find the length of the jet.

8. The jet has a wingspan of 59.7 m. Find the wingspan of the model.

For a supersonic jet, the ratio of wingspan to length is 5 to 12.

9. A supersonic jet is 60 m long. Find the wingspan.

10. A model of a supersonic jet has a wingspan of 20 cm. Find the length of the model.

A passenger jet is 40 m long and has a wingspan of 30 m. Find the scale used to construct a model that is

★11. 80 cm long.

★12. 4.5 m long.

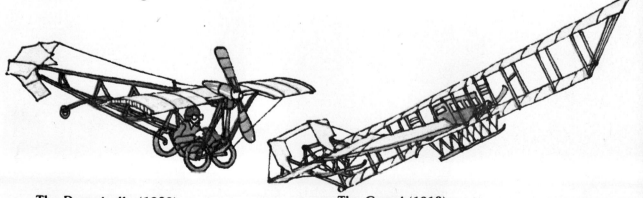

The *Demoiselle* (1909)   **The *Grand* (1913)**

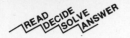

Problem Solving: Proportions

Often the results taken from a sample, or cross section, of the population are used to predict such things as the outcome of an election, the number of viewers of a TV program, or the quality of a product.

READ During a TV special, pollsters found that 75 out of 200 people were watching the special. Predict the number of viewers out of 10,000 people.

DECIDE Write a proportion.

Number of viewers ⟶ $\dfrac{75}{200} = \dfrac{n}{10{,}000}$
Number of people ⟶

SOLVE

$$\frac{75}{200} = \frac{n}{10{,}000}$$

$$75 \times 10{,}000 = 200 \times n$$

$$750{,}000 = 200n$$

$$3750 = n$$

ANSWER About 3750 people out of 10,000 watched the special.

For exercises 1–12, write a proportion. Then give the answer. If necessary, round to the nearest one.

Out of a sample of 25 students, 9 plan to vote for Candidate A, 11 plan to vote for Candidate B, and 5 plan to vote for Candidate C.

Out of 450 students, how many votes would you predict for

1. Candidate A?   2. Candidate B?   3. Candidate C?

Last month, 300 people in a sample were asked which cereal they liked better, Brand X or Brand Y. 175 liked Brand X, 80 liked Brand Y, and 45 liked neither brand.

Out of 10,000 people, how many would you predict to select

4. Brand X?   5. Brand Y?   6. neither brand?

Out of a sample of 200 nonvoters, 75 were too young to vote, 40 were not registered, and 85 were not interested in the election.

Out of 25,000 nonvoters, how many would you predict did not vote because they were

7. too young?   8. not registered?   9. not interested?

A manufacturer of light bulbs tested a sample of 500 bulbs. Two bulbs were found to be defective.

How many defective bulbs would you predict out of

10. 10,000 bulbs?   11. 100,000 bulbs?   12. 1,000,000 bulbs?

*13. Before an election, a pollster found that out of a sample of 250 people, 110 planned to vote for Candidate Z. After the election, it was found that Candidate Z received 4 out of 10 votes. Did Candidate Z do better or worse than expected?

Problem Solving: Proportions

READ   There are about 2,800,000 cars registered in Mexico. The population of Mexico is about 66,000,000. Find the approximate number of people per car. Round to the nearest one.

DECIDE   You can write either of the proportions shown below, since 2,800,000 out of 66,000,000 is the same as 28 out of 660.

Cars $\longrightarrow$
People $\longrightarrow$
$$\frac{2{,}800{,}000}{66{,}000{,}000} = \frac{1}{n}$$

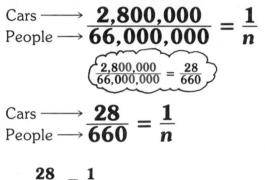

$$\frac{2{,}800{,}000}{66{,}000{,}000} = \frac{28}{660}$$

Cars $\longrightarrow$
People $\longrightarrow$
$$\frac{28}{660} = \frac{1}{n}$$

SOLVE
$$\frac{28}{660} = \frac{1}{n}$$

$$28 \times n = 660 \times 1$$

$$28n = 660$$

$$n \approx 24$$

ANSWER   In Mexico, there are about 24 people per car.

For each exercise, use a proportion to find the number of people per car. If necessary, round to the nearest one.

	Country	Number of cars	Population
1.	France	17,000,000	54,000,000
2.	United Kingdom	14,000,000	56,000,000
3.	Canada	9,800,000	23,000,000
4.	Poland	1,500,000	35,000,000
5.	Brazil	6,800,000	113,000,000
6.	Australia	5,200,000	14,000,000
7.	U.S.S.R.	5,600,000	259,000,000
8.	Venezuela	1,200,000	13,000,000
9.	United States	114,000,000	218,000,000
10.	Japan	20,000,000	114,000,000
11.	India	830,000	635,000,000
12.	Tanzania	34,000	16,000,000
13.	Philippines	550,000	45,000,000
14.	Kenya	93,000	14,200,000
15.	Ecuador	40,000	7,300,000
16.	China	40,000	950,000,000

★17. There are about 286,018,000 cars registered in the world. The world population is about 4,111,746,000. To the nearest one, find the number of people per car.

★18. There are about 362,638,000 vehicles (cars, trucks, and buses) registered in the world. To the nearest one, find the number of people per vehicle.

Problem Solving: Write a Problem

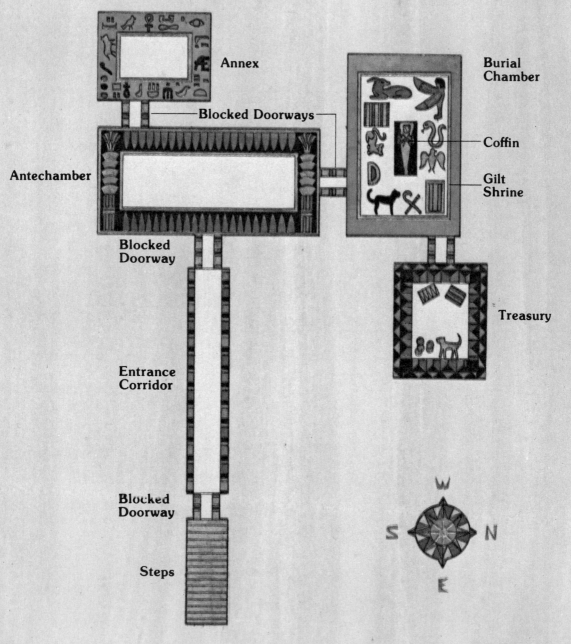

Tomb of Tutankhamen
Scale: 3 cm ⟶ 4 m

Annex

Blocked Doorways

Antechamber

Blocked Doorway

Entrance Corridor

Blocked Doorway

Steps

Burial Chamber

Coffin

Gilt Shrine

Treasury

224

Tutankhamen lived 3300 years ago and ruled Egypt from about 1347 to 1339 B.C. In 1922, a team of archaeologists led by Howard Carter discovered the tomb of King Tut.

In the burial chamber, they found the coffin of the king surrounded by gilt shrines, the largest of which was about 3.3 meters wide, 5.2 meters long, and 2.7 meters high. The coffin itself was made of 1114 kilograms of 22-karat gold.

Write a problem about the Annex.

Find the area of the Annex. First use your ruler and the scale to find the actual length and width.

Write a problem about

1. finding the actual dimensions of one of the rooms.

2. comparing the lengths of two of the rooms.

3. finding the area of one of the rooms.

4. comparing the areas of two of the rooms.

5. the Treasury.

6. the Antechamber.

7. the length of the coffin.

8. the scale-drawing dimensions of the largest gilt shrine.

9. fitting the largest gilt shrine in another room.

10. the time King Tut ruled.

11. the year the tomb was discovered.

*12. the value of the gold in the coffin.

Park Naturalist

As a naturalist, Judi Falk often studies wildlife population. She uses a method called "capture-recapture" to estimate the number of a species in a particular area.

In one study, 150 elk in a wildlife preserve were captured, tagged, and then released. Later, 200 elk were captured. It was found that 16 of these elk were tagged. Using this information, Judi estimated the number of elk in the preserve.

$$\text{Number tagged} \longrightarrow \quad \frac{16}{200} = \frac{150}{n} \quad \longleftarrow \text{Total number}$$

Number tagged $\longrightarrow$ $\dfrac{16}{200} = \dfrac{150}{n}$
Total number $\longrightarrow$

$$16 \times n = 200 \times 150$$
$$16n = 30{,}000$$
$$n = 1875$$

Judi estimated that there are about 1875 elk in the preserve.

Over a period of several weeks, the naturalists took more samples of elk from the preserve. For each exercise, use the data given and estimate the number of elk in the preserve.

	Sample size	Number of tagged elk in sample
1.	96	8
2.	150	9
3.	160	12
4.	175	15
5.	300	20

6. Find the average of your estimates in exercises 1–5. This is the average estimate of the size of the elk population.

7. Would it be possible to count all the elk in the preserve? Would it be practical to do so?

8. At Long Lake, the naturalists tagged 120 trout. Later, they took a sample of 308 trout and found 8 of them tagged. Estimate the number of trout in the lake.

9. At Cedar Marsh, 250 ducks were tagged. In a later sample, 13 out of 325 ducks were found to be tagged. Estimate the number of ducks in the marsh.

Time Out

Copy the diagram below.

Try to connect point A to A, point B to B, point C to C, and point D to D by following the lines of the grid. No path can cross another path.

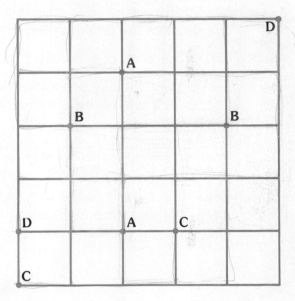

Lab Activity

Estimating with Ratios

You can use the capture-recapture method to estimate
the number of border pieces in a jigsaw puzzle.

Step 1   Get a puzzle with a large number of pieces.
The box will tell you how many pieces there are.

Step 2   Mix up the pieces. Pick a sample of about
one tenth of the total number of pieces.

Step 3   Count the number of border pieces in the sample.

Step 4   Set up the following proportion and solve to
find an estimate of the number of border pieces.

$$\frac{\text{Number of border pieces in sample}}{\text{Number of pieces in sample}} = \frac{\text{Total number of border pieces}}{\text{Number of pieces in puzzle}}$$

Step 5   Return the sample to the box and mix up the
pieces. Repeat steps 2, 3, and 4 three more times.
Then find the average estimate.

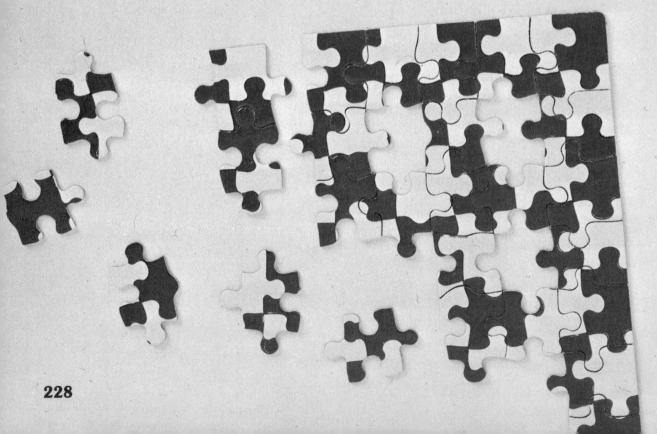

228

Chapter 11 Test
Ratio and Proportion, pages 214–228

Do the ratios form a proportion? Write *yes* or *no*.

1. $\dfrac{5}{6}$ $\dfrac{25}{30}$
2. $\dfrac{25}{30}$ $\dfrac{9}{10}$

3. $\dfrac{50}{70}$ $\dfrac{6}{9}$
4. $\dfrac{16}{20}$ $\dfrac{12}{15}$

5. $\dfrac{1.8}{27}$ $\dfrac{1.0}{15}$
6. $\dfrac{0.8}{1.2}$ $\dfrac{16}{25}$

Solve each proportion.

7. $\dfrac{2}{3} = \dfrac{t}{12}$
8. $\dfrac{9}{15} = \dfrac{6}{n}$

9. $\dfrac{x}{33} = \dfrac{7}{11}$
10. $\dfrac{14}{18} = \dfrac{21}{a}$

11. $\dfrac{9}{12} = \dfrac{y}{32}$
12. $\dfrac{r}{68} = \dfrac{15}{17}$

13. $\dfrac{0.7}{2.1} = \dfrac{n}{42}$
14. $\dfrac{0.2}{5} = \dfrac{z}{7.5}$

Use proportions to find each answer.

15. The diagram for a birdhouse is drawn to a scale of 2 to 15. If the height on the diagram is 4.2 cm, what is the actual height?

16. Stereo tapes are on sale at 3 for $14.85. How much would 5 tapes cost?

17. A model train is built to a scale of 1 to 32. If the actual train car is 1490 cm long, what is the length of the model to the nearest centimeter?

18. During a test, 100 cars were selected at random. 27 of them were found to be defective. Out of 5000 cars, how many would you predict to be defective?

19. There are about 11,000,000 people in Illinois, and the area of the state is about 144,000 square kilometers. To the nearest one, find the number of people per square kilometer.

20. Joel can do pushups at a rate of 25 in 60 seconds. At this rate, how long will it take him to do 20 pushups?

21. Write a problem about finding the area of the Treasury.

Treasury

Scale: 3 cm ⟶ 4 m

Percents and Decimals

A. In a survey, 39 out of every 100 people contacted said they read only newspapers or magazines.

39 out of 100 is 39 hundredths, or 39 **percent.**
Percent means hundredths.

$$\frac{39}{100} = 0.39 = 39\%$$

B. Write a decimal for each percent. Remember, percent means hundredths.

$21\% = 0.21$	$7\% = 0.07$	$80\% = 0.8$
$62.5\% = 0.625$	$33\frac{1}{3}\% = 0.33\frac{1}{3}$	$100\% = 1$

■*To write a decimal for a percent, move the decimal point two places to the left, and omit the percent sign.*

c. Write a percent for each decimal.

$0.52 = 52\%$ $0.03 = 3\%$ $0.9 = 90\%$

$0.1 = 10\%$ $0.763 = 76.3\%$ $0.66\frac{2}{3} = 66\frac{2}{3}\%$

■ *To write a percent for a decimal, move the decimal point two places to the right, and use a percent sign.*

● **Discuss**   100% of your class is how many students?
0% of your class is how many students?

Write a decimal for each percent.

1. 13%   2. 16%   3. 30%   4. 90%   5. 8%   6. 9%

7. 12.6%   8. 19.8%   9. 26.7%   10. 40.4%   11. 3.8%   12. 4.2%

13. 1.4%   14. 5.9%   15. $12\frac{1}{2}\%$ 16. $33\frac{1}{3}\%$ 17. $81\frac{2}{3}\%$ 18. $37\frac{1}{2}\%$

19. $6\frac{3}{4}\%$ 20. $1\frac{2}{3}\%$ 21. 56.75%   22. 48.25%   23. 0%   24. 100%

Write a percent for each decimal.

25. 0.72   26. 0.41   27. 0.93   28. 0.57   29. 0.09   30. 0.01

31. 0.4   32. 0.7   33. 0.834   34. 0.682   35. 0.309   36. 0.803

37. $0.16\frac{1}{3}$ 38. $0.78\frac{2}{3}$ 39. $0.45\frac{1}{2}$ 40. $0.92\frac{1}{2}$ 41. $0.03\frac{2}{3}$ 42. $0.06\frac{1}{2}$

43. 0.5   44. 0.05   45. 0.063   46. 0.63   47. 0.041   48. 0.033

49. 53% of the people in the survey read books, newspapers, and magazines. This is how many out of every 100 people?

50. 6 out of every 100 people in the survey do not read newspapers. What percent is this?

*51. 31% of the people in the survey have library cards. What percent do not have library cards?

Percents, Decimals, and Fractions

A. About 20% of the earth's land area is in Africa. What fraction of the earth's land area is this?

Write a fraction for 20%.

$20\% = \frac{20}{100}$ Percent means hundredths.

$\frac{20}{100} = \frac{1}{5}$ Write the fraction in lowest terms.

$20\% = \frac{1}{5}$

About $\frac{1}{5}$ of the earth's land area is in Africa.

B. Write a fraction for $66\frac{2}{3}\%$.

$66\frac{2}{3}\% = \frac{66\frac{2}{3}}{100}$ Percent means hundredths.

$66\frac{2}{3} \div 100$ $\frac{66\frac{2}{3}}{100}$ means $66\frac{2}{3} \div 100$.

$\frac{200}{3} \div 100$

$\frac{\overset{2}{\cancel{200}}}{3} \times \frac{1}{\underset{1}{\cancel{100}}} = \frac{2}{3}$

$66\frac{2}{3}\% = \frac{2}{3}$

C. Write a fraction for 37.5%.

$37.5\% = \frac{37.5}{100}$

$\frac{37.5}{100} = \frac{375}{1000} = \frac{3}{8}$ Multiply both 37.5 and 100 by 10. Write the fraction in lowest terms.

$37.5\% = \frac{3}{8}$

D. Write a percent for $\frac{5}{8}$.

$\frac{5}{8}$ means $5 \div 8$.

$$\begin{array}{r} 0.62\frac{4}{8} = 0.62\frac{1}{2} \\ 8\overline{)5.00} \\ -4\,8 \\ \hline 20 \\ -16 \\ \hline 4 \end{array}$$

Divide until the quotient shows hundredths.

Write the remainder in a fraction.

$0.62\frac{1}{2} = 62\frac{1}{2}\%$

$\frac{5}{8} = 62\frac{1}{2}\%$, or 62.5%

Copy and complete this table.

Fraction in lowest terms	Decimal	Percent
$\frac{1}{2}$	1.	2.
3.	$0.33\frac{1}{3}$	4.
$\frac{2}{3}$	5.	6.
7.	8.	25%
9.	0.75	10.
$\frac{1}{5}$	11.	12.
13.	14.	40%
$\frac{3}{5}$	15.	16.
17.	0.8	18.
19.	$0.16\frac{2}{3}$	20.
21.	22.	$83\frac{1}{3}$%
$\frac{1}{8}$	23.	24.
25.	0.375	26.
$\frac{5}{8}$	27.	28.
29.	30.	87.5%
31.	32.	10%
33.	0.3	34.
$\frac{7}{10}$	35.	36.
37.	0.9	38.
$\frac{10}{10}$	39.	40.

Write a fraction in lowest terms for each percent.

41. 39%   42. 45%   43. 24%

44. 2%   45. 57.5%   46. $41\frac{2}{3}$%

Write a percent for each fraction.

47. $\frac{7}{25}$ 48. $\frac{14}{20}$ 49. $\frac{33}{40}$

50. $\frac{49}{200}$ 51. $\frac{4}{7}$ 52. $\frac{8}{9}$

Complete this table.

	Earth's Land Area		
	Continent	Fraction	Percent
	Africa	$\frac{1}{5}$	20%
53.	Asia	$\frac{3}{10}$	30%
54.	North America	$\frac{4}{25}$	16%
55.	South America	$\frac{3}{25}$	12%
56.	Europe	$\frac{13}{200}$	6.5%
57.	Australia	$\frac{1}{20}$	5%
58.	Antarctica	$\frac{19}{200}$	

*59. Find the sum of the fractions in the table. Then find the sum of the percents.

More practice
Set 43, page 413

Percents Greater Than 100% and Less Than 1%

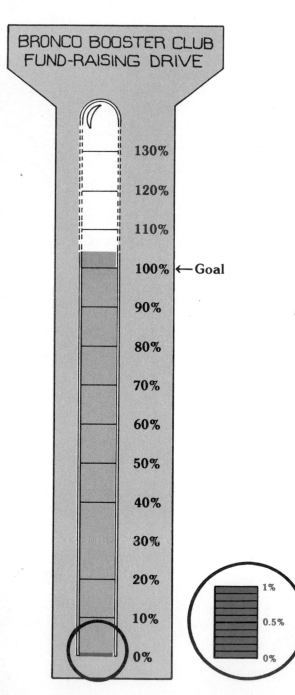

BRONCO BOOSTER CLUB
FUND-RAISING DRIVE

130%
120%
110%
100% ← Goal
90%
80%
70%
60%
50%
40%
30%
20%
10%
0%

1%
0.5%
0%

A. The members of the Bronco Booster Club raised money to help send the band to the basketball tournament. After the first week, they had reached more than 100% of their goal.

If the goal was $125, this means that they raised more than $125.

If the goal was $500, this means that they raised more than $500.

In the picture, percents greater than 100% are shown in red.

• *Discuss* Sometimes percents greater than 100% do not make sense. Could 110% of the band members go to the tournament? Why not?

B. If the fund-raising goal was $100, then $1 is 1% of the goal. An amount less than $1 is less than 1% of the goal.

In the picture, percents less than 1% are shown in the enlarged section. 0.5% is read "five tenths of one percent."

234

c. In the tables below, percents greater than 100%
and less than 1% are shown in color.

Percent	Decimal	Fraction or whole number
500%	5	5
50%	0.5	$\frac{5}{10} = \frac{1}{2}$
5%	0.05	$\frac{5}{100} = \frac{1}{20}$
0.5% or $\frac{1}{2}$%	0.005	$\frac{5}{1000} = \frac{1}{200}$

Percent	Decimal	Fraction or mixed number
150%	1.5	$1\frac{5}{10} = 1\frac{1}{2}$
15%	0.15	$\frac{15}{100} = \frac{3}{20}$
1.5% or $1\frac{1}{2}$%	0.015	$\frac{15}{1000} = \frac{3}{200}$
0.15%	0.0015	$\frac{15}{10,000} = \frac{3}{2000}$

Write a decimal for each percent.

1. 120%   2. 183%   3. 500%   4. 215%   5. 308%   6. 480%

7. 0.2%   8. 0.7%   9. 0.1%   10. 0.75%   11. 0.23%   12. 0.01%

Write a fraction, a mixed number, or a whole number
for each percent.

13. 140%   14. 225%   15. 400%   16. 675%   17. 200%   18. 879%

19. 0.4%   20. 0.8%   21. 0.3%   22. 0.75%   23. 0.16%   24. 0.25%

Write a percent for each number.

25. 7.5   26. 6.8   27. 3   28. 9.27   29. 4.15   30. $3\frac{7}{10}$

31. $8\frac{3}{5}$ 32. $13\frac{1}{2}$ 33. 0.004   34. 0.009   35. 0.006   36. 0.0025

37. $\frac{7}{1000}$ 38. $\frac{3}{500}$ 39. $\frac{1}{200}$ 40. $\frac{1}{250}$ ★41. $\frac{9}{2000}$ ★42. $\frac{3}{25,000}$

Select the percent that makes more sense.

43. On a test, Mario had (80%, 130%) of the items correct.

44. (4%, 140%) of the eighth graders were absent yesterday.

45. The enrollment decreased (0.5%, 120%) last year.

Finding a Percent of a Number

To help you solve percent problems, think about the data given in the problem as ___% of ____ is ____. Then write an equation. Use a decimal or a fraction for the percent. Use a letter for the unknown number.

A. The Aoki family bought a tent for $220 plus 5% sales tax. What was the amount of the sales tax?

5% of 220 is ____.

$$0.05(220) = n \quad \text{(5\% = 0.05)} \quad \text{or} \quad \frac{1}{20}(220) = n \quad \left(5\% = \frac{1}{20}\right)$$
$$11 = n \qquad\qquad\qquad\qquad\quad 11 = n$$

The sales tax was $11.00.

B. Find $66\frac{2}{3}\%$ of 180.

$66\frac{2}{3}\%$ of 180 is ____.

$$\frac{2}{3}(180) = n \quad \left(66\frac{2}{3}\% = \frac{2}{3}\right)$$
$$120 = n$$

$66\frac{2}{3}\%$ of 180 is 120.

c. Find 150% of 300.

150% of 300 is ____.

$1.5(300) = t$ ⟨150% = 1.5⟩

$450 = t$

150% of 300 is 450.

D. Find 0.6% of 25.

0.6% of 25 is ____.

$0.006(25) = a$ ⟨0.6% = 0.006⟩

$0.150 = a$

0.6% of 25 is 0.15.

•**Discuss** Is 225% of 37 greater than or less than 37?
Is 75% of 19 greater than or less than 19?

Find each answer.

1. 30% of 140
2. 35% of 80
3. 17% of 400
4. 25% of 172

5. 200% of 75
6. 100% of 13
7. 125% of 44
8. 110% of 60

9. 92% of 45
10. 60% of 112
11. 48% of 125
12. 32% of 65

13. 140% of 6
14. 175% of 4
15. 300% of 18
16. 500% of 9

17. $12\frac{1}{2}$% of 80
18. $62\frac{1}{2}$% of 24
19. $33\frac{1}{3}$% of 162
20. $16\frac{2}{3}$% of 78

21. $83\frac{1}{3}$% of 126
22. $66\frac{2}{3}$% of 90
23. 0.2% of 800
24. 0.8% of 300

25. 7.5% of 84
26. 2.5% of 96
27. 0.4% of 1200
28. 0.7% of 5600

29. 0.08% of 900
30. 0.05% of 700
★31. $\frac{1}{8}$% of 16
★32. $133\frac{1}{3}$% of 15

For each item, find the amount of the sales tax.

33. Camp stove: $47
    Sales tax: 7%
34. Lantern: $40
    Sales tax: 6%
35. Cookware: $11
    Sales tax: 4%

36. Fishing rod: $14
    Sales tax: 4.5%
37. Casting reel: $26
    Sales tax: 3.5%
38. Fishing net: $12
    Sales tax: 4.25%

**More practice
Set 44, page 413**

Computing Interest

A. Derek purchased a $250 bond that pays 10.5% interest per year. How much interest will he earn in 2 years?

You can find the interest for one year and then multiply this number by 2.

10.5% of 250 is ____.

0.105(250) = n

26.25 = n

2(26.25) = 52.50

The interest will be $52.50.

You can also use the **simple interest formula** to find the answer.

Principal $250

Rate 10.5%

Time in years 2

Interest = (Principal)(Rate)(Time)

I = PRT

I = (250)(0.105)(2)

I = 52.50

The interest will be $52.50.

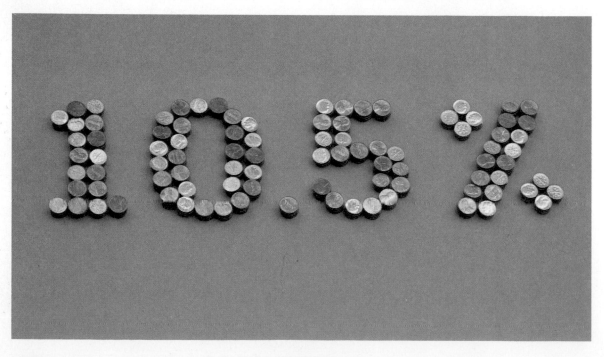

B. Molly borrowed $800 for 6 months. She paid $72 in interest. What was the interest rate per year?

$$I = PRT$$
$$72 = (800)(R)(0.5)$$
$$72 = 400R$$
$$0.18 = R$$
$$18\% = R$$

6 months = 0.5 year

The interest rate was 18% per year.

Find the interest earned on each investment.

1. $200 at 6% for 1 year
2. $100 at 5% for 1 year
3. $1000 at 8% for 2 years
4. $600 at 4% for 2 years
5. $800 at 7.5% for 3 years
6. $400 at 9.5% for 2 years
7. $1500 at 18% for 6 months
8. $2500 at 12% for 6 months
9. $6200 at 9% for 1.5 years
10. $4800 at 10% for 2.5 years
11. $900 at 15% for 3 months
12. $800 at 16% for 9 months

Find each missing number.

	Interest	Principal	Rate	Time
13.	$540	$2000	9%	
14.	$144	$600	12%	
15.	$96		8%	? years
16.	$280		7%	2 years
17.	$42	$700		1 year
18.	$70	$1400		1 year
19.	$135	$1500	18%	
20.	$180	$1200	12%	
21.	$680		8.5%	2 years
22.	$3240		7.2%	3 years
*23.	$900		$6\frac{2}{3}\%$	6 months
*24.	$1125	$18,000	$8\frac{1}{0}\%$	

Problem Solving: Multiple-Step Problems

READ   The Melody Music Shop is having a sale.
Guitars that originally cost $89 are on sale
at a 20% discount. What is the sale price?

DECIDE   There are two ways to solve this problem.

First Method

Find the amount of the discount.

20% of 89 is ____.

Then subtract the discount from the original price.

Second Method

Subtract the percent of discount from 100% to find what percent the sale price is of the original price.

Then multiply the original price by this percent.

SOLVE

$0.2(89) = x$

$17.8 = x$

$89.00 - 17.80 = 71.20$

$100\% - 20\% = 80\%$

$0.8(89) = x$

$71.2 = x$

ANSWER   The sale price is $71.20.

The sale price is $71.20.

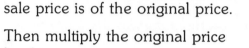

240

Find the sale price of each item.

	Item	Original price	Percent of discount
1.	Record album	$7	10%
2.	Record case	$4	12%
3.	Brass cymbals	$16	20%
4.	Tape recorder	$35	25%
5.	Headphones	$17	8%
6.	Record changer	$78	15%
7.	Stereo speakers	$129	$33\frac{1}{3}\%$
8.	Record stand	$34	$12\frac{1}{2}\%$
9.	Amplifier	$72	16%
10.	Guitar	$36	$16\frac{2}{3}\%$
11.	Color TV	$418	30%
12.	Black/white TV	$115	20%
13.	Console stereo	$395	15%
14.	Drum set	$654	$33\frac{1}{3}\%$
15.	Piano	$1295	30%
16.	Organ	$1595	35%

*17. Radios that originally sold for $55 were on sale at a 20% discount. Later, in a clearance sale, the radios were sold for 15% off the sale price. What was the final price?

*18. Is the final price in exercise 17 the same as 35% off the original price?

Keeping Skillful

Write the prime factorization of each number.

1. 6   2. 8

3. 12   4. 20

5. 32   6. 45

7. 75   8. 80

9. 94   10. 108

11. 200   12. 1000

Find the GCF of each pair of numbers.

13. 5; 10   14. 6; 42

15. 3; 27   16. 11; 13

17. 15; 18   18. 24; 32

19. 7; 23   20. 16; 28

21. 50; 120   22. 90; 162

Find the LCM of each pair of numbers.

23. 5; 25   24. 8; 12

25. 6; 20   26. 9; 27

27. 5; 9   28. 7; 11

29. 24; 42   30. 36; 40

31. 45; 81   32. 35; 56

Finding What Percent One Number Is of Another

A. This wide-bodied jet has 32 first-class seats. On one flight, 28 of these seats were filled. What percent of the seats were filled?

____% of 32 is 28.

$$k(32) = 28 \quad \text{Write an equation.}$$

$$\frac{32k}{32} = \frac{28}{32} \quad \text{Divide both sides by 32.}$$

$$k = \frac{7}{8} \quad \text{Write the fraction in lowest terms.}$$

$$k = 0.875 \quad \text{Divide.}$$

$$k = 87.5\% \quad \text{Write a percent for the decimal.}$$

87.5% of the first-class seats were filled.

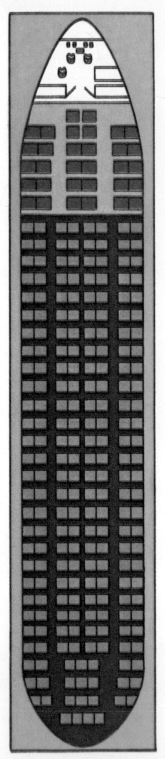

B. What percent of 25 is 35?

____% of 25 is 35.

$$n(25) = 35$$

$$\frac{25n}{25} = \frac{35}{25}$$

$$n = \frac{7}{5}$$

$$n = 1.4$$

$$n = 140\%$$

35 is 140% of 25.

C. To the nearest whole percent, 136 is what percent of 175?

____% of 175 is 136.

$$x(175) = 136$$

$$\frac{175x}{175} = \frac{136}{175}$$

$$x = \frac{136}{175}$$

$$x \approx 0.777$$

$$x \approx 78\%$$

136 is about 78% of 175.

Find each percent.

1. 9 is what percent of 15?

2. 21 is what percent of 30?

3. 28 is what percent of 50?

4. 12 is what percent of 25?

5. 7 is what percent of 5?

6. 19 is what percent of 10?

7. What percent of 25 is 16?

8. What percent of 20 is 17?

9. What percent of 200 is 16?

10. What percent of 250 is 15?

11. What percent of 81 is 54?

12. What percent of 96 is 32?

13. What percent of 75 is 225?

14. What percent of 125 is 500?

15. 3.5 is what percent of 28?

16. 12.5 is what percent of 20?

17. 16.8 is what percent of 10.5?

18. 32.4 is what percent of 21.6?

Give each answer to the nearest tenth of one percent.

19. 5 is what percent of 625?

20. 9 is what percent of 1800?

*21. What percent of 42 is 74.9?

*22. What percent of 65.9 is 0.3?

*23. What percent of 1.25 is 0.002?

Round each answer to the nearest whole percent.

24. There are 257 seats on the airplane shown. 225 of them are in the economy section. What percent of the seats are in the economy section?

25. Thirty-two of the 257 seats are in the first-class section. What percent of the seats are in the first-class section?

26. In the economy section, 56 of the 225 seats are window seats. What percent of the economy seats are window seats?

27. In the first-class section, 10 of the 32 seats are window seats. What percent of the first-class seats are window seats?

28. On one flight, 216 of the 225 economy seats were filled. What percent of the economy seats were filled?

29. On another flight, 5 of the 257 seats on the airplane were empty. What percent of the seats were empty?

30. Sometimes, an airline will sell more seats than are available. On one flight, 273 seats were sold. Only 257 seats were available. What percent of the available seats were sold?

More practice
Set 45, page 413

Problem Solving: Percent

Large amounts of energy are often measured in exajoules. One year, the United States consumed about 80 exajoules of energy. The graph shows how this energy was used.

Energy Consumption—U.S.

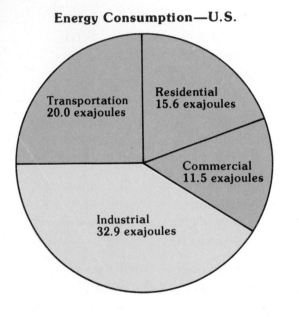

Transportation 20.0 exajoules

Residential 15.6 exajoules

Commercial 11.5 exajoules

Industrial 32.9 exajoules

READ About 32.9 of the 80 exajoules were used by industry. What percent of the total energy consumed was used by industry? Round to the nearest whole percent.

DECIDE Think: ___% of 80 is 32.9. Then write an equation.

$$n(80) = 32.9$$

SOLVE

$$n(80) = 32.9$$

$$\frac{80n}{80} = \frac{32.9}{80}$$

$$n \approx 0.411$$

$$n \approx 41\%$$

ANSWER About 41% of the total energy was consumed by industry.

For exercises 1–8, round each answer to the nearest whole percent.

1. The 15.6 exajoules used by the residential sector is what percent of the total consumption of 80 exajoules?

2. The 11.5 exajoules used by the commercial sector is what percent of the 80 exajoules?

3. The 20 exajoules used by transportation is what percent of the 80 exajoules?

4. About 19 of the 20 exajoules used by transportation came from fuel. What percent is this?

5. Space heating accounted for about 5.3 of the 11.5 exajoules used by the commercial sector. What percent is this?

6. The 5.3 exajoules used for space heating is what percent of the 80 exajoules?

7. About 6.2 of the 15.6 exajoules used by the residential sector came from natural gas. What percent is this?

8. About 0.9 of the 11.5 exajoules used by the commercial sector were used for water heating. What percent is this?

For exercises 9–10, round to the nearest tenth of one percent.

9. Residential and commercial air conditioning accounted for about 2 of the 80 exajoules. What percent is this?

10. Residential and commercial cooking accounted for about 1 of the 80 exajoules. What percent is this?

The graph below shows how 15.6 exajoules of energy were consumed by the residential sector.

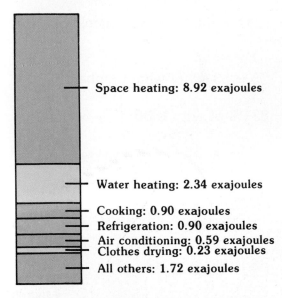

Space heating: 8.92 exajoules

Water heating: 2.34 exajoules

Cooking: 0.90 exajoules
Refrigeration: 0.90 exajoules
Air conditioning: 0.59 exajoules
Clothes drying: 0.23 exajoules
All others: 1.72 exajoules

*11. What percent of the energy consumed by the residential sector is used by each item shown on the graph? Round to the nearest tenth of one percent.

*12. What is the sum of the percents in exercise 11?

Finding a Number When a Percent of It Is Known

A. At Lincoln Junior High School, 65% of the students eat lunch at school. 403 students eat lunch at school. How many students attend Lincoln School?

65% of _____ is 403.

$$0.65x = 403$$

Write an equation.
$65\% = 0.65$

$$\frac{0.65x}{0.65} = \frac{403}{0.65}$$

Divide both sides by 0.65.

$$x = 620$$

620 students attend Lincoln School.

B. 35 is $83\frac{1}{3}\%$ of what number?

$83\frac{1}{3}\%$ of _____ is 35.

$$\frac{5}{6}n = 35$$

Write an equation.
$83\frac{1}{3}\% = \frac{5}{6}$

$$\left(\frac{6}{5}\right)\frac{5}{6}n = \left(\frac{6}{5}\right)35$$

Multiply both sides by the reciprocal of $\frac{5}{6}$.

$$n = 42$$

35 is $83\frac{1}{3}\%$ of 42.

Find each answer.

1. 80% of what number is 12?

2. 40% of what number is 22?

3. 15% of what number is 48?

4. 25% of what number is 36?

5. 95% of what number is 38?

6. 75% of what number is 69?

7. 4% of what number is 18?

8. 7% of what number is 35?

9. 15 is $33\frac{1}{3}\%$ of what number?

10. 13 is $12\frac{1}{2}\%$ of what number?

11. 135 is 180% of what number?

12. 110 is 125% of what number?

13. 44.8 is 56% of what number?

14. 14.3 is 22% of what number?

15. 60 is $37\frac{1}{2}\%$ of what number?

16. 72 is $66\frac{2}{3}\%$ of what number?

17. 33.48 is 9% of what number?

18. 20.75 is 5% of what number?

246

19. 120% of what number is 67.2?

20. 160% of what number is 124.8?

21. $83\frac{1}{3}$% of what number is 105?

22. $16\frac{2}{3}$% of what number is 64?

23. 9 is 0.3% of what number?

24. 12 is 0.8% of what number?

*25. 2.31 is 0.3% of what number?

*26. $166\frac{2}{3}$% of what number is 441?

*27. 0.25% of what number is 0.23?

28. One day, 9 eighth graders were absent. This is 4% of the class. How many students are in the class?

29. There are 84 eighth-grade boys. This is 48% of the class. How many students are in the class?

30. The 78 girls in intramurals make up 40% of the group. How many students are in intramurals?

31. At the Variety Show, 85% of all the available seats were filled. If 629 seats were filled, how many seats were available?

32. 75% of the students in the Drama Club were in the school play. If 27 Drama Club members were in the play, how many members are in the club?

More practice
Set 46, page 413

Lab Activity

Letters Used in Written English

This table shows the frequency of letters in written English.

E	13%	D	4%	G	1.5%
T	9%	L	3.5%	B	1.5%
A	8%	C	3%	V	1%
O	8%	U	3%	K	0.5%
N	7%	M	3%	X	0.5%
R	6.5%	F	2%	J	0.5%
I	6.5%	P	2%	Q	0.3%
S	6%	Y	2%	Z	0.2%
H	6%	W	1.5%		

Select a paragraph from a book. For each letter below, find the percent of use in the paragraph. Is your percent close to the percent in the table?

1. *E*   2. *S*   3. *K*   4. *X*   5. *M*

6. Write a word in which exactly 40% of the letters are the letter *T*.

7. Write a sentence in which more than 10% of the letters are the letter *Z*.

8. Write a sentence in which exactly 10% of the letters are the letter *A*.

Problem Solving: Percent

READ   Rose used 75% of her savings to buy a microscope. The microscope cost $31.50. How much money had Rose saved?

DECIDE   Think: 75% of ___ is 31.50. Then write an equation.

$$0.75x = 31.50$$

SOLVE $0.75x = 31.50$

$$\frac{0.75x}{0.75} = \frac{31.50}{0.75}$$

$$x = 42$$

ANSWER   Rose had saved $42.

248

Find each answer.

1. Renting buses for a field trip cost $150. This was 80% of the total cost of the trip. What was the total cost?

2. Each member of the Science Club paid $2.00 for the newsletter. This was 40% of the membership dues. How much were the dues?

3. Peter put a deposit of $39.75 on a telescope. This was 25% of the total price. What was the total price?

4. Linda made a 30% deposit on an electronics kit. The deposit was $13.50. How much did the kit cost?

5. The 6% sales tax on a radio kit was $0.87. How much did the kit cost without the tax?

6. The 5% sales tax on a battery amounted to $0.08. How much did the battery cost without the tax?

A 20% discount on a chemistry set was $7.99.

7. What was the original price?

8. What was the discounted price?

A 12% discount on microscope slides was $0.75.

9. What was the original price?

10. What was the discounted price?

The price of a scientific encyclopedia increased 15%, or $18.

11. What was the original price?

12. What was the new price?

★13. In a fund-raising drive, the Science Club earned $72 by washing cars. This was 75% of the total amount they received from the drive. 10% of the total came from science fair winnings, and 15% came from donations. How much came from donations?

Time Out

In the work at the right, each letter represents a different digit. What digit does A represent?

Hint: The sum of A, B, and C is the same as the sum of A, D, and E.

Problem Solving: Percent

READ   **A.** During the hockey season, Kevin took 195 shots and scored 39 goals. What percent of his shots resulted in goals?

DECIDE   Think: ___% of 195 is 39.
Then write an equation.

$$n(195) = 39$$

SOLVE $n(195) = 39$

$$\frac{195n}{195} = \frac{39}{195}$$

$$n = 0.2$$

$$n = 20\%$$

ANSWER   Kevin scored on 20% of his shots.

B. In a basketball game, Heidi made 9 free throws. This was 60% of the free throws that she tried. How many did she try?

60% of ___ is 9.

$$\tfrac{3}{5}n = 9$$

$$\left(\tfrac{5}{3}\right)\tfrac{3}{5}n = \left(\tfrac{5}{3}\right)9$$

$$n = 15$$

Heidi tried 15 free throws.

C. During the baseball season, Kate was at bat 125 times. She got a hit 48% of the time. How many hits did she get?

48% of 125 is ___.

$$0.48(125) = n$$

$$60 = n$$

Kate got 60 hits.

Find the missing numbers.

Wildcats' Baseball Team Hitting Record

	Name	Times at bat	Hits	Percent
1.	Kristen	75	21	
2.	Jill	48	30	
3.	Michelle	60		30%
4.	Kim		20	25%
5.	Pedro	72		$33\frac{1}{3}\%$
6.	Gina		36	37.5%
7.	Diego	63		$66\frac{2}{3}\%$
8.	Lee	54	18	
9.	Maria		27	60%

Jets' Basketball Team Field Goal Record

	Name	Number attempted	Number completed	Percent
10.	Takeo		126	42%
11.	George	250		32%
12.	Greta	156	78	
13.	Manuel		70	$62\frac{1}{2}\%$
14.	Jan	200		35%
15.	Irene		88	44%
16.	Wally	180	54	
17.	Don	192	72	
18.	Anuko	150		48%

Find each answer.

19. The Falcons won 56% of the 25 games that they played. How many games did they win?

20. The Rangers played 20 games away from home. They won 11 of them. What percent of the away games did the Rangers win?

21. The Tigers had a total of 54 points. Lori scored 18 of them. What percent of the points were scored by Lori?

22. The Hawks attempted 48 free throws. They made 62.5% of them. How many did they make?

23. The Lions won 28 home games. This was 80% of their home games. How many home games did they play?

★24. The Eagles won 33 games, tied 6 games, and lost 1 game on home ice. What percent of the games did the visiting teams win?

★25. The Mustangs completed 14 out of 35 free throws. What percent were not completed?

Compound Interest

A bank usually pays **compound interest.** This means that each time interest is paid, the bank adds the interest to the principal. The next time the interest is paid, it is paid on the new principal.

Suppose $1000 is invested in a bank that pays 6% per year interest compounded semiannually (every 6 months, or 0.5 year). The work below shows how you can find the new principal after 6 months and after 1 year.

First 6 months	Second 6 months
I = PRT	*I = PRT*
I = (1000)(0.06)(0.5)	*I* = (1030)(0.06)(0.5)
I = 30	*I* = 30.9

New principal

1000 + 30 = 1030

$1030.00

New principal

1030 + 30.90 = 1060.90

$1060.90

1. Use your calculator and continue this table until the principal has doubled. When necessary, round to the nearest cent.

Year	Principal	Interest	New principal
0.5	$1000.00	$30.00	$1030.00
1.0	$1030.00	$30.90	$1060.90
1.5	$1060.90		
2.0			

2. After how many years will a $1000 investment double if it is invested at 6% per year with interest compounded semiannually?

Teacher

Mr. Williams is a junior high school teacher. When he gives a letter grade on a test or a report card, he follows these guidelines.

A 93%—100%

B 87%—92%

C 78%—86%

D 70%—77%

F Below 70%

On a Spanish test, Karin had 26 out of 29 answers correct. What was her percent grade and her letter grade?

____% of 29 is 26.

$$n(29) = 26$$

$$n \approx 0.896$$

$$n \approx 90\%$$

Karin's grade was 90%, or a B.

For each student, the number of correct answers is given. Find a percent grade to the nearest whole percent. Then find the letter grade for that percent.

Science Test (50 questions)

1. Susan 43   2. Carmen 44

3. Max 38   4. Joseph 49

History Test (30 questions)

5. Chris 27   6. Rose 18

7. Henry 26   8. Matsuko 25

Math Test (80 problems)

9. John 64   10. Joel 63

11. Kazuko 72   12. Mary Kay 77

Spelling Test (125 words)

13. Lisa 100   14. Brian 121

15. Frank 97   16. Anita 115

Chapter 12 Test
Percent, pages 230–253

Write a decimal for each percent.

1. 23%   2. 12.5%

3. 180%   4. 0.3%

Write a mixed number or a fraction in lowest terms for each percent.

5. 25%   6. 87.5%

7. $66\frac{2}{3}$%   8. 150%

Write a percent for each number.

9. 0.84   10. 0.07

11. 0.6   12. 3.5

13. $\frac{4}{5}$ 14. $\frac{1}{3}$

15. $\frac{3}{1000}$ 16. $1\frac{7}{10}$

Find each answer.

17. 75% of 60

18. 125% of 68

19. 13 is what percent of 26?

20. 42 is what percent of 30?

21. 18 is 90% of what number?

22. 6 is $33\frac{1}{3}$% of what number?

23. Find the interest on $900 invested for 2 years in an account that pays 8% interest per year. Use $I = PRT$.

24. Tennis rackets are on sale at a 20% discount. What is the sale price of a racket that originally cost $16.95?

25. A radio cost $57.50 plus 4% sales tax. What was the amount of the sales tax?

26. Last season, Shawn made 63 out of 150 free throws. What percent of the free throws did he make?

27. The 12% discount on a record album is $1.02. What is the original cost of the album?

Problems Around Us

1. The Oroville Dam is an earthen dam. It weighs about 12×10^{10} kilograms. A cubic meter of earth weighs about 2×10^5 kilograms. About how many cubic meters of earth are in the dam? Compute using scientific notation. Then give the answer in standard form.

2. On a map of Indiana, 18 mm represents an actual distance of 50 km. Gary and Indianapolis are 81 mm apart on the map. How many kilometers is Gary from Indianapolis?

3. A manufacturer of electric hair dryers tested a sample of 400 dryers and found 2 dryers to be defective. At this rate, how many defective dryers should the manufacturer expect out of 10,000 dryers?

4. A *parsec* is a distance of 3.0857×10^{16} meters. The star Proxima is about 1.31 parsecs from Earth. How many meters from Earth is Proxima? Compute using scientific notation. Then give the answer in standard form.

5. Brown's Department Store is having a sale. Sweaters are on sale for a 30% discount. What is the sale price of a sweater that originally sold for $14?

6. The liner *Queen Elizabeth 2* can carry 1815 passengers. She sailed with 80% of this number of passengers. How many passengers was she carrying?

7. From 1.5 cubic meters of a crude oil, 0.7 cubic meters of gasoline can be produced. How many cubic meters of gasoline can be produced from 27 cubic meters of this crude oil?

8. Ruth invested $15,000 in an account that pays 11% interest per year. How much interest will she receive after 1 year?

9. Tina bought a new coat. The original price of the coat was $129. The coat was on sale for 20% off. What was the sale price of the coat?

10. A rocket ship travels at a rate of 2.6×10^4 kilometers per hour. At this rate, how far will this rocket ship travel in one day? (24 hours = 1 day) Compute using scientific notation. Then give the answer in standard form.

255

Individualized Skills Maintenance

Diagnose

A *pages 156–159*

$\frac{3}{7} \times \frac{7}{9}$

$10 \times \frac{2}{5}$

$5\frac{1}{2} \times 2\frac{2}{3}$

B *pages 162–165*

$15 \div \frac{3}{4}$

$\frac{5}{9} \div \frac{10}{11}$

$5\frac{1}{4} \div 3\frac{1}{2}$

Practice

A

1. $\frac{1}{2} \times \frac{8}{9}$
2. $\frac{4}{7} \times \frac{14}{15}$
3. $\frac{6}{7} \times \frac{9}{14}$
4. $\frac{4}{5} \times \frac{3}{4}$
5. $\frac{5}{6} \times \frac{5}{6}$

6. $\frac{2}{3} \times 15$
7. $\frac{1}{9} \times 11$
8. $\frac{3}{4} \times 6$
9. $12 \times \frac{9}{16}$
10. $\frac{5}{9} \times \frac{7}{10}$

11. $\frac{3}{14} \times \frac{20}{27}$
12. $8 \times \frac{3}{16}$
13. $5 \times 1\frac{3}{5}$
14. $3\frac{2}{3} \times 6$
15. $2\frac{1}{2} \times \frac{2}{5}$

16. $\frac{8}{15} \times 1\frac{1}{4}$
17. $4\frac{1}{4} \times 2\frac{2}{3}$
18. $2\frac{4}{7} \times 1\frac{1}{9}$
19. $6\frac{3}{4} \times 5\frac{1}{3}$
20. $1\frac{1}{5} \times 4\frac{1}{6}$

B

21. $7 \div \frac{1}{4}$
22. $15 \div \frac{3}{8}$
23. $\frac{1}{2} \div \frac{1}{4}$
24. $\frac{1}{4} \div \frac{1}{2}$
25. $\frac{5}{9} \div \frac{2}{3}$

26. $\frac{2}{7} \div \frac{2}{7}$
27. $4\frac{3}{4} \div \frac{5}{8}$
28. $\frac{7}{10} \div \frac{14}{15}$
29. $9\frac{2}{5} \div \frac{2}{15}$
30. $7\frac{7}{8} \div \frac{7}{9}$

31. $11 \div 4$
32. $8 \div 1\frac{1}{3}$
33. $20 \div 3\frac{3}{4}$
34. $\frac{11}{16} \div 8\frac{1}{4}$
35. $\frac{9}{8} \div \frac{8}{9}$

36. $6\frac{1}{4} \div 1\frac{7}{8}$
37. $15\frac{3}{5} \div 2\frac{1}{2}$
38. $8\frac{2}{3} \div 1\frac{5}{9}$
39. $4\frac{1}{2} \div 6\frac{2}{9}$
40. $5\frac{1}{2} \div 13\frac{3}{4}$

Unit 4 Review

Chapter 10, pages 194–212

1. Write 0.001 as a power of 10.

2. Write 10^6 in standard form.

3. Find this product.

   3.7×10^{-4}

4. Write $10^4 \times 10^5$ as a power of 10.

5. Write $\dfrac{10^{-6}}{10^{-4}}$ as a power of 10.

Compute using exponents. Give each answer in standard form.

6. $\dfrac{1000}{0.001}$ 7. $100,000 \times 0.01$

Write in scientific notation.

8. 256,000   9. 0.0007

10. Find $7,200,000 \times 0.0006$ using scientific notation. Give the answer in standard form.

Chapter 11, pages 214–228
Solve each proportion.

11. $\dfrac{6}{8} = \dfrac{x}{44}$ 12. $\dfrac{9}{m} = \dfrac{1.2}{7.6}$

Use proportions for exercises 13–15.

13. Three stereo tapes cost $17.85. How much would 5 tapes cost?

14. On a map, 4 cm represents 75 km. An island is 15 cm long on the map. To the nearest kilometer, what is the actual length?

15. Out of a sample of 400 people, 225 said they like Brand A better than Brand B. Out of 1000 people, how many would you predict to select Brand A?

Chapter 12, pages 230–253
Complete this table.

Fraction or mixed number	Decimal	Percent
16.	0.66	17.
18.	19.	120%
$\frac{1}{200}$	20.	21.

22. Find 65% of 32.

23. 42 is what percent of 126?

24. 36 is 150% of what number?

25. One day, 4 out of 32 students were absent. What percent is this?

26. Skis are on sale at a 30% discount. What is the sale price of skis that originally cost $159.00?

Unit 4 Test
Chapters 10–12, pages 194–254

1. Write 10,000 as a power of 10.

2. Write 10^{-3} in standard form.

3. Find this product.

   0.053×10^3

4. Write $10^{-6} \times 10^4$ as a power of 10.

5. Write $\dfrac{10^{-4}}{10^2}$ as a power of 10.

Compute using exponents. Give the answer in standard form.

6. $\dfrac{10,000}{100}$ 7. 0.0001×1000

Write in scientific notation.

8. 0.0074 9. $450,000$

10. Find $0.00032 \times 400,000$ using scientific notation. Give the answer in standard form.

Solve each proportion.

11. $\dfrac{n}{16} = \dfrac{21}{24}$ 12. $\dfrac{1.5}{3.6} = \dfrac{5}{y}$

Use proportions for exercises 13–15.

13. Patio chairs are on sale at 2 for $39. How much would 3 chairs cost?

14. On a scale drawing, a house is 4.5 cm long. If 3 cm on the drawing represents 8 meters, what is the actual length of the house?

15. During a road test, 150 bicycles were picked at random. 36 of them were defective. Out of 1000 bicycles, how many would you predict to be defective?

Complete this table.

Fraction or mixed number	Decimal	Percent
$\frac{1}{6}$	16.	17.
18.	0.75	19.
20.	21.	150%

22. Find 6% of 900.

23. 30 is what percent of 45?

24. 18 is 45% of what number?

25. Larry made 21 free throws. This was 60% of the free throws he tried. How many free throws did he try?

26. A football that originally cost $14.75 is on sale at a 12% discount. What is the sale price?

Unit 5

Chapter 13   Geometry

Basic Geometric Ideas

A. Three basic ideas in geometry are **point, line,** and **plane.**
True points, lines, and planes exist only in the mind.

A flat surface suggests a plane.
A true plane is endless.

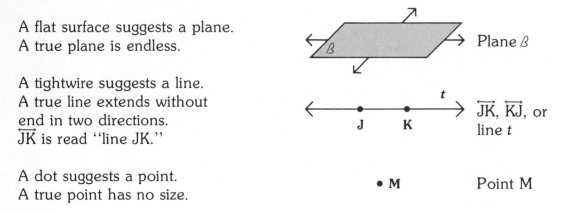

Plane *B*

A tightwire suggests a line.
A true line extends without
end in two directions.
$\overleftrightarrow{JK}$ is read "line JK."

$\overleftrightarrow{JK}$, $\overleftrightarrow{KJ}$, or
line *t*

A dot suggests a point.
A true point has no size.

• **M**   Point M

B. In space, two planes are parallel, or they intersect.

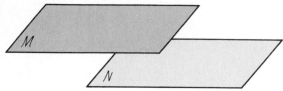

Parallel planes never meet.
plane *M* ‖ plane *N*
‖ is read "is parallel to."

Intersecting planes meet in a line.
Planes *C* and *D* meet in line x.

C. In a plane, two lines are parallel, or they intersect.

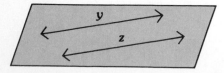

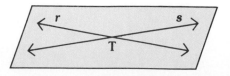

Parallel lines never meet.
line *y* ‖ line *z*

Intersecting lines meet at a point.
Line *r* intersects line *s* at point T.

D. Segments and **rays** are parts of a line.

A segment has two **endpoints.** The endpoints are used to name the segment.

Segment XY or segment YX

$\overline{XY}$ or $\overline{YX}$

A ray has one endpoint and extends endlessly in one direction. The endpoint is given first when naming a ray.

Ray YX

$\overrightarrow{YX}$

Think of the carton dividers as planes.

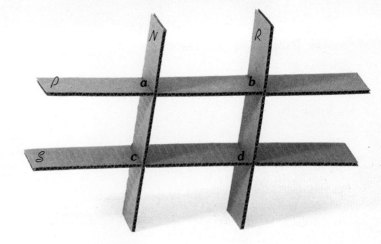

1. Name two pairs of parallel planes.

2. Name four pairs of intersecting planes, and give the line of intersection for each pair.

3. Name six pairs of parallel lines.

For each exercise, make a sketch.

4. $\overrightarrow{GH}$ 5. $\overline{YZ}$ 6. $\overleftrightarrow{LK}$ 7. $\overleftrightarrow{MN} \parallel \overleftrightarrow{WX}$

8. $\overleftrightarrow{RS}$ intersecting $\overleftrightarrow{PQ}$ at T

9. $\overline{AB}$ intersecting $\overleftrightarrow{CD}$ at C

10. $\overrightarrow{HG}$ and $\overrightarrow{HF}$ with common endpoint H

11. Line m parallel to line t with both lines intersecting line n

Think of the top, bottom, and sides of a box as suggesting planes.

*12. How many pairs of parallel planes are suggested?

*13. How many pairs of intersecting planes are suggested?

261

Angles and Angle Measurement

A. $\overrightarrow{GF}$ and $\overrightarrow{GH}$ are the **sides** of an
angle. Point G is the **vertex**
of this angle.

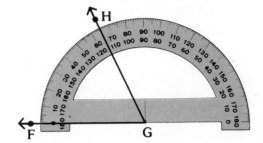

The angle can be named ∠FGH, or
∠HGF, or ∠G.

A **protractor** is used to measure
an angle or to draw an angle.

The measure of ∠FGH is 65 degrees.

m ∠FGH = 65°

B. Angles can be classified according to their measures.

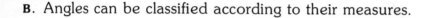

An **acute angle** is an
angle with a measure less
than 90°.

A **right angle** is an angle
with a measure of 90°. The
symbol ⌐ is used to show a
right angle.

An **obtuse angle** is an angle
with a measure greater than
90° and less than 180°.

C. Sometimes angles are named with numbers.
In the diagram, since *n* is a line, the sum
of the measures of ∠1, ∠2, and ∠3 is 180°.

m∠1 + m∠2 + m∠3 = 75 + 45 + 60 = 180

D. If lines, segments, or rays intersect to
form right angles, they are **perpendicular.**
⊥ is read "is perpendicular to."

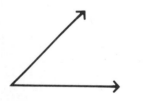

$\overleftrightarrow{XY} \perp \overrightarrow{ST}$ $\overrightarrow{XS} \perp \overrightarrow{ST}$ $\overrightarrow{SX} \perp \overrightarrow{ST}$

Use this diagram for
exercises 1–18.

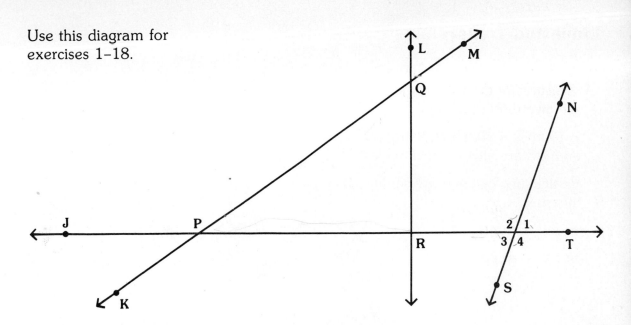

Use a protractor to measure each angle. Then tell
if the angle is acute, right, or obtuse.

1. ∠RPQ   **2.** ∠PRQ   **3.** ∠PQR   **4.** ∠JPQ   **5.** ∠PQL   **6.** ∠MQR

7. ∠QRT   **8.** ∠JPK   **9.** ∠1   **10.** ∠2   **11.** ∠3   **12.** ∠4

13. Give another name for ∠PQR.

14. Name the sides of ∠JPQ.

15. Are any lines perpendicular? If so, name them

16. Are any lines parallel? If so, name them.

17. Without measuring, give the sum of the measures of ∠3 and ∠4.

18. Name two angles for which the sum of the measures is 180°.

Use a protractor to draw an angle with the given measure.

19. 45°   **20.** 115°   **21.** 80°   **22.** 64°   **23.** 175°   **24.** 90°

★25. In the figure at the right, m∠5 = 75°.
Without using a protractor, give the
measure of each of the other angles.

Lines and Transversals

A. Lines *c* and *d* intersect. The measures of the four angles formed are given in the table.

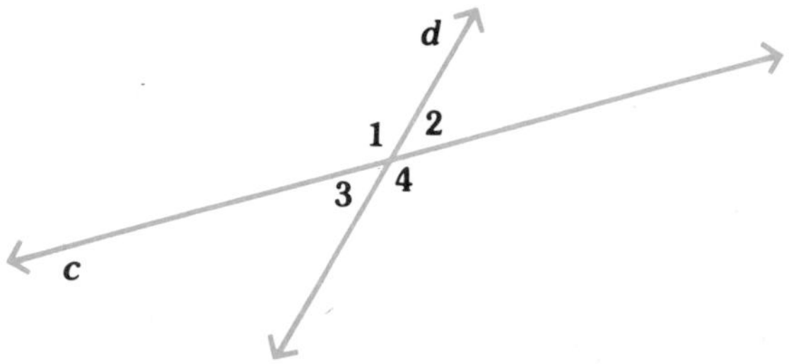

∠1 and ∠4 are **vertical angles.** ∠2 and ∠3 are also vertical angles.

Vertical angles have the same measure.

m∠1 = m∠4

m∠2 = m∠3

Angle	1	2	3	4
Measure	135°	45°	45°	135°

B. Line *z* is a **transversal** on lines *x* and *y*. Lines *x* and *y* are parallel. The measures of the angles formed are given in the table.

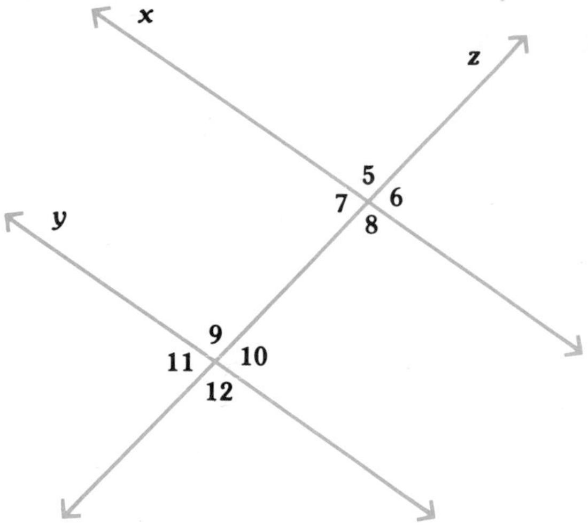

∠8 and ∠9 are **alternate interior angles.** ∠7 and ∠10 are also alternate interior angles.

When a transversal cuts parallel lines, the alternate interior angles have the same measure.

m∠8 = m∠9

m∠7 = m∠10

Angle	5	6	7	8	9	10	11	12
Measure	100°	80°	80°	100°	100°	80°	80°	100°

• **Discuss** Which of angles 5–12 are vertical angles? Do the angles in each pair have the same measure?

For exercises 1–3, use the diagram showing transversal t on parallel lines r and s.

1. Give the measure of each angle.

2. Name the vertical angles. Do the angles in each pair have the same measure?

3. Name the alternate interior angles. Do the angles in each pair have the same measure?

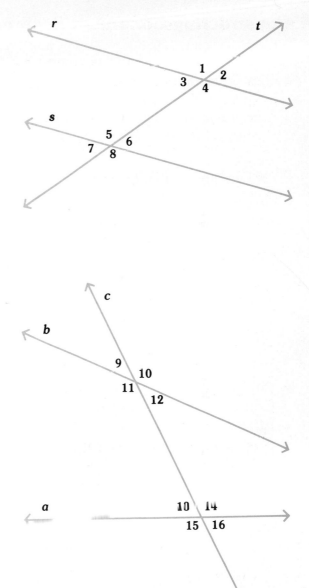

For exercises 4–6, use the diagram showing transversal c on lines a and b. Lines a and b are not parallel.

4. Give the measure of each angle.

5. Name the vertical angles. Do the angles in each pair have the same measure?

6. Name the alternate interior angles. Do the angles in each pair have the same measure?

7. Do alternate interior angles always have the same measure?

★8. Line h is a transversal on parallel lines j and k. Suppose the angles are named as shown in the diagram for exercises 1–3, and m∠7 = 30°. Give the measure of each of the other angles.

265

Constructing Congruent Segments and Angles

To make a **construction** in geometry means to make a drawing using only a compass and straightedge.

A. **Congruent segments** have the same measure.
   Construct a segment congruent to $\overline{MN}$.

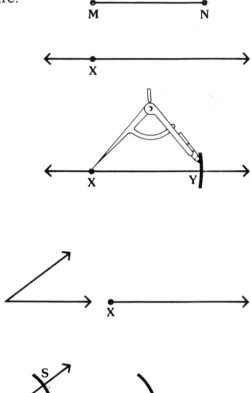

Step 1
Draw a line. Label point X.

Step 2
Open the compass to the length of $\overline{MN}$.
With X as center, draw an arc that intersects the line at point Y.

$\overline{XY}$ and $\overline{MN}$ have the same measure.
$\overline{XY}$ is congruent to $\overline{MN}$.
$\overline{XY} \cong \overline{MN}$

B. **Congruent angles** have the same measure.
   Construct an angle congruent to $\angle B$.

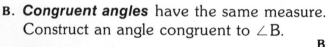

Step 1
Draw a ray with endpoint X.

Step 2
With B as center, draw an arc that intersects the sides of $\angle B$ at points R and S. Using the same opening and X as center, draw an arc that intersects the ray at D.

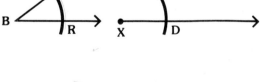

Step 3
Set the compass to the length of $\overline{RS}$. With D as center, draw an intersecting arc. Label point E.

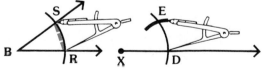

Step 4
Draw $\overrightarrow{XE}$.

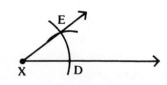

$\angle X$ and $\angle B$ have the same measure.
$\angle X \cong \angle B$

Trace each segment and angle below. Then use only a compass and a straightedge to make the constructions.

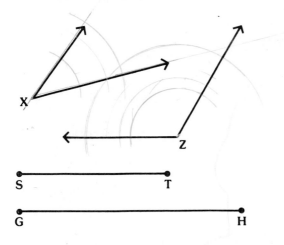

X

Z

S   T

G   H

1. Construct a segment congruent to $\overline{GH}$.

2. Construct a segment that is twice as long as $\overline{ST}$.

3. Construct a segment whose length is equal to the sum of the measures of $\overline{GH}$ and $\overline{ST}$.

4. Construct an angle congruent to $\angle Z$.

5. Construct an angle whose measure is twice the measure of $\angle X$.

6. Construct an angle whose measure is equal to the sum of the measures of $\angle X$ and $\angle Z$.

★7. Construct $\overline{AB} \cong \overline{GH}$.
At A, construct $\angle A \cong \angle X$.
At B, construct $\angle B \cong \angle Z$, so that a ray of $\angle B$ intersects a ray of $\angle A$. What figure is formed?

Keeping Skillful

Multiply.

1. $\frac{3}{5} \times \frac{2}{3}$ 2. $\frac{1}{3} \times \frac{3}{7}$

3. $\frac{2}{9} \times \frac{1}{2}$ 4. $\frac{1}{5} \times \frac{1}{2}$

5. $\frac{3}{8} \times \frac{8}{3}$ 6. $\frac{3}{4} \times \frac{5}{6}$

7. $\frac{1}{2} \times 1\frac{1}{3}$ 8. $1\frac{1}{5} \times 3\frac{1}{2}$

9. $2\frac{2}{3} \times 4$ 10. $1\frac{3}{5} \times 1\frac{7}{8}$

11. $2\frac{1}{12} \times \frac{1}{3}$ 12. $\frac{14}{33} \times \frac{3}{7}$

Divide.

13. $\frac{1}{2} \div \frac{2}{3}$ 14. $\frac{5}{6} \div \frac{3}{4}$

15. $\frac{4}{5} \div \frac{1}{3}$ 16. $\frac{3}{7} \div \frac{4}{7}$

17. $3 \div \frac{2}{3}$ 18. $1\frac{7}{8} \div 2$

19. $\frac{4}{5} \div 1\frac{3}{5}$ 20. $2\frac{3}{4} \div \frac{1}{3}$

21. $1\frac{5}{6} \div 2\frac{1}{2}$ 22. $3\frac{1}{3} \div 1\frac{5}{9}$

23. $4\frac{9}{10} \div 2\frac{1}{3}$ 24. $5\frac{1}{2} \div 5\frac{3}{4}$

Write each fraction as a decimal.

25. $\frac{3}{4}$ 26. $\frac{8}{10}$ 27. $\frac{1}{5}$ 28. $\frac{19}{25}$

29. $\frac{3}{8}$ 30. $\frac{2}{3}$ 31. $\frac{5}{6}$ 32. $\frac{4}{7}$

Bisecting Segments and Angles

To **bisect** a segment or an angle means to divide it into two congruent segments or angles.

A. Construct the perpendicular bisector of $\overline{MN}$.

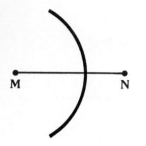
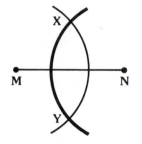

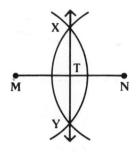

Step 1
With the compass point on M, draw an arc that intersects $\overline{MN}$.

Step 2
Using the same opening and N as center, draw an arc that intersects the first arc in two points. Label them X and Y.

Step 3
Draw $\overleftrightarrow{XY}$.

$\overleftrightarrow{XY}$ is the perpendicular bisector of $\overline{MN}$. Point T is the **midpoint** of $\overline{MN}$.
$\overline{MT} \cong \overline{TN}$

B. Construct the bisector of $\angle XYZ$.

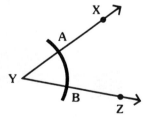
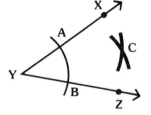
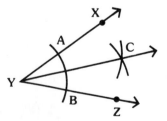

Step 1
With the compass point on Y, draw an arc that intersects both rays of the angle. Label points A and B.

Step 2
With the compass point on A, draw an arc. Using the same opening and B as center, draw an intersecting arc. Label point C.

Step 3
Draw $\overrightarrow{YC}$.

$\overrightarrow{YC}$ bisects $\angle XYZ$.
$\angle XYC \cong \angle CYZ$
$m\angle XYC + m\angle CYZ = m\angle XYZ$

268

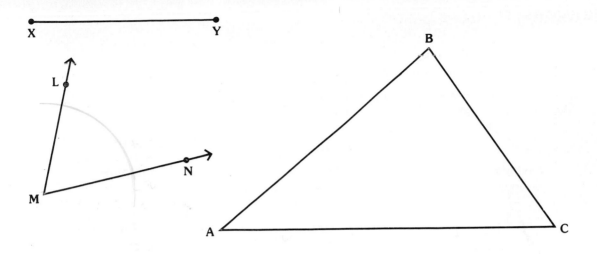

Use only a compass and straightedge to make these constructions.

1. Trace $\overline{XY}$. Construct the perpendicular bisector. Label the midpoint W, and name two congruent segments.

2. Trace $\angle LMN$. Construct the bisector. Label the bisector $\overrightarrow{MZ}$, and name two congruent angles.

3. Trace triangle ABC. Construct the perpendicular bisector of each side.

4. Draw a different triangle. Repeat exercise 3.

5. Trace triangle ABC again. Construct the bisector of each angle.

6. Draw a different triangle. Repeat exercise 5.

★7. Construct a 45° angle.

★8. Construct a 135° angle.

Time Out

1. Make 100 using exactly four 9s.

2. Make 1000 using exactly eight 8s.

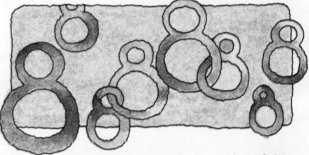

Polygons

A. The figures below are examples of **polygons.** The name of a polygon is determined by the number of its sides.

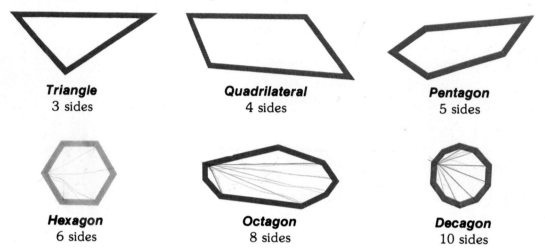

Triangle
3 sides

Quadrilateral
4 sides

Pentagon
5 sides

Hexagon
6 sides

Octagon
8 sides

Decagon
10 sides

B. Triangles can be classified according to the length of their sides.

Scalene Triangle
no congruent sides

Isosceles Triangle
at least 2 congruent sides

Equilateral Triangle
3 congruent sides

Triangles can also be classified according to their angle measures.

Acute Triangle
3 acute angles

Right Triangle
1 right angle

Obtuse Triangle
1 obtuse angle

C. Some quadrilaterals have special names.

Trapezoid
a quadrilateral with
exactly 2 parallel sides

Parallelogram
a quadrilateral with
opposite sides parallel

Rhombus
a parallelogram with
4 congruent sides

Rectangle
a parallelogram
with 4 right angles

Square
a rectangle with
4 congruent sides

Does the exercise describe a polygon?
If so, sketch the polygon. If not,
write *not possible*.

1. Scalene-acute triangle

2. Equilateral-acute triangle

3. Scalene-right triangle

4. Right-isosceles triangle

5. Scalene-equilateral triangle

6. Acute-isosceles triangle

7. Rectangle with obtuse angles

8. Square with 1 acute angle

9. Pentagon with 5 congruent angles

10. Hexagon with 5 angles

11. Rhombus with 4 congruent angles

12. Triangle with 2 right angles

13. Equilateral-obtuse triangle

14. Rectangle with 4 congruent sides

15. Parallelogram with at least
1 right angle

16. Parallelogram with 4 congruent
sides

What is another name for the

17. rhombus in exercise 11?

18. rectangle in exercise 14?

19. parallelogram in exercise 16?

★20. Why is it impossible to have
a scalene-isosceles triangle?

271

The Sum of the Measures of the Angles of a Triangle

A. You can show that the sum of the measures of the angles of any triangle is 180°.

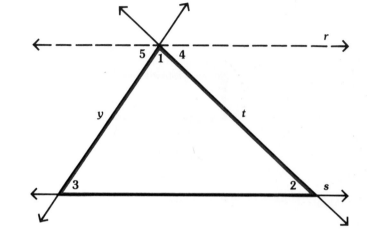

In the diagram, the angles of the triangle are $\angle 1$, $\angle 2$, and $\angle 3$. Line r is parallel to line s.

Line t is a transversal on the parallel lines, so the alternate interior angles have the same measure.

m $\angle 4$ = m $\angle 2$

Line y is another transversal on the parallel lines.

m $\angle 5$ = m $\angle 3$

Since r is a line, **m $\angle 4$ + m $\angle 1$ + m $\angle 5$ = 180.**

By substituting, **m $\angle 2$ + m $\angle 1$ + m $\angle 3$ = 180.**

■ *In any triangle, the sum of the measures of the angles is 180°.*

B. In triangle XYZ, m $\angle$ X = 82°, m $\angle$ Y = 47°. Find m $\angle$ Z.

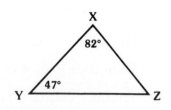

m $\angle$ X + m $\angle$ Y = 82 + 47 = 129

m $\angle$ Z = 180 − 129 = 51

m $\angle$ Z = 51°

c. The **diagonals** drawn from one vertex of a polygon separate it into triangles.

The two diagonals separate the pentagon into three triangles. The sum of the measures of the angles of a pentagon is $3 \times 180°$, or 540°.

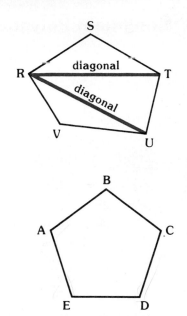

D. In a **regular polygon,** all the sides are congruent and all the angles are congruent.

Pentagon ABCDE is a regular pentagon. The measure of each angle is $540° \div 5$, or 108°.

● **Discuss**   What is another name for a regular triangle? for a regular quadrilateral?

Complete the table.

Polygon	Number of sides	Number of diagonals from one vertex	Number of triangles	Sum of measures of all angles	Measure of each angle in a regular figure
Triangle	3	0	1	$1 \times 180°$, or 180°	$180° \div 3$, or 60°
Quadrilateral	4	1.	2.	3.	4.
Pentagon	5	2	3	$3 \times 180°$, or 540°	$540° \div 5$, or 108°
Hexagon	6	5.	6.	7.	8.
Heptagon	7	9.	10.	11.	12.
Octagon	8	13.	14.	15.	16.
Nonagon	9	17.	18.	19.	20.
Decagon	10	21.	22.	23.	24.
Dodecagon	12	25.	26.	27.	28.

*29. Write an expression for the sum of the measures of the angles of a polygon with n sides. Use it to find the sum for a polygon with 102 sides.

Congruent Polygons

Congruent polygons have the same size and shape.

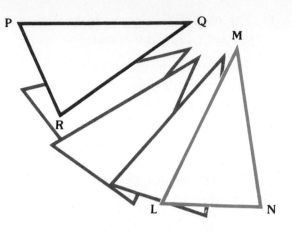

A. Triangles PQR and LMN have the same size and shape. They are congruent triangles.

△PQR ≅ △LMN

The first diagram shows that △PQR can be placed over △LMN so the parts fit exactly. The matching parts are called the **corresponding parts.** These parts are marked in the second diagram.

The corresponding sides and angles of congruent triangles are congruent.

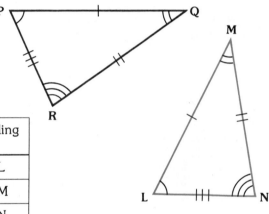

Corresponding vertices	Corresponding sides	Corresponding angles
P and L	$\overline{PQ} \cong \overline{LM}$	∠P ≅ ∠L
Q and M	$\overline{QR} \cong \overline{MN}$	∠Q ≅ ∠M
R and N	$\overline{PR} \cong \overline{LN}$	∠R ≅ ∠N

B. Polygons ABCD and JKLM do not have the same size and shape. They are not congruent.

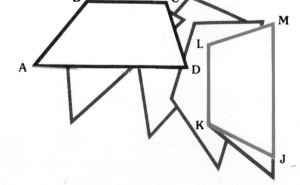

■*In congruent polygons, the corresponding angles are congruent and the corresponding sides are congruent.*

274

Do the polygons appear to be congruent? Write *yes* or *no*.

1. 2.

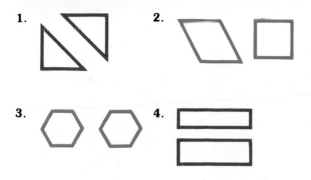

3. 4.

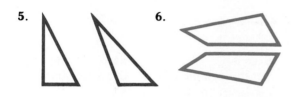

5. 6.

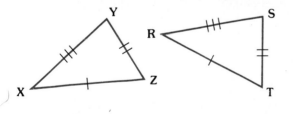

For each pair of congruent polygons, name all the corresponding sides and all the corresponding angles.

7. △XYZ ≅ △RST

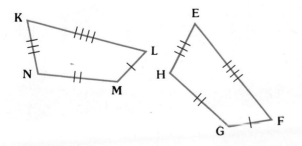

8. Polygon KLMN ≅ polygon EFGH

Triangles ABC and DEF are congruent.

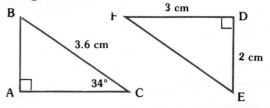

Give the measures of these segments and angles.

9. $\overline{AC}$ 10. $\overline{AB}$ 11. $\overline{EF}$

12. ∠F   13. ∠B   14. ∠E

Triangles JKL and NML are congruent.

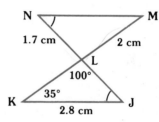

Give the measures of these segments and angles.

15. $\overline{MN}$ 16. $\overline{LK}$ 17. $\overline{JL}$

18. ∠J   19. ∠N   20. ∠MLN

*21. If three angles of one triangle are congruent to three angles of another triangle, can you be sure that the triangles are congruent? Draw a picture to explain your answer.

275

Constructing Congruent Triangles

A. If three sides of one triangle are congruent to three sides of another triangle, the triangles are congruent.

Construct a triangle congruent to △XYZ using only three sides.

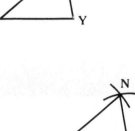

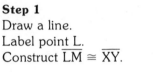

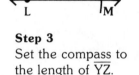

Step 1
Draw a line.
Label point L.
Construct $\overline{LM} \cong \overline{XY}$.

Step 2
Set the compass to the length of $\overline{XZ}$.
With L as center, draw an arc.

Step 3
Set the compass to the length of $\overline{YZ}$.
With M as center, draw an intersecting arc. Label point N.

Step 4
Draw $\overline{LN}$ and $\overline{MN}$.

△LMN ≅ △XYZ

B. If two angles and the side between them of one triangle are congruent to the corresponding parts of another, the triangles are congruent.

Construct a triangle congruent to △FGH using only two angles and the side between them.

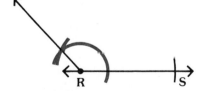

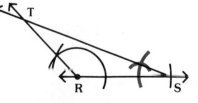

Step 1
Draw a line.
Label point R.
Construct $\overline{RS} \cong \overline{FG}$.

Step 2
At R, construct ∠R ≅ ∠F.

Step 3
At S, construct ∠S ≅ ∠G.
Label point T.

△RST ≅ △FGH

Remember, to make a construction, use only a compass and straightedge.

Trace △ABC. Construct a triangle congruent to △ABC using only the parts given.

1. $\overline{AB}$, $\overline{BC}$, and $\overline{AC}$

2. ∠A, $\overline{AB}$, and ∠B

3. $\overline{AB}$, ∠B, and $\overline{BC}$

Trace the segments and angles shown at the right. Can you construct a triangle using only the parts given? If you can, make the construction. If you cannot, write *not possible*.

4. Sides w, x, and y

5. Sides x, y, and z

6. Sides w, x, and z

7. Sides w, y, and z

8. Side y and two sides with the length of segment x

9. ∠T between sides w and x

10. Side y between ∠R and ∠S

11. Side z between ∠S and ∠T

★12. A right triangle with the right angle between sides x and y

★13. △FGH in which ∠F ≅ ∠R, $\overline{FG}$ is congruent to segment x, and $\overline{GH}$ is congruent to segment y

★14. △LMN in which ∠L ≅ ∠S, ∠N ≅ ∠R, and $\overline{LM}$ is congruent to segment y

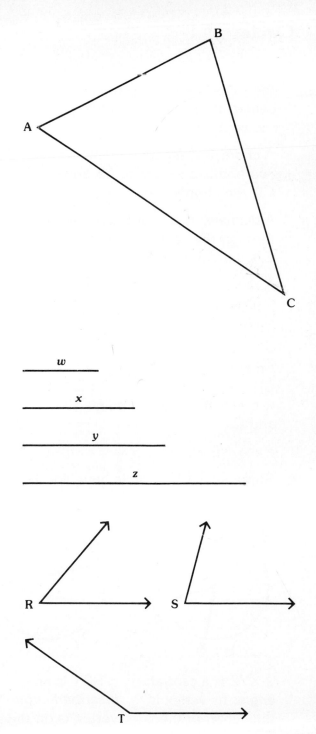

Circles

A. All of the points on a **circle** are
the same distance from the
center of the circle. Point N is
the center of circle N.

A **chord** is a segment that joins
two points on a circle. $\overline{AB}$ and
$\overline{CD}$ are chords.

A **diameter** is a chord that passes
through the center of the circle.
$\overline{CD}$ is a diameter.

A **radius** is a segment that has
the center and a point on the
circle as endpoints. $\overline{NR}$, $\overline{NC}$, and
$\overline{ND}$ are radii.

An **arc** is part of a circle. $\overset{\frown}{RC}$, or
$\overset{\frown}{CR}$, names the shorter of the
two arcs that contain points R
and C.

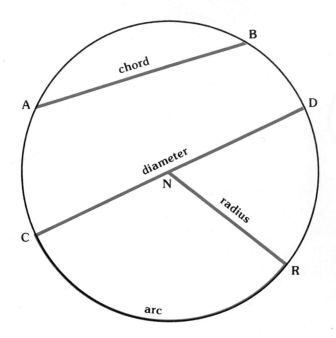

B. Some angles in a circle have special
names.

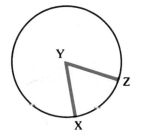

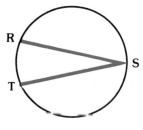

∠XYZ is a **central**
angle. Its vertex is
the center of the
circle and it cuts
off $\overset{\frown}{XZ}$.

∠RST is an
inscribed angle. Its
vertex is on the
circle and it cuts
off $\overset{\frown}{RT}$.

C. Two perpendicular diameters
are drawn in circle H. Each
of the four central angles is a
right angle.

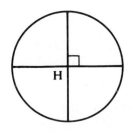

The number of degrees
around the center of a
circle is 360°.

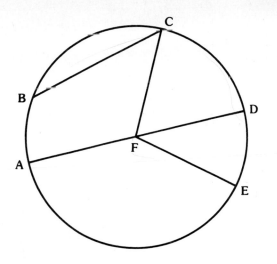

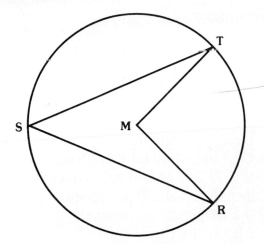

Use circle F.

1. Name a diameter.

2. Name three radii.

3. Name three arcs, each containing point B.

4. Name two chords.

5. In a circle, how are the measures of the radius and the diameter related?

6. The sum of the measures of ∠EFD, ∠DFC, and ∠CFA is 220°. What is the measure of ∠AFE?

Use circle M.

7. Measure central angle RMT.

8. Measure inscribed angle RST.

Draw four circles. Label their centers A, B, C, and D. In each, draw a central angle and an inscribed angle that cut off the same arc. Complete the table.

Circle	Measure of central angle	Measure of inscribed angle
A	9.	10.
B	11.	12.
C	13.	14.
D	15.	16.

17. If a central angle and an inscribed angle cut off the same arc, how are the measures of the angles related?

In circle Z, m∠MZL = 100°. Without using a protractor, give these measures.

*18. m∠MKL

*19. m∠KZL

*20. m∠KML

*21. m∠KLM

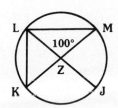

Bisecting by Paper Folding

Find the perpendicular bisectors of the sides of a triangle.

Step 1 Draw △ABC on a piece of paper.

Step 2 Hold the paper to the light. Fold so that point A coincides with B and half of $\overline{AB}$ is over the other half. This fold shows the perpendicular bisector of $\overline{AB}$.

Step 3 Repeat step 2 for $\overline{BC}$ and $\overline{AC}$.

Repeat steps 1, 2, and 3 for other triangles. What do you notice about the perpendicular bisectors of the sides of a triangle?

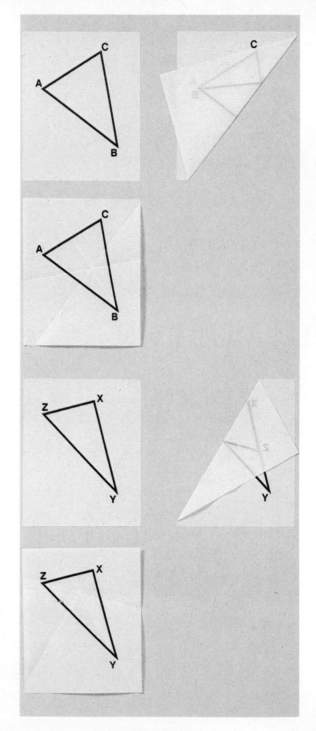

Find the bisectors of the angles of a triangle.

Step 4 Draw △XYZ.

Step 5 Hold the paper to the light. Fold so that one ray of ∠X coincides with the other ray of the angle. This fold shows the bisector of ∠X.

Step 6 Repeat step 5 for ∠Y and ∠Z.

Repeat steps 4, 5, and 6 for other triangles. What do you notice about the bisectors of the angles of a triangle?

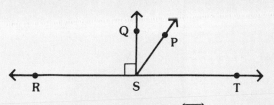

1. Name a segment on $\overleftrightarrow{RT}$.

2. Name a ray perpendicular to $\overleftrightarrow{ST}$.

3. Name an obtuse angle.

In the figure below, $a \parallel b$, $a \perp d$, and $m\angle 1 = 75°$. For each exercise, give the measure of the angle.

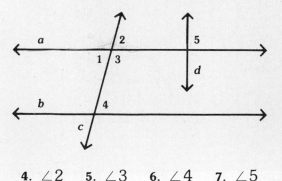

4. $\angle 2$ 5. $\angle 3$ 6. $\angle 4$ 7. $\angle 5$

Use circle D.

8. Name two chords.

9. Name three radii.

10. Name an inscribed angle.

11. Is $\angle EFG \cong \angle EDG$? Write *yes* or *no*.

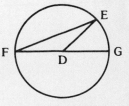

Write *true* or *false*.

12. A rhombus is a parallelogram.

13. A pentagon has six sides.

14. An isosceles triangle can be a right triangle.

15. A square is a regular quadrilateral.

16. An acute triangle can have one obtuse angle.

17. An equilateral triangle has three acute angles.

In the figures below, $\triangle ABC \cong \triangle XYZ$. Give the missing measures.

18. $\overline{XY}$

19. $\overline{XZ}$

20. $\overline{YZ}$

21. $\angle Z$

22. $\angle B$

23. $\angle Y$

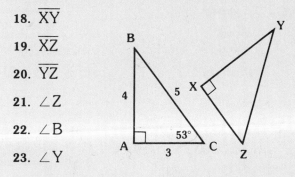

Trace $\angle M$, $\angle N$, and $\overline{MN}$.

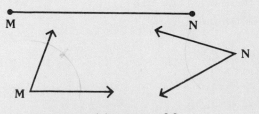

24. Copy and bisect $\angle M$.

25. Construct $\triangle LMN$.

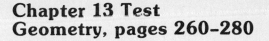

Chapter 14   Perimeter, Area, and Volume

Perimeter

The distance around a polygon is its **perimeter.**

A. To find the perimeter of this cabinet top, add the lengths of its sides.

P = 154 + 28 + 36 + 102 + 36 + 28

P = 384

Perimeter: 384 cm

B. Formulas can be used to find the perimeters of certain polygons.

Rhombus	Rectangle	Parallelogram
	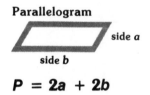	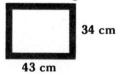
side *s*	length *l*	side *b*
P = 4s	**P = 2l + 2w**	**P = 2a + 2b**

C. Find the perimeter of a square, 3.2 mm on a side.

Since a square is a rhombus, use the formula $P = 4s$.

P = 4s

P = 4(3.2)

P = 12.8

Perimeter: 12.8 mm

D. Find the perimeter of this rectangle.

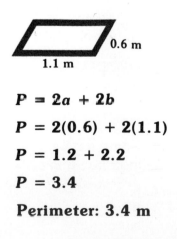

34 cm

43 cm

P = 2l + 2w

P = 2(43) + 2(34)

P = 86 + 68

P = 154

Perimeter: 154 cm

E. Find the perimeter of this parallelogram.

0.6 m

1.1 m

P = 2a + 2b

P = 2(0.6) + 2(1.1)

P = 1.2 + 2.2

P = 3.4

Perimeter: 3.4 m

• **Discuss**   Can the formula $P = 2a + 2b$ be used to find the perimeter of a rectangle? Explain.

Find the perimeter of each polygon.

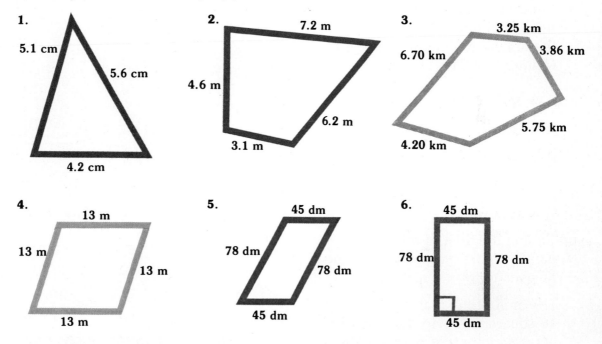

1.
5.1 cm
5.6 cm
4.2 cm

2.
7.2 m
4.6 m
6.2 m
3.1 m

3.
3.25 km
6.70 km
3.86 km
4.20 km
5.75 km

4.
13 m
13 m
13 m
13 m

5.
45 dm
78 dm
78 dm
45 dm

6.
45 dm
78 dm
78 dm
45 dm

7. A rectangle, 4.3 dm by 2.1 dm

8. A rectangle, 0.2 cm by 4.1 cm

9. A square, 670 mm on a side

10. A square, 78 m on a side

11. A parallelogram with sides of 46 cm and 420 cm

12. A parallelogram with sides of 0.22 dm and 0.68 dm

13. A rhombus, 2.3 m on a side

14. A rhombus, 46.1 mm on a side

15. A snapshot, 9.0 cm by 12.6 cm

16. A flag, 0.75 m by 1.12 m

★17. The formula $P = 2l + 2w$ can also be written $P = 2(l + w)$. Use each formula to find the perimeter of a rectangle, 18.1 m by 22.4 m.

★18. Find another way to write the formula $P = 2a + 2b$.

283

Area of a Rectangle and a Parallelogram

The number of square units enclosed
by a figure is its *area.*

A. Recall the area of a rectangle equals
the length times the width. To find
the area of this window, use the
formula $A = lw$.

$A = lw$

$A = 8.1(4.7)$

$A = 38.07$

Area: 38.07 m²

B. To find the area of this
parallelogram, you can "rearrange"
its parts to form a rectangle.

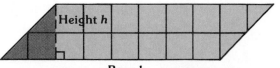

The area of the rectangle is
16 square units. So the area of the
parallelogram is also 16 square
units.

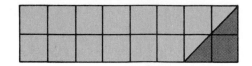

■*For any parallelogram, the area is
equal to the base times the height.* $A = bh$

C. Find the area of this parallelogram.

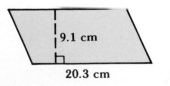

$A - bh$

$A = 20.3(9.1)$

$A = 184.73$

Area: 184.73 cm²

• **Discuss** Can the formula
$A = bh$ be used to find the
area of a rectangle? Explain.

Find the area of each polygon.

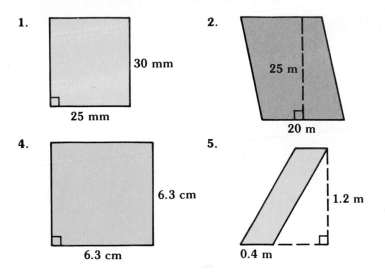

1. 30 mm
   25 mm

2. 25 m
   20 m

3. 2.1 cm
   2.3 cm
   2.4 cm

4. 6.3 cm
   6.3 cm

5. 1.2 m
   0.4 m

6. 25 mm
   30 mm
   35 mm

7. Find the area of a square mirror, 170 cm on a side.

8. Find the area of a rectangular carpet, 2.7 m by 3.6 m.

9. Find the area of a sheet of wall paneling, 122 cm by 244 cm.

10. Find the area of a square floor tile, 20 cm on a side.

11. Use your answer to exercise 10. About how many of these floor tiles are needed to cover a floor, 320 cm by 360 cm?

★12. Find the area of the shaded region.

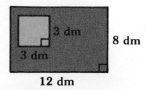

3 dm
3 dm
8 dm
12 dm

★13. Find the length of segment GH.

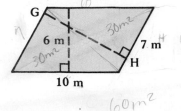

G
6 m
7 m
H
10 m

★14. The area and perimeter of a certain square are the same number. What is the length of a side of the square?

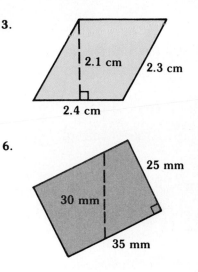

285

Area of a Triangle and a Trapezoid

A. To find the area of a triangle, think of the triangle as half of a parallelogram.

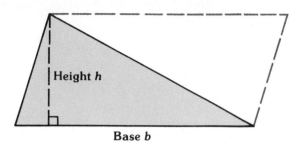

Area of parallelogram: *bh*

Area of triangle: $\frac{1}{2}bh$

■ *For any triangle, the area is equal to one half the base times the height.*

$$A = \frac{1}{2}bh$$

B. To find the area of a trapezoid, think of the trapezoid as half of a parallelogram.

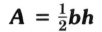

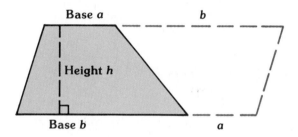

Base of this parallelogram: $a + b$

Area of parallelogram: $(a + b)h$

Area of trapezoid: $\frac{1}{2}(a + b)h$

■ *For any trapezoid, the area is equal to one half the height times the sum of the bases.*

$$A = \frac{1}{2}h(a + b)$$

C. Find the area of this triangle.

$A = \frac{1}{2}bh$

$A = \frac{1}{2}(4)(12)$

$A = 2(12)$

$A = 24$

Area: 24 cm²

D. Find the area of this trapezoid.

$A = \frac{1}{2}h(a + b)$

$A = \frac{1}{2}(12)(15 + 22)$

$A = 6(37)$

$A = 222$

Area: 222 dm²

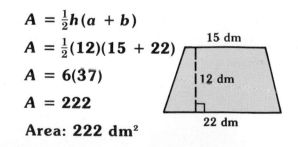

E. Find the area of this trapezoid.

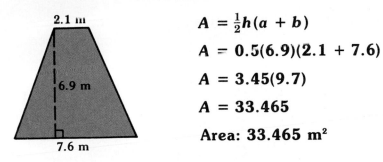

$A = \frac{1}{2}h(a + b)$

$A = 0.5(6.9)(2.1 + 7.6)$

$A = 3.45(9.7)$

$A = 33.465$

Area: 33.465 m²

When multiplying decimals, use 0.5 for $\frac{1}{2}$.

Find the area of each polygon.

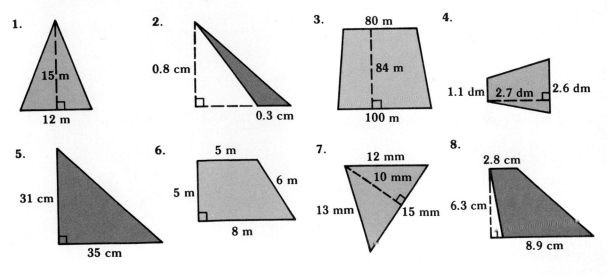

1.

15 m
12 m

2.

0.8 cm
0.3 cm

3.

80 m
84 m
100 m

4.

1.1 dm   2.7 dm   2.6 dm

5.

31 cm
35 cm

6.

5 m
5 m
6 m
8 m

7.

12 mm
10 mm
13 mm   15 mm

8.

2.8 cm
6.3 cm
8.9 cm

*9. Fran's dock is at F, and Harumi's dock is at H. The two swam from Fran's dock to Harumi's dock. How far did they swim?

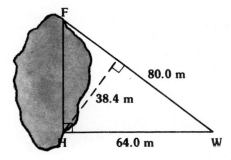

F
80.0 m
38.4 m
H   64.0 m   W

Circumference of a Circle

A. Mr. and Mrs. Cortez are building a log cabin. Mr. Cortez is looking for trees with trunks that are 20 cm in diameter. Mrs. Cortez reminds him that the **circumference** of each trunk should measure about 63 cm.

Mrs. Cortez remembered that the ratio of the circumference C to the diameter d of any circle is a number named by the Greek letter π, or *pi*.

$$\frac{C}{d} = \pi$$

π is a decimal that never ends and has no repeating pattern.

$$\pi = \textbf{3.141592653589793238} \ldots$$

3.14 is often used as an approximation for π.

- *For any circle, the circumference is equal to π times the diameter.* $C = \pi d$

- *For any circle, the circumference is equal to 2 times π times the radius.* $C = 2\pi r$

B. The diameter of a tree trunk is 25 cm. Find the circumference. Use 3.14 for π.

$C = \pi d$

$C \approx 3.14(25)$

$C \approx 78.5$

Circumference: About 78.5 cm

c. The radius of a circle is 3.7 mm. Find the circumference. Use 3.14 for π.

$$C = 2\pi r$$
$$C \approx 2(3.14)(3.7)$$
$$C \approx 23.236$$

Circumference: About 23.236 mm

Find the circumference of a circle with the given diameter or radius. Use 3.14 for π.

1. Diameter: 10 cm
2. Diameter: 40 m
3. Radius: 8 cm
4. Radius: 10 cm
5. Diameter: 2.5 dm
6. Radius: 0.3 mm
7. Radius: 4.2 km
8. Diameter: 8.4 km
9. Diameter: 1 m
10. Radius: 6.1 cm
11. Radius: 13 mm
12. Diameter: 61 cm
13. Diameter: 110 m
14. Radius: 300 mm

15. The diameter of a tree trunk is 30 cm. Find the circumference.

*16. Will a nail 11 cm long go completely through a log with circumference 33.69 cm?

*17. In the 1800s, students used either $\frac{355}{113}$ or 3.14159 as an approximation for π. Which number is closer to π as given on page 288?

Trace this diagram and cut it out.

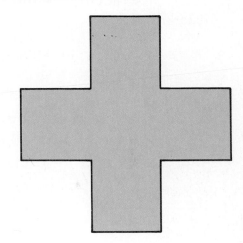

Can you make 2 straight cuts across the figure so that the pieces can be arranged to form a square?

Area of a Circle

A. Study these three diagrams.

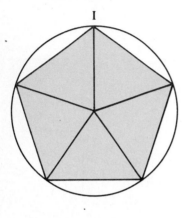

I

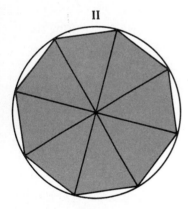

II

III

Notice that as a circle's interior is "divided" into more and more congruent triangles, the total area of these triangles gets closer and closer to the area of the circle.

To understand the formula for finding the area of a circle, consider diagram III. The total area of the 20 triangles is just about the same as the area of the circle. The base of each triangle is about $\frac{1}{20}$ of the circumference of the circle. The height of each triangle is about the same as the radius.

Recall the area of a triangle is equal to $\frac{1}{2}bh$.

Area of 20 triangles $= 20\left(\frac{1}{2}bh\right)$

We can actually arrive at the formula for finding the area of a circle by using $\frac{1}{20}C$ for b and r for h in the above product.

Area of circle $= 20\left(\frac{1}{2}\right)\left(\frac{1}{20}C\right)(r)$

$A = \frac{1}{2}Cr$	$20\left(\frac{1}{20}\right) = 1$
$A = \frac{1}{2}(2\pi r)(r)$	$C = 2\pi r$
$A = \pi rr$	$\frac{1}{2}(2) = 1$
$A = \pi r^2$	

■ *For any circle, the area is equal to π times the radius squared.*

$$A = \pi r^2$$

h

$\leftarrow b \rightarrow$

B. Neferelli's Show Spectacular is a traveling three-ring circus. The radius of the center ring is 8 m. Find the area. Use 3.14 for π.

$A = \pi r^2$

$A \approx 3.14(8^2)$

$A \approx 3.14(64)$

$A \approx 200.96$

Area: About 200.96 m²

Find the area of a circle with the given diameter or radius. Use 3.14 for π.

1. Radius: 3 cm
2. Radius: 4 mm
3. Diameter: 20 m
4. Diameter: 18 dm
5. Radius: 1 km
6. Radius: 10 mm
7. Diameter: 4.2 km
8. Diameter: 7.6 m
9. Radius: 0.13 dm
10. Radius: 0.5 m

11. The floor of the circus tent is circular with a radius of 30 m. What is the area of the floor?

12. Henri the Magnificent dives into a pool with a diameter of 1.6 m. Find the area.

13. Reggie the elephant performs on a circular platform 110 cm in diameter. What is the area of the platform?

★14. The circumference of a circle is about 25.12 cm. Find the area.

★15. What is the area of the shaded region?

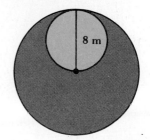

8 m

Surface Area of a Polyhedron

A. A space figure with faces that are polygonal regions is called a **polyhedron.**

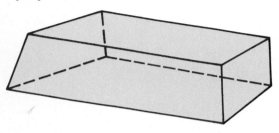

A **prism** is a polyhedron with two parallel and congruent **bases.** Its other faces are determined by parallelograms.

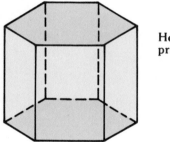

Hexagonal prism

A **pyramid** is a polyhedron with one base. Its other faces are triangular regions.

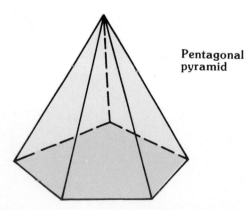

Pentagonal pyramid

B. The total **surface area** of a polyhedron is the sum of the areas of all the faces.

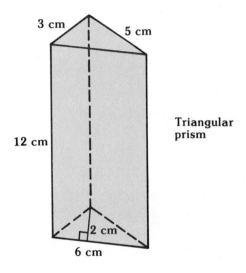

Triangular prism

To find the total surface area of this prism, it may be helpful to make a table.

Shape of face	Area in cm²
Triangle	$\frac{1}{2}(2)(6) = 6$
Triangle	$\frac{1}{2}(2)(6) = 6$
Rectangle	$(12)(6) = 72$
Rectangle	$(12)(3) = 36$
Rectangle	$(12)(5) = 60$
	Total 180

Total surface area: 180 cm²

Find the total surface area of each polyhedron.

1. Rectangular prism

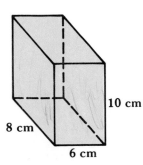

10 cm
8 cm
6 cm

2. Cube

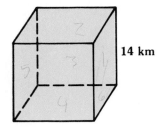

14 km

3. Square pyramid

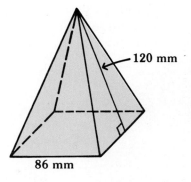

120 mm
86 mm

4. Rectangular pyramid

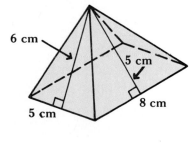

6 cm
5 cm
5 cm
8 cm

5. Triangular prism

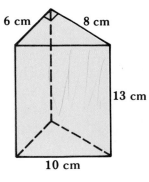

6 cm   8 cm
13 cm
10 cm

6. Rectangular prism

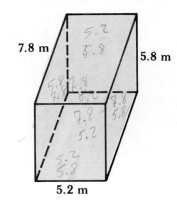

7.8 m
5.8 m
5.2 m

7. How many square meters of glass are there in the walls and roof of this greenhouse?

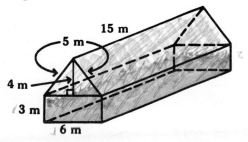

15 m
5 m
4 m
3 m
6 m

*8. How many square meters of tile are needed to tile the sides and bottom of this swimming pool?

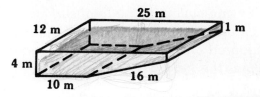

25 m
12 m
1 m
4 m
10 m
16 m

293

Surface Area of a Cylinder and a Cone

A. The total surface area of a **cylinder** is the sum of the areas of the bases and the area of the curved surface.

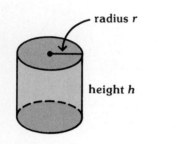

radius *r*

height *h*

The circular bases are congruent. Since each has area πr^2, the total area of the two bases is $2\pi r^2$.

If a cylinder is "opened up," the curved surface flattens out to be a rectangle.

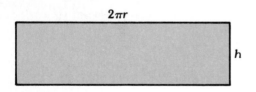

2πr

h

The area of the curved surface is $2\pi rh$.

■ *For any cylinder, the total surface area is equal to twice π times the radius squared plus twice π times the radius times the height.*

$$A = 2\pi r^2 + 2\pi rh$$

B. A **cone** has one circular base. The area of the base is πr^2.

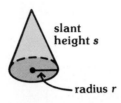

slant height *s*

radius *r*

If a cone is "opened up," the curved surface looks like a piece of pie.

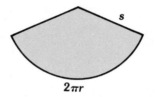

s

2πr

This region can be divided into smaller pie-shaped pieces and rearranged to look like a parallelogram.

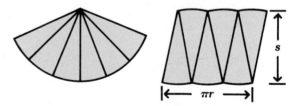

s

πr

The area of the curved surface is πrs.

■ *For any cone, the total surface area is equal to π times the radius squared plus π times the radius times the slant height.*

$$A = \pi r^2 + \pi rs$$

C. Find the total surface area of a cylinder with radius 6 m and height 13 m. Use 3.14 for π and give your answer to the nearest tenth.

$A = 2\pi r^2 + 2\pi rh$

$A \approx 2(3.14)(6^2) + 2(3.14)(6)(13)$

$A \approx 226.08 + 489.84$

$A \approx 715.92$

Area: About 715.9 m²

D. Find the total surface area of a cone with diameter 16 cm and slant height 20 cm. Use 3.14 for π and give your answer to the nearest tenth.

$A = \pi r^2 + \pi rs$

$A \approx 3.14(8^2) + 3.14(8)(20)$

$A \approx 200.96 + 502.40$

$A \approx 703.36$

Area: About 703.4 cm²

Find each total surface area. Use 3.14 for π and give your answer to the nearest tenth.

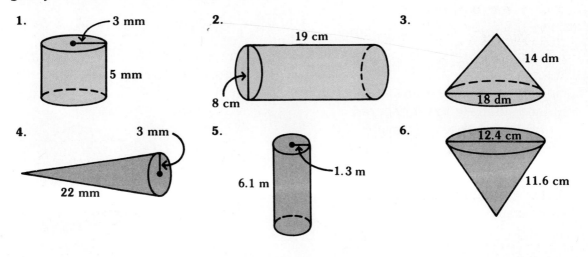

1. 3 mm, 5 mm

2. 19 cm, 8 cm

3. 14 dm, 18 dm

4. 3 mm, 22 mm

5. 1.3 m, 6.1 m

6. 12.4 cm, 11.6 cm

7. How many square centimeters of metal are needed to make a soup can 8 cm in diameter and 13 cm in height?

*8. Find the surface area of this lampshade.

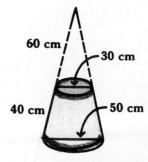

60 cm, 30 cm, 40 cm, 50 cm

295

Wallpaper Hanger

Lisa Raddatz is a wallpaper hanger. Before she orders the wallpaper for a room, she must calculate the total area of the surfaces to be papered.

The Hendersons hired Ms. Raddatz to paper the four walls of their family room.

1. The family room is 7 m long, 4.5 m wide, and 2.5 m high. What is the total surface area of the 4 walls?

2. What is the total area of the following surfaces which are not to be papered?

   door, 1.0 m by 2.1 m
   door, 0.8 m by 2.1 m
   1 window, 0.7 m by 1.5 m
   3 windows, each 0.6 m by 2.0 m

3. Find the total area of the wall surfaces that are to be papered. (Subtract the answer to exercise 2 from the answer to exercise 1.)

4. The wallpaper Ms. Raddatz uses covers 2.7 square meters per roll. She always orders at least one half roll extra to allow for matching the patterns. She can order full rolls only. How many rolls of wallpaper should Ms. Raddatz order for the family room?

Ms. Raddatz is going to paper the wall of this stairway.

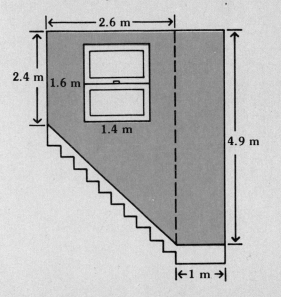

To calculate the wall area, Ms. Raddatz "divided" it into regions shaped like a trapezoid and a rectangle.

5. What is the area of the wall? (Disregard the window.)

6. What is the area of the window?

7. Find the area of the wall surface to be papered.

8. How many rolls of paper should Ms. Raddatz order for this job?

Keeping Skillful

Compare. Use >, <, or =.

1. $\frac{3}{4}$ ⬤ $\frac{1}{4}$ 2. $\frac{14}{16}$ ⬤ $\frac{7}{8}$

3. $\frac{5}{8}$ ⬤ $\frac{1}{2}$ 4. $\frac{1}{3}$ ⬤ $\frac{5}{9}$

5. $8\frac{4}{5}$ ⬤ $9\frac{2}{5}$ 6. $3\frac{4}{9}$ ⬤ $3\frac{2}{9}$

7. $7\frac{4}{8}$ ⬤ $7\frac{2}{4}$ 8. $6\frac{5}{6}$ ⬤ $3\frac{5}{6}$

9. $1\frac{1}{4}$ ⬤ $1\frac{1}{3}$ 10. $4\frac{9}{10}$ ⬤ $4\frac{7}{8}$

Add or subtract.

11. $\frac{5}{10} + \frac{2}{10}$ 12. $\frac{3}{4} + \frac{1}{4}$

13. $\frac{7}{8} - \frac{3}{8}$ 14. $\frac{13}{20} - \frac{3}{20}$

15. $\frac{1}{3} + \frac{5}{12}$ 16. $\frac{7}{16} - \frac{1}{4}$

17. $\frac{1}{8} + \frac{1}{6}$ 18. $\frac{3}{5} - \frac{1}{3}$

19. $\frac{1}{2} + \frac{3}{4} + \frac{5}{6}$ 20. $\frac{1}{5} + \frac{5}{6} + \frac{3}{10}$

21. $2\frac{2}{3} + 3\frac{1}{7}$ 22. $5\frac{9}{10} - 2\frac{3}{4}$

23. $4\frac{1}{6} - 2\frac{3}{4}$ 24. $15 + 3\frac{4}{7}$

25. $8 - 4\frac{1}{6}$ 26. $10\frac{8}{9} - 7$

Volume of a Prism and a Pyramid

The number of cubic units enclosed by a space figure is its **volume.**

A. There are 8×5 or 40 cubic centimeters in the top layer of this prism.

There are 3 layers of cubic centimeters.

The volume is 3×40 or 120 cm³.

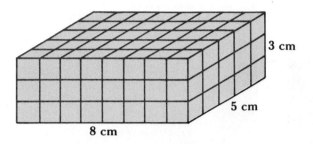

■ *For any prism, the volume is equal to the area of the base times the height.*

$$V = Bh$$

B. The volume of a pyramid is one third the volume of a prism with base and height the same size as in the pyramid.

The volume of this pyramid is $\frac{1}{3} \times 120$ or 40 cm³.

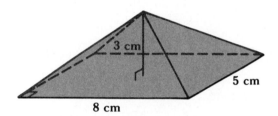

■ *For any pyramid, the volume is equal to one third the area of the base times the height.*

$$V = \tfrac{1}{3}Bh$$

C. Find the volume of this prism.

$V = Bh$

$V = \frac{1}{2}(5)(2)(4)$

$V = 20$

Volume: 20 m³

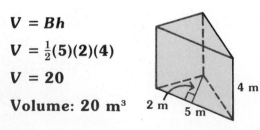

D. Find the volume of this pyramid.

$V = \frac{1}{3}Bh$

$V = \frac{1}{3}\left(\frac{1}{2}\right)(12)(7)(8)$

$V = 112$

Volume: 112 mm³

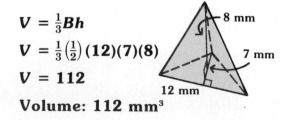

298

Find each volume.

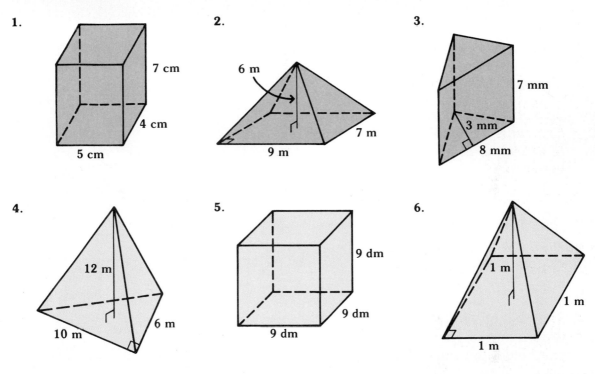

1. 7 cm, 4 cm, 5 cm

2. 6 m, 7 m, 9 m

3. 7 mm, 3 mm, 8 mm

4. 12 m, 10 m, 6 m

5. 9 dm, 9 dm, 9 dm

6. 1 m, 1 m, 1 m

7. A cord of wood is stacked as a rectangular prism about 1.2 m wide, 1.2 m high, and 2.4 m long. To the nearest tenth of a cubic meter, how much space does a cord of wood occupy?

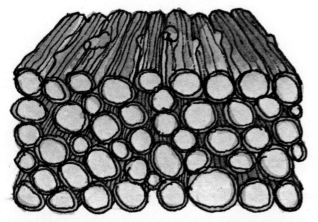

8. The Great Pyramid of Egypt has a square base 227 m on a side. Its height is 144 m. Find its volume.

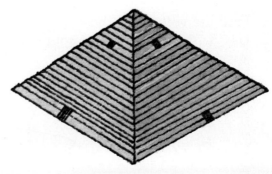

Volume of a Cylinder and a Cone

A. Recall the volume of a prism is equal to the area of the base times the height. The volume of a cylinder is found the same way.

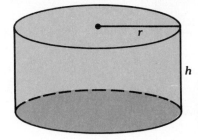

Since the area of the base of a cylinder is equal to πr^2, the volume of a cylinder can be found as follows.

■ *For any cylinder, the volume is equal to π times the radius squared times the height.*

$$V = \pi r^2 h$$

B. The volume of a cone is one third the volume of a cylinder with base and height the same size as in the cone.

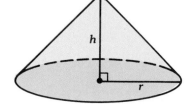

■ *For any cone, the volume is equal to one third times π times the radius squared times the height.*

$$V = \tfrac{1}{3}\pi r^2 h$$

C. Find the volume of this cylinder. Use 3.14 for π and give your answer to the nearest tenth.

$$V = \pi r^2 h$$
$$V \approx 3.14(2.0^2)(3.8)$$
$$V \approx 47.728$$

Volume: About 47.7 cm³

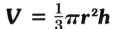

2.0 cm

3.8 cm

D. Find the volume of this cone. Use 3.14 for π and give your answer to the nearest tenth.

$$V = \tfrac{1}{3}\pi r^2 h$$
$$V \approx \tfrac{1}{3}(3.14)(4^2)(12)$$
$$V \approx 200.96$$

Volume: About 201.0 m³

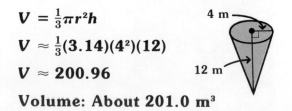

4 m

12 m

Find each volume. Use 3.14 for π and give your answers to the nearest tenth.

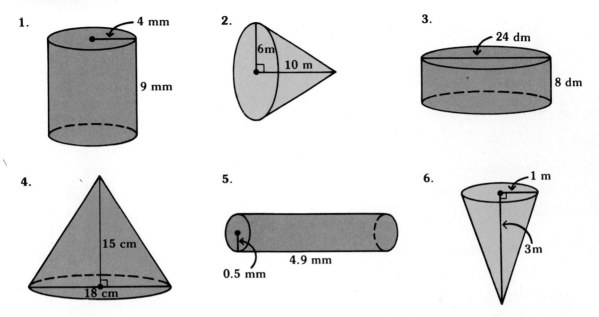

1. 4 mm, 9 mm

2. 6 m, 10 m

3. 24 dm, 8 dm

4. 15 cm, 18 cm

5. 0.5 mm, 4.9 mm

6. 1 m, 3 m

7. What is the volume of this paper cup?

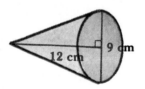

12 cm, 9 cm

8. What is the volume of this can?

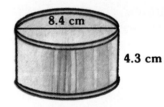

8.4 cm, 4.3 cm

9. What is the volume of this water storage tank?

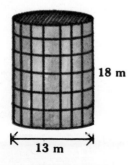

18 m, 13 m

*10. Will the contents of the round canister fit into the square canister?

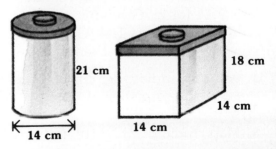

21 cm, 14 cm, 18 cm, 14 cm, 14 cm

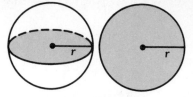

Spheres

A. The surface area of a **sphere** is 4 times the area of a circle with the same radius.

Since the area of a circle is equal to πr^2, the surface area of a sphere is equal to $4\pi r^2$.

$$A = 4\pi r^2$$

B. The volume of a sphere is $\frac{2}{3}$ the volume of a cylinder with the same radius and a height equal to twice the radius.

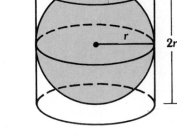

Since the volume of the cylinder is equal to $\pi r^2(2r)$ or $2\pi r^3$, the volume of the sphere is equal to $\frac{2}{3}(2\pi r^3)$ or $\frac{4}{3}\pi r^3$.

$$V = \frac{4}{3}\pi r^3$$

C. Find the surface area and volume. Use 3.14 for π.

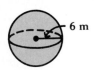

6 m

$A = 4\pi r^2$

$A \approx 4(3.14)(6^2)$

$A \approx 452.16$

Area: About 452.16 m²

$V = \frac{4}{3}\pi r^3$

$V \approx \frac{4}{3}(3.14)(6^3)$

$V \approx 904.32$

Volume: About 904.32 m³

Find the surface area and volume of each sphere. Use 3.14 for π. Give your answers to the nearest tenth for exercises 1–4. Give your answers in scientific notation for exercises 5–6.

1. golf ball, radius: 2.1 cm

2. tennis ball, diameter: 6.6 cm

3. basketball, radius: 12 cm

4. marble, radius: 0.63 cm

5. Mars, radius: 3.3×10^3 km

6. Venus, diameter: 1.2×10^4 km

Chapter 14 Test
Perimeter, Area, and Volume, pages 282–302

Find the perimeter of each polygon.

1. A rectangle, 18 m by 11 m

2. A rhombus, 4.1 mm on a side

3. A triangle with sides of 12 cm, 15 cm, and 19.2 cm

Find the area of each polygon.

4.

5.

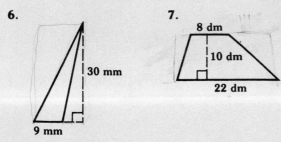

6.

7.

8. The diameter of a circle is 15 cm. Find the circumference. Use 3.14 for π.

9. The radius of a circle is 17 m. Find the area. Use 3.14 for π.

Find the surface area of each figure. Use 3.14 for π. Round your answers to the nearest tenth.

10.

11.

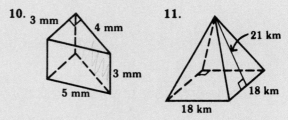

12.

13.

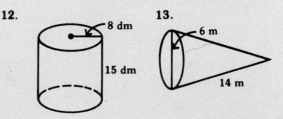

Find the volume of each figure. Use 3.14 for π. Round your answers to the nearest tenth.

14.

15.

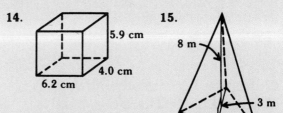

16.

17.

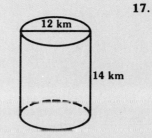
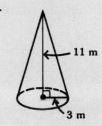

303

Chapter 15   Square Roots and Right-Triangle Geometry

Meaning of Square Root

A. What is the length of a side of a square that has an area of 16 cm²?

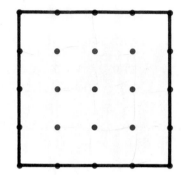

From the picture, you can see that the side of the square is 4 cm. $4^2 = 4 \times 4 = 16$

It is also true that $(-4)^2 = (-4) \times (-4) = 16$.

16 is the **square** of 4 and -4.

4 and -4 are **square roots** of 16.

Area: 16 cm²

$\sqrt{16}$ means "the positive square root of 16."
Only positive square roots will be studied in this book.

B. $6^2 = 6 \times 6 = 36$, so $\sqrt{36} = 6$.

$10^2 = 10 \times 10 = 100$, so $\sqrt{100} = 10$.

$15^2 = 15 \times 15 = 225$, so $\sqrt{225} = 15$.

C. There is no whole number whose square is 10. Therefore, $\sqrt{10}$ is not a whole number.

Between which two consecutive whole numbers is $\sqrt{10}$?

$3^2 = 9$ and $4^2 = 16$.
10 is between 9 and 16.
So, $\sqrt{10}$ is between $\sqrt{9}$ and $\sqrt{16}$.

$\sqrt{10}$ is between 3 and 4.

D. Is $\sqrt{275}$ between 16 and 17?

$16^2 = 256$ and $17^2 = 289$.
275 is between 256 and 289.
So, $\sqrt{275}$ is between $\sqrt{256}$ and $\sqrt{289}$.

$\sqrt{275}$ is between 16 and 17.

If the square root is a whole number, give the number. Otherwise, write *not a whole number.*

1. $\sqrt{4}$ 2. $\sqrt{8}$ 3. $\sqrt{9}$

4. $\sqrt{12}$ 5. $\sqrt{16}$ 6. $\sqrt{25}$

7. $\sqrt{36}$ 8. $\sqrt{39}$ 9. $\sqrt{42}$

10. $\sqrt{49}$ 11. $\sqrt{56}$ 12. $\sqrt{60}$

13. $\sqrt{64}$ 14. $\sqrt{75}$ 15. $\sqrt{81}$

*16. $\sqrt{324}$ *17. $\sqrt{450}$ *18. $\sqrt{576}$

Between which two consecutive whole numbers is each of the following?

19. $\sqrt{3}$ 20. $\sqrt{5}$ 21. $\sqrt{7}$

22. $\sqrt{15}$ 23. $\sqrt{20}$ 24. $\sqrt{30}$

25. $\sqrt{34}$ 26. $\sqrt{38}$ 27. $\sqrt{60}$

28. $\sqrt{72}$ 29. $\sqrt{88}$ 30. $\sqrt{96}$

Write *yes* or *no.*

31. Is $\sqrt{105}$ between 10 and 11?

32. Is $\sqrt{198}$ between 14 and 15?

33. Is $\sqrt{333}$ between 18 and 19?

34. Is $\sqrt{464}$ between 22 and 23?

35. Is $\sqrt{648}$ between 25 and 26?

36. Is $\sqrt{950}$ between 30 and 31?

37. Is $\sqrt{3500}$ between 59 and 60?

38. Is $\sqrt{5420}$ between 75 and 76?

39. Is $\sqrt{8500}$ between 91 and 92?

Keeping Skillful

Write each product as a power of 10.

1. $10^2 \times 10^3$ 2. $10^4 \times 10^5$

3. $10^{-2} \times 10^{-4}$ 4. $10^{-6} \times 10^{-1}$

5. $10^3 \times 10^{-5}$ 6. $10^{-6} \times 10^2$

Find each product using exponents. Give answers in standard form.

7. 100×10 8. $100 \times 10,000$

9. 0.1×0.001 10. 0.01×0.001

11. 100×0.001 12. $0.01 \times 10,000$

Write each quotient as a power of 10.

13. $\dfrac{10^5}{10^2}$ 14. $\dfrac{10^6}{10^4}$ 15. $\dfrac{10^2}{10^4}$

16. $\dfrac{10^3}{10^{-7}}$ 17. $\dfrac{10^{-3}}{10^{-4}}$ 18. $\dfrac{10^{-2}}{10^5}$

Find each quotient using exponents. Give answers in standard form.

19. $\dfrac{10,000}{100}$ 20. $\dfrac{1000}{100,000}$

21. $\dfrac{0.1}{0.01}$ 22. $\dfrac{0.0001}{0.01}$

23. $\dfrac{1000}{0.01}$ 24. $\dfrac{0.001}{100}$

Approximating Square Roots

A calculator can help you approximate $\sqrt{5}$ as a decimal.

The following method can be used for finding the square root of a number on a calculator that does not have a square-root key.

$2^2 = 4$ and $3^2 = 9$, so $\sqrt{5}$ is between 2 and 3.

Since 5 is closer to 4 than to 9, start with 2.1.

$2.1^2 = 4.41$, so $2.1 = \sqrt{4.41}$.
$2.2^2 = 4.84$, so $2.2 = \sqrt{4.84}$. ← $\sqrt{5}$ is between 2.2 and 2.3.
$2.3^2 = 5.29$, so $2.3 = \sqrt{5.29}$.

You can start at 2.21 or 2.29. Try 2.21.

$2.21^2 = 4.8841$, so $2.21 = \sqrt{4.8841}$.
$2.22^2 = 4.9284$, so $2.22 = \sqrt{4.9284}$.
$2.23^2 = 4.9729$, so $2.23 = \sqrt{4.9729}$. ← $\sqrt{5}$ is between 2.23 and 2.24.
$2.24^2 = 5.0176$, so $2.24 = \sqrt{5.0176}$.

You can start at 2.231 or 2.239. Try 2.239.

$2.239^2 = 5.013121$, so $2.239 = \sqrt{5.013121}$.
$2.238^2 = 5.008644$, so $2.238 = \sqrt{5.008644}$.
$2.237^2 = 5.004169$, so $2.237 = \sqrt{5.004169}$. ← $\sqrt{5}$ is between 2.237 and
$2.236^2 = 4.999696$, so $2.236 = \sqrt{4.999696}$. 2.236. Rounded to the nearest hundredth, $\sqrt{5}$ is 2.24.

Use your calculator to find the square root of each number to the nearest hundredth.

1. 2	2. 3	3. 6	4. 7	5. 10	6. 17
7. 29	8. 32	9. 45	10. 57	11. 75	12. 91
13. 137	14. 150	15. 177	16. 190	17. 200	18. 250
19. 1500	20. 2947	21. 3969	22. 68.3	23. 711.54	24. 5438.21

Multiplying and Dividing Square Roots

A. Evaluate $\sqrt{9} \times \sqrt{16}$ and $\sqrt{9 \times 16}$.

$$\sqrt{9} \times \sqrt{16} = 3 \times 4 = 12$$

$$\sqrt{9 \times 16} = \sqrt{144} = 12$$

Therefore, $\sqrt{9} \times \sqrt{16} = \sqrt{9 \times 16}$.

■ $\sqrt{a} \times \sqrt{b} = \sqrt{a \times b}$ when a and b are positive.

B. Multiply $\sqrt{3} \times \sqrt{12}$.

$$\sqrt{3} \times \sqrt{12} = \sqrt{3 \times 12} = \sqrt{36} = 6$$

C. Evaluate $\dfrac{\sqrt{64}}{\sqrt{16}}$ and $\sqrt{\dfrac{64}{16}}$.

$$\frac{\sqrt{64}}{\sqrt{16}} = \frac{8}{4} = 2$$

$$\sqrt{\frac{64}{16}} = \sqrt{4} = 2$$

Therefore, $\dfrac{\sqrt{64}}{\sqrt{16}} = \sqrt{\dfrac{64}{16}}$.

■ $\dfrac{\sqrt{a}}{\sqrt{b}} = \sqrt{\dfrac{a}{b}}$ when a and b are positive.

D. Divide $\dfrac{\sqrt{2}}{\sqrt{8}}$.

$$\frac{\sqrt{2}}{\sqrt{8}} = \sqrt{\frac{2}{8}} = \sqrt{\frac{1}{4}} = \frac{1}{2}$$

Multiply.

1. $\sqrt{4} \times \sqrt{9}$ 2. $\sqrt{4} \times \sqrt{16}$

3. $\sqrt{2} \times \sqrt{8}$ 4. $\sqrt{2} \times \sqrt{18}$

5. $\sqrt{3} \times \sqrt{12}$ 6. $\sqrt{5} \times \sqrt{20}$

7. $\sqrt{3} \times \sqrt{27}$ 8. $\sqrt{2} \times \sqrt{32}$

9. $\sqrt{4} \times \sqrt{25}$ 10. $\sqrt{2} \times \sqrt{50}$

11. $\sqrt{3} \times \sqrt{3}$ 12. $\sqrt{7} \times \sqrt{7}$

13. $(\sqrt{5})^2$ 14. $(\sqrt{11})^2$

15. $(\sqrt{23})^2$ 16. $(\sqrt{46})^2$

Divide.

17. $\dfrac{\sqrt{36}}{\sqrt{9}}$ 18. $\dfrac{\sqrt{100}}{\sqrt{4}}$

19. $\dfrac{\sqrt{8}}{\sqrt{32}}$ 20. $\dfrac{\sqrt{25}}{\sqrt{100}}$

21. $\dfrac{\sqrt{50}}{\sqrt{2}}$ 22. $\dfrac{\sqrt{98}}{\sqrt{2}}$

23. $\dfrac{\sqrt{27}}{\sqrt{3}}$ 24. $\dfrac{\sqrt{48}}{\sqrt{3}}$

25. $\dfrac{\sqrt{2025}}{\sqrt{81}}$ 26. $\dfrac{\sqrt{6000}}{\sqrt{60}}$

Simplifying Expressions Involving Square Roots

A. Simplify $\sqrt{20}$.

$$\sqrt{20} = \sqrt{4 \times 5}$$
$$= \sqrt{4} \times \sqrt{5}$$
$$= 2\sqrt{5}$$

$2\sqrt{5}$ is usually considered to be in simpler form than $\sqrt{20}$ because 20 has a factor that is a square. 5 has no square factor greater than 1.

B. Simplify $\dfrac{15\sqrt{42}}{3\sqrt{6}}$.

$$\frac{15\sqrt{42}}{3\sqrt{6}} = \frac{15}{3} \times \frac{\sqrt{42}}{\sqrt{6}}$$
$$= 5 \times \sqrt{\frac{42}{6}}$$
$$= 5\sqrt{7}$$

C. Simplify $\sqrt{576}$.

$576 = 2 \times 2 \times 2 \times 2 \times 2 \times 2 \times 3 \times 3$ — Use prime factoring to help simplify.

$576 = 2^2 \times 2^2 \times 2^2 \times 3^2$ — Pair the common factors.

$\sqrt{576} = \sqrt{2^2 \times 2^2 \times 2^2 \times 3^2}$

$\sqrt{576} = \sqrt{2^2} \times \sqrt{2^2} \times \sqrt{2^2} \times \sqrt{3^2}$

$\sqrt{576} = 2 \times 2 \times 2 \times 3$ — $\sqrt{2^2} = \sqrt{4} = 2; \sqrt{3^2} = \sqrt{9} = 3$

$\sqrt{576} = 24$

Simplify.

1. $\sqrt{8}$ 2. $\sqrt{12}$ 3. $\sqrt{18}$

4. $\sqrt{20}$ 5. $\sqrt{24}$ 6. $\sqrt{27}$

7. $\sqrt{28}$ 8. $\sqrt{32}$ 9. $\sqrt{40}$

10. $\sqrt{45}$ 11. $\sqrt{48}$ 12. $\sqrt{50}$

13. $\sqrt{54}$ 14. $\sqrt{63}$ 15. $\sqrt{75}$

16. $\sqrt{80}$ 17. $\sqrt{90}$ 18. $\sqrt{96}$

19. $2\sqrt{45}$ 20. $5\sqrt{75}$

21. $3\sqrt{32}$ 22. $6\sqrt{27}$

23. $2\sqrt{3} \times \sqrt{3}$ 24. $3\sqrt{5} \times 2\sqrt{5}$

25. $2\sqrt{2} \times 3\sqrt{8}$ 26. $3\sqrt{6} \times 2\sqrt{8}$

27. $\dfrac{4\sqrt{10}}{2\sqrt{2}}$ 28. $\dfrac{3\sqrt{21}}{9\sqrt{3}}$

29. $\dfrac{10\sqrt{75}}{5\sqrt{3}}$ 30. $\dfrac{12\sqrt{8}}{4\sqrt{2}}$

31. $\dfrac{\sqrt{72}}{\sqrt{6}}$ 32. $\dfrac{\sqrt{192}}{\sqrt{6}}$

★33. $\dfrac{3\sqrt{24}}{2\sqrt{3}}$ ★34. $\dfrac{5\sqrt{60}}{2\sqrt{5}}$

★35. $3\sqrt{\dfrac{32}{9}}$ ★36. $5\sqrt{\dfrac{6}{50}}$

Write as a whole number.

37. $\sqrt{196}$ 38. $\sqrt{256}$ 39. $\sqrt{324}$

40. $\sqrt{225}$ 41. $\sqrt{676}$ 42. $\sqrt{441}$

43. $\sqrt{729}$ 44. $\sqrt{1024}$ 45. $\sqrt{2025}$

Time Out

The members of a band are lined up in a column, single file, one behind the other. You know only these two things about the line:

- If any band member in line has red hair, the band member behind that one has red hair.
- The fifth band member in line has red hair.

Which of these conclusions have to be true?

1. All the band members have red hair.

2. Only two band members have red hair.

3. The sixth band member in line has red hair.

4. The fourth band member in line has red hair.

5. All the band members after the fourth one in line have red hair.

309

Using Tables to Find Square Roots

The table on page 311 gives squares and square roots. The square roots are given to the nearest thousandth.

A. To the nearest tenth of a kilometer, how far can you see from a plane at an altitude of 10 km?

Use the formula $K = 112\sqrt{A}$, where K is the distance you can see in kilometers and A is the altitude of the plane in kilometers.

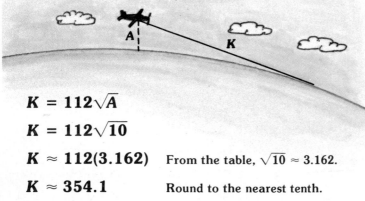

$K = 112\sqrt{A}$

$K = 112\sqrt{10}$

$K \approx 112(3.162)$ From the table, $\sqrt{10} \approx 3.162$.

$K \approx 354.1$ Round to the nearest tenth.

You can see about 354.1 km.

B. Find $\sqrt{676}$.

The table shows that $26^2 = 676$, so $\sqrt{676} = 26$.

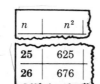

n	n^2
25	625
26	676

C. Find $\sqrt{275}$ to the nearest tenth.

$\sqrt{275} = \sqrt{5 \times 55}$ or $\sqrt{275} = \sqrt{5 \times 5 \times 11}$

$\qquad = \sqrt{5} \times \sqrt{55} \qquad\qquad = \sqrt{5^2} \times \sqrt{11}$

$\qquad \approx 2.236(7.416) \qquad\qquad \approx 5(3.317)$

$\qquad \approx 16.6 \qquad\qquad\qquad\quad \approx 16.6$

Use the table on page 311. Round to the nearest tenth.

1. $\sqrt{3}$ 2. $\sqrt{12}$

3. $\sqrt{34}$ 4. $\sqrt{76}$

5. $\sqrt{130}$ 6. $\sqrt{142}$

7. $\sqrt{121}$ 8. $\sqrt{289}$

9. $\sqrt{784}$ 10. $\sqrt{1296}$

11. $\sqrt{2916}$ 12. $\sqrt{9801}$

13. $\sqrt{165}$ 14. $\sqrt{250}$

15. $\sqrt{310}$ 16. $\sqrt{425}$

17. $\sqrt{600}$ 18. $\sqrt{1000}$

19. $\sqrt{7500}$ 20. $\sqrt{3750}$

★21. $\sqrt{11^3}$ ★22. $\sqrt{42^3}$

★23. $\sqrt{17^4}$ ★24. $\sqrt{53^4}$

Use $K = 112\sqrt{A}$. To the nearest tenth of a kilometer, how far can you see from a plane at an altitude of

25. 6 km?

26. 12 km?

27. 14 km?

28. 22 km?

29. 50 km?

30. 105 km?

Squares and Square Roots

n	n^2	$\sqrt{n}$	n	n^2	$\sqrt{n}$	n	n^2	$\sqrt{n}$	n	n^2	$\sqrt{n}$
1	1	1.000	51	2601	7.141	101	10,201	10.050	151	22,801	12.288
2	4	1.414	52	2704	7.211	102	10,404	10.100	152	23,104	12.329
3	9	1.732	53	2809	7.280	103	10,609	10.149	153	23,409	12.369
4	16	2.000	54	2916	7.348	104	10,816	10.198	154	23,716	12.410
5	25	2.236	55	3025	7.416	105	11,025	10.247	155	24,025	12.450
6	36	2.449	56	3136	7.483	106	11,236	10.296	156	24,336	12.490
7	49	2.646	57	3249	7.550	107	11,449	10.344	157	24,649	12.530
8	64	2.828	58	3364	7.616	108	11,664	10.392	158	24,964	12.570
9	81	3.000	59	3481	7.681	109	11,881	10.440	159	25,281	12.610
10	100	3.162	60	3600	7.746	110	12,100	10.488	160	25,600	12.649
11	121	3.317	61	3721	7.810	111	12,321	10.536	161	25,921	12.689
12	144	3.464	62	3844	7.874	112	12,544	10.583	162	26,244	12.728
13	169	3.606	63	3969	7.937	113	12,769	10.630	163	26,569	12.767
14	196	3.742	64	4096	8.000	114	12,996	10.677	164	26,896	12.806
15	225	3.873	65	4225	8.062	115	13,225	10.724	165	27,225	12.845
16	256	4.000	66	4356	8.124	116	13,456	10.770	166	27,556	12.884
17	289	4.123	67	4489	8.185	117	13,689	10.817	167	27,889	12.923
18	324	4.243	68	4624	8.246	118	13,924	10.863	168	28,224	12.961
19	361	4.359	69	4761	8.307	119	14,161	10.909	169	28,561	13.000
20	400	4.472	70	4900	8.367	120	14,400	10.954	170	28,900	13.038
21	441	4.583	71	5041	8.426	121	14,641	11.000	171	29,241	13.077
22	484	4.690	72	5184	8.485	122	14,884	11.045	172	29,584	13.115
23	529	4.796	73	5329	8.544	123	15,129	11.091	173	29,929	13.153
24	576	4.899	74	5476	8.602	124	15,376	11.136	174	30,276	13.191
25	625	5.000	75	5625	8.660	125	15,625	11.180	175	30,625	13.229
26	676	5.099	76	5776	8.718	126	15,876	11.225	176	30,976	13.266
27	729	5.196	77	5929	8.775	127	16,129	11.269	177	31,329	13.304
28	784	5.292	78	6084	8.832	128	16,384	11.314	178	31,684	13.342
29	841	5.385	79	6241	8.888	129	16,641	11.358	179	32,041	13.379
30	900	5.477	80	6400	8.944	130	16,900	11.402	180	32,400	13.416
31	961	5.568	81	6561	9.000	131	17,161	11.446	181	32,761	13.454
32	1024	5.657	82	6724	9.055	132	17,424	11.489	182	33,124	13.491
33	1089	5.745	83	6889	9.110	133	17,689	11.533	183	33,489	13.528
34	1156	5.831	84	7056	9.165	134	17,956	11.576	184	33,856	13.565
35	1225	5.916	85	7225	9.220	135	18,225	11.619	185	34,225	13.601
36	1296	6.000	86	7396	9.274	136	18,496	11.662	186	34,596	13.638
37	1369	6.083	87	7569	9.327	137	18,769	11.705	187	34,969	13.675
38	1444	6.164	88	7744	9.381	138	19,044	11.747	188	35,344	13.711
39	1521	6.245	89	7921	9.434	139	19,321	11.790	189	35,721	13.748
40	1600	6.325	90	8100	9.487	140	19,600	11.832	190	36,100	13.784
41	1681	6.403	91	8281	9.539	141	19,881	11.874	191	36,481	13.820
42	1764	6.481	92	8464	9.592	142	20,164	11.916	192	36,864	13.856
43	1849	6.557	93	8649	9.644	143	20,449	11.958	193	37,249	13.892
44	1936	6.633	94	8836	9.695	144	20,736	12.000	194	37,636	13.928
45	2025	6.708	95	9025	9.747	145	21,025	12.042	195	38,025	13.964
46	2116	6.782	96	9216	9.798	146	21,316	12.083	196	38,416	14.000
47	2209	6.856	97	9409	9.849	147	21,609	12.124	197	38,809	14.036
48	2304	6.928	98	9604	9.899	148	21,904	12.166	198	39,204	14.071
49	2401	7.000	99	9801	9.950	149	22,201	12.207	199	39,601	14.107
50	2500	7.071	100	10,000	10.000	150	22,500	12.247	200	40,000	14.142

Square Roots, Sides of Squares, and Right Triangles

You can use segments on dot paper to show square roots.

Given $\overline{RS}$, draw a square on $\overline{RS}$.

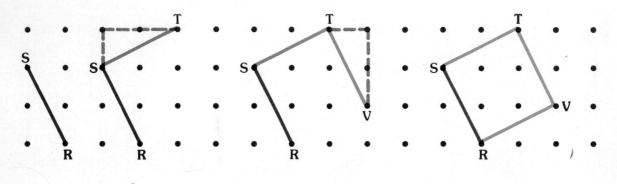

| Given. | To go from S to T, go up 1 unit and right 2 units. | To go from T to V, go right 1 unit and down 2 units. | Draw $\overline{RV}$ to complete the square. |

You can find the area of square RSTV and the length of $\overline{RS}$. Draw a square around square RSTV.

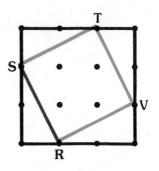

The difference between the area of the outer square and the area of the four triangles is the area of square RSTV.

Area of outer square: **9 square units**

Area of 4 triangles: $4\left(\frac{1}{2}\right)(2)(1)$ or **4 square units**

Subtract to find the area of square RSTV.

Area of outer square	Area of 4 triangles	Area of square RSTV
9	− 4	= 5

Since the area of square RSTV is 5 square units, the length of $\overline{RS}$ is $\sqrt{5}$.

Draw each triangle below on dot paper or graph paper. Follow the steps shown in this example.

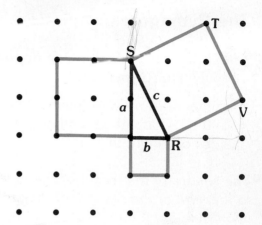

Step 1 Draw a square on each side of the triangle. Use the method on page 312 to draw the square on the slanted side.

Step 2 Find the area of each square. By counting, $a^2 = 4$ and $b^2 = 1$. By the method on page 312, $c^2 = 5$.

Step 3 Record the area of the square on each side in a chart like this.

a^2	b^2	c^2
4	1	5

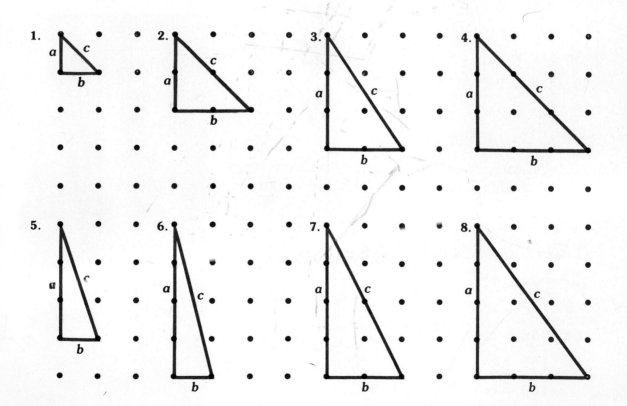

1.

2.

3.

4.

5.

6.

7.

8.

9. Study the chart. Write an equation using a^2, b^2, and c^2.

The Pythagorean Relation

A. In a right triangle, the side opposite the right angle is the **hypotenuse.**

Pythagoras, a Greek mathematician in about 500 B.C., described a relationship between the sides of a right triangle.

■ *The square of the length of the hypotenuse is equal to the sum of the squares of the lengths of the other two sides, or $c^2 = a^2 + b^2$.*

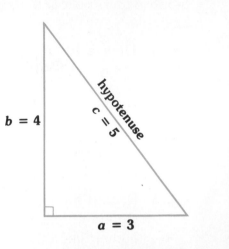

Apply the Pythagorean relation to the right triangle shown.

$$a^2 + b^2 = c^2$$
$$3^2 + 4^2 = 5^2$$
$$9 + 16 = 25$$
$$25 = 25$$

B. An escalator moves between floors that are 6 m apart. On each floor, the horizontal distance from the front of the escalator to the back is 8 m. How far would a person travel between floors on the escalator?

$$a^2 + b^2 = c^2$$
$$8^2 + 6^2 = c^2$$
$$64 + 36 = c^2$$
$$100 = c^2$$
$$\sqrt{100} = c$$
$$10 = c$$

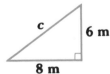

A person would travel 10 m.

c. For this right triangle, find a.

$$a^2 + b^2 = c^2$$
$$a^2 + 3^2 = 7^2$$
$$a^2 + 9 = 49$$
$$a^2 + 9 - 9 = 49 - 9$$
$$a^2 = 40$$
$$a = \sqrt{40}$$
$$a \approx 6.325 \quad \text{From table on page 311.}$$

a is about 6.325.

Can a right triangle have these sides? Write *yes* or *no*.

1. $a = 8$, $b = 15$, $c = 17$ **2.** $a = 16$, $b = 12$, $c = 20$

3. $a = 20$, $b = 21$, $c = 29$ **4.** $a = 30$, $b = 18$, $c = 36$

For each right triangle, find the length of the missing side.

5. $a = 2$, $b = 3$ **6.** $a = 3$, $b = 5$ **7.** $a = 4$, $b = 2$

8. $a = 8$, $b = 10$ **9.** $a = 7$, $b = 12$ **10.** $a = 5$, $b = 12$

11. $a = 3$, $c = 8$ **12.** $a = 15$, $c = 17$ **13.** $a = 2$, $c = 10$

14. $b = 8$, $c = 12$ **15.** $b = 12$, $c = 15$ **16.** $b = 10$, $c = 16$

17.

18.

19.

*20. If the bottom of a 15-meter ramp is 12 m from a loading platform, how high is the platform?

*21. Would a 7-meter ladder reach a height of 6 m if the bottom of it is 4 m from the wall?

Problem Solving: The Pythagorean Relation

READ   **A.** Charlie took a homing pigeon 6 km north of home and then 2 km west. The pigeon flew straight home. To the nearest hundredth of a kilometer, how far did the pigeon fly?

READ   **B.** A 5-meter rope is attached to the top of a 2-meter tent pole. If the rope is stretched to the ground and fastened, how far from the base of the tent pole is it fastened?

DECIDE   Draw a sketch. Solve the Pythagorean relation for c.

DECIDE   Draw a sketch. Solve the Pythagorean relation for a.

SOLVE

$$a^2 + b^2 = c^2$$
$$2^2 + 6^2 = c^2$$
$$4 + 36 = c^2$$
$$40 = c^2$$
$$\sqrt{40} = c$$
$$6.325 \approx c$$

SOLVE

$$a^2 + b^2 = c^2$$
$$a^2 + 2^2 = 5^2$$
$$a^2 + 4 = 25$$
$$a^2 + 4 - 4 = 25 - 4$$
$$a^2 = 21$$
$$a = \sqrt{21}$$
$$a \approx 4.583$$

ANSWER   The pigeon flew about 6.33 km.

ANSWER   The pole is about 4.58 m from the base of the tent pole.

316

Solve each of the following. Round each answer to the nearest hundredth.

1. The campsite is 4 km north of a store. The store is 6 km east of a bridge. As a crow flies, how far is the campsite from the bridge?

2. Glen walked 4 km due east and then 2 km due south. How far was he from his starting point?

3. How much rope must be used to hold a 3-meter pole if the rope is attached to the top of the pole and to the ground 2 m from the foot of the pole?

4. Iyo walked south 4 km from camp to the store. Colette walked west the same distance from camp. How far apart were they?

5. A raft is 2 m long and 1.5 m wide. The diagonal of the raft is 2.5 m. Is the raft a rectangle?

6. A tent pole is 3 m long. Will it fit flat in a car trunk that is 2.5 m by 1.5 m?

7. As Takeo rowed a boat across a 24 m stream, the current carried the boat 3 m downstream. How far was the boat from the starting point?

8. The campsite is a rectangular area 100 m long and 50 m wide. Jan walked diagonally from one corner to another. How far did she walk?

9. Colette let out 100 m of string while flying a kite. She is 20 m from a point under the kite. How high is the kite?

*10. A telegraph pole is 10 m high. How long is the wire from the top of this pole to the top of another pole which is 12 m high? The poles are 30 m apart.

Similar Triangles

A. Triangle ABC is **similar** to triangle XYZ. Similar triangles have the same shape.

We write $\triangle ABC \sim \triangle XYZ$.

In similar triangles, the corresponding angles are congruent.

$\angle A \cong \angle X$
$\angle B \cong \angle Y$
$\angle C \cong \angle Z$

In similar triangles, the lengths of the corresponding sides are proportional.

$$\frac{AB}{XY} = \frac{AC}{XZ} = \frac{BC}{YZ}$$

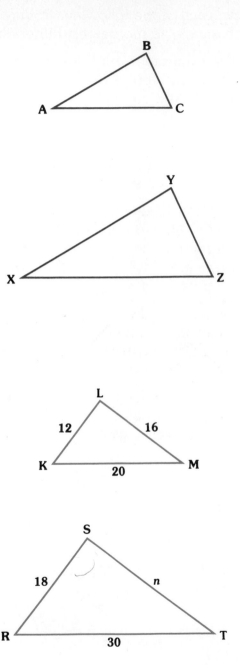

B. These triangles are similar. Find the missing length.

$$\frac{KL}{RS} = \frac{LM}{ST}$$

$$\frac{12}{18} = \frac{16}{n}$$

$12 \times n = 18 \times 16$ Write the cross-products.

$12n = 288$

$$\frac{12n}{12} = \frac{288}{12}$$

$n = 24$

318

In each exercise, the two triangles are similar.
Find the missing length.

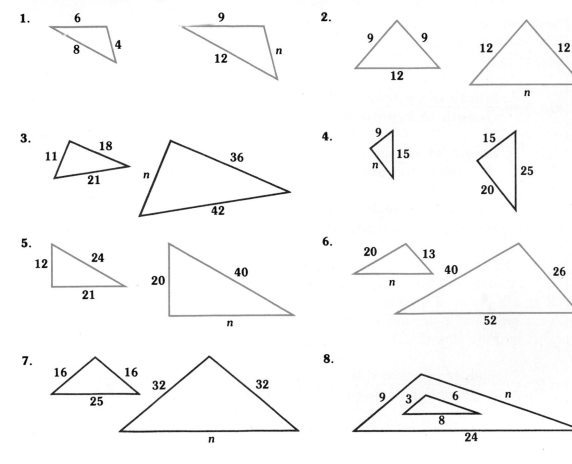

1.
6
8   4
9
12   n

2.
9   9
12   12
12
n

3.
11   18
21
n   36
42

4.
9
n   15
15
20   25

5.
12   24
21
20   40
n

6.
20   13
n
40   26
52

7.
16   16
25
32   32
n

8.
9   3   6   n
8
24

*9. The triangles formed by Don and
his shadow and the tree and its
shadow are similar. Find the
height of the tree.

1.6 m

0.5 m

1 m

*10. The triangles are similar.
Find the distance across the
river.

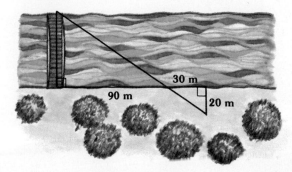

30 m
90 m
20 m

Sine, Cosine, and Tangent

A. In any right triangle, three **trigonometric ratios** can be written for each acute angle. They are **sine** (sin), **cosine** (cos), and **tangent** (tan).

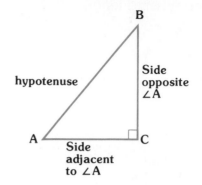

$$\sin A = \frac{\text{length of opposite side}}{\text{length of hypotenuse}}$$

$$\cos A = \frac{\text{length of adjacent side}}{\text{length of hypotenuse}}$$

$$\tan A = \frac{\text{length of opposite side}}{\text{length of adjacent side}}$$

B. For the triangles at the right, you know $\angle R \cong \angle X$ because the triangles are similar. Give a ratio and a decimal for the sine of $\angle R$ and the sine of $\angle X$.

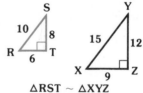

△RST ~ △XYZ

$$\sin R = \frac{\text{length of opposite side}}{\text{length of hypotenuse}} \qquad \sin X = \frac{\text{length of opposite side}}{\text{length of hypotenuse}}$$

$$\sin R = \frac{8}{10} = 0.8 \qquad\qquad \sin X = \frac{12}{15} = 0.8$$

$\sin R = \sin X$
Any angle with the same measure as $\angle R$ has the same sine, cosine, and tangent.

C. Give the cosine of $\angle R$ for the triangle above.

$$\cos R = \frac{\text{length of adjacent side}}{\text{length of hypotenuse}}$$

$$\cos R = \frac{6}{10} = 0.6$$

D. Give the tangent of $\angle S$ for the triangle above.

$$\tan S = \frac{\text{length of opposite side}}{\text{length of adjacent side}}$$

$$\tan S = \frac{6}{8} = 0.75$$

320

Use these triangles for exercises 1–48.

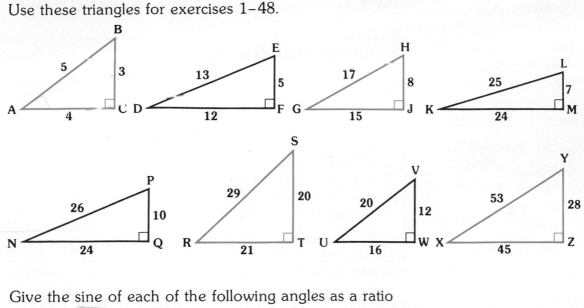

Give the sine of each of the following angles as a ratio
and as a decimal to the nearest hundredth.

1. ∠A   2. ∠B   3. ∠D   4. ∠E   5. ∠G   6. ∠H   7. ∠K   8. ∠L

9. ∠N   10. ∠P   11. ∠R   12. ∠S   13. ∠U   14. ∠V   15. ∠X   16. ∠Y

Give the cosine of each of the following angles as a ratio
and as a decimal to the nearest hundredth.

17. ∠A   18. ∠B   19. ∠D   20. ∠E   21. ∠G   22. ∠H   23. ∠K   24. ∠L

25. ∠N   26. ∠P   27. ∠R   28. ∠S   29. ∠U   30. ∠V   31. ∠X   32. ∠Y

Give the tangent of each of the following angles as a
ratio and as a decimal to the nearest hundredth.

33. ∠A   34. ∠B   35. ∠D   36. ∠E   37. ∠G   38. ∠H   39. ∠K   40. ∠L

41. ∠N   42. ∠P   43. ∠R   44. ∠S   45. ∠U   46. ∠V   47. ∠X   48. ∠Y

★49. Measure $\overline{BC}$ and $\overline{AB}$ and give a ratio for sine A.
Measure $\overline{DE}$ and $\overline{AD}$ and give another ratio
for sine A. Measure $\overline{FG}$ and $\overline{AF}$ and give a
third ratio for sine A. What do you notice
about these ratios?

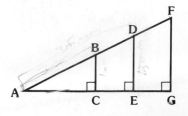

Finding Sides of Right Triangles Using Trigonometric Ratios

This is part of the table from page 427. It gives values for tangent, sine, and cosine to the nearest thousandth.

Trigonometric Ratios

Measure of angle	tan	sin	cos	Measure of angle	tan	sin	cos
1°	0.017	0.017	1.000	46°	1.036	0.719	0.695
2°	0.035	0.035	0.999	47°	1.072	0.731	0.682
3°	0.052	0.052	0.999	48°	1.111	0.743	0.669
4°	0.070	0.070	0.998	49°	1.150	0.755	0.656
5°	0.087	0.087	0.996	50°	1.192	0.766	0.643
6°	0.105	0.105	0.995	51°	1.235	0.777	0.629
7°	0.123	0.122	0.993	52°	1.280	0.788	0.616
8°	0.141	0.139	0.990	53°	1.327	0.799	0.602
9°	0.158	0.156	0.988	54°	1.376	0.809	0.588
10°	0.176	0.174	0.985	55°	1.428	0.819	0.574

A. Use the table to write cos 9° and tan 48° as decimals.

cos 9° ≈ 0.988

tan 48° ≈ 1.111

B. You can use trigonometric ratios to find lengths of sides in right triangles.

Find n to the nearest hundredth.

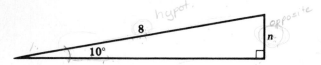

$$\sin = \frac{\text{length of opposite side}}{\text{length of hypotenuse}}$$

$$\sin 10° = \frac{n}{8}$$

$$0.174 \approx \frac{n}{8} \quad \text{From the table,} \atop \text{sin 10° ≈ 0.174.}$$

$$8(0.174) \approx 8\left(\frac{n}{8}\right)$$

$$1.392 \approx n$$

n is about 1.39.

C. Find t to the nearest hundredth.

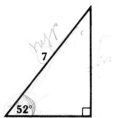

$$\cos = \frac{\text{length of adjacent side}}{\text{length of hypotenuse}}$$

$$\cos 52° = \frac{t}{7}$$

$$0.616 \approx \frac{t}{7} \quad \text{From the table,} \atop \text{cos 52° ≈ 0.616.}$$

$$7(0.616) \approx 7\left(\frac{t}{7}\right)$$

$$4.312 \approx t$$

t is about 4.31.

Use the table on page 427 to give each of the
following as a decimal.

1. $\cos 17°$ **2.** $\sin 6°$ **3.** $\tan 56°$ **4.** $\sin 56°$ **5.** $\cos 60°$

6. $\sin 35°$ **7.** $\tan 87°$ **8.** $\cos 33°$ **9.** $\tan 66°$ **10.** $\cos 89°$

Use sine, cosine, or tangent to find n to the
nearest hundredth. Use the table on page 427.

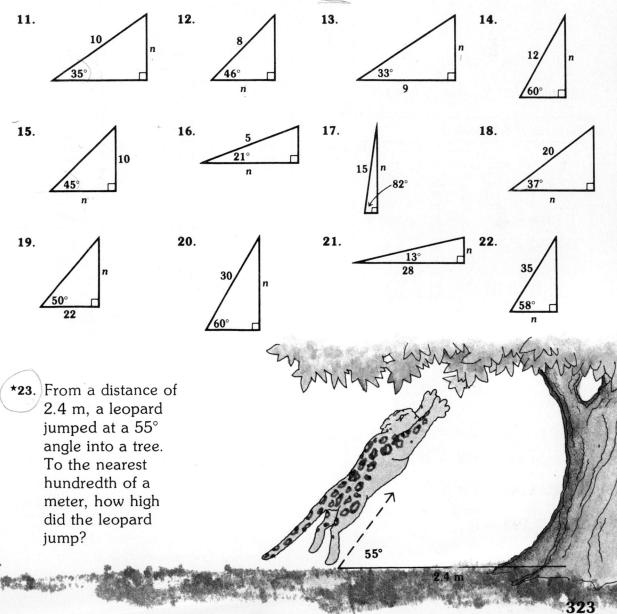

11. 10, 35°, n

12. 8, 46°, n

13. 33°, 9, n

14. 12, 60°, n

15. 10, 45°, n

16. 5, 21°, n

17. 15, 82°, n

18. 20, 37°, n

19. 50°, 22, n

20. 30, 60°, n

21. 13°, 28, n

22. 35, 58°, n

★23. From a distance of
2.4 m, a leopard
jumped at a 55°
angle into a tree.
To the nearest
hundredth of a
meter, how high
did the leopard
jump?

55°

2.4 m

Chapter 15 Test
Square Roots and Right-Triangle Geometry, pages 304–323

1. Between which two consecutive whole numbers is $\sqrt{45}$?

Simplify.

2. $\sqrt{16}$ **3.** $\sqrt{72}$ **4.** $\sqrt{576}$

5. $\sqrt{12} \times \sqrt{3}$ **6.** $\dfrac{\sqrt{72}}{\sqrt{8}}$ **7.** $\dfrac{\sqrt{54}}{\sqrt{2}}$

Use this table for exercises 8–13.

Squares and Square Roots					
n	n^2	$\sqrt{n}$	n	n^2	$\sqrt{n}$
1	1	1.000	51	2601	7.141
2	4	1.414	52	2704	7.211
3	9	1.732	53	2809	7.280
4	16	2.000	54	2916	7.348
5	25	2.236	55	3025	7.416
6	36	2.449	56	3136	7.483
7	49	2.646	57	3249	7.550
8	64	2.828	58	3364	7.616
9	81	3.000	59	3481	7.681
10	100	3.162	60	3600	7.746

Round to the nearest hundredth.

8. $\sqrt{8}$ **9.** $\sqrt{59}$

10. $\sqrt{2704}$ **11.** $\sqrt{600}$

Find the length of the missing side.

12. Right triangle: $u = 4$, $h = 6$

13. Right triangle: $a = 3$, $c = 8$

14. $\triangle ABC \sim \triangle DEF$

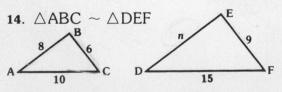

For exercises 15–17, give each as a ratio and as a decimal.

15. sin A

16. cos B

17. tan B

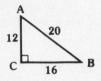

Use this table for exercises 18–21.

Measure of angle	tan	sin	cos
26°	0.488	0.438	0.899
27°	0.510	0.454	0.891
28°	0.532	0.469	0.883
29°	0.554	0.485	0.875
30°	0.577	0.500	0.866
31°	0.601	0.515	0.857
32°	0.625	0.530	0.848
33°	0.649	0.545	0.839
34°	0.675	0.559	0.829
35°	0.700	0.574	0.819

Give each of the following as a decimal.

18. sin 26°   **19.** tan 34°

Use sine, cosine, or tangent to find n to the nearest hundredth.

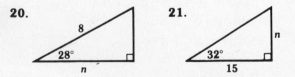

20.   **21.**

22. Rosa walked 3 km north and 7 km east. To the nearest tenth of a kilometer, how far was she from her starting point? Use the square-root table on this page.

Problems Around Us

1. The population of the United States was about 204 million in 1970. By 1979, the population had increased 7.9%. What was the population in 1979?

2. In 1977, the United States imports were 157 billion dollars. The exports were 119 billion dollars. To the nearest whole percent, the exports were what percent of the imports?

3. Red Lake has an area of 1171 km². The Great Salt Lake is 3.18 times as large. To the nearest square kilometer, what is the area of the Great Salt Lake?

4. In 1979, Australia had 79 phones for every 200 people. The population of Australia was 14,408,000. How many phones were there?

5. The highest recorded temperature on earth was 57.8°C in 1922 in Libya. The lowest recorded temperature was ⁻67.7°C in 1933 in the Soviet Union. What was the difference between these temperatures?

6. The price of a $475 television set increased 15%. What was the price after the increase?

7. To the nearest ten meters, Mt. Everest is 8850 m high. Mt. Wilson is 0.49 times as high. To the nearest ten meters, how high is Mt. Wilson?

8. The regular price of a piano is $630. What would the sale price be after a 30% discount?

9. Mel rode his bicycle $6\frac{2}{3}$ miles in $\frac{5}{12}$ hour. What was his speed in miles per hour?

10. Fall Creek Falls in Tennessee is 78 m high. Akaka Falls in Hawaii is $1\frac{3}{4}$ times as high. How high is Akaka Falls?

Individualized Skills Maintenance

Diagnose

A *pages 216–217*

Solve each proportion.

$$\frac{3}{7} = \frac{x}{21}$$

$$\frac{0.6}{4.2} = \frac{9}{y}$$

B *pages 176–179*

$$\frac{1}{4} + \frac{3}{8}$$

$$2\frac{2}{3} + 1\frac{1}{5}$$

$$9\frac{5}{6} + 8\frac{2}{9}$$

Practice

A Solve each proportion.

1. $\frac{2}{9} = \frac{x}{18}$　　2. $\frac{56}{8} = \frac{a}{2}$　　3. $\frac{77}{35} = \frac{11}{y}$　　4. $\frac{15}{18} = \frac{c}{24}$

5. $\frac{30}{m} = \frac{5}{21}$　　6. $\frac{63}{35} = \frac{45}{y}$　　7. $\frac{24}{f} = \frac{60}{15}$　　8. $\frac{60}{72} = \frac{m}{36}$

9. $\frac{17.6}{4} = \frac{h}{8}$　　10. $\frac{0.4}{1.6} = \frac{m}{20}$　　11. $\frac{3.9}{r} = \frac{0.3}{1.2}$　　12. $\frac{a}{2.3} = \frac{87}{0.3}$

B

13. $\frac{1}{8}$
    $+\frac{5}{6}$

14. $\frac{2}{3}$
    $+\frac{5}{8}$

15. $\frac{3}{5}$
    $+\frac{1}{4}$

16. $\frac{1}{2}$
    $+\frac{5}{12}$

17. $\frac{2}{7}$
    $+\frac{1}{3}$

18. $\frac{1}{4}$
    $+\frac{9}{10}$

19. $\frac{1}{6}$
    $+\frac{7}{9}$

20. $3\frac{1}{3}$
    $+4\frac{2}{3}$

21. $8\frac{5}{6}$
    $+6\frac{2}{3}$

22. $16\frac{2}{7}$
    $+5\frac{1}{2}$

23. $9\frac{3}{4}$
    $+10\frac{5}{6}$

24. $21\frac{5}{8}$
    $+2\frac{1}{2}$

25. $11\frac{4}{5} + 7\frac{1}{2}$　　26. $7\frac{1}{6} + 22\frac{1}{2}$　　27. $13\frac{5}{8} + 15\frac{1}{6}$　　28. $26\frac{1}{9} + 18\frac{5}{12}$

Unit 5 Review

Chapter 13, pages 260–280

Use this diagram for exercises 1–4.
$j \parallel k$ and $m\angle 1 = 135°$.

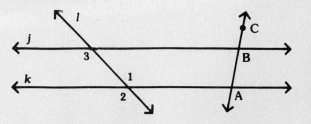

1. Name a ray with endpoint B.

2. Is $\angle 1$ acute, right, or obtuse?

3. Give the measure of $\angle 2$.

4. Give the measure of $\angle 3$.

In the figures below, $\triangle ABC \cong \triangle JKL$.
For exercises 5–7, give the measure of
the angle or segment.

5. $\angle C$

6. $\angle K$

7. $\overline{KL}$

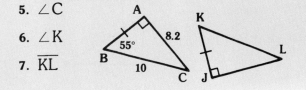

Write true or false.

8. An octagon has seven sides.

9. A scalene triangle has no
   congruent sides.

10. Name an
    inscribed
    angle in
    circle A.

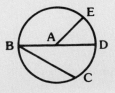

Chapter 14, pages 282–302

11. Find the perimeter of a rhombus,
    2.3 cm on a side.

Find the area of each figure.
Use 3.14 for π.

12.

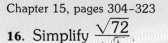

13.

12 cm

Use the diagram for exercises 14–15.
Use 3.14 for π.

14. Find the
    surface
    area.

15. Find the
    volume.

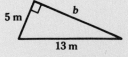

Chapter 15, pages 304–323

16. Simplify $\dfrac{\sqrt{72}}{\sqrt{6}}$

17. Find the
    length of
    the missing
    side.

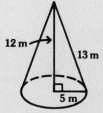

18. Find n to the
    nearest hundredth.

Measure of angle	tan	sin	cos
52°	1.280	0.788	0.616

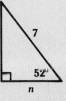

327

Unit 5 Test
Chapters 13–15, pages 260–324

Use this diagram for exercises 1–4.
$a \parallel b$ and $m\angle 1 = 80°$.

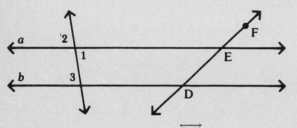

1. Name a segment on $\overrightarrow{DF}$.

2. Is $\angle 1$ acute, right, or obtuse?

3. Give the measure of $\angle 2$.

4. Give the measure of $\angle 3$.

In the figure below, $\triangle DEF \cong \triangle GEH$. For exercises 5–7, give the measure of the angle or segment.

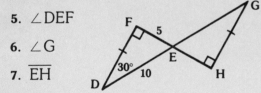

5. $\angle DEF$

6. $\angle G$

7. $\overline{EH}$

Write *true* or *false*.

8. An obtuse triangle has three obtuse angles.

9. A parallelogram is a quadrilateral.

10. Name a chord in circle T.

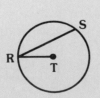

11. Find the perimeter of a rectangle, 2.6 cm by 1.4 cm.

12. The diameter of a circle is 9 m. Find the circumference. Use 3.14 for π.

Find the area of each figure. Use 3.14 for π.

13.

14.

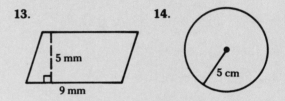

Use the diagram for exercises 15–16.

15. Find the surface area.

16. Find the volume.

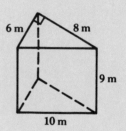

17. Simplify $\sqrt{80}$.

18. Give the sine of $\angle A$ as a ratio.

19. Lucy biked 12 km due south and then 16 km due east. How far was she from her starting point?

Unit 6

Chapter 16 Statistics and Graphs

Collecting and Organizing Data

Statistics are numerical facts, or **data,** that have been organized. A census or a sample often provides data.

A. A **census** is an examination or a count of everything that is to be studied. For example, if you wanted to know the favorite TV show of the students in your class, you would ask each student.

A **sample** is an examination of only a portion of the objects or people to be studied. To find the favorite TV show of the students in your school, you would probably ask a sample of the students. The sample should be representative of the whole school's preferences. For example, the school drama club would probably not be a representative sample for finding the favorite TV show of the students in your school.

● **Discuss** How would you pick a representative sample of the students in your school?

B. A **frequency table** is often used to show counts from either a census or a sample.

Juana took a census of the students in her math class. She made this frequency table to display the number of last names that begin with each letter.

Letter	Tally	Frequency
A	II	2
B	I	1
C		0
D	I	1
E		0
F	II	2
G	I	1
H	III	3
I		0
J		0
K		0
L	IIII	5
M	II	2
N	I	1
O	I	1
P	I	1
Q		0
R	II	2
S	IIII	4
T	I	1
U		0
V		0
W	III	3
X		0
Y	I	1
Z		0

In each case, tell whether you would use a census or a sample to find

1. the number of students in your math class who ride the school bus.

2. the number of students in your state who ride a school bus.

3. the favorite teacher in your school.

4. the number of hairs on your head.

5. the average monthly income in your community.

6. the most popular sport of the students in your science class.

Choose the sample that is more likely to be representative of the entire school population.

7. You wish to find the favorite subject of the students in your school. Should your sample be

   a. the band students, or
   b. the students whose last names begin with the letter *M*?

8. You wish to find the percent of honor-roll students in your school. Should your sample be

   a. the students in the library, or
   b. the students with locker numbers ending in 5?

9. Complete this frequency table of the number of birthdays in each month of the year for the students in your math class.

Month	Tally	Frequency
January		
February		
March		
April		
May		
June		

10. Make a frequency table of the number of boys and the number of girls in your math class.

11. Make a frequency table of these test grades.

    A, A, C, B, C, C, D, B, C, B, A, C, C, D, F, C, C, C, F, D, B, C

Many times, percents are calculated from the data in frequency tables. Find the missing percents.

Hair Color of Students in Art Class

	Color	Frequency	Percent
	Black	5	$15\frac{5}{8}\%$
★12.	Brown	14	
★13.	Auburn	4	
★14.	Red	2	
★15.	Blond	7	

Sample Statistics

A. For collecting data, a sample would be better to use than a census if the census would be

1. impossible.

2. possible, but too expensive.

3. destructive of what is being tested.

4. unnecessary, because a sample gives enough information.

B. In a sample, 1000 people were asked to name their favorite brand of rye bread. The results are given below.

Favorite Rye Breads

Brand name	Percent of sample
Porter's Rye Bread	46%
Fresh-Baked Rye Bread	24%
Pearlman's Rye Bread	20%
Century Rye Bread	11%

Mr. Juarez orders 2200 loaves of rye bread each week for Sunshine Supermarket. He orders the four brands named above. Based on the sample, how many loaves of Porter's Rye Bread should he order?

Find 46% of 2200.

$$0.46(2200) = n$$

$$1012 = n$$

Mr. Juarez should order 1012 loaves of Porter's Rye Bread.

• **Discuss** Is the sum of the percents in the table 100%? What reason might there be for this?

Use one or more of the reasons given in example A to tell why a sample would be preferable to a census in each situation.

1. Testing the water in a pool for chlorine content

2. Mailing tubes of toothpaste to people to get customer reactions

3. Taking a public-opinion poll of the President's popularity

4. Seeing if the soup needs more salt

5. Testing the safety of a new jet engine

6. Testing a patient's blood

Use the table in example B for exercises 7–11.

When Mr. Juarez orders 2200 loaves of rye bread, about how many loaves should be

7. Fresh-Baked Rye Bread?

8. Pearlman's Rye Bread?

9. Century Rye Bread?

★10. 25 of the people who named Pearlman's Rye Bread prefer it without seeds. What percent of the sample is this?

★11. When Mr. Juarez orders from Pearlman's, how many loaves should be with seeds and how many should be without seeds?

Keeping Skillful

Do these ratios form a proportion? Write *yes* or *no.*

1. $\dfrac{2}{3}$ $\dfrac{12}{18}$ 2. $\dfrac{21}{28}$ $\dfrac{3}{4}$

3. $\dfrac{36}{48}$ $\dfrac{9}{16}$ 4. $\dfrac{8}{9}$ $\dfrac{56}{72}$

5. $\dfrac{8}{12}$ $\dfrac{10}{15}$ 6. $\dfrac{8}{5}$ $\dfrac{40}{30}$

7. $\dfrac{33}{44}$ $\dfrac{9}{10}$ 8. $\dfrac{33}{22}$ $\dfrac{9}{6}$

9. $\dfrac{5}{0.2}$ $\dfrac{25}{1}$ 10. $\dfrac{0.5}{0.8}$ $\dfrac{0.25}{4}$

Solve each proportion.

11. $\dfrac{3}{8} = \dfrac{x}{32}$ 12. $\dfrac{4}{5} = \dfrac{24}{r}$

13. $\dfrac{15}{21} = \dfrac{5}{t}$ 14. $\dfrac{36}{27} = \dfrac{n}{18}$

15. $\dfrac{8}{17} = \dfrac{s}{34}$ 16. $\dfrac{k}{9} = \dfrac{16}{72}$

17. $\dfrac{4}{n} = \dfrac{48}{60}$ 18. $\dfrac{z}{18} = \dfrac{18}{12}$

19. $\dfrac{54}{a} = \dfrac{6}{8}$ 20. $\dfrac{c}{0.6} = \dfrac{1}{1.5}$

21. $\dfrac{7.2}{2.7} = \dfrac{1.6}{d}$ 22. $\dfrac{3.6}{9} = \dfrac{4.8}{f}$

Mean, Median, and Mode

Mean, median, and mode are three statistical measures used to give a quick description of a set of data.

A. **Mean** is another name for "average." To find the mean of a set of numbers, first find the sum of the numbers. Then divide by the number of numbers.

Find the mean of the estimated earnings of the athletes listed in this table.

Estimated Earnings of Athletes—1977

Athlete	Sport	Earnings
Jimmy Connors	Tennis	$922,000
Chris Evert	Tennis	$503,000
Anders Hedbarg	Hockey	$500,000
Bob Lanier	Basketball	$450,000
Bob McAdoo	Basketball	$500,000
Ulf Nilsson	Hockey	$500,000
Bobby Orr	Hockey	$600,000
Mike Schmidt	Baseball	$560,000
O. J. Simpson	Football	$733,000

The sum of the earnings is $5,268,000. Divide the sum by 9, the number of athletes listed.

$$9\overline{)5268000}^{\textstyle 585333\frac{1}{3}}$$

The mean of the estimated earnings is about $585,333.

B. The **median** is the middle value of a set of data when the numbers are listed in order.

Find the median of the estimated earnings of the athletes listed in the table.

$450,000   Arrange the earnings in order.
$500,000
$500,000
$500,000
$503,000   Find the middle number.
$560,000
$600,000
$733,000
$922,000

The median is $503,000.

C. When a set of data has an even number of numbers, the median is the average of the two middle numbers.

Find the median of this set of numbers.

3, 4, 6, 9, 12, 13, 16, 18

The numbers are listed in order. There are two numbers in the middle, 9 and 12.

$9 + 12 = 21$ Find the average of 9 and 12.
$21 \div 2 = 10\frac{1}{2}$

The median is $10\frac{1}{2}$.

D. The *mode* is the number that occurs most often in a set of data. In the list of athletes' earnings, the mode is $500,000.

E. In some sets of data, there is no mode. This set of data has no mode.

16, 17, 19, 24, 29, 36, 38, 46

Sometimes there are two or more modes. This set of data has two modes.

3, 5, 5, 6, 7, 8, 8, 9, 14, 16

This set of data shows the number of games played in each World Series for the years 1956–1979.

7, 7, 7, 6, 7, 5, 7, 4, 7, 7, 4, 7, 7, 5, 5, 7, 7, 7, 5, 7, 4, 6, 6, 7

Find the

1. mean.   2. median.   3. mode.

Here are the scores of each winning team in the Super Bowls for the years 1970–1979.

23, 16, 24, 14, 24, 16, 21, 32, 27, 35

Find the

4. mean.   5. median.   6. mode.

Here are the average speeds (in kilometers per hour) of the winning cars at the Indianapolis Speedway for the years 1967–1979.

242, 245, 251, 249, 252, 262, 254, 254, 239, 238, 258, 258, 254

Find the

7. mean.   8. median.   9. mode.

Here are the approximate seating capacities of the seven largest baseball stadiums.

56,000; 60,000; 58,700; 58,000; 76,700; 57,100; 59,100

Find the

10. mean.   11. median.   12. mode.

More practice
Set 47, page 413

335

Range

The *range* of a set of data is the difference between the least and the greatest numbers in the data.

Maximum Recorded Life Spans of Animals

Column 1		Column 2	
Horse	46 years	Parakeet	25 years
Orangutan	54 years	Trout	41 years
Mussel	60 years	Hippopotamus	51 years
Condor	72 years	Whale	87 years
Turtle	88 years	Tortoise	116 years
Mean life span: 64 years		**Mean life span: 64 years**	

The ages in column 1 go from 46 years through 88 years, so the range is 88 − 46, or 42 years.

The ages in column 2 go from 25 years through 116 years, so the range is 116 − 25, or 91 years.

Even though the sets of data in the table have the same mean, the life spans in column 2 have the greater range.

Find the range of each set of data.

1. 5, 9, 7, 22, 14, 4, 36, 7, 7, 8
2. 51, 66, 44, 87, 62, 33, 47, 41
3. 4.2, 5.9, 0.4, 3.9, 5.0, 7.0, 4.1
4. 4.98, 0.03, 2.11, 123.42, 0.20

5.

Animal	Adult length (without tail)
Red spider monkey	62 cm
Gorilla	180 cm
Chacma baboon	105 cm
Orangutan	150 cm
Chimpanzee	68 cm

6.

Animal	Adult weight
Puma	105 kg
Leopard	90 kg
Tiger	270 kg
Lion	225 kg
Cheetah	65 kg

7.

Animal	Length of newborn
Bottle-nosed dolphin	1.05 m
Humpback whale	3.90 m
Blue whale	7.50 m

*8.

Animal	Adult weight
Flying lemur	1.8 kg
Flying fox	0.9 kg
Vampire bat	42.0 g

Lab Activity

Collecting and Organizing Data

1. Get a copy of your local newspaper. Find an article about your city or town and another article from the sports section.

2. For each article, count and then list the number of letters in each of the first 50 words.

3. Now record your data in a frequency table like this.

Size of word	News article		Sports article	
	Tally	Frequency	Tally	Frequency
1 letter				
2 letters				
3 letters				
4 letters				
5 letters				
6 letters				
7 letters				
8 letters				
More than 8 letters				

4. For each article, list the number of letters in each of the 50 words from the least to the greatest. (Each list should have 50 numbers.)

5. For each list, find the mean, the median, the mode, and the range.

337

Bar Graphs

Many kinds of graphs are used to picture data.

This **bar graph** shows some of the weather conditions during a recent year for Indianapolis, Indiana. There were about 97 clear days.

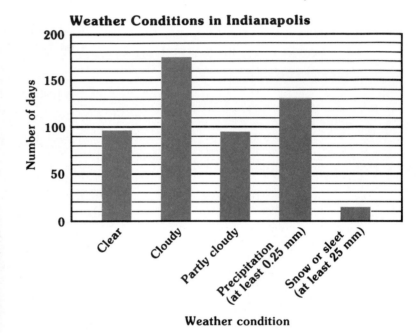

Weather Conditions in Indianapolis

Number of days

Weather condition

Approximately how many days

1. were cloudy?
2. were partly cloudy?
3. had at least 0.25 mm of precipitation?
4. had at least 25 mm of snow or sleet?

5. During a recent year in Dallas, Texas, there were 135 clear days, 121 cloudy days, 109 partly cloudy days, 68 days with at least 0.25 mm of precipitation, and 2 days with at least 25 mm of snow or sleet. Make a bar graph.

This graph shows the duration of sunlight for Boston, Massachusetts. On January 1, the sun rises at about 7:15 A.M. and sets at about 4:20 P.M.

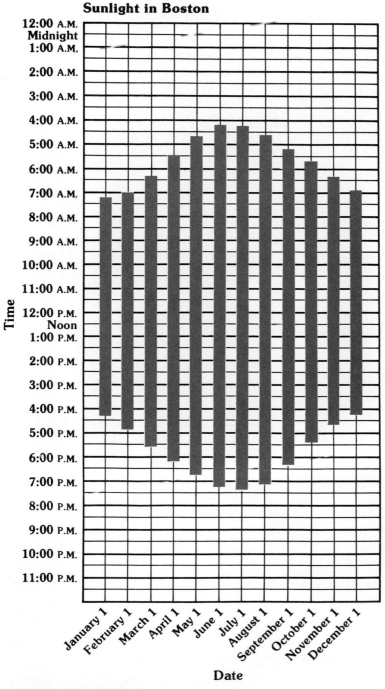

Sunlight in Boston

6. For each of the other dates shown on the bar graph for Boston, give the approximate times of sunrise and sunset.

Which of the dates shown has

7. the latest sunrise?

8. the earliest sunset?

9. the longest day?

10. Make a bar graph showing these hours of sunlight in Kingston, Ontario.

Date	Times
Jan. 1	7:43–4:36
Feb. 1	7:26–5:13
Mar. 1	6:44–5:53
Apr. 1	5:49–6:32
May 1	4:56–7:11
June 1	4:23–7:44
July 1	4:24–7:56
Aug. 1	4:50–7:33
Sept. 1	5:28–6:44
Oct. 1	6:03–5:48
Nov. 1	6:43–4:55
Dec. 1	7:23–4:27

Broken-Line Graphs

Changes in data over a period of time can be pictured in a **broken-line graph.**

This graph shows the increase in the average number of daily telephone conversations in the United States.

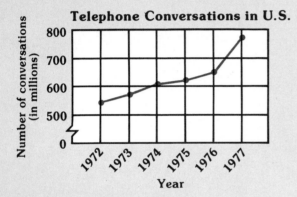

About how many daily telephone conversations were there in

1. 1972?   2. 1974?   3. 1976?

During what year was there

4. the smallest increase in the number of phone conversations?

5. the largest increase in the number of phone conversations?

6. This table shows the number of telephones in the town of Poplar Creek. Make a broken-line graph.

Year	Number of telephones
1973	34,482
1974	35,209
1975	35,003
1976	37,880
1977	40,582
1978	41,830
1979	43,716

These graphs show the average number of daily telephone calls for the first six months of the year at the Dorman Company. The red graph shows the number of incoming calls. The blue graph shows the number of outgoing calls.

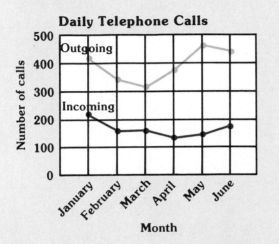

Daily Telephone Calls

Number of calls (y-axis): 0, 100, 200, 300, 400, 500

Month (x-axis): January, February, March, April, May, June

Outgoing

Incoming

About how many incoming calls were there per day in

7. January?   8. March?

About how many outgoing calls were there per day in

9. February?   10. June?

11. During what month were there about 380 outgoing calls per day?

12. During what month were there about 140 incoming calls per day?

*13. Estimate the total number of daily telephone calls at the Dorman Company for each month.

14. Mrs. Lin recorded the amount of time each of her children spent on the telephone. Here are her results for one week. Make a broken-line graph.

Day	Number of minutes Sue talked	Number of minutes Lee talked
Sunday	65	30
Monday	20	0
Tuesday	16	21
Wednesday	38	16
Thursday	45	8
Friday	52	35
Saturday	74	18

Circle Graphs

Circle graphs are often used to picture percents.

Meredith used the data in the table below to make a circle graph.

Commercial Television Broadcasting

Type of broadcast	Percent of broadcast time (6:00 A.M. to midnight)
News	9%
Public affairs	4%
Advertising	12%
Entertainment and sports	75%

First, she computed the size of each central angle for the graph. Remember, there are 360° in a circle.

News $\quad\quad\quad$ $0.09(360°) = 32.4° \approx 32°$

Public affairs $\quad$ $0.04(360°) = 14.4° \approx 14°$

Advertising $\quad\quad$ $0.12(360°) = 43.2° \approx 43°$

Entertainment
and sports $\quad\quad$ $0.75(360°) = 270°$

Then Meredith drew a circle and one radius. She used a protractor to draw the central angles. Here is her completed graph.

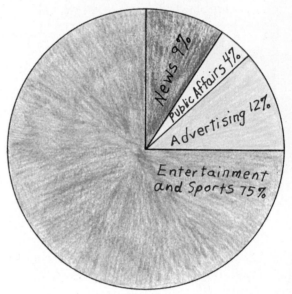

Commercial Television Broadcasting

News 9%
Public Affairs 4%
Advertising 12%
Entertainment and Sports 75%

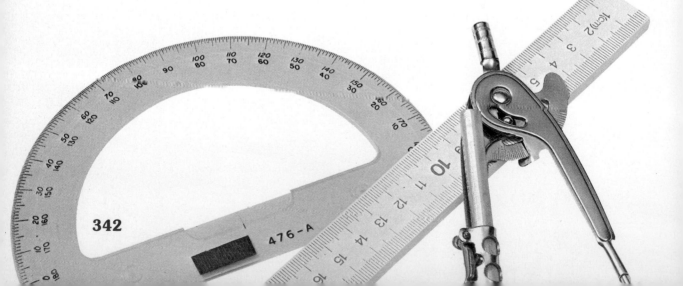

476-A

There are 18 hours of broadcast time each day.
Use the information on page 342 to find how many
hours are spent broadcasting

1. news. (Find 9% of 18 hours.)   2. public affairs.   3. advertising.

4. entertainment and sports.   *5. all programing except advertising.

This circle graph shows how Louise's
Foods spent about $45,000,000 for
television advertising. About how much
money was spent to advertise on

6. daytime programing?

7. news broadcasts?

8. weekend sports shows?

9. evening dramas?

10. situation comedies?

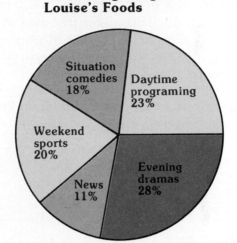

Advertising Budget for Louise's Foods

Julio polled 500 students to find their
favorite type of television program.
Complete this table. Round each
percent to the nearest whole percent.

TV Preferences of 500 Students

Type of program	Number of votes	Percent of votes
Sports	104	21% (___%___ of 500 is 104.)
Drama	66	11.
Game shows	68	12.
Situation comedies	150	13.
Musical-variety	90	14.
News and information	22	15.

16. Make a circle graph to show Julio's results.

Predictions

A. In making predictions, statisticians sometimes plot points for the items of data as shown below. Then an attempt is made to draw a straight line as close to the points as possible. This line is called the **line of best fit.**

On the basis of the line of best fit for the graph below, a prediction was made that someone would swim the 100-meter freestyle in 50 seconds or less in 1976. Actually, Jim Montgomery of the United States swam 100 meters in 49.99 seconds at the 1976 Olympics.

Olympic Records for Men's 100-Meter Freestyle Swimming

Year	Time (seconds)
1948	57.3
1952	57.4
1956	55.4
1960	55.2
1964	53.4
1968	52.2
1972	51.2

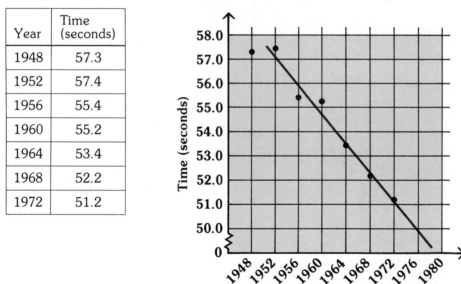

B. Predictions are often based on samples.

In a school of 2204 students, 40 students were selected at random. They were asked to name their favorite event in the Summer Olympics. Swimming was chosen by 17.5% of the sample. Predict how many students in the whole school would choose swimming.

Find 17.5% of 2204.

$$0.175(2204) = n$$

$$385.7 = n$$

About 386 students would choose swimming.

Use this table for exercises 1 and 2.

Olympic Records—Women's 400-Meter Freestyle

Year	Time (minutes and seconds)
1948	5:17.8
1952	5:12.1
1956	4:54.6
1960	4:50.6
1964	4:43.3
1968	4:31.8
1972	4:19.0

1. On grid paper, plot the points for the data in the table. Label the vertical axis with time in minutes and seconds: 4:05, 4:10, 4:15, . . . , 5:20.

2. Try to draw the line of best fit. Make a prediction for the winning time for 1976.

This table shows the favorite event of the Summer Olympics chosen by the sample of students in example B.

Event	Percent of sample
Swimming	17.5%
Diving	20%
Cycling	7.5%
Weight lifting	15.5%
Boxing	9.5%
Gymnastics	30%

Predict how many of the 2204 students in the school would choose

3. diving.   4. cycling.

5. weight lifting.   6. boxing.

7. gymnastics.   *8. a water sport.

Scattergrams and Correlations

A. Mr. Benson, the school counselor, listed the reading and mathematics scores for a class of 20 students. Then he plotted the ordered pairs (reading score, mathematics score) on a graph. For example, point A gives the location of (50, 38).

Reading	Math	Reading	Math
84	79	72	73
85	84	88	78
76	76	73	73
72	80	70	60
70	65	50	38
85	75	84	79
94	90	69	65
80	70	78	64
77	73	98	91
61	63	74	76

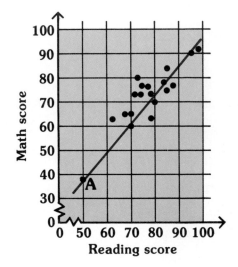

Such a graph is called a **scattergram.** The position of the points indicates how reading and mathematics scores are related.

This scattergram shows a **positive correlation.** In general terms, as the numbers in one set of data increase, the numbers in the other set also increase. If the line of best fit were drawn, the points would be close to the line and the line would slant upward from left to right.

B. This scattergram shows *negative correlation.* As the numbers in one set of data increase, the numbers in the other set decrease. The line of best fit slants downward from left to right.

You could expect a negative correlation in a graph that shows points for the ordered pairs (age of infant, hours of sleep).

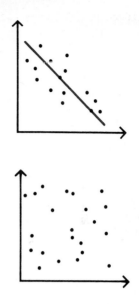

C. This scattergram shows no correlation. There is no definite pattern to the points.

You could expect no correlation in a graph that shows points for the ordered pairs (adult weight, phone bill).

What kind of correlation would you expect in scattergrams showing points for these ordered pairs?

1. (child's age, child's weight)

2. (weight of car, kilometers per liter)

3. (English score, weight)

4. (income, expenditures)

5. (altitude, moisture content of air)

6. (outdoor temperature, heating bill)

7. This table lists the speeds and life spans of nine animals. Plot a scattergram.

Speed (km/h)	80	18	40	72	0.25	40	0.4	20	22
Life span (years)	15	10	40	15	45	72	1	35	20

8. What kind of correlation does your graph suggest?

9. Twelve children ran a 50-meter race. Their ages in years and times in seconds are shown below. Plot a scattergram.

Age	Time	Age	Time
12	8.1	12	7.8
6	13.4	7	11.0
13	8.3	5	14.1
8	11.7	9	9.2
10	9.4	11	8.5
11	7.9	6	13.8

10. What kind of correlation does your graph suggest?

Interpreting Statistics

A. This advertisement is misleading because information is missing. Here are some examples of what "save 20%" might mean.

Save 20% of the original ticket price.

Save 20% of the ticket price when you buy two.

Save 20% of another airline's ticket price.

**Fly...
Celestial
Airlines**

Save 20%

B. This advertisement gives the mean salary, but this may be misleading. Suppose these are the salaries for the other salespeople.

$8000; $8000; $8000; $8000; $10,000; $60,000;
$8000; $8000; $8000; $8000; $10,000; $60,000;
$8000; $8000; $8000; $8000; $50,000; $74,000

The mean does not represent the typical salary. Either the mode or the median would be more representative of these salaries.

**Wanted:
SALESPERSON**

for

**Walter's Furniture
Store**

Good Benefits

**Average Salary
$20,000**

C. Each graph shows the increase in sales for a magazine.

Sports Weekly **Sales Rise Sharply**

Slow Growth for *Sports Weekly*

Each of the graphs above displays the data correctly. However, by adjusting the vertical scale, the impression given by each graph changes.

Explain what is missing in each of these advertising claims.

1. Has 25% less fat
2. Lasts 50% longer
3. Is 3 times thicker
4. Guaranteed for life

For each set of numbers, calculate the mean, median, and mode. Which of the three statistical measures is least representative of the data?

5. 30, 30, 30, 30, 30, 50, 50, 60, 200, 4000
6. 1400, 1400, 1700, 2400, 6200, 9200, 12,000
7. 200, 230, 250, 260, 270, 500, 500, 680, 800

Refer to the graphs in example C. Which graph do you think was prepared by

8. a sales executive of *Sports Weekly*?
9. a sales executive of a competing magazine?

Use the data in the table below to make a graph that should appeal to a sales representative from

*10. Wake-Up Cereal.
*11. a competing cereal company.

Sales of Wake-Up Breakfast Cereal

Year	Boxes sold (in millions)
1976	25
1977	23
1978	22
1979	20

Time Out

In 10 moves or less, rearrange the squares to form a well-known tongue twister.

You can slide the squares in the box, but you must not remove and replace any of them.

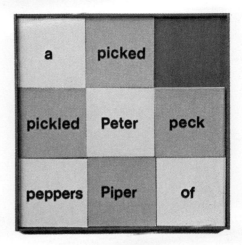

Quality-Control Engineer

Quality-control engineers use various statistical measures to see that products meet certain standards.

Ray Manatowa is a quality-control engineer in the packaging division of Crane Raisins. The boxes of raisins are to be filled to these specifications.

Mean weight	470 g
Expected weight	450–489 g
Guaranteed minimum weight	440 g

Once a month, a sample of 30 boxes is taken. Here is the graph Mr. Manatowa made last month from the list of weights. Four boxes weighed 440–449 g. Eight boxes weighed 470–479 g.

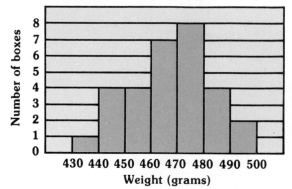

Weights of Sample Boxes

How many boxes weighed

1. 460–469 g?   2. less than 480 g?

What percent of the boxes weighed

3. less than the guaranteed minimum weight?

4. less than the expected weight?

5. more than the expected weight?

About 54,000 boxes of raisins were packaged last month. Predict how many of these weighed

6. less than the guaranteed minimum weight.

7. more than the expected weight.

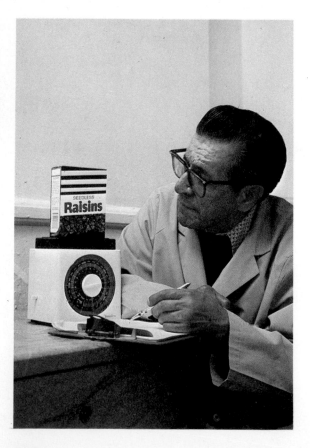

Chapter 16 Test
Statistics and Graphs, pages 330-350

1. Make a frequency table of these test grades.

   A, B, B, C, D, F, C, C, D,
   B, B, C, C, D, A, F, C, D

2. Suppose you wish to find the average number of seeds per orange in a crate of oranges. Would you use a census or sample?

Here are the weights in grams of the six puppies in Brownie's litter.

120, 115, 146, 140, 120, 124

Find the

3. mean.   4. median.

5. mode.   6. range.

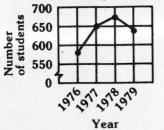

Average Daily Attendance at Cooper School

7. What was the average daily attendance for 1977?

8. In what year was the average daily attendance about 640?

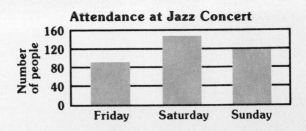

Attendance at Jazz Concert

9. How many people attended the concert on Sunday?

10. What day had the greatest attendance at the concert?

11. Cindy is making a circle graph to show how she spends her spare time. How many degrees should be in the part of her graph that represents 30% of her time?

12. In a sample of 120 students, 35% of the students speak at least two languages. Predict how many of the school's 1140 students speak at least two languages.

13. Does this scattergram suggest a positive correlation, a negative correlation, or no correlation?

14. For this data, find the mean, median, and mode. Then tell which is most representative of the data.

    20, 25, 25, 26, 37, 47, 51

Chapter 17   Probability

Counting and Tree Diagrams

Michelle and Craig Hahn own a farm. Each year they plant one of three crops: beans B, corn C, or wheat W. Corn is harsh on the soil, so after planting corn, they always plant beans the next year. After planting wheat, they plant only beans or wheat. After planting beans, they can plant any of the three crops.

This year, their crop is wheat. To count the crop choices for the next three years, Michelle made a **tree diagram.** She found that there are 11 possible **outcomes.**

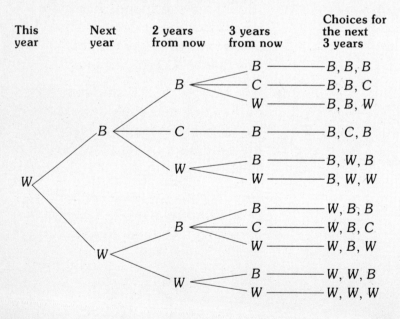

This year	Next year	2 years from now	3 years from now	Choices for the next 3 years
			B	B, B, B
		B	C	B, B, C
			W	B, B, W
	B	C	B	B, C, B
			B	B, W, B
		W	W	B, W, W
W			B	W, B, B
		B	C	W, B, C
			W	W, B, W
	W		B	W, W, B
		W	W	W, W, W

How many crop choices for the
3 years after planting wheat have

1. all 3 crops alike?

2. at least 2 crops alike?

3. 3 different crops?

4. beans occurring at least once?

5. corn occurring at least once?

6. wheat occurring at least once?

7. Make a tree diagram to show the crop choices for 3 years after planting beans.

8. How many possible crop choices are there for the 3 years after planting beans?

How many crop choices for the
3 years after planting beans have

9. 3 different crops?

10. at least 2 crops alike?

11. corn occurring at least once?

12. Make a tree diagram to show the crop choices for the 3 years after planting corn.

13. If it is decided not to plant the same crop 3 years in a row, how many possible crop choices are there for the 3 years after planting beans?

Louise L, Alice A, and Clem C are going to play Chinese checkers. They started a tree diagram showing the possible outcomes for 2 games.

Winner of the first game	Winner of the second game	Possible outcomes for 2 games

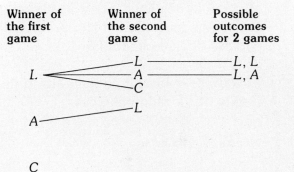

14. Complete the diagram.

15. How many possible outcomes are there?

16. Guess the number of possible outcomes for 3 games. Make a tree diagram to verify your guess.

*17. Guess the number of possible outcomes for 4 games.

Tex can travel from El Paso to New Orleans by bus, train, or airplane. He can travel from New Orleans to Tampico, Mexico, by airplane or ship.

18. How many choices for the trip to Tampico are there?

19. Tex can continue on to Veracruz, Mexico, by bus, airplane, or ship. How many possible travel choices are there for the trip from El Paso to Veracruz via New Orleans and Tampico?

353

Counting: Multiplication

A. A bowling team bowls on Mondays and Thursdays. Vista Alleys, Topple Ten, and Midway Lanes have alleys available on Mondays and Thursdays. How many possible location choices does the team have?

Alexandra made a tree diagram to find the total number of location choices.

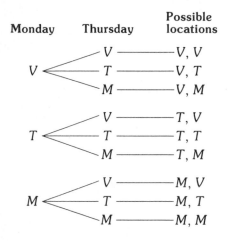

| | | Possible |
| Monday | Thursday | locations |

```
        V ——————— V, V
V <     T ——————— V, T
        M ——————— V, M

        V ——————— T, V
T <     T ——————— T, T
        M ——————— T, M

        V ——————— M, V
M <     T ——————— M, T
        M ——————— M, M
```

Marion found the total number of location choices by multiplying.

Number of choices for Monday	Number of choices for Thursday	Total number of possible locations
3 ×	**3** =	**9**

Both Alexandra and Marion found that there were 9 possible location choices.

■ *If successive choices are to be made, then the total number of choices can be found by multiplying the number of choices at each stage.*

B. Moss has 4 bowling trophies that he plans to display on a shelf. In how many ways can he arrange the trophies on the shelf?

Number of choices for left	Number of choices for left center	Number of choices for right center	Number of choices for right	Total number of arrangements
4 ×	3 ×	2 ×	1 =	24

He can arrange the trophies 24 ways.

Multiply to find the answers.

1. Marion wants to have her new bowling ball coded with 3 different letters chosen from her first name. How many codes are possible?

Number of choices for the first letter	Number of choices for the second letter	Number of choices for the third letter	Total number of choices
▦ ×	▦ ×	▦ =	▦

How many codes can Marion make using the letters in her first name if she wants to use

2. any 3 letters?   3. 4 different letters?

4. any 4 letters?   5. 2 different letters?

How many codes can Alberto make using the letters in his first name if he wants to use

6. 3 different letters?   7. any 3 letters?

8. 4 different letters?   9. any 4 letters?

10. In how many ways can the team of Alexandra, Roger, Alberto, Marion, and Moss stand in a line to have their picture taken?

Measuring Chances

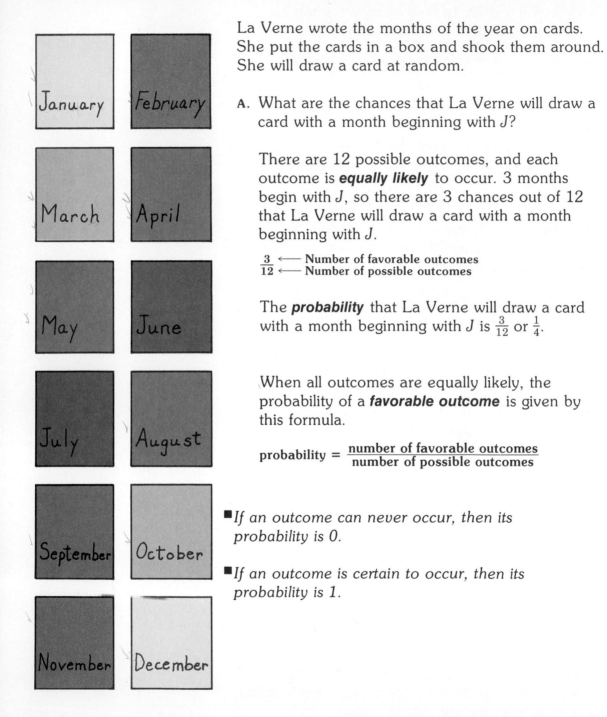

La Verne wrote the months of the year on cards. She put the cards in a box and shook them around. She will draw a card at random.

A. What are the chances that La Verne will draw a card with a month beginning with *J*?

There are 12 possible outcomes, and each outcome is **equally likely** to occur. 3 months begin with *J*, so there are 3 chances out of 12 that La Verne will draw a card with a month beginning with *J*.

$$\frac{3}{12} \begin{array}{l} \longleftarrow \text{ Number of favorable outcomes} \\ \longleftarrow \text{ Number of possible outcomes} \end{array}$$

The **probability** that La Verne will draw a card with a month beginning with *J* is $\frac{3}{12}$ or $\frac{1}{4}$.

When all outcomes are equally likely, the probability of a **favorable outcome** is given by this formula.

$$\text{probability} = \frac{\text{number of favorable outcomes}}{\text{number of possible outcomes}}$$

■ *If an outcome can never occur, then its probability is 0.*

■ *If an outcome is certain to occur, then its probability is 1.*

356

B. Find the probability that La Verne will draw a card with a month beginning with J, A, or M.

Again there are 12 possible outcomes, and each outcome is equally likely to occur. 3 months begin with J, 2 months begin with A, and 2 months begin with M. So there are 7 favorable outcomes.

$\dfrac{7}{12}$ ⟵ **Number of favorable outcomes**
⟵ **Number of possible outcomes**

The probability that La Verne will draw a card with a month beginning with J, A, or M is $\frac{7}{12}$.

Whenever a card is drawn, it is replaced before another is drawn. Find the probability of drawing a card showing a month that

1. begins with M.   **2.** begins with N.   **3.** begins with M or N.

4. ends in t.   **5.** ends in r.   **6.** ends in y.

7. ends in t, r, or y.   **8.** is 3 letters long.   **9.** is 5 letters long.

10. is 7 letters long.   **11.** is 9 letters long.   **12.** is 10 letters long.

13. is 3, 5, 7, or 9 letters long.   **14.** contains a letter of your name.

Lennie will draw a card showing a day of the week. Find the probability of drawing a card showing a day that

15. begins with T.   **16.** begins with S.   **17.** begins with S or T.

18. ends in y.   **19.** begins with M.   **20.** ends in r.

21. is 6 letters long.   **22.** is 9 letters long.   **23.** is 3 letters long.

24. is 3, 6, or 9 letters long.   **25.** begins with M or ends in y.

●**Discuss**   Can the probability of an outcome ever be less than 0? Can the probability of an outcome ever be greater than 1?

Computing Probabilities

Ms. Hubbard will choose 2 students at random from the orchestra to accompany her to the statewide music festival.

The name of each orchestra member is on a card. Ms. Hubbard will draw a card to select the first student. Then, without replacing the first card, she will draw a second card to select another student.

There are 49 students in the orchestra and 22 are violinists. Find the probability that both the students chosen are violinists.

First find the number of possible outcomes.

Number of choices for the first student	Number of choices for the second student	Number of possible outcomes
49	× **48**	= **2352**

There are 2352 possible outcomes.

Next find the number of favorable outcomes.

Number of choices of a violinist for the first student	Number of choices of a violinist for the second student	Number of favorable outcomes
22	× **21**	= **462**

There are 462 favorable outcomes.

All the outcomes are equally likely.

$$\text{probability} = \frac{\text{number of favorable outcomes}}{\text{number of possible outcomes}}$$

The probability that both students chosen are violinists is $\frac{462}{2352}$ or $\frac{11}{56}$.

Use the information in this table to help you answer the exercises.

Number of Students in the Orchestra

	Seventh graders	Eighth graders
Boys	12	14
Girls	7	16

Suppose that only eighth graders can attend the festival. Answer exercises 1–5 to find the probability that both students chosen from among the eighth graders are boys.

1. How many eighth graders are in the orchestra?

2. Find the number of possible outcomes.

3. How many eighth-grade boys are in the orchestra?

4. Find the number of favorable outcomes.

5. Find the probability that both students chosen are eighth-grade boys.

6. Suppose that only seventh graders can attend the festival. Find the probability that both students chosen from among the seventh graders are girls.

7. Suppose that only girls can attend the festival. Find the probability that the first student chosen from among the girls is an eighth-grade girl.

8. Suppose that only boys can attend the festival. Find the probability that the first student chosen from among the boys is a seventh-grade boy.

In the orchestra, 20 members play wind instruments and 7 members play percussion instruments. If all members are eligible to attend the festival, find the probability that

9. both students chosen play wind instruments.

10. both students chosen play percussion instruments.

Suppose that all the orchestra members are eligible to attend the festival. Find the probability that

11. both students chosen are boys.

12. both students chosen are girls.

13. the first student chosen is a boy and the second student chosen is a girl.

14. the first student chosen is a girl and the second student chosen is a boy.

15. the first student chosen is a seventh grader and the second student chosen is an eighth grader.

16. the first student chosen is an eighth grader and the second student chosen is a seventh grader.

359

Making Predictions

Probabilities can help you make predictions about future events.

Wendy wants to predict the number of times she will get a two-digit number in 25 spins.

First, she computes the probability that the spinner will stop on a two-digit number.

$\frac{11}{20}$ ←—— **Number of favorable outcomes**
←—— **Number of possible outcomes**

Then, she multiplies the probability and the number of spins to find the **expected number** of favorable outcomes.

Probability of getting a two-digit number	Number of spins	Expected number of favorable outcomes

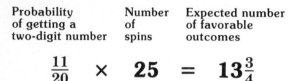

$$\frac{11}{20} \times 25 = 13\frac{3}{4}$$

Wendy predicts that the spinner will stop on a two-digit number about 14 times.

On a single spin, find the probability of getting

1. an even number.
2. a single-digit number.
3. a number in the blue sector.
4. a number that has a factor of 3.
5. a number with 1 for one of its digits.

Predict the number of times you would get

6. an even number in 40 spins.
7. a single-digit number in 60 spins.
8. a number in the blue sector in 35 spins.
9. a number that has a factor of 3 in 48 spins.
10. a number with 5 for one of its digits in 80 spins.
11. a prime number in 75 spins.

The manager of the Silver Dollar Restaurant knows
that about 75% of the customers order a baked potato.

12. What is the probability that a customer selected at random will order a baked potato?

13. What is the expected number of baked potatoes needed to serve 250 customers?

● *Discuss* Is the expected number of favorable outcomes usually obtained?

Lab Activity

Probability in Guessing

Just for fun, take this multiple-choice test.

1. Mildred "Babe" Didrikson won the 1932 Olympic Javelin Throw with a throw of
  a. 142 ft. 11 in.   **b.** 143 ft. 4 in.   **c.** 144 ft. 6 in.

2. The *kantar* is a unit of weight in Turkey which is equivalent to
  a. 124.45 lb.   **b.** 124.54 lb.   **c.** 125.44 lb.

3. The capital city of the Republic of Nauru is
  a. Renar.   **b.** Yaren.   **c.** Areyn.

4. The seventeenth longest railway tunnel in the world is named
  a. Ricken.   **b.** Otira.   **c.** Tauem.

5. The U.S. Curling Champion in 1971 was
  a. LaBonte   **b.** Brunson.   **c.** Dalziel.

6. A color not found in the flag of the Republic of Djibouti is
  a. yellow.   **b.** green.   **c.** red.

7. The Department of the Interior was created by Congress on
  a. January 14, 1849.   **b.** March 3, 1849.
  c. April 9, 1849.

8. The number of votes McGovern received in 1972 in Adams County, Idaho, was
  a. 347.   **b.** 319.   **c.** 293.

9. Ronveig Ernst recently moved to New Mexico from
  a. Wisconsin.   **b.** Ohio.   **c.** Illinois.

1. What is the probability of guessing correctly on any one item on this test?

2. What is the expected number of correct answers?

3. The answers are at the bottom of this page. Did you get the expected number of correct answers?

4. Find the expected number of correct answers for the entire class.

5. Find the actual number of correct answers in the entire class. How does this number compare with your answer to exercise 4?

Answers: 1. b   **2.** a   **3.** b   **4.** c   **5.** c   **6.** a   **7.** b   **8.** c   **9.** a

361

Career

Simulation Consultant

You know there are ten digits: 0, 1, 2, 3, 4, 5, 6, 7, 8, and 9. Suppose ten cards are placed in a hat with a different digit written on each card. If you were to draw a card, record its digit, replace it, scramble the cards, draw again, and so on, you would get a **table of random digits.** Here is such a table.

```
1 9 1 0 3 8 8 3 4 4 3 7 2 1 3 9 0 2 3 5 5 3 2 2
7 9 5 1 6 7 8 8 3 5 3 1 4 3 6 5 0 2 6 1 7 1 3 3
5 2 8 4 3 3 7 3 1 0 5 2 6 9 2 0 1 0 5 4 7 0 7 1
3 1 2 3 9 1 6 3 5 8 1 6 8 3 5 5 3 4 7 9 5 5 2 8
2 0 0 4 6 3 9 0 2 2 4 4 0 7 6 1 3 5 8 2 3 8 8 4
4 3 0 0 1 9 9 0 7 4 3 7 1 8 0 1 9 5 7 0 2 3 0 0
2 2 7 6 3 9 6 8 5 3 6 4 2 2 2 5 6 2 9 8 8 6 3 5
9 5 6 6 7 5 0 6 4 8 8 6 7 5 4 2 0 7 0 8 3 5 2 8
4 1 2 0 2 4 5 9 1 1 0 1 1 1 3 6 6 8 6 5 8 9 9 8
7 5 4 7 5 6 8 8 7 9 6 5 5 9 6 3 9 2 6 8 8 2 6 3
1 0 1 4 5 7 0 0 8 6 9 1 2 8 2 9 8 3 3 0 2 3 6 5
3 9 2 3 3 5 8 1 9 0 9 9 5 0 5 0 7 3 5 0 3 7 7 5
3 1 5 9 5 7 6 5 8 3 3 3 7 4 1 8 8 5 2 7 1 5 4 2
6 4 7 0 4 8 7 9 9 5 6 9 7 9 3 9 7 9 5 6 8 5 1 2
9 2 3 4 7 9 7 6 9 9 0 5 3 1 1 6 5 8 2 8 4 8 0 5
```

Nick Caruso uses tables of random digits in his job as a simulation consultant. Simulate means imitate.

A baseball coach asks Mr. Caruso how likely it is for a player who hits 0.400, or 40%, to get a hit three or more times in a row.

Since there are ten digits, Mr. Caruso picks the first four digits (0, 1, 2, and 3) to represent "hits." This mimics the 0.400, or 40%. Then he circles the "hits" in the table.

For the first 120 digits, the following hits are circled.

This simulation of 120 times at bat shows that the coach can expect the player to get three or more hits in sequence about 10 times. A better estimate would use more numbers from the table.

1. What is the longest string of hits that seems likely in 120 times at bat?

2. Did the "player" ever go four times to bat without a hit?

3. Use the entire table of random digits. Now what is the longest string of hits that seems likely?

4. Use the columns of the entire table instead of the rows. What is the longest string of hits that seems likely?

5. For a player who hits 0.250, or 25%, Mr. Caruso ignores the digits 0 and 1 so that he can work with eight digits. He calls 2 and 3 "hits" to simulate 25%. Refer to all the rows of the table of random digits and use simulation. What is the longest string of hits that seems likely?

Many manufacturers test a sample, or portion, of their products.

A tire manufacturer wants to test 1% of the tires as they come off the line. Rather than take every 100th tire, he asks Mr. Caruso to advise him on how to take a 1% sample randomly.

If the table of random digits were printed with the digits paired, the table would have random numbers from 00 through 99. The first two rows of the table would appear as follows.

```
19 10 38 83 44 37 21 39 02 35 53 22
79 51 67 88 35 31 43 65 02 61 71 33
```

Referring to this new table, the first tire that comes off the line is assigned the number 19, the second tire is assigned the number 10, and so on. Mr. Caruso decides that every tire numbered 44 will be tested. Since 44 is one of the 100 numbers from 00 through 99, it should appear about 1% of the time in a very large table of random digits.

6. The fifth tire is numbered 44, so it will be tested. What is the next tire that will be tested?

7. Pick your own number between 00 and 99. Which tires would you check?

8. Suppose every tire numbered 75 will be tested. What are the first four tires that will be tested?

9. Describe how to choose a random 2% sample.

Multiplying Probabilities: Independent Choices

Mr. Kenoi has 14 girls and 10 boys in his class. Each day, he chooses a student at random to help him. Each choice is **independent** because a choice any one day has no effect on the choice of any other day.

A. What is the probability that a girl will be chosen two days in a row?

The probability of choosing a girl on any one day is $\frac{14}{24}$ or $\frac{7}{12}$.

Multiply this probability by itself to find the chances that a girl will be chosen two days in a row.

Probability of choosing a girl one day	Probability of choosing a girl the next day	Probability of choosing a girl both days
$\frac{7}{12}$ $\times$	$\frac{7}{12}$ $=$	$\frac{49}{144}$

The probability of choosing a girl two days in a row is $\frac{49}{144}$.

B. What is the probability that a boy will be chosen one day and a girl the next day?

The probability of choosing a boy on any one day is $\frac{10}{24}$ or $\frac{5}{12}$.

The probability of choosing a girl on any one day is $\frac{14}{24}$ or $\frac{7}{12}$.

Multiply these probabilities.

$$\frac{5}{12} \times \frac{7}{12} = \frac{35}{144}$$

The probability of choosing a boy one day and a girl the next day is $\frac{35}{144}$.

In Mr. Kenoi's class, what is the probability that

1. the helper will be a boy two days in a row?
2. the helper will be a girl three days in a row?
3. the helper will be a boy three days in a row?
4. the helper will be a girl one day and a boy the next two days?

One day, 2 girls and 2 boys were absent.

5. What is the probability that the helper was a girl?
6. The next day, the same people were absent. What is the probability that the helper both days was a girl?

Lisa put the six cards in a bag. She drew one, replaced it, and drew another card. What is the probability that

7. both cards showed the letter P?
8. both cards showed the letter E?
9. both cards showed the letter R?
10. after three draws, all draws showed E?
11. after three draws, all draws showed R?
12. after three draws, all draws showed P?
13. the first draw showed E, the second draw showed P, and the third draw showed R?

Time Out

There are 3 big boxes of books high on a shelf in a storeroom.

They are labeled as shown.

The principal has been told that all three labels are wrong.

After a bit of thought, he took one book from one of the boxes and looked at its title. Then he was able to put the right label on each box.

From which box did he take the book?

365

Multiplying Probabilities: Dependent Choices

The table shows the number of students in a tennis tournament. The tournament schedule is set by selecting each of the 36 players at random.

Tennis Tournament

	Seventh graders	Eighth graders
Boys	6	10
Girls	8	12

Find the probability that the first two players selected are eighth-grade girls.

The probability of selecting an eighth-grade girl on the first draw is $\frac{12}{36}$ or $\frac{1}{3}$.

If an eighth-grade girl is selected on the first draw, there remain 35 students to be selected, 11 of whom are eighth-grade girls. Thus, the probability of selecting an eighth-grade girl this time is $\frac{11}{35}$.

Multiply these two probabilities.

$$\frac{1}{3} \times \frac{11}{35} = \frac{11}{105}$$

The probability that the first two players are eighth-grade girls is $\frac{11}{105}$.

Since the outcome of the first draw influences the outcome of the second draw, the two draws are **dependent**.

Use the table on page 366 for exercises 1–8. For the tennis tournament, what is the probability that

1. the first two players selected are seventh-grade boys?

2. the first two players selected are girls?

3. the first player selected is an eighth-grade boy and the second player selected is a seventh-grade girl?

4. the first player selected is a boy and the second player selected is a girl?

5. the first four players selected are eighth-grade girls?

6. the first two players selected are girls and the next two players selected are boys?

7. the first three players selected are girls and the fourth is a boy?

8. the first player selected is a seventh-grade girl, the second is an eighth-grade girl, and the next two are seventh-grade boys?

There is 1 white ball, 2 orange balls, and 3 yellow balls to use in one game. If used at random, what is the probability that

9. the first two balls used are orange?

10. the first ball used is white and the second ball used is yellow?

11. the first three balls used are yellow?

12. the first ball used is yellow, the second ball used is white, and the third ball used is orange?

*13. if 5 balls are used, the white ball is not used?

Probability

Once a probability problem is set up, use of a calculator can make the multiplications easier.

A. The combinations on the gym lockers at Hammerville Junior High have three numbers ranging from 0 to 39. For example, one combination is 13–36–27. If a combination is chosen at random from all possible combinations, what is the probability that the first two numbers are multiples of 11 and the third number is even?

Use your calculator to find this product.

Probability of multiple of 11		Probability of multiple of 11		Probability of even number
$\frac{3}{40}$	$\times$	$\frac{3}{40}$	$\times$	$\frac{1}{2}$

The probability is $\frac{9}{3200}$, or 0.0028125.

B. What is the probability that an archer with 90% accuracy will hit a bull's-eye 7 times in a row?

Use your calculator to find this product.

$(0.9)^7$

The probability is 0.4782969. It is not as likely as you might think!

Use your calculator to answer each question. Refer to example A for exercises 1–3.

1. If a combination is chosen at random from all those possible, what is the probability that each number contains the digit 3?

2. If a combination is chosen at random from all those possible, what is the probability that the first number is prime, the second number is odd, and the third number is a single digit?

3. What is the probability of correctly guessing a particular combination?

4. What is the probability, to the nearest thousandth, that an archer with 85% accuracy will hit a bull's-eye 4 times in a row? 5 times? 6 times? 7 times?

Chapter 17 Test
Probability, pages 352–368

1. A school cafeteria menu has the following items. A student chooses one item from each group. Make a tree diagram to show the possible luncheon choices.

Group A	Group B	Group C
Chicken leg	Lettuce salad	Apple
Tuna salad	Fruit gelatin	Banana
Hot dog		Orange

2. Carlota is choosing a pair of bowling shoes. In her size, the shoes come in 3 different styles and 5 different colors. Use multiplication to tell how many possible pairs of shoes she has to choose from.

A jar contains 100 pennies. 25 of the pennies are from the Denver mint, 65 are from the Philadelphia mint, and 10 are from the San Francisco mint.

Answer exercises 3–5 to find the probability that a penny drawn is from the Denver mint.

3. How many possible outcomes are there?

4. How many favorable outcomes are there?

5. What is the probability that a penny drawn is from the Denver mint?

Suppose that each time a penny is drawn, it is returned to the jar.

6. What is the probability that the first three pennies drawn are from the San Francisco mint?

7. What is the probability that the first penny drawn is from the Denver mint and the second is from the Philadelphia mint?

8. Find the expected number of pennies from the San Francisco mint you would get in 38 draws.

Danny has 50 light bulbs in a carton. He knows that 5 bulbs are defective, but the defective bulbs are not marked. He begins testing the bulbs. As he tests them he does not return them to the carton.

9. What is the probability that he selects a defective bulb on the first draw?

10. What is the probability that he selects a defective bulb on each of the first two draws?

Chapter 18 Algebra

Rational Numbers

A. Remember that the whole numbers and their opposites are *integers*.

The sum of an integer and its opposite is 0.

The opposite of 10 is -10.

$$10 + (-10) = 0$$

The opposite of -5 is 5.

$$-5 + 5 = 0$$

B. A *rational number* is a number that *can be written* as a quotient of two integers, with the divisor not equal to 0.

These numbers are rational.

$$\frac{2}{3} \quad \frac{5}{-6} \quad \frac{-16}{7} \quad \frac{0}{4} \quad \frac{-9}{-25} \quad \frac{3}{3}$$

C. Every integer is a rational number.

$$5 = \frac{5}{1} \quad -4 = \frac{-4}{1} \quad 0 = \frac{0}{1}$$

Mixed numbers and some decimals are also rational numbers.

$$2\frac{1}{2} = \frac{5}{2} \quad 0.7 = \frac{7}{10} \quad 0.\overline{3} = \frac{1}{3}$$

WELCOME TO THE LAND OF RATIONAL NUMBERS

CITY OF INTEGERS

Give each missing number.

1. $17 + \blacksquare = 0$ 2. $-1 + \blacksquare = 0$

3. $0 + \blacksquare = 0$ 4. $\blacksquare + (-6) = 0$

Write each number as a quotient of two integers.

5. 8   6. -5 7. 15

8. 0.3   9. 0.04   10. 1.2

11. 0.25   12. $1\frac{3}{4}$ 13. $3\frac{1}{5}$

14. $5\frac{1}{2}$ ★15. $0.\overline{6}$ ★16. $1.\overline{3}$

Write each number as a quotient of two integers in 3 different ways.

17. 5   18. -3 19. 1   20. 0

21. $3\frac{1}{3}$ 22. $1\frac{5}{6}$ 23. $4\frac{1}{4}$ 24. 1.8

For each number, write as many of these phrases as apply: *whole number, integer, rational number.*

Here's how

-13

integer, rational number

25. 22   26. -7 27. 0

28. 4.5   29. 8.0   30. $2.\overline{3}$

31. $10\frac{2}{7}$ 32. $\frac{-16}{-8}$ 33. $\frac{6}{6}$

Keeping Skillful

1. $-6 + 2$ 2. $8 + (-10)$

3. $9 + (-4)$ 4. $-8 + 13$

5. $-7 + (-19)$ 6. $-12 + (-9)$

7. $-47 + 92$ 8. $-63 + 15$

9. $-37 + (-46)$ 10. $75 + (-58)$

11. $8 - (-2)$ 12. $-6 - 9$

13. $-4 - (-3)$ 14. $-7 - 5$

15. $12 - 15$ 16. $-24 - 8$

17. $13 - (-28)$ 18. $-34 - (-16)$

19. $-53 - 29$ 20. $94 - (-18)$

21. $80 - 90$ 22. $-47 - 8$

23. $5(-6)$ 24. $(-8)(-3)$

25. $(-9)(7)$ 26. $(-12)(-4)$

27. $24(-11)$ 28. $(-32)(5)$

29. $(-18)(-6)$ 30. $7(-13)$

31. $14(22)$ 32. $(-60)(-8)$

33. $(-12) \div 4$ 34. $(-12) \div (-4)$

35. $20 \div (-5)$ 36. $(-20) \div (-5)$

37. $32 \div 16$ 38. $60 \div (-10)$

39. $(-34) \div 17$ 40. $63 \div (-7)$

41. $(-56) \div 8$ 42. $(-72) \div (-9)$

43. $(-51) \div (-3)$ 44. $51 \div 17$

Comparing and Ordering Rational Numbers

A. There are different ways to represent the same rational number.

$$\frac{8}{-2} = 8 \div (-2) = -4$$

$$-\frac{8}{2} = -(8 \div 2) = -4$$

$$\frac{-8}{2} = (-8) \div 2 = -4$$

So, $\frac{8}{-2} = -\frac{8}{2} = \frac{-8}{2}$.

> Each quotient equals −4.

B. $\frac{-8}{-2} = (-8) \div (-2) = 4$

$$\frac{8}{2} = 8 \div 2 = 4$$

So, $\frac{-8}{-2} = \frac{8}{2}$.

■ *Every rational number can be written with a positive denominator.*

C. Compare $\frac{3}{-4}$ and $\frac{-2}{3}$.

$$\frac{3}{-4} \quad \bullet \quad \frac{-2}{3}$$

$$\frac{-3}{4} \quad \bullet \quad \frac{-2}{3} \qquad \text{Write each number with a positive denominator.}$$

$$\frac{-9}{12} \quad \bullet \quad \frac{-8}{12} \qquad \text{Write the numbers with a common denominator.}$$

$$\frac{-9}{12} < \frac{-8}{12} \qquad \begin{array}{l}\text{Compare the numerators.}\\ -9 < -8\end{array}$$

$$\frac{3}{-4} < \frac{-2}{3}$$

D. Compare -1.5 and -2.4.

Think of a number line.

-1.5 is 1.5 units left of 0.
-2.4 is 2.4 units left of 0.

$$-2.4 < -1.5$$

E. List these numbers in order from the least to the greatest. $\frac{-2}{5}$ $\frac{7}{-15}$ $\frac{-1}{-6}$

$\frac{-2}{5}$ $\frac{7}{-15}$ $\frac{-1}{-6}$

$\frac{-2}{5}$ $\frac{-7}{15}$ $\frac{1}{6}$ Write each number with a positive denominator.

$\frac{-12}{30}$ $\frac{-14}{30}$ $\frac{5}{30}$ Write the numbers with a common denominator.

$\frac{-14}{30}$ $\frac{-12}{30}$ $\frac{5}{30}$ Write the numbers so that
  ↓   ↓   ↓   the numerators are in order.
                    $-14 < -12 < 5$

$\frac{7}{-15}$ $\frac{-2}{5}$ $\frac{-1}{-6}$ Write the original numbers in order.

Write each number with a positive denominator.

1. $\frac{6}{-3}$ **2.** $\frac{-10}{-2}$ **3.** $\frac{-12}{5}$ **4.** $\frac{3}{-4}$ **5.** $\frac{-7}{-9}$ **6.** $\frac{1}{-2}$ **7.** $\frac{-22}{-35}$ **8.** $\frac{-8}{11}$

Compare. Use >, <, or =.

9. $\frac{4}{-5}$ ⬤ $\frac{-3}{4}$ **10.** $\frac{-1}{3}$ ⬤ $\frac{-1}{-2}$ **11.** $\frac{2}{-5}$ ⬤ $\frac{-4}{10}$ **12.** $\frac{3}{-10}$ ⬤ $\frac{-4}{9}$

13. -2.1 ⬤ -1.2 **14.** -5.7 ⬤ -5.9 **15.** 3.4 ⬤ -3.4 **16.** -0.8 ⬤ -0.7

★17. -1.24 ⬤ -1.2 **★18.** -0.01 ⬤ -0.1 **★19.** $-1\frac{1}{3}$ ⬤ $-1\frac{1}{2}$ **★20.** $-4\frac{3}{4}$ ⬤ $-4\frac{1}{2}$

List the numbers in order from the least to the greatest.

21. $\frac{3}{-8}$ $\frac{-5}{6}$ $\frac{-3}{-4}$ **22.** $\frac{-1}{6}$ $\frac{1}{-5}$ $\frac{-1}{4}$ **23.** $\frac{-7}{-8}$ $\frac{6}{-4}$ $\frac{-1}{2}$

24. $\frac{4}{-5}$ $\frac{-2}{3}$ $\frac{11}{-15}$ **25.** $\frac{-5}{2}$ -2 $\frac{3}{-2}$ **26.** 0 $\frac{-1}{-2}$ $\frac{1}{-2}$

★27. -1.4 -1.7 -1.5 **★28.** $-3\frac{1}{2}$ $-3\frac{2}{3}$ -4 **★29.** $-8\frac{1}{5}$ $-7\frac{1}{8}$ -8

Adding and Subtracting Rational Numbers

A. Rational numbers can be added as you add fractions, using the usual sign rules for addition.

Find $\frac{-3}{8} + \frac{2}{-5}$.

$\frac{-3}{8} + \frac{2}{-5}$

$\frac{-3}{8} + \frac{-2}{5}$ Write each number with a positive denominator.

$\frac{-15}{40} + \frac{-16}{40}$ Write the numbers with a common denominator.

$\frac{-31}{40}$ or $-\frac{31}{40}$ Add.

B. Subtracting a number is the same as adding its opposite.

Find $\frac{-7}{8} - \frac{-2}{3}$.

$\frac{-7}{8} - \frac{-2}{3}$

$\frac{-7}{8} - \left(-\frac{2}{3}\right)$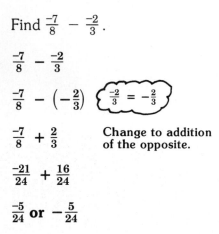

$\frac{-7}{8} + \frac{2}{3}$ Change to addition of the opposite.

$\frac{-21}{24} + \frac{16}{24}$

$\frac{-5}{24}$ or $-\frac{5}{24}$

C. Evaluate $t - \frac{5}{6}$ for $t = -\frac{4}{9}$.

$t - \frac{5}{6}$

$-\frac{4}{9} - \frac{5}{6}$ Substitute $-\frac{4}{9}$ for t.

$\frac{-4}{9} - \frac{5}{6}$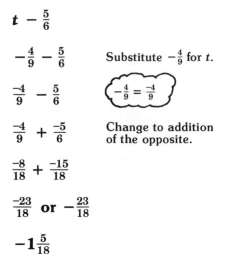

$\frac{-4}{9} + \frac{-5}{6}$ Change to addition of the opposite.

$\frac{-8}{18} + \frac{-15}{18}$

$\frac{-23}{18}$ or $-\frac{23}{18}$

$-1\frac{5}{18}$

D. Evaluate $-n - 1.4$ for $n = -3.7$.

$-n - 1.4$

$-(-3.7) - 1.4$

$3.7 - 1.4$ $-(-3.7)$ means "the opposite of -3.7."

$3.7 + (-1.4)$ Change to addition of the opposite.

2.3

374

Find each answer.

1. $\frac{-4}{5} + \frac{1}{-3}$

2. $\frac{-3}{4} + \frac{-1}{2}$

3. $\frac{3}{-8} + \frac{-1}{-4}$

4. $\frac{5}{-6} + \frac{2}{3}$

5. $\frac{2}{7} - \frac{5}{6}$

6. $\frac{-2}{5} - \frac{1}{4}$

7. $\frac{-1}{10} - \frac{-3}{5}$

8. $\frac{5}{9} - \frac{-1}{6}$

9. $\frac{7}{-8} + 1$

10. $-3 + \frac{-4}{9}$

11. $\frac{-15}{7} - 2$

12. $-\frac{1}{2} - 3$

13. $-5.2 + 1.4$

14. $2.8 - 9.1$

15. $-8 - 1.6$

16. $3.17 - (-4.35)$

★17. $-1\frac{1}{3} + \frac{3}{4}$

★18. $-2\frac{2}{5} - 3\frac{1}{2}$

★19. $6\frac{1}{8} - 9$

★20. $-1\frac{3}{8} + 4$

Evaluate each expression for $a = -\frac{3}{4}$.

21. $a + \frac{1}{5}$

22. $a - \frac{4}{7}$

23. $\frac{2}{3} + a$

24. $-a + \frac{1}{2}$

25. $-2 - a$

★26. $a + 1\frac{1}{2}$

★27. $a - 2\frac{2}{3}$

★28. $4\frac{3}{5} - a$

★29. $-1\frac{1}{6} - a$

★30. $-a - 4\frac{1}{8}$

Evaluate each expression for $s = -1.5$.

31. $s + 0.5$

32. $s - 1.25$

33. $-s - 0.67$

34. $0.4 + s$

Time Out

Toby will not fail to deny Moby's request for no pickles in his sandwich, if Moby forgets to wear sneakers that have no laces.

But Moby wears sneakers with laces. Will his sandwich have pickles?

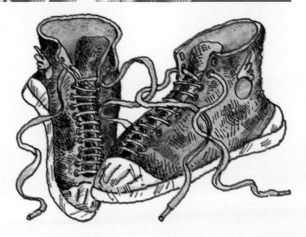

Solving Addition Equations

A. The water level in Timberlake Reservoir went down 52.1 cm in June. The total change in the water level for May and June together was −12.9 cm. Find the change in the water level for May.

May change	June change	Total change

$$c + (-52.1) = -12.9$$

Write an equation.

$$c + (-52.1) + 52.1 = -12.9 + 52.1$$

To get c by itself, add the opposite of −52.1 to both sides of the equation.

$$c + 0 = 39.2$$

$$c = 39.2$$

The water level rose 39.2 cm in May.

B. Solve $t + 8 = -2$.

$$t + 8 = -2$$
$$t + 8 + (-8) = -2 + (-8)$$
$$t + 0 = -10$$
$$t = -10$$

C. Solve $-1.5 + a = 2.3$.

$$-1.5 + a = 2.3$$
$$-1.5 + a + 1.5 = 2.3 + 1.5$$
$$a + 0 = 3.8$$
$$a = 3.8$$

Solve each equation.

1. $x + 9 = 7$ **2.** $-2 + a = 5$ **3.** $-8 + r = -11$ **4.** $v + 32 = -90$

5. $-4 + b = 2$ **6.** $-8 + p = -7$ **7.** $m + 5.5 = -4$ **8.** $16 + q = 13$

9. $-7 + c = 3$ **10.** $6 + n = -9$ **11.** $-3 + q = 7.6$ **12.** $-25 + d = -32$

13. $y + 1 = -5$ **14.** $v + 3.4 = 1$ **15.** $9.2 + x = 4.1$ **16.** $6.1 + z = 2.8$

17. $d + \frac{2}{3} = \frac{1}{2}$ **18.** $f + 5 = 1.7$ **19.** $\frac{-3}{8} + n = \frac{-1}{4}$ **20.** $\frac{8}{11} + a = -\frac{1}{2}$

21. $\frac{3}{4} + t = 0$ **22.** $\frac{-6}{7} + g = \frac{-3}{5}$ **23.** $\frac{3}{10} + b = -4$ **24.** $-5\frac{2}{3} + v = -2$

25. $\frac{7}{8} + z = -1$ **★26.** $k + 4\frac{1}{3} = 2\frac{1}{2}$ **★27.** $-1\frac{1}{4} + t = -7$ **★28.** $y + 8\frac{3}{4} = 5\frac{7}{8}$

Find each answer by solving an addition equation.

29. In a year's time, the water level in a reservoir dropped 99.26 cm. The level had risen 152 cm during the first half of the year. Find the change in the water level during the last half of the year.

30. Barbara's bank balance increased by $18.20 in two months. During the second month, her balance had decreased by $34.56. Find the change in her balance for the first month.

Solving Subtraction Equations

To solve a subtraction equation, first change
the subtraction to addition of the opposite.

A. Solve $x - 5 = -8$.

$$x - 5 = -8$$

$$x + (-5) = -8 \qquad \text{Change to addition of the opposite.}$$

$$x + (-5) + 5 = -8 + 5 \qquad \begin{array}{l}\text{To get } x \text{ by itself, add the opposite of } -5 \\ \text{to both sides of the equation.}\end{array}$$

$$x + 0 = -3$$

$$x = -3$$

B. Solve $2 - n = -7$.

$$2 - n = -7$$

$$2 + (-n) = -7 \qquad \text{Change to addition of the opposite.}$$

$$2 + (-n) + (-2) = -7 + (-2) \qquad \begin{array}{l}\text{To get } -n \text{ by itself, add the opposite of } 2 \\ \text{to both sides of the equation.}\end{array}$$

$$-n + 0 = -9$$

$$-n = -9 \qquad -n \text{ means "the opposite of } n\text{."}$$

$$n = 9 \qquad \begin{array}{l}\text{Since the opposite of } n \text{ is } -9, \\ n \text{ must be } 9.\end{array}$$

C. Solve $-4.8 - t = -1.6$.

$$-4.8 - t = -1.6$$

$$-4.8 + (-t) = -1.6$$

$$-4.8 + (-t) + 4.8 = -1.6 + 4.8$$

$$-t + 0 = 3.2$$

$$-t = 3.2$$

$$t = -3.2$$

Solve each equation.

1. $x - 3 = 2$ 2. $b - 12 = -5$

3. $n - 7 = -3$ 4. $r - 22 = -9$

5. $t - 4 = -6$ 6. $-5 - s = -4$

7. $y - 5 = 0$ 8. $1 - z = -10$

9. $9 - a = -1$ 10. $-14 - f = 8$

11. $-8 - d = 3$ 12. $-2 - w = -9$

13. $c - 8.2 = -2.6$

14. $g - (-0.5) = -0.2$

15. $k - 1.27 = 0.902$

16. $7.6 - m = -4.3$

17. $0.15 - w = -2.8$

18. $-5.9 - e = 3$

19. $x - \frac{3}{5} = -\frac{1}{4}$

20. $\frac{2}{3} - t = -\frac{1}{6}$

21. $a - \left(-\frac{5}{8}\right) = \frac{1}{2}$

22. $\frac{7}{16} - p = \frac{-5}{8}$

★23. $y - 4\frac{1}{3} = -2\frac{2}{5}$

★24. $6\frac{1}{2} - c = 8\frac{3}{7}$

★25. $-1\frac{9}{10} - z = -7$

★26. $45\frac{2}{5} - x = -17\frac{5}{9}$

Time Out

Anabel, Landon, and Irma will each get one of these prizes: money, a horse, a bicycle. There is only one of each prize.

If Anabel gets the horse, then Landon will get the money.

If Irma gets the horse, then Anabel will get the bicycle.

If Landon gets the horse, then Irma will get the bicycle.

If Anabel gets the bicycle, then Irma will get the money.

If Landon gets the money, then Irma will get the horse.

Who gets the money?

Multiplying and Dividing Rational Numbers

Rational numbers can be multiplied and divided using fraction techniques and the usual sign rules.

A. Find $\left(\frac{-4}{5}\right)\left(\frac{6}{-7}\right)$ and $\left(\frac{4}{-3}\right)\left(\frac{1}{6}\right)$.

$$\left(\tfrac{-4}{5}\right)\left(\tfrac{6}{-7}\right) = \tfrac{-24}{-35} = \tfrac{24}{35}$$

$$\left(\tfrac{4}{-3}\right)\left(\tfrac{1}{6}\right) = \left(\tfrac{\overset{2}{\cancel{4}}}{-3}\right)\left(\tfrac{1}{\underset{3}{\cancel{6}}}\right) = \tfrac{2}{-9} = -\tfrac{2}{9}$$

Note that the answers are written with positive denominators.

B. The product of a rational number and its **reciprocal** is 1.

$-\frac{2}{3}$ and $-\frac{3}{2}$ are reciprocals.

$$\left(-\tfrac{2}{3}\right)\left(-\tfrac{3}{2}\right) = \left(-\tfrac{\overset{1}{\cancel{2}}}{\underset{1}{\cancel{3}}}\right)\left(-\tfrac{\overset{1}{\cancel{3}}}{\underset{1}{\cancel{2}}}\right) = 1$$

-2 and $-\frac{1}{2}$ are reciprocals.

$$(-2)\left(-\tfrac{1}{2}\right) = \left(-\tfrac{\overset{1}{\cancel{2}}}{1}\right)\left(-\tfrac{1}{\underset{1}{\cancel{2}}}\right) = 1$$

C. Find $\left(-\frac{15}{16}\right) \div \frac{5}{6}$.

$$\left(-\tfrac{15}{16}\right) \div \tfrac{5}{6}$$

$$\left(-\tfrac{15}{16}\right)\left(\tfrac{6}{5}\right)$$ **Change to multiplication by the reciprocal of $\frac{5}{6}$.**

$$\left(-\tfrac{\overset{3}{\cancel{15}}}{\underset{8}{\cancel{16}}}\right)\left(\tfrac{\overset{3}{\cancel{6}}}{\underset{1}{\cancel{5}}}\right)$$

$$-\tfrac{9}{8} = -1\tfrac{1}{8}$$

D. Evaluate the expression $\frac{2}{3}x$ for $x = -\frac{3}{8}$.

$$\tfrac{2}{3}x$$

$$\tfrac{2}{3}\left(-\tfrac{3}{8}\right)$$ **Substitute $-\frac{3}{8}$ for x.**

$$\tfrac{\overset{1}{\cancel{2}}}{3}\left(-\tfrac{\overset{1}{\cancel{3}}}{\underset{4}{\cancel{8}}}\right)$$

$$-\tfrac{1}{4}$$

Give each answer.

1. $\frac{-2}{5}\left(\frac{5}{-6}\right)$ 2. $\frac{7}{-15}\left(\frac{-10}{-21}\right)$ 3. $\left(-\frac{3}{8}\right)\left(-\frac{6}{7}\right)$ 4. $\frac{5}{9}\left(\frac{-3}{20}\right)$

5. $\frac{-2}{3} \div \frac{1}{4}$ 6. $\frac{-5}{8} \div \frac{-2}{5}$ 7. $\frac{7}{15} \div \frac{-4}{25}$ 8. $\frac{7}{9} \div \frac{-7}{9}$

9. $-7\left(\frac{-3}{14}\right)$ 10. $\frac{-2}{7} \div 3$ 11. $1 \div \left(-\frac{1}{2}\right)$ 12. $\left(-\frac{6}{11}\right)\left(-\frac{3}{10}\right)$

Evaluate each expression for $t = -\frac{3}{4}$.

13. $\frac{1}{2}t$ 14. $\frac{-8}{15}t$ 15. $-12t$ 16. $\frac{8}{9}t$ 17. $-\frac{2}{5} \div t$ 18. $t \div \frac{9}{10}$

Evaluate each expression for $r = -2.7$.

19. $5.1r$ 20. $-1.3r$ 21. $0.07r$ 22. $-135 \div r$ 23. $r \div 0.18$

On a typical winter day in Montana or South Dakota, the variation in temperature is about 10°C. Here are some record temperature changes. For each exercise, divide to find the average change per hour. Give the answer to the nearest tenth of a degree.

24. Browning, Montana: January 23–24, 1916
    −55.6° in 24 hours (from 6.7°C to −48.9°C)

25. Fairfield, Montana: December 24, 1924
    −46.6° in 12 hours (from 17.2°C to −29.4°C)

For these record temperature changes, find the average change per minute. Give the answers to the nearest tenth of a degree.

26. Spearfish, South Dakota: January 22, 1943
    −32.2° in 27 minutes (from 12.2°C to −20°C)

27. Rapid City, South Dakota: January 10, 1911
    −26.1° in 15 minutes (from 12.8°C to −13.3°C)

Expressions with Rational Numbers

A. Expressions with rational numbers can be written in different ways.

$$\tfrac{2}{3}n = \tfrac{2}{3}\left(\tfrac{n}{1}\right) = \frac{2n}{3} \qquad \left(n = \tfrac{n}{1}\right)$$

So, $\tfrac{2}{3}n$ is the same as $\dfrac{2n}{3}$.

B. Write each expression given below as the product of a rational number and a variable.

$$\frac{-2a}{5} = \tfrac{-2}{5}a \text{ or } -\tfrac{2}{5}a$$

$$\frac{n}{2} = \frac{1n}{2} = \tfrac{1}{2}n \qquad \left(n = 1n\right)$$

$$\frac{-n}{3} = \frac{-1n}{3} = \tfrac{-1}{3}n \text{ or } -\tfrac{1}{3}n \qquad \left(-n = -1n\right)$$

C. Evaluate $2a + b$ for $a = -\tfrac{1}{4}$ and $b = -\tfrac{2}{3}$.

$2a + b$

$\tfrac{2}{1}\left(-\tfrac{1}{4}\right) + \left(-\tfrac{2}{3}\right)$ — Substitute $-\tfrac{1}{4}$ for a and $-\tfrac{2}{3}$ for b.

$-\tfrac{1}{2} + \left(-\tfrac{2}{3}\right)$ — Multiply.

$-\tfrac{3}{6} + \left(-\tfrac{4}{6}\right)$ — Write the numbers with a common denominator.

$-\tfrac{7}{6} = -1\tfrac{1}{6}$ — Add.

D. Evaluate $\dfrac{3n}{4}$ for $n = -\tfrac{1}{2}$.

$\dfrac{3n}{4} = \tfrac{3}{4}n$ — Write a product with n as one factor.

$\tfrac{3}{4}\left(-\tfrac{1}{2}\right)$ — Substitute $-\tfrac{1}{2}$ for n.

$-\tfrac{3}{8}$ — Multiply.

Write each expression as a product of a rational number and a variable.

1. $\dfrac{3u}{5}$ 2. $\dfrac{-4x}{7}$ 3. $\dfrac{c}{3}$ 4. $\dfrac{b}{2}$ 5. $\dfrac{-2y}{9}$ 6. $\dfrac{g}{7}$

7. $\dfrac{-v}{12}$ 8. $\dfrac{4c}{13}$ 9. $-\dfrac{5s}{11}$ 10. $\dfrac{6t}{-7}$ 11. $-\dfrac{r}{5}$ 12. $\dfrac{a}{-6}$

13. $-n$ 14. t 15. $\dfrac{-k}{4}$ 16. $-\dfrac{4b}{13}$ 17. $\dfrac{-x}{10}$ 18. $\dfrac{-2n}{-5}$

Evaluate each expression for $a = \frac{-3}{5}$, $b = -\frac{1}{2}$, and $c = \frac{2}{3}$.

19. $a + 3b$

20. $-2a - b$

21. $a(b + 1)$

22. $-a(1 - c)$

23. $ab + c$

24. $a(b + c)$

25. abc **26.** $-abc$

27. $\frac{2a}{3}$ **28.** $\frac{b}{5}$

29. $\frac{-c}{8}$ **30.** $\frac{-a}{10}$

★31. $\frac{5a}{6} - b + \frac{c}{8}$

Evaluate each expression for $x = -3.5$, $y = -0.7$, and $z = 1.4$.

32. $2x - y$

33. $x(y + z)$

34. $xy + xz$

35. $0.4x - 5.1z$

★36. $y^2 + 0.51$

★37. $x^2 + 2x + 1$

Side Trip

Density of Rational Numbers

Between every two rational numbers, there is another rational number.

Find a rational number between $\frac{1}{3}$ and $\frac{1}{2}$.

$\frac{1}{3} = \frac{2}{6} = \frac{4}{12}$ Write the numbers with a common denominator so that the numerators differ by at least 2.

$\frac{1}{2} = \frac{3}{6} = \frac{6}{12}$

$\frac{4}{12} < \frac{5}{12} < \frac{6}{12}$, so $\frac{1}{3} < \frac{5}{12} < \frac{1}{2}$.

Find a rational number between the numbers in each pair.

1. $\frac{1}{4}$ and $\frac{1}{5}$ **2.** $\frac{1}{8}$ and $\frac{1}{7}$ **3.** $\frac{1}{10}$ and $\frac{2}{10}$

4. $\frac{4}{9}$ and $\frac{5}{9}$ **5.** 0 and $\frac{1}{8}$ **6.** $3\frac{1}{4}$ and $3\frac{1}{3}$

7. -2 and -1 **8.** $-\frac{1}{2}$ and 0

9. $-\frac{2}{3}$ and $-\frac{1}{4}$ **10.** $-\frac{1}{2}$ and $-\frac{1}{3}$

11. $-\frac{1}{2}$ and $\frac{1}{2}$ **12.** $-2\frac{2}{3}$ and $-2\frac{1}{3}$

13. 1.1 and 1.2 **14.** 0 and 0.1

Find a positive number that is closer to 0

15. than 0.1.   **16.** than 0.01.   **17.** than 0.001.

18. Can you find the smallest positive rational number? Explain your answer.

Using Reciprocals to Solve Equations

Reciprocals can be used to solve many equations.

A. Solve $\dfrac{-3n}{5} = 2$.

$$\dfrac{-3n}{5} = 2$$

$$-\tfrac{3}{5}n = 2 \qquad \text{Write the left side of the equation as a product with } n \text{ as one factor.}$$

$$\left(-\tfrac{5}{3}\right)\left(-\tfrac{3}{5}\right)n = \left(-\tfrac{5}{3}\right)\tfrac{2}{1} \qquad \text{To get } n \text{ by itself, multiply both sides of the equation by the reciprocal of } -\tfrac{3}{5}.$$

$$1n = -\tfrac{10}{3}$$

$$n = -3\tfrac{1}{3}$$

B. Solve $\dfrac{-x}{4} = -16$.

$$\dfrac{-x}{4} = -16$$

$$-\tfrac{1}{4}x = -16$$

$$(-4)\left(-\tfrac{1}{4}\right)x = (-4)(-16)$$

$$1x = 64$$

$$x = 64$$

Solve these equations using reciprocals.

1. $-\frac{2}{3}n = \frac{1}{5}$

2. $\frac{1}{2}t = \frac{-5}{6}$

3. $-\frac{3}{4}a = -8$

4. $-\frac{3}{8}y = \frac{6}{25}$

5. $\frac{-4x}{9} = \frac{2}{3}$

6. $\frac{-5w}{7} = \frac{-10}{21}$

7. $\frac{3d}{11} = -9$

8. $\frac{-5e}{6} = 5$

9. $\frac{s}{4} = -3$

10. $\frac{r}{3} = \frac{2}{3}$

11. $\frac{b}{12} = -\frac{1}{5}$

12. $\frac{v}{5} = \frac{-3}{8}$

13. $\frac{-t}{2} = -\frac{2}{7}$

14. $\frac{-c}{8} = \frac{13}{16}$

15. $\frac{-p}{16} = \frac{-7}{12}$

16. $\frac{-k}{3} = 7$

17. $\frac{-4f}{15} = -\frac{8}{25}$

18. $-\frac{7}{18}r = \frac{4}{21}$

19. $\frac{-y}{21} = 1$

20. $\frac{x}{30} = \frac{-9}{15}$

21. $-3x = \frac{2}{7}$

22. $-8z = \frac{-3}{11}$

23. $-24a = \frac{16}{21}$

24. $14b = \frac{-35}{41}$

25. $-\frac{11}{16}n = -\frac{33}{64}$

26. $-\frac{m}{17} = \frac{15}{34}$

27. $\frac{27t}{32} = -\frac{81}{128}$

28. $\frac{-k}{51} = \frac{-3}{17}$

Solve these equations to find a mathematical
term that tells what the acorn said when it grew up.

29. $\frac{-x}{2} = 7$ **R**

30. $-7c = \frac{1}{2}$ **Y**

31. $-\frac{3a}{4} = \frac{-1}{3}$ **O**

32. $-\frac{5d}{3} = \frac{-5}{12}$ **E**

33. $\frac{3n}{2} = -\frac{3}{8}$ **M**

34. $\frac{3y}{-35} = \frac{-7}{105}$ **G**

35. $\frac{4t}{7} = 2$ **T**

36. $\underline{}\ \underline{}\ \underline{}\ \underline{}\ \underline{}\ \underline{}\ \underline{}\ \underline{}$
$\quad\quad\ \ \frac{7}{9}\ \ \ \frac{1}{4}\ \ \ \frac{4}{9}\ \ \ -\frac{1}{4}\ \ \ \frac{1}{4}\ \ \ 3\frac{1}{2}\ \ -14\ \ -\frac{1}{14}$

Solving Two-Step Equations

A. Mrs. Proudfoot is buying antique lamps. She can resell 6 of the lamps for a total of $730. She wants to make a total profit of $100 on the sale. How much can she pay for each lamp?

Let c represent the amount Mrs. Proudfoot pays for each lamp. Then her total cost is $6c$.

Total resale amount	Total cost	Total profit	
$730 - 6c = 100$			Write an equation.
$730 + (-6c) = 100$			Change the subtraction to addition of the opposite.
$730 + (-6c) + (-730) = 100 + (-730)$			To get $-6c$ by itself, add -730 to both sides of the equation.
$-6c + 0 = -630$			
$\left(-\frac{1}{6}\right)(-6c) = \left(-\frac{1}{6}\right)(-630)$			To get c by itself, multiply both sides of the equation by the reciprocal of -6.
$1c = 105$			
$c = 105$			

Mrs. Proudfoot can pay $105 for each lamp.

B. Solve $-2x + 3 = -1$.

$$-2x + 3 = -1$$

$$-2x + 3 \atop +(-3) \qquad = -1 \atop +(-3)$$

To get $-2x$ by itself, add -3 to both sides of the equation.

$$-2x + 0 = -4$$

$$-2x = -4$$

$$\left(-\tfrac{1}{2}\right) \, (-2x) = \left(-\tfrac{1}{2}\right) \, (-4)$$

$$1x = 2$$

To get x by itself, multiply both sides of the equation by the reciprocal of -2.

$$x = 2$$

Solve each equation.

1. $4x - 9 = -1$
2. $6y - 8 = -20$
3. $-3 + 5t = -18$
4. $27 + 7c = -29$
5. $9 - 4x = -11$
6. $8 - 9z = 26$
7. $-3d - 6 = 4$
8. $-6x - 7 = 8$
9. $12 - 3y = -9$
10. $14 - 5x = -1$
11. $-3y + 7 = -4$
12. $-10x + 8 = -12$
13. $-2b - 7 = -7$
14. $-8 = -4n + 8$
15. $-11e + 21 = 32$
16. $13x + 26 = 39$
17. $-2k - 1 = 3$
18. $-4h - 7 = 6$
19. $5x - 6 = -7$
20. $7x - 8 = -9$
21. $8 - 12g = -3$
22. $17 - 15x = -3$
23. $-4y - 27 = -15$
24. $-8c - 41 = -25$
25. $26 = -1 - 6m$
26. $-31 = 4 - 8x$
27. $-13n - 17 = 9$
28. $7x - 1 = 0.4$
*29. $-0.21y + 1 = -3.2$
*30. $2.6x + 0.4 = -2.2$

31. One of Mrs. Proudfoot's customers is willing to pay $370 for 5 matching bowls. Mrs. Proudfoot will have to purchase the bowls from other dealers. If she wants to make a total profit of $60, how much can she pay for each bowl?

Graphing Inequalities

Mathematical sentences using the words "is less than" or "is greater than" are called **_inequalities._**

A. Ramon said, "More than 50 people are invited to the party." Write his sentence as an inequality.

You can think of Ramon's sentence as "The number of people invited is more than 50."

$x > 50$

Sonia said, "So far, fewer than 30 people have replied to the invitation." Write her sentence as an inequality.

You can think of Sonia's sentence as "The number of replies is less than 30."

$y < 30$

B. Graph $x > 3$.

Every number to the right of 3 on the number line will make this sentence true. For example, $4 > 3$, $7.5 > 3$, and $3.01 > 3$ are all true.

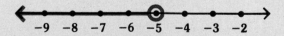

Use a circle to show that 3 is not in the graph.

C. Graph $y < -5$.

Every number to the left of -5 on the number line will make this sentence true. For example, $-6 < -5$, $-8.3 < -5$, and $-21 < -5$ are all true.

Use a circle to show that -5 is not in the graph

D. Graph $x \leq -2$.

This inequality is read "x is less than or equal to −2."

Use a filled-in circle to show that −2 is included in the graph.

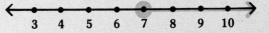

E. Graph $x \geq 7$.

This inequality is read "x is greater than or equal to 7."

Use a filled-in circle to show that 7 is included in the graph.

Write each sentence as an inequality.

1. More than 100 balloons have been ordered for the party.

2. The refreshment committee has spent less than $60.

3. The temperature is expected to be less than 10°C.

4. More than 5 people have volunteered for the clean-up committee.

Graph each inequality.

5. $x < -4$ 6. $y < -6$ 7. $c > 8$ 8. $b > 0$ 9. $z \leq -5$

10. $n \geq -1$ 11. $x \leq 0$ 12. $x \leq -13$ 13. $d > 11$ 14. $s < -7$

15. $b \geq -5$ 16. $c < 10$ 17. $t > -2$ 18. $z \leq 15$ 19. $x \leq -8$

Rules for Inequalities

A. Add -3 to both sides of the inequality $2 < 7$. Write the new inequality formed.

$$2 < 7$$

$$2 + (-3) \bullet 7 + (-3)$$

$$-1 \bullet 4$$

$$-1 < 4$$

Notice that the new inequality has the same symbol as the original inequality.

The **order of the inequality** $2 < 7$ is not changed by adding -3 to both sides.

B. Multiply both sides of the inequality $-4 < 3$ by -2. Write the new inequality formed.

$$-4 < 3$$

$$(-2)(-4) \bullet (-2)3$$

$$8 \bullet -6$$

$$8 > -6$$

Notice that the direction of the inequality symbol is changed in the new inequality.

The order of the inequality $-4 < 3$ is *reversed* when both sides are multiplied by -2.

Add the given number to both sides of the inequality. Write the new inequality formed.

1. $3 < 8$, add 2
2. $0 < 5$, add 6
3. $-1 > -4$, add 3
4. $-7 < -5$, add 2
5. $-6 < 2$, add 3.1
6. $3 > -3$, add 2.5
7. $-3.4 < 12$, add 3.4
8. $1 > -4.7$, add 4.7
9. $10 > 5$, add -6
10. $12 > 4$, add -8
11. $-2 < -1$, add -4.5
12. $-2 > -10$, add -1.5
13. $5.5 > -3$, add 3
14. $-6 < 4.1$, add -4
15. $-1.5 < 0$, add 1.5

16. Study your answers to exercises 1–15. Which of the rules on page 391 have you discovered?

Multiply both sides of the inequality by the given number. Write the new inequality formed.

17. $10 < 12$, multiply by 2

18. $0 < 6$, multiply by 4

19. $6.5 > -1$, multiply by 3

20. $-5 > -9$, multiply by 5

21. $-8 < -7$, multiply by 4

22. $-18 < -6$, multiply by 1.5

23. $0 > -2$, multiply by 2.1

24. $4 > -12$, multiply by 0.25

25. $-3 < 2$, multiply by 0.5

26. $14 > -7$, multiply by 2

27. Does the order of an inequality change when both sides are multiplied by the same positive number?

Multiply both sides of the inequality by the given number. Write the new inequality formed.

28. $7 > 5$, multiply by -1

29. $4 < 9$, multiply by -1

30. $2 > -6$, multiply by -2

31. $-9 < 1$, multiply by -3

32. $-3 < 5$, multiply by -3

33. $10 > -10$, multiply by -4

34. $-5.1 < -1.4$, multiply by -1

35. $-3.2 > -7.4$, multiply by -5

36. $-6 < 2$, multiply by -0.5

37. $-4 > -12$, multiply by -0.25

38. Does the order of an inequality change when both sides are multiplied by the same negative number?

Rules for Inequalities

1. If the same number is added to both sides of an inequality, the order of the inequality does not change.

2. If both sides of an inequality are multiplied by the same positive number, the order of the inequality does not change.

3. If both sides of an inequality are multiplied by the same negative number, the order of the inequality is reversed.

Solving Inequalities

The methods used to solve equations can be applied to inequalities.

A. Aiko earns $75 plus commissions each week. How much must she make in commissions to earn more than $215 each week?

Solve $75 + c > 215$.

$$75 + c > 215$$
$$75 + c + (-75) > 215 + (-75)$$
$$c + 0 > 140$$
$$c > 140$$

Adding the same number to both sides did not change the order of the inequality.

Aiko must earn more than $140 in commissions.

B. Solve $-3.2 \leq x - 6$.

$$-3.2 \leq x - 6$$
$$-3.2 \leq x + (-6)$$
$$-3.2 + 6 \leq x + (-6) + 6$$
$$2.8 \leq x + 0$$
$$2.8 \leq x$$

c. Solve $\frac{1}{3}y \geq -10$.

$$\frac{1}{3}y \geq -10$$
$$(3)\frac{1}{3}y \geq (3)(-10)$$
$$1y \geq -30$$
$$y \geq -30$$

Since both sides were multiplied by a positive number, 3, the order of the inequality did not change.

D. Solve $-2x < 18$.

$$-2x < 18$$
$$\left(-\frac{1}{2}\right)(-2x) > \left(-\frac{1}{2}\right)18$$
$$1x > -9$$
$$x > -9$$

Since both sides were multiplied by a negative number, $-\frac{1}{2}$, the order of the inequality was reversed.

Solve each inequality.

1. $x + 7 < 5$

2. $y + 9 < 3$

3. $z - 8 > 16$

4. $a - 3 < 8$

5. $d + (-2) \geq -6$

6. $x + (-10) \leq -16$

7. $14 < x - 2.1$

8. $3 < h - 4.7$

9. $-1.6 > -4 + r$

10. $-5.3 > -5 + x$

11. $0 \leq t - 2.7$

12. $0 > y - 1.1$

13. $-1.3 + z \geq -1.7$

14. $-2.5 + m > -3.3$

15. $x + 2.6 < 0.21$

16. $10n < 50$

17. $8x \geq 48$

18. $-5c > -30$

19. $-7e < -28$

20. $6g \leq -36$

21. $-2x > 26$

22. $-8h < 56$

23. $6x < -9$

24. $5n > -18$

25. $\frac{2}{3}s \geq -8$

26. $\frac{4}{5}k > -16$

27. $-\frac{7}{8}t < -14$

28. $\frac{-3x}{4} \leq -12$

29. $\frac{-5y}{4} < 5$

30. $-\frac{2}{5}t > 6$

★**31.** Noreen earns $75 per week and a commission of $25 for each sale. How many sales must she make in order to earn more than $250 per week?

Chapter 18 Test
Algebra, pages 370–393

Write each number as a quotient of two integers.

1. -4 **2.** $5\frac{2}{3}$

Compare. Use $>$, $<$, or $=$.

3. $\frac{-3}{4}$ ● $\frac{5}{-7}$ **4.** -1.6 ● -1.8

5. List these numbers in order from the least to the greatest.

$\frac{2}{-5}$ $\frac{-1}{4}$ $\frac{-2}{-3}$

Find each answer.

6. $-\frac{1}{2} + \frac{-3}{4}$ **7.** $\frac{4}{-5} - \frac{1}{9}$

8. $\left(\frac{-3}{5}\right)\left(\frac{1}{2}\right)$ **9.** $\left(-\frac{14}{5}\right) \div \left(-\frac{7}{15}\right)$

Evaluate each expression for $t = \frac{-2}{5}$.

10. $t + 3$ **11.** $2t - \frac{1}{5}$

12. $-\frac{1}{2}t$ **13.** $t \div 4$

Solve each equation.

14. $x + 3 = -7$

15. $c - \frac{2}{3} = -\frac{1}{2}$

16. $-\frac{2}{3}n = 6$

17. $3a + 5 = -4$

18. Graph $x > -3$.

19. Graph $y \leq 6$.

Multiply both sides of the inequality by the given number. Write the new inequality formed.

20. $-5 < -3$, multiply by 2

21. $6 > -4$, multiply by -1

Solve each inequality.

22. $-3x > 6$

23. $y + 7 \leq -7$

24. $2t \geq -9$

25. $4 < n - 3$

Problems Around Us

1. In 1976, the African country of Zaïre produced 30% of the world's diamonds. World diamond production that year was 42,700,000 carats. How many carats of diamonds did Zaïre produce in 1976?

2. During his basketball career, Wilt Chamberlain scored 31,419 points in 1045 games. To the nearest tenth, what was his average number of points per game?

3. An automobile averages 12 kilometers per liter of gas. How far can this car go on 50 liters of gas?

4. The Sears Tower is 30.8 meters taller than the World Trade Center. The height of the World Trade Center is 412.4 meters. How tall is the Sears Tower?

5. George bought a shirt for $9.50 and a tie for $6.00. The sales tax rate is 6%. What was his total bill?

6. A rectangular lot is 30 meters wide and 40 meters long. How long is a path that cuts diagonally across the lot?

7. A car goes 550 kilometers on 40 liters of gas. How many kilometers per liter did this car average?

8. Mr. Kleber received a 7% raise in salary. The amount of the raise was $1295. What was his salary before the raise?

9. The ratio of width to length for a United States flag must be 10 to 19. If a flag is 100 cm long, how wide should it be? Give the answer to the nearest tenth of a centimeter.

10. In its orbit about the earth, the moon travels about 8.83×10^4 kilometers each day. It completes one orbit in approximately 2.73×10^1 days. Find the length of the moon's orbit.

Individualized Skills Maintenance

Diagnose

A *pages 176–177, 180–181*

$$\frac{3}{4} - \frac{1}{8}$$

$$\frac{5}{6} - \frac{3}{7}$$

$$5\frac{3}{11} - 2\frac{1}{2}$$

B *pages 230–231*

Write a decimal for 16.5%.

Write a percent for 0.471.

C *pages 232–233*

Write a fraction for 32.5%.

Write a percent for $\frac{9}{40}$.

Practice

A

1. $\frac{9}{10}$ $-\frac{1}{5}$
2. $\frac{6}{7}$ $-\frac{2}{3}$
3. $\frac{5}{8}$ $-\frac{3}{16}$
4. $\frac{4}{5}$ $-\frac{1}{6}$
5. $\frac{5}{6}$ $-\frac{3}{8}$
6. $\frac{3}{4}$ $-\frac{1}{6}$

7. $10\frac{2}{3}$ $- 5\frac{1}{2}$
8. $4\frac{1}{3}$ $-4\frac{1}{4}$
9. 5 $- 2\frac{3}{11}$
10. $12\frac{1}{10}$ $- 6\frac{7}{10}$
11. $8\frac{1}{2}$ $-1\frac{3}{4}$
12. $11\frac{3}{5}$ $- 3\frac{5}{8}$

B Write a decimal for each percent.

13. 23%   14. 6%   15. 40%   16. 21.5%   17. $4\frac{1}{2}$%   18. $37\frac{1}{3}$%

Write a percent for each decimal.

19. 0.4   20. 0.08   21. 0.87   22. 0.632   23. $0.27\frac{2}{3}$ 24. $0.01\frac{1}{2}$

C Write a fraction for each percent.

25. 35%   26. 3%   27. 19.5%   28. $66\frac{2}{3}$%   29. $83\frac{1}{3}$%   30. $37\frac{1}{2}$%

Write a percent for each fraction.

31. $\frac{4}{5}$ 32. $\frac{3}{25}$ 33. $\frac{7}{20}$ 34. $\frac{99}{200}$ 35. $\frac{1}{7}$ 36. $\frac{5}{9}$

Unit 6 Review

Chapter 16, pages 330–350

1. The adult men in a sample had these heights given in centimeters.

    180, 168, 165, 180, 180, 198, 178, 183, 173, 183

    What is the mode for this data?

2. What is the median for the data in exercise 1?

3. What is the mean for the data in exercise 1?

4. In exercise 1, 30% of the men in the sample had a height of 180 cm. Predict how many men in a group of 50 would be 180 cm tall.

5. Make a bar graph for this data.

Year	'76	'77	'78	'79	'80
Number of graduates	58	65	78	71	75

6. Use the line of best fit in the graph below to predict the number of interceptions for 275 attempted passes.

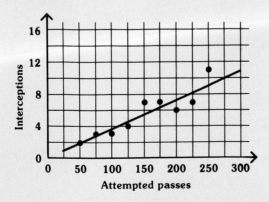

Chapter 17, pages 352–368

7. How many different 5-digit numbers are there if each number uses all of these digits: 7, 2, 9, 1, 5?

8. Mike chooses a digit at random. What is the probability that the name of the digit he chose has three letters?

9. Maria and Inez have each written a letter of the alphabet. Neither girl has seen what the other wrote. What is the probability that they both wrote vowels?

Chapter 18, pages 370–393

10. Write 1.5 as a quotient of two integers.

11. Compare. Use $>$, $<$, or $=$.

    $\frac{-4}{5}$ ● $\frac{7}{-9}$

Find each answer.

12. $-\frac{1}{2} + \frac{1}{4}$ 13. $\left(\frac{-1}{3}\right)\left(\frac{-6}{11}\right)$

Solve.

14. $x - 5 = -2$

15. $4x - 3 = -1$

16. $-5c \geq 10$

Unit 6 Test
Chapters 16–18, pages 330–394

1. Make a frequency table for these scores.

   85, 75, 92, 83, 80, 97, 90, 81, 93, 76, 84, 83, 90, 73, 79, 83

2. Give the range for the data in exercise 1.

3. Give the median for the data in exercise 1.

4. Give the mean for the data in exercise 1.

5. In exercise 1, 25% of the scores are below 80. Predict how many scores in a group of 40 would be below 80.

6. Does the scattergram below show a negative correlation, a positive correlation, or no correlation between number of absences and test scores?

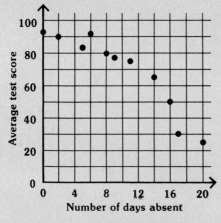

7. What is missing in this advertising claim?

   > Guaranteed 40% longer

8. Tim chose a day of the week at random. What is the probability that he chose a day that does not begin with S?

9. Mr. Happ asked each of 30 pupils to secretly write an odd digit. Use probability to predict the number of students who wrote the digit 7.

10. Fran chose 2 different vowels. What is the probability that she chose a and e?

11. List in order from the least to the greatest.

    $\frac{-4}{-7}$ $\frac{1}{2}$ $\frac{-3}{5}$

Find each answer.

12. $\frac{-2}{5} - \frac{-1}{3}$ 13. $(-4) \div \frac{-2}{3}$

Evaluate each expression for $a = \frac{-1}{2}$.

14. $a + 1$ 15. $-2a$

16. Graph $x \geq -4$.

Solve.

17. $-12 + n = -5$

18. $-3n = 51$

19. $-8 < y + 2$

End-of-Book Test

Add or subtract.

1. $\begin{array}{r} 19{,}285 \\ +\ 3{,}672 \\ \hline \end{array}$
2. $\begin{array}{r} 5023 \\ -3947 \\ \hline \end{array}$

Multiply or divide.

3. 263×74
4. $6345 \div 47$

5. Round 38,258 to the nearest thousand.

Add or subtract.

6. $68.2 + 85.73$
7. $15 - 6.92$

Multiply or divide.

8. 3.85×0.23
9. $2.04 \div 6$

10. Find $5.326 \div 0.35$. Round the quotient to the nearest tenth.

11. Compare. Use >, <, or =.

    63.5 ● 63.380

12. Find the missing number.

    $2468 \text{ g} = \blacksquare \text{ kg}$

13. Which measurement is more precise, 16 L or 168 mL?

Solve for x.

14. $32 + x = 48$
15. $4x = 48$

Add or subtract.

16. $-3 + (-8)$
17. $6 - (-4)$

18. Compare. Use > or <.

    -7 ● -9

19. Complete this table for the equation $y = x - 5$.

x	-2	-1	0	2	6
y	-7				

20. Draw a graph for the equation in exercise 19. Use your table.

21. Give the LCM of 24 and 36.

Add or subtract.

22. $\begin{array}{r} 5\frac{2}{3} \\ +3\frac{4}{5} \\ \hline \end{array}$
23. $\begin{array}{r} 2\frac{5}{9} \\ -1\frac{2}{3} \\ \hline \end{array}$

Multiply or divide.

24. $\frac{3}{8} \times \frac{2}{3}$
25. $2\frac{2}{5} \div 1\frac{1}{5}$

26. Write $\frac{24}{32}$ in lowest terms.

27. Write $3\frac{1}{2}$ as a fraction.

28. Write $\frac{3}{4}$ and $\frac{7}{10}$ with a common denominator.

29. Compare. Use >, <, or =.

    $3\frac{2}{3}$ ● $3\frac{5}{8}$

Continued on next page.

Write each number in scientific notation.

30. 63,500,000   31. 0.0000028

32. Solve. $\frac{3}{18} = \frac{x}{24}$

33. Write a decimal for 17%.

34. Find 80% of 20.

35. 15 is what percent of 60?

Use this figure for
exercises 36 and 37.

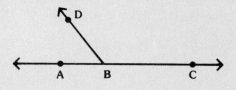

36. Name a segment on $\overleftrightarrow{AC}$.

37. Name an obtuse angle in the figure above.

38. Find the
perimeter
of this
rectangle.

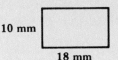

10 mm

18 mm

39. Find the area
of this circle.
Use 3.14 for π.

7 m

40. Simplify. $\sqrt{2} \times \sqrt{8}$

41. Find the length of the missing side of a right triangle with $a = 12$ and $c = 13$.

42. Make a frequency table for these ages.

11, 12, 12, 13, 15, 13, 12, 11,
14, 13, 13, 13, 12, 13, 14, 13

43. There are 6 black socks, 8 brown socks, and 2 green socks in a drawer. If you remove two socks without looking, what is the probability that they are both black?

44. Multiply. $\left(-\frac{3}{8}\right)\left(\frac{5}{6}\right)$

45. A bus carries 47 students. How many buses are needed to carry 562 students?

46. At the start of a trip to Peoria, Jeri was 320 km away. After driving 159 km, how far did she still have to drive?

47. The model of a car is built to a scale of 2 to 75. If the car is 500 cm long, what is the length of the model to the nearest centimeter?

48. Coats are on sale at a 20% discount. What is the sale price of a coat that originally sold for $150?

49. The height of a kangaroo is $1\frac{5}{7}$ times the length of its $3\frac{1}{2}$-foot tail. What is the height of the kangaroo?

Acknowledgments

For permission to reproduce photographs on the following pages, acknowledgment is made to:

Photos on 4 and 16, J. R. Holland/STOCK BOSTON. Photo on 26, NASA. Photo on 32, Flip Schulke/BLACK STAR. Photo on 72, Jerry Cooke/SPORTS ILLUSTRATED. Photo on 75, Diana Lifton. Photo on 97, Dr. E. R. Degginger. Photo on 98, J. P. Laffont/SYGMA. Photo on 114, Co Rentmeester/SPORTS ILLUSTRATED. Photo on 164, James H. Carmichael/BRUCE COLEMAN. Photo on 166, Library of Congress. Photo on 176, Gus Giordano Dance Co.; Jon Randolph/WTTW-TV. Photo on 186, Jack Weiss. Photo on 189, U.S. National Museum. Photo on 195, Clay Adams, Inc., Division of Becton, Dickinson & Co. Photo on 200, courtesy of Bell Laboratories. Photo on 211, Grant Heilman Photography. Photo on 222–223, Carl Frank/PHOTO RESEARCHERS. Photo on 226, Yellowstone National Park/National Park Service. Puzzle in photo on 228, Museum of Modern Art Puzzle No. 6830, Copyright 1979 William Anastasi. Photo on 244, Mary Elyse Ebright. Photo on 325, Gene Dekovic. Photo on 335, Heinz Kluetmeier/SPORTS ILLUSTRATED. Photo on 338, Jack Weiss. Photos on 366 and 381, H. Armstrong Roberts Photography. Photo on 395, Mt. Wilson & Palomar Observatories.

Photo on cover, courtesy of International Harvester.

More Practice

Set 1 *pages 8–9*

1. 527
+396

2. 3827
+ 883

3. 12,485
+ 2,717

4. 66,260
+28,154

5. 103,463
+ 37,546

6. 213,523
+618,435

7. 631
−424

8. 4375
− 712

9. 59,049
−47,550

10. 40,000
−33,127

11. 642,132
−581,640

12. 594,958
− 2,163

13. 627
+357

14. 6071
− 268

15. 14,894
+ 9,658

16. 95,102
− 5,247

17. 498,476
+ 25,449

18. 715,802
− 51,264

19. 653 + 47 + 709   **20.** 600 − 436   **21.** 40,715 + 296   **22.** 74,383 − 6,815

23. 359,182 + 50,827   **24.** 5025 − 829   **25.** 7139 + 9207   **26.** 45,003 − 7593

Set 2 *pages 12–13*

1. 50
× 9

2. 48
× 7

3. 670
× 4

4. 872
× 8

5. 90
×60

6. 349
× 52

7. 400
× 7

8. 19
× 4

9. 76
× 3

10. 501
× 36

11. 319
× 41

12. 57
×68

13. 755
×902

14. 3916
× 51

15. 700 × 7   **16.** 80 × 920   **17.** 631 × 48   **18.** 414 × 39   **19.** 37 × 72 × 50

20. 85 × 46   **21.** 734 × 61   **22.** 509 × 72   **23.** 616 × 300   **24.** 9219 × 78

Set 3 *pages 16–17*

1. 6)437   **2.** 5)895   **3.** 9)747   **4.** 4)1076   **5.** 8)4161

6. 7)592   **7.** 43)891   **8.** 25)675   **9.** 3)4192   **10.** 12)3496

11. 52)7790   **12.** 137)683   **13.** 44)12346   **14.** 253)6016   **15.** 19)48137

16. 8291 ÷ 11   **17.** 22,456 ÷ 32   **18.** 816 ÷ 373   **19.** 76,608 ÷ 342

20. 92,673 ÷ 50   **21.** 390,980 ÷ 65   **22.** 5046 ÷ 841   **23.** 863,560 ÷ 410

Set 4 *pages 26–27*

Compare these decimals. Use >, <, or =.

1. 0.76 ● 0.72   2. 0.34563 ● 0.3456   3. 0.647 ● 0.6470
4. 0.238 ● 0.283   5. 14.356 ● 14.357   6. 2.084 ● 2.089
7. 0.5163 ● 0.516   8. 3.040 ● 3.04   9. 0.6999 ● 0.7

List these decimals in order from the least to the greatest.

10. 7.37 9.12 9.21   11. 0.361 0.219 0.36 0.214
12. 0.63 0.59 0.632   13. 8.27 4.361 6.18 4.18
14. 6.01 6.1 6.02   15. 0.943 0.937 0.944 0.932

Set 5 *pages 32–33*

1. 9.273   2. 2.56   3. 8.7   4. 7.93   5. 28.96   6. 54.8
   +6.801   +5.385   +1.26   +4.78   +28.05   +75.6

7. 10.43   8. 61.5   9. 9.32   10. 4.61   11. 6.014   12. 45.00
   − 8.28   −58.39   −7.92   −4.49   −3.819   − 6.23

13. 54.37   14. 0.8   15. 1.28   16. 7.1   17. 6.76   18. 82.69
   +26.73   −0.026   +0.19   −5.36   +3.593   −64.63

19. 53.254 + 4.2 + 7.23   20. 454.6 − 7.121   21. 7 + 25.0002 + 6.00807

Set 6 *pages 36–37*

1. 92   2. 0.038   3. 84.7   4. 0.0047   5. 0.0019   6. 31.63
  ×0.08   × 0.05   × 0.6   × 0.03   ×0.0006   × 0.4

7. 8.31   8. 0.66   9. 16.8   10. 0.0168   11. 0.0078   12. 80.01
  × 1.1   × 4.8   ×0.42   × 20.7   ×0.0078   ×0.002

13. 5.8 × 3.1   14. 4.63 × 9.2   15. 8.5 × 0.007   16. 1.96 × 0.037
17. 5.783 × 100   18. 9.1 × 1000   19. 0.05 × 10,000   20. 0.81 × 1000

More Practice

Set 7 *pages 40–41*

Divide until the remainder is zero.

1. $23\overline{)32.2}$ 2. $8\overline{)0.36}$ 3. $86\overline{)3637.8}$ 4. $51\overline{)260.1}$ 5. $35\overline{)7256.9}$

6. $74\overline{)2.59}$ 7. $8\overline{)21.6}$ 8. $130\overline{)60.84}$ 9. $37\overline{)26.64}$ 10. $46\overline{)94.76}$

11. $32\overline{)2.08}$ 12. $10\overline{)829.2}$ 13. $100\overline{)52.3}$ 14. $1000\overline{)4.26}$ 15. $1000\overline{)731.1}$

Set 8 *pages 42–43*

Divide until the remainder is zero.

1. $0.03\overline{)2.4}$ 2. $0.07\overline{)0.91}$ 3. $0.6\overline{)3.3}$ 4. $3.02\overline{)19.63}$ 5. $0.68\overline{)0.272}$

6. $0.5\overline{)0.029}$ 7. $6.05\overline{)48.4}$ 8. $0.01\overline{)4}$ 9. $0.25\overline{)7.5}$ 10. $0.37\overline{)0.0222}$

Divide. Round each quotient to the nearest tenth.

11. $0.6\overline{)2.791}$ 12. $2.1\overline{)5.27}$ 13. $3.5\overline{)3.81}$ 14. $0.7\overline{)47.21}$ 15. $3.26\overline{)0.8068}$

Divide. Round each quotient to the nearest hundredth.

16. $0.9\overline{)3.83}$ 17. $0.03\overline{)0.472}$ 18. $0.5\overline{)0.316}$ 19. $0.7\overline{)45.72}$ 20. $0.273\overline{)0.1739}$

Set 9 *pages 68–69*

Evaluate $121 - m$ for

1. $m = 0$.   2. $m = 93$.   3. $m = 101$.   4. $m = 54$.   5. $m = 27$.   6. $m = 79$.

Evaluate each expression for $x = 23$.

7. $x + 9$ 8. $146 + x$ 9. $x - 16$ 10. $30 - x$ 11. $14 + x$ 12. $120 - x$

13. $x - 5$ 14. $23 + x$ 15. $72 - x$ 16. $x - 19$ 17. $x + 57$ 18. $x + 132$

Set 10 *pages 72–73*

Solve each equation.

1. $m + 13 = 52$ 2. $101 = k - 19$ 3. $a - 3.72 = 9.31$ 4. $c + 4.72 = 11.98$

5. $28 = h - 79$ 6. $t - 38 = 127$ 7. $41.16 = w + 15.74$ 8. $26.83 = c - 11.17$

Set 11 *pages 76–77*

Evaluate each expression for $n = 8$.

1. $13n$ **2.** $96 \div n$ **3.** $8 \div n$ **4.** $n \div 2$ **5.** $\dfrac{32}{n}$ **6.** $\dfrac{5n}{2}$ **7.** $n(n)$

Evaluate each expression for $y = 12$.

8. $12y$ **9.** $192 \div y$ **10.** $24 \div y$ **11.** $y \div 6$ **12.** $\dfrac{36}{y}$ **13.** $\dfrac{3y}{4}$ **14.** $\dfrac{5y}{y}$

Evaluate each expression for $a = 11$ and $c = 22$.

15. ac **16.** $c \div a$ **17.** $a(a)$ **18.** $\dfrac{ac}{2}$ **19.** $\dfrac{ac}{c}$ **20.** $\dfrac{c(c)}{4}$ **21.** $\dfrac{8a}{c}$

Set 12 *pages 80–81*

Solve each equation.

1. $8m = 168$ **2.** $13x = 91$ **3.** $185 = 5y$ **4.** $384 = 16w$

5. $44.8 = 16a$ **6.** $44.2w = 132.6$ **7.** $31m = 12.71$ **8.** $7r = 252$

9. $\dfrac{a}{13} = 19$ **10.** $\dfrac{m}{23} = 15$ **11.** $\dfrac{x}{6} = 11.8$ **12.** $2.9 = \dfrac{a}{12}$ **13.** $\dfrac{k}{32} = 2.16$

14. $8.03 = \dfrac{w}{20}$ **15.** $\dfrac{h}{55} = 31$ **16.** $47 = \dfrac{e}{68}$ **17.** $\dfrac{s}{207} = 5.2$ **18.** $1.96 = \dfrac{c}{9}$

Set 13 *pages 84–85*

Solve each equation.

1. $6a + 17 = 65$ **2.** $3w - 52 = 17$ **3.** $41 + 7m = 608$

4. $12n + 43 = 259$ **5.** $2x - 2.94 = 20$ **6.** $83.08 = 5.86 + 11y$

7. $14x - 12.48 = 69$ **8.** $2.55 + 31m = 125$ **9.** $52c - 149 = 267$

10. $647 = 227 + 35e$ **11.** $3.8r + 19.2 = 76.2$ **12.** $16.9 + 9.3f = 119.2$

13. $32t - 107.5 = 394.9$ **14.** $387.8 = 17b - 152.8$ **15.** $19k - 15.3 = 150$

More Practice

Set 14   *pages 96–97*

Compare these integers. Use >, <, or =.

1. 8 ● 1   2. 6 ● 12   3. 4 ● −2   4. −7 ● 6   5. −35 ● −30
6. −5 ● 0   7. −4 ● −13   8. −27 ● −29   9. −2 ● −12   10. −17 ● −18
11. −9 ● −1   12. 5 ● −8   13. −6 ● −16   14. −22 ● −18   15. −56 ● −52

List in order from the least to the greatest.

16. 0 −9 −3   17. 7 −2 −1   18. 4 −4 0
19. 6 −4 4 −6   20. −10 −17 −21 15   21. 15 −18 −1 3
22. −3 −20 −11 5 0   23. 12 −2 5 −13 −14   24. 7 −8 −10 9 −4

Set 15   *pages 98–99*

1. −6 + (−9)   2. −5 + (−7)   3. −13 + 13   4. 11 + (−4)
5. −11 + 4   6. −6 + (−19)   7. −12 + 4   8. −45 + (−13)
9. 57 + (−31)   10. −46 + (−34)   11. −35 + 0   12. 16 + (−15)
13. −15 + 14   14. 23 + (−23)   15. 40 + (−22)   16. −32 + (−58)

Set 16   *pages 100–101*

1. 10 − 4   2. 11 − (−3)   3. −11 − 3   4. −11 − (−5)
5. 17 − 20   6. −40 − 11   7. −5 − (−6)   8. 10 − 25
9. −24 − (−24)   10. −12 − (−18)   11. 0 − 50   12. −41 − (−36)
13. 48 − (−54)   14. −36 − 27   15. 6 − (−3)   16. 0 − (−38)

Set 17   *pages 104–105*

1. (−6)(9)   2. (−8)(−7)   3. 13(−3)   4. (−2)(−37)   5. (−6)(−6)
6. 5(−5)   7. (−1)(0)   8. (−11)(−4)   9. $(−1)^4$ 10. $(−2)^3$
11. 6(−2)(−4)   12. 9(−7)(10)   13. (−4)(0)(−1)   14. (−3)(−4)(−1)
15. 2(−9)(−2)   16. (−6)(3)(4) 17. (−5)(−3)(−7)   18. 20(−8)(−1)

406

Set 18 *pages 106–107*

1. $19 \div (-1)$
2. $54 \div 9$
3. $20 \div (-5)$
4. $(-36) \div 4$
5. $(-55) \div (-11)$
6. $0 \div (-15)$
7. $(-49) \div (-7)$
8. $(-120) \div 15$
9. $168 \div (-14)$
10. $(-855) \div (-19)$
11. $(-45) \div 3$
12. $60 \div (-12)$
13. $47 \div (-47)$
14. $(-63) \div (-63)$
15. $(-91) \div 91$
16. $(-156) \div (-6)$

Set 19 *pages 108–109*

Evaluate each expression for $n = -8$.

1. $7n$
2. $-3n$
3. $4n + 2$
4. $10 - n$
5. $6 - 2n$
6. $-40 - 5n$
7. $2(n + 3)$
8. $-6(n - 4)$
9. $-n - 4$
10. $9n - 15$

Evaluate each expression for $x = -18$.

11. $\dfrac{x}{3}$
12. $\dfrac{36}{x}$
13. $\dfrac{-x}{6}$
14. $\dfrac{x}{18} + \dfrac{x}{9}$
15. $\dfrac{x}{2} - \dfrac{x}{6}$
16. $16 - \dfrac{x}{3}$
17. $\dfrac{10 - x}{7}$
18. $\dfrac{2x + 6}{10}$
19. $\dfrac{-4(x + 10)}{8}$
20. $\dfrac{4x}{9} - 13$

Set 20 *pages 138–139*

Write the prime factorization.

1. 40
2. 126
3. 432
4. 490
5. 725
6. 168
7. 726
8. 1008
9. 396
10. 882
11. 770
12. 4356
13. 2500
14. 10,584

Set 21 *pages 140–141*

Find the greatest common factor of each pair of numbers.

1. 18; 24
2. 25; 60
3. 14; 49
4. 32; 48
5. 52; 58
6. 77; 50
7. 38; 133
8. 24; 56
9. 15; 105
10. 27; 72
11. 74; 111
12. 375; 875

Set 22 *pages 142–143*

Find the least common multiple of each pair of numbers.

1. 10; 15
2. 15; 20
3. 3; 7
4. 7; 11
5. 15; 18
6. 9; 27
7. 4; 6
8. 42; 63
9. 48; 15
10. 44; 45
11. 68; 69
12. 9; 75

More Practice

Set 23 *pages 150–151*

Write each fraction in lowest terms.

1. $\frac{12}{22}$ **2.** $\frac{30}{48}$ **3.** $\frac{12}{124}$ **4.** $\frac{77}{84}$ **5.** $\frac{30}{125}$ **6.** $\frac{500}{810}$ **7.** $\frac{72}{144}$ **8.** $\frac{83}{93}$

9. $\frac{60}{105}$ **10.** $\frac{47}{141}$ **11.** $\frac{12}{13}$ **12.** $\frac{128}{144}$ **13.** $\frac{40}{44}$ **14.** $\frac{36}{54}$ **15.** $\frac{75}{99}$ **16.** $\frac{78}{96}$

Set 24 *pages 152–153*

Write a mixed number or a whole number for each fraction.

1. $\frac{13}{4}$ **2.** $\frac{12}{5}$ **3.** $\frac{36}{9}$ **4.** $\frac{37}{7}$ **5.** $\frac{75}{20}$ **6.** $\frac{53}{9}$ **7.** $\frac{63}{6}$ **8.** $\frac{143}{11}$

9. $\frac{13}{11}$ **10.** $\frac{22}{3}$ **11.** $\frac{200}{24}$ **12.** $\frac{89}{40}$ **13.** $\frac{621}{9}$ **14.** $\frac{17}{2}$ **15.** $\frac{65}{12}$ **16.** $\frac{120}{14}$

Write a fraction for each mixed number.

17. $1\frac{1}{3}$ **18.** $2\frac{3}{4}$ **19.** $3\frac{4}{7}$ **20.** $10\frac{5}{6}$ **21.** $7\frac{1}{8}$ **22.** $2\frac{13}{25}$ **23.** $5\frac{4}{15}$ **24.** $8\frac{3}{11}$

25. $9\frac{3}{5}$ **26.** $3\frac{1}{10}$ **27.** $11\frac{1}{12}$ **28.** $4\frac{3}{16}$ **29.** $1\frac{27}{28}$ **30.** $2\frac{2}{29}$ **31.** $8\frac{6}{7}$ **32.** $9\frac{1}{9}$

Set 25 *pages 156–157*

1. $\frac{1}{3} \times \frac{6}{7}$ **2.** $\frac{1}{8} \times \frac{4}{9}$ **3.** $\frac{2}{5} \times \frac{1}{2}$ **4.** $\frac{5}{7} \times \frac{2}{3}$ **5.** $\frac{4}{9} \times \frac{9}{11}$ **6.** $\frac{1}{7} \times \frac{1}{7}$

7. $\frac{7}{10} \times \frac{10}{21}$ **8.** $\frac{4}{15} \times \frac{5}{12}$ **9.** $\frac{5}{8} \times \frac{5}{8}$ **10.** $\frac{8}{11} \times \frac{11}{12}$ **11.** $\frac{1}{4} \times 16$ **12.** $\frac{3}{7} \times 28$

13. $8 \times \frac{1}{3}$ **14.** $\frac{1}{6} \times 9$ **15.** $15 \times \frac{2}{25}$ **16.** $\frac{7}{18} \times 6$ **17.** $\frac{5}{9} \times \frac{2}{15}$ **18.** $\frac{3}{14} \times \frac{7}{9}$

Set 26 *pages 158–159*

1. $6 \times 1\frac{2}{3}$ **2.** $8 \times 3\frac{1}{2}$ **3.** $12 \times 6\frac{3}{4}$ **4.** $2\frac{4}{5} \times 5$ **5.** $9\frac{3}{10} \times 16$ **6.** $4\frac{1}{9} \times 9$

7. $5\frac{1}{4} \times \frac{4}{21}$ **8.** $8\frac{2}{3} \times \frac{3}{7}$ **9.** $1\frac{1}{9} \times \frac{2}{5}$ **10.** $\frac{3}{11} \times 3\frac{1}{7}$ **11.** $\frac{2}{15} \times 4\frac{2}{7}$ **12.** $\frac{5}{9} \times 3\frac{3}{20}$

13. $1\frac{2}{3} \times 1\frac{1}{20}$ **14.** $2\frac{3}{4} \times 3\frac{1}{5}$ **15.** $4\frac{7}{8} \times 1\frac{7}{13}$ **16.** $2\frac{1}{2} \times 4\frac{4}{5}$ **17.** $3\frac{1}{3} \times 3\frac{1}{3}$ **18.** $4\frac{3}{8} \times 5\frac{1}{7}$

Set 27 *pages 162–163*

1. $5 \div \frac{1}{4}$ 2. $6 \div \frac{2}{3}$ 3. $8 \div \frac{5}{6}$ 4. $21 \div \frac{3}{7}$ 5. $\frac{1}{4} \div \frac{3}{8}$ 6. $\frac{4}{5} \div \frac{6}{25}$

7. $\frac{4}{5} \div \frac{4}{5}$ 8. $\frac{7}{16} \div \frac{3}{8}$ 9. $\frac{3}{8} \div \frac{7}{16}$ 10. $\frac{9}{10} \div \frac{4}{7}$ 11. $\frac{25}{36} \div \frac{5}{6}$ 12. $2\frac{3}{8} \div \frac{3}{4}$

13. $3\frac{1}{2} \div \frac{1}{7}$ 14. $4\frac{1}{6} \div \frac{1}{3}$ 15. $2\frac{1}{7} \div \frac{3}{14}$ 16. $2\frac{1}{10} \div \frac{14}{15}$ 17. $5\frac{3}{5} \div \frac{3}{5}$ 18. $6\frac{1}{6} \div \frac{3}{4}$

Set 28 *pages 164–165*

1. $8 \div 1\frac{1}{3}$ 2. $3\frac{1}{5} \div 6$ 3. $\frac{3}{4} \div 3\frac{1}{8}$ 4. $11 \div 6$ 5. $4\frac{1}{3} \div 1\frac{1}{6}$ 6. $5\frac{1}{4} \div 7\frac{1}{2}$

7. $15\frac{3}{4} \div 5\frac{1}{4}$ 8. $3\frac{1}{6} \div 2\frac{1}{2}$ 9. $2\frac{1}{4} \div 3\frac{2}{3}$ 10. $10\frac{2}{3} \div 1\frac{7}{9}$ 11. $1\frac{7}{9} \div 10\frac{2}{3}$ 12. $9\frac{4}{7} \div 1\frac{1}{2}$

13. $\frac{1}{2} \div 2\frac{1}{2}$ 14. $\frac{3}{7} \div 1\frac{13}{14}$ 15. $12 \div 5\frac{1}{4}$ 16. $7\frac{1}{5} \div 2\frac{2}{5}$ 17. $7\frac{1}{7} \div 11\frac{1}{4}$ 18. $10\frac{3}{4} \div 3\frac{1}{5}$

Set 29 *pages 174–175*

Compare. Use $>$, $<$, or $=$.

1. $\frac{9}{16} \bullet \frac{5}{16}$ 2. $\frac{11}{14} \bullet \frac{3}{14}$ 3. $\frac{7}{8} \bullet \frac{1}{2}$ 4. $\frac{12}{16} \bullet \frac{3}{4}$ 5. $\frac{4}{7} \bullet \frac{3}{5}$

6. $3\frac{1}{6} \bullet 3\frac{3}{8}$ 7. $4\frac{7}{10} \bullet 4\frac{21}{30}$ 8. $6\frac{1}{4} \bullet 3\frac{1}{8}$ 9. $5\frac{3}{4} \bullet 5\frac{3}{5}$ 10. $9\frac{11}{20} \bullet 9\frac{3}{4}$

List in order from the least to the greatest.

11. $\frac{2}{3}$ $\frac{1}{4}$ $\frac{1}{2}$ 12. $\frac{1}{3}$ $\frac{2}{5}$ $\frac{2}{15}$ 13. $\frac{2}{3}$ $\frac{13}{16}$ $\frac{5}{8}$ 14. $\frac{1}{2}$ $\frac{2}{3}$ $\frac{4}{7}$ 15. $\frac{5}{6}$ $\frac{7}{9}$ $\frac{3}{4}$

16. $1\frac{1}{2}$ $3\frac{1}{4}$ $2\frac{1}{3}$ 17. $2\frac{1}{6}$ $2\frac{2}{5}$ $2\frac{3}{10}$ 18. $4\frac{1}{8}$ $4\frac{1}{3}$ $4\frac{1}{6}$ 19. $3\frac{4}{7}$ $3\frac{3}{5}$ $3\frac{1}{2}$ 20. $5\frac{7}{12}$ $5\frac{5}{8}$ $5\frac{3}{4}$

Set 30 *pages 176–177*

1. $\frac{5}{6}$ 2. $\frac{2}{3}$ 3. $\frac{3}{4}$ 4. $\frac{4}{7}$ 5. $\frac{1}{3}$ 6. $\frac{5}{9}$ 7. $\frac{3}{5}$ 8. $\frac{1}{2}$
$+\frac{1}{3}$ $+\frac{3}{5}$ $+\frac{1}{6}$ $+\frac{5}{8}$ $+\frac{5}{8}$ $+\frac{5}{12}$ $+\frac{3}{4}$ $+\frac{3}{14}$

9. $\frac{7}{8}$ 10. $\frac{1}{2}$ 11. $\frac{5}{6}$ 12. $\frac{6}{7}$ 13. $\frac{3}{4}$ 14. $\frac{3}{8}$ 15. $\frac{3}{4}$ 16. $\frac{11}{12}$
$-\frac{3}{4}$ $-\frac{3}{10}$ $-\frac{1}{4}$ $-\frac{1}{6}$ $-\frac{5}{9}$ $-\frac{3}{10}$ $-\frac{2}{7}$ $-\frac{2}{3}$

More Practice

Set 31 *pages 178-179*

1. $5\frac{1}{2}$
   $+4\frac{1}{4}$

2. $9\frac{3}{8}$
   $+\frac{3}{4}$

3. $5\frac{5}{6}$
   $+11\frac{5}{6}$

4. $21\frac{2}{3}$
   $+19$

5. $5\frac{3}{10}$
   $+4\frac{3}{5}$

6. $6\frac{2}{3}$
   $+9\frac{1}{5}$

7. $8\frac{3}{7}$
   $+9\frac{4}{7}$

8. $10\frac{1}{4}$
   $+23\frac{5}{6}$

9. $9\frac{1}{3}$
   $+6\frac{3}{7}$

10. $4\frac{11}{15}$
    $+1\frac{1}{3}$

11. $2\frac{3}{8}$
    $+3\frac{5}{6}$

12. $20\frac{3}{8}$
    $+\frac{1}{8}$

13. $8\frac{7}{10}$
    $+3\frac{2}{7}$

14. $\frac{1}{2}$
    $+7\frac{3}{5}$

Set 32 *pages 180-181*

1. $10\frac{1}{2}$
   $-4\frac{1}{8}$

2. $9\frac{2}{5}$
   $-1\frac{1}{3}$

3. $8\frac{5}{6}$
   $-7\frac{11}{12}$

4. $9\frac{7}{8}$
   -4

5. 9
   $-4\frac{7}{8}$

6. $17\frac{1}{4}$
   $-12\frac{2}{3}$

7. $7\frac{1}{3}$
   $-\frac{5}{9}$

8. $17\frac{4}{7}$
   $-9\frac{6}{7}$

9. 21
   $-19\frac{2}{11}$

10. $33\frac{1}{6}$
    $-33\frac{1}{9}$

11. $4\frac{3}{4}$
    $-3\frac{2}{5}$

12. $6\frac{2}{7}$
    $-5\frac{9}{14}$

13. $8\frac{3}{10}$
    $-4\frac{1}{15}$

14. $20\frac{1}{2}$
    $-15\frac{5}{11}$

Set 33 *page 182*

Evaluate each expression for $x = \frac{5}{6}$.

1. $x + 3\frac{5}{12}$
2. $x - \frac{1}{3}$
3. $4\frac{1}{2} - x$
4. $x + 6\frac{1}{5}$
5. $\left(x - \frac{1}{6}\right) - \frac{1}{4}$

Evaluate each expression for $y = 5\frac{1}{4}$.

6. $y + 6\frac{1}{4}$
7. $8\frac{7}{8} - y$
8. $12 - y$
9. $8\frac{1}{8} - \left(y - 3\frac{1}{2}\right)$
10. $\left(9\frac{4}{5} - y\right) - 3\frac{1}{2}$

Set 34 *pages 184-185*

Solve each equation.

1. $a - \frac{3}{4} = \frac{1}{2}$
2. $4\frac{3}{7} + c = 8$
3. $h + \frac{5}{7} = 1\frac{2}{7}$
4. $9 + m = 17\frac{1}{2}$

5. $\frac{5}{8} + w = 5\frac{1}{4}$
6. $r - \frac{2}{3} = 11$
7. $n - 2\frac{1}{6} = 5\frac{4}{5}$
8. $11\frac{3}{5} = r + 9\frac{3}{4}$

9. $11\frac{1}{8} = u - 4\frac{3}{8}$
10. $6\frac{1}{2} = x - \frac{5}{12}$
11. $c + 10\frac{9}{10} = 11\frac{3}{10}$
12. $11\frac{7}{8} + k = 20$

Set 35 *pages 196–197*

1. 9.276×10^2 **2.** 0.048×10^1 **3.** 723.9×10^8 **4.** 0.0003×10^6

5. 244.3×10^{-1} **6.** 625.3×10^{-7} **7.** 0.25×10^{-4} **8.** 0.00021×10^{-2}

Set 36 *pages 198–199*

Write each number in scientific notation.

1. 253   **2.** 9400   **3.** 444,000   **4.** 3,120,000   **5.** 61.1   **6.** 56.37

7. 7070   **8.** 11,000   **9.** 29,030   **10.** 10,000,000   **11.** 6.26   **12.** 536.51

Set 37 *pages 200–201*

Write each number in scientific notation.

1. 0.3   **2.** 0.06   **3.** 0.0018   **4.** 0.000732   **5.** 0.012   **6.** 0.0000568

7. 0.1   **8.** 0.083   **9.** 0.00055   **10.** 0.000098   **11.** 0.000006   **12.** 0.00000072

Set 38 *pages 202–203*

Write each product as a power of 10.

1. $10^5 \times 10^6$ **2.** $10^{-1} \times 10^9$ **3.** $10^{-3} \times 10^{-7}$ **4.** $10^2 \times 10^{-8}$ **5.** $10^{-6} \times 10^6$

6. $10^4 \times 10^9$ **7.** $10^{-8} \times 10^4$ **8.** $10^{-4} \times 10^{-4}$ **9.** $10^5 \times 10^5$ **10.** $10^{-9} \times 10^7$

Find each product, using exponents.
Give answers in standard form.

11. 1000×1000 **12.** 0.1×10 **13.** 10×0.01 **14.** $0.0001 \times 1000 \times 10$

15. 0.01×0.001 **16.** 0.1×0.1 **17.** $100,000 \times 0.01$ **18.** $0.01 \times 0.001 \times 100$

Set 39 *pages 204–205*

Multiply, using scientific notation.
Then give the answers in standard form.

1. $410,000 \times 6500$ **2.** 0.83×1300 **3.** 2000×35

4. $0.00052 \times 34,000$ **5.** $47,000 \times 2200$ **6.** 0.006×0.3001

7. 0.00002×6900 **8.** $0.0000039 \times 40,000$ **9.** 0.00091×87

10. $490,000 \times 5000$ **11.** $54,500 \times 0.0011$ **12.** 0.183×0.103

More Practice

Set 40   *pages 206–207*

Write each quotient as a power of 10.

1. $\dfrac{10^7}{10^2}$ 2. $\dfrac{10^9}{10^9}$ 3. $\dfrac{10^6}{10^{-5}}$ 4. $\dfrac{10^8}{10^{-1}}$ 5. $\dfrac{10^{-7}}{10^2}$ 6. $\dfrac{10^{-4}}{10^{-8}}$ 7. $\dfrac{10^{-6}}{10^6}$

8. $\dfrac{10^{-2}}{10^{-9}}$ 9. $\dfrac{10^{12}}{10^3}$ 10. $\dfrac{10^{-5}}{10^{-5}}$ 11. $\dfrac{10^{-6}}{10^{-2}}$ 12. $\dfrac{10^{-1}}{10^{-7}}$ 13. $\dfrac{10^{11}}{10^2}$ 14. $\dfrac{10^2}{10^{-11}}$

Find each quotient, using exponents.
Give the answers in standard form.

15. $\dfrac{10,000}{100}$ 16. $\dfrac{10}{10,000}$ 17. $\dfrac{1000}{0.1}$ 18. $\dfrac{1000}{1000}$ 19. $\dfrac{10}{0.01}$ 20. $\dfrac{0.01}{10}$

21. $\dfrac{0.0001}{0.1}$ 22. $\dfrac{0.01}{0.01}$ 23. $\dfrac{1000}{0.001}$ 24. $\dfrac{0.01}{0.001}$ 25. $\dfrac{0.1}{100}$ 26. $\dfrac{0.001}{0.01}$

Set 41   *pages 208–209*

Divide, using scientific notation. Round the quotient of the decimals
to the nearest tenth. Give the answers in standard form.

1. $\dfrac{5.6 \times 10^4}{7 \times 10^2}$ 2. $\dfrac{6,000,000}{0.35}$ 3. $\dfrac{0.00804}{120}$ 4. $\dfrac{250,000}{0.62}$ 5. $\dfrac{0.0053}{0.018}$

6. $\dfrac{7 \times 10^{-3}}{2.1 \times 10^2}$ 7. $\dfrac{28,300,000}{4500}$ 8. $\dfrac{9000}{0.96}$ 9. $\dfrac{0.506}{0.29}$ 10. $\dfrac{320}{48,000}$

Set 42   *pages 216–217*

Solve each proportion.

1. $\dfrac{10}{15} = \dfrac{n}{9}$ 2. $\dfrac{6}{12} = \dfrac{c}{10}$ 3. $\dfrac{12}{42} = \dfrac{14}{h}$ 4. $\dfrac{24}{64} = \dfrac{9}{r}$ 5. $\dfrac{18}{x} = \dfrac{8}{20}$

6. $\dfrac{p}{24} = \dfrac{12}{9}$ 7. $\dfrac{15}{n} = \dfrac{50}{60}$ 8. $\dfrac{15}{s} = \dfrac{40}{56}$ 9. $\dfrac{14}{56} = \dfrac{a}{4}$ 10. $\dfrac{12}{96} = \dfrac{8}{z}$

11. $\dfrac{18}{w} = \dfrac{45}{55}$ 12. $\dfrac{v}{130} = \dfrac{14}{20}$ 13. $\dfrac{0.5}{14} = \dfrac{1.5}{d}$ 14. $\dfrac{0.8}{1.6} = \dfrac{1.5}{m}$ 15. $\dfrac{9}{k} = \dfrac{1.8}{2}$

16. $\dfrac{y}{1.1} = \dfrac{4}{5.5}$ 17. $\dfrac{b}{4} = \dfrac{0.9}{0.12}$ 18. $\dfrac{1.5}{t} = \dfrac{2}{0.8}$ 19. $\dfrac{7.5}{8} = \dfrac{m}{1.6}$ 20. $\dfrac{5.7}{6} = \dfrac{x}{0.8}$

Set 43 *pages 232–233*

Write a fraction for each percent.

1. 37% **2.** 74% **3.** 85% **4.** 9% **5.** 42.5% **6.** $91\frac{2}{3}$% **7.** 8.2%

Write a percent for each fraction.

8. $\frac{11}{20}$ **9.** $\frac{21}{25}$ **10.** $\frac{7}{12}$ **11.** $\frac{3}{14}$ **12.** $\frac{19}{40}$ **13.** $\frac{123}{200}$ **14.** $\frac{11}{18}$

Set 44 *pages 236–237*

1. 25% of 68 is ____. **2.** 47% of 500 is ____. **3.** 6% of 95 is ____.

4. 120% of 60 is ____. **5.** 200% of 41 is ____. **6.** $37\frac{1}{2}$% of 40 is ____.

7. $16\frac{2}{3}$% of 84 is ____. **8.** 1.7% of 700 is ____. **9.** 0.9% of 2300 is ____.

Set 45 *pages 242–243*

1. ____% of 50 is 24. **2.** ____% of 55 is 33. **3.** ____% of 350 is 14.

4. ____% of 400 is 60. **5.** ____% of 72 is 12. **6.** ____% of 80 is 240.

7. ____% of 36 is 13.5. **8.** ____% of 60 is 52.5. **9.** ____% of 14.5 is 26.1.

Set 46 *pages 246–247*

1. 75% of ____ is 18. **2.** 30% of ____ is 42. **3.** 5% of ____ is 8.

4. $62\frac{1}{2}$% of ____ is 40. **5.** 14% of ____ is 10.5. **6.** 160% of ____ is 72.

7. 6% of ____ is 15.12. **8.** 0.4% of ____ is 8. **9.** 140% of ____ is 92.4.

10. $16\frac{2}{3}$% of ____ is 30. **11.** $12\frac{1}{2}$% of ____ is 9.6. **12.** $83\frac{1}{3}$% of ____ is 75.

Set 47 *pages 334–335*

For each set of data, find the mean, the median, and the mode.

1. 1, 3, 7, 9, 2, 7, 7, 8, 1 **2.** 4, 3, 11, 10, 15, 13, 1, 7, 56

3. 3, 3, 3, 21, 21, 30 **4.** 5, 5, 3, 16, 12, 80, 12

5. 1, 4, 50, 50 **6.** 2, 4, 8, 10, 6, 8, 2, 1, 9, 2

7. 7, 10, 30, 15, 11 **8.** 143, 50, 9, 205, 102

9. 80, 72, 49, 72, 3, 3 **10.** 340, 262, 262, 4, 2, 5, 28

Answers to Odd-Numbered Exercises

Chapter 1

Pages 2-3 **1.** 10,000 **3.** 1000
5. 10,000,000 **7.** 1,000,000 **9.** 49 **11.** 125
13. 1296 **15.** 81 **17.** 10^3 **19.** 10^2 **21.** 6^2
23. 3^1 **25.** 2 **27.** 5 **29.** 2 **31.** 3
33. $(1 \times 10^6) + (7 \times 10^3) + (3 \times 10^2) +$
$(2 \times 10^1) + (8 \times 10^0)$ **35.** $(1 \times 10^6) +$
$(5 \times 10^5) + (2 \times 10^4) + (5 \times 10^3) +$
$(3 \times 10^2) + (1 \times 10^1) + (1 \times 10^0)$
37. 8,000,000,000 **39.** 345,082,000,000,000

Pages 4-5 **1.** 360 **3.** 3600 **5.** 15,470
7. 57,440 **9.** 31,700 **11.** 42,000
13. 46,700 **15.** 540,000 **17.** 600,000
19. 8,000,000 **21.** 330,000,000 **23.** 100,000
25. 135,000 **27.** 200,000 **29.** 216,000
31. 200,000 **33.** 219,000 **35.** 200,000
37. 186,000 **39.** 900,000 **41.** 858,000
43. 900,000 **45.** 879,000 **47.** 600,000
49. 560,000 **51.** 134,999; 125,000

Pages 6-7 **1.** 900 **3.** 500 **5.** 800 **7.** 600
9. 500 **11.** 9000 **13.** 5000 **15.** 14,000
17. 90,000 **19.** 10,000 **21.** 700,000
23. 400,000 **25.** 150,000

Pages 8-9 **1.** 613 **3.** 10,861 **5.** 90,322
7. 1877 **9.** 6035 **11.** 1466 **13.** 222,003
15. 60,621 **17.** 186 **19.** 829 **21.** 589
23. 3064 **25.** 23,518 **27.** 1359 **29.** 2285
31. 21,893 **33.** 63,135 **35.** 74,121 **37.** 22,353

Pages 10-11 **1.** 160,000 **3.** 240,000
5. 140,000 **7.** 40,000 **9.** 300,000
11. 12,000,000 **13.** 18,000,000
15. 24,000,000 **17.** 40,000,000
19. 18,000,000

Pages 12-13 **1.** 360 **3.** 234 **5.** 2880
7. 3652 **9.** 2400 **11.** 2380 **13.** 1968
15. 4370 **17.** 22,555 **19.** 1500 **21.** 20,500
23. 36,240 **25.** 7500 **27.** 42,048
29. 345,600 **31.** 53,970 **33.** 95,418
35. 46,632 **37.** 104,571 **39.** 63,112
41. 15,930 **43.** 2,007,000 liters **45.** 1472;
1472 **47.** 1850; 2444 **49.** 2924; 2924
51. 945; 648

Pages 14-15 **1.** 3 **3.** 13 **5.** 12 **7.** 60
9. 15 **11.** 14 **13.** 72 **15.** 260 **17.** 156
19. 1 **21.** 141 **23.** 34 **25.** 9 **27.** 19
29. 195 **31.** 227 **33.** $6 \times (7 + 9) = 96$
35. $6 \times 9 - (2 \times 7) = 40$

Pages 16-17 **1.** 53 R3 **3.** 157 **5.** 403 R3
7. 700 R2 **9.** 21 R7 **11.** 82 **13.** 253 R10
15. 380 R25 **17.** 169 R39 **19.** 916
21. 2 R159 **23.** 22 R188 **25.** 409 R53
27. 53 **29.** 68 km/h

Pages 18-19 **1.** 27 programs **3.** 52 months
5. 33 pages **7.** 17 students **9.** $975

Pages 20-21 **1.** 9 **3.** 2 **5.** 14 **7.** 10 **9.** 4
11. 1 **13.** 7 **15.** 2 **17.** 14 **19.** 10 **21.** 13
23. 22 **25.** 5 **27.** 6
29. $\dfrac{5(8)}{2} = 20$ **31.** $\dfrac{12(3 - 1)}{4 - 2} = 12$

Chapter 2

Pages 24-25 **1.** 8 thousandths **3.** 8 ones
5. Answers will vary. An example is 6.666066.
7. Answers will vary. An example is 0.222225.
9. Fifty-four and nine thousand three hundred
eighty ten-thousandths **11.** Fifty-eight and
nine thousand three hundred thirty-two
ten-thousandths **13.** 0.65 **15.** 0.097
17. 5400.3 **19.** 2,600,000
21. 4,500,000,000,000,000,000,000

Pages 26-27 **1.** 0.50 **3.** 4.76 **5.** 64.90
7. 16.00 **9.** 27.000 **11.** 2.840 **13.** 46.623
15. < **17.** > **19.** < **21.** > **23.** <
25. 0.134 0.135 0.261 **27.** 3.241 3.369 3.418
3.836 **29.** 9.8657

Pages 28-29 **1.** 6 **3.** 60 **5.** 1 **7.** 7 **9.** 6
11. 73 **13.** 2.16 **15.** 9.00 **17.** 0.73
19. 0.99 **21.** 9.06 **23.** 2.56 **25.** 200.005
27. 0.736 **29.** 2.005 **31.** 0.783 **33.** 0.436
35. 324.6720 **37.** 3.8889 **39.** 10.2323
41. 54.0000 **43.** 8.2 m **45.** 4.9 m **47.** 0.2 m

Pages 30-31 **1.** 15 **3.** 15 **5.** 26 **7.** 4
9. 15 **11.** 13 **13.** 1 **15.** $21 **17.** $39
19. $6 **21.** $1 **23.** $4.50; $5.49

Pages 32-33 **1.** 6.382 **3.** 15.29 **5.** 19.60
7. 36.56 **9.** 40.97 **11.** 8.338 **13.** 22.20831
15. 17.70726 **17.** 20.02439 **19.** 10.78
21. 0.6516 **23.** 0.0701 **25.** 188.59
27. 0.196 **29.** 30.48 cm **31.** 0.18 cm

Pages 34-35 **1.** $4.10 **3.** Too little information
5. Too little information **7.** Too little
information **9.** 6203 km

Pages 36–37 **1.** 0.82 **3.** 3.54 **5.** 0.00126
7. 0.00000315 **9.** 0.00000752 **11.** 5.67
13. 0.192 **15.** 7.28 **17.** 33.088 **19.** 0.258
21. 97.686 **23.** 4281 **25.** 50,000
27. $22.79 **29.** 0.000002 **31.** 2.6 **33.** 84.0

Pages 38–39 **1.** 17.2 **3.** 10.45 **5.** 0.4664
7. 12 **9.** 80 **11.** 300 **13.** 0.05 **15.** 600
17. 280 **19.** 1200 **21.** 80 **23.** 0.000045
25. $2.40

Pages 40–41 **1.** 2.4 **3.** 3.6 **5.** 0.156
7. 63.2 **9.** 3.5 **11.** 1.42 **13.** 0.72 **15.** 1.2
17. 1.09 **19.** 15.84 **21.** 0.09865
23. 0.2 cm **25.** 0.012 cm

Pages 42–43 **1.** 90 **3.** 3.5 **5.** 80 **7.** 4
9. 9000 **11.** 5 **13.** 0.3 **15.** 8.1 **17.** 137.33
19. 7.55 **21.** 4194 kilowatt-hours

Chapter 3

Pages 46–47 **1.** -gram **3.** meter **5.** -liter
7. -gram **9.** -gram **11.** -meter **13.** -gram
15. meter **17.** meter **19.** centimeter
21. millimeter **23.** kilometer **25.** 100
27. 0.01 **29.** 10 **31.** 0.001 **33.** 100
35. 0.01 **37.** 1000

Pages 48–49 **1.** 9.24 **3.** 6230 **5.** 5200
7. 3000 **9.** 4.36 **11.** 0.00421 **13.** 1.532
15. 90 **17.** 1200 **19.** 3.2 **21.** 69.4
23. 6800 **25.** 84.1 **27.** 182 **29.** 3 m
31. 20 cm **33.** 38 cm **35.** 66 cm **37.** 1 m
39. 1.5 m **41.** 3.8 cm **43.** 0.36 m
45. 1.46 km

Pages 50–51 **1.** 0.305 **3.** 15,400
5. 0.013892 **7.** 651,000 **9.** 0.7168
11. 5.12 **13.** 46 g **15.** 1 g **17.** 500 g
19. 1 kg **21.** 75 kg **23.** 188 g **25.** 95 mg

Pages 52–53 **1.** 0.768 **3.** 65,300
5. 0.07815 **7.** 0.648 **9.** 470 **11.** 250 mL
13. 400 L **15.** 1 L **17.** 8 L **19.** 60 kL
21. 6000 L

Pages 54–55 **1.** 8 m² **3.** 1.8 m² **5.** 144 cm²
7. 30,000 **9.** 73.85 **11.** 0.1328
13. 4,000,000 **15.** 0.015563 **17.** 3,800,000

Pages 56–57 **1.** 23,000,000 **3.** 0.0048
5. 0.568 **7.** 120 m³ **9.** 216 dm³
11. 140,000 mm³ or 140 cm³

Page 58 **1.** −10°C **3.** 37°C **5.** 40°C
7. 78°C **9.** 30°C **11.** −5°C

Page 59 **1.** 144 L, 144 kg **3.** 315 mL, 315 g
5. 11,700 L, 11,700 kg **7.** 403,200 mL,
403,200 g, or 403.2 L, 403.2 kg

Pages 60–61 **1.** 1 kg **3.** 0.1 cm **5.** 0.01 kg
7. 1 mL **9.** 0.01 L **11.** 0.1 mL **13.** 3.24 kg
15. 14.32 L **17.** 145 mL **19.** 32.15 cm
21. 32.4 g **23.** 56 mL **25.** 19.0 cm
27. 25.8 L **29.** 4.61 g

Chapter 4

Pages 68–69 **1.** 26 **3.** 39 **5.** 12 **7.** 145
9. 16 **11.** 20 **13.** 24 **15.** 11 **17.** 65
19. 145 **21.** 126 **23.** 135 **25.** 9, J
27. 21, N **29.** 43, E **31.** 34, F **33.** 28, O
35. 48, G **37.** 24, R **39.** 66, A **41.** 43, E
43. 66, A

Pages 70–71 **1.** $m + 29$ **3.** $d - 41$
5. $33 - t$ **7.** $54 + s$ **9.** $3 + r$ **11.** $8 - m$
13. $b + 3$ **15.** $232 - x$ **17.** $d + 5$
19. $b + d - 27$

Pages 72–73 **1.** $k = 27$ **3.** $h = 65$
5. $q = 85$ **7.** $s = 45$ **9.** $w = 103$
11. $z = 203$ **13.** $m = 34.9$ **15.** $a = 11.97$
17. $x = 37$ **19.** $b + 26 = 47, b = 21$
21. $y + 34 = 112, y = 78$ **23.** 4745 points
25. 591.8 dm

Pages 74–75 **1.** $x + 32 = 189$ or $189 - 32 = x$;
157 people **3.** $x - 53.75 = 32.46$ or
$32.46 + 53.75 = x$; $86.21 **5.** $x + 19.5 = 36$
or $36 - 19.5 = x$; 16.5 hours
7. $7.75 + x = 9.50$ or $9.50 - 7.75 = x$;
$1.75 **9.** $x - 15,389.68 = 3156.94$ or
$15,389.68 + 3156.94 = x$; $18,546.62

Pages 76–77 **1.** 84 **3.** 14 **5.** 1 **7.** 1 **9.** 60
11. 5 **13.** 1 **15.** 3 **17.** 3 **19.** 49 **21.** 7
23. 2 **25.** 60, I **27.** 60, I **29.** 4, L
31. 9, E **33.** 36, D **35.** 18, T **37.** 72, N
39. 1, Y **41.** 9, E **43.** 18, T **45.** 3, R

Pages 78–79 **1.** $18w$ **3.** $14x$ **5.** $\frac{g}{4}$ **7.** $\frac{32}{v}$
9. $\frac{b}{12}$ **11.** rs **13.** $24c$ **15.** $\frac{d}{3}$ **17.** $\frac{29.6}{n}$
19. $\frac{hs}{5}$

Pages 80–81 **1.** $t = 12$ **3.** $p = 14$
5. $w = 187$ **7.** $y = 190.8$ **9.** $k = 1.2$
11. $y = 2.71$ **13.** $n = 3366.33$ **15.** $d = 30$
17. $7c = 168$, $c = 24$ **19.** $19s = 43.7$,
$s = 2.3$ **21.** $53y = 10.07$, $y = 0.19$
23. $1.78 **25.** $36.79

Pages 82–83 **1.** $x + 68 = 143$ or $143 - 68 = x$,

75 customers **3.** $\frac{x}{48} = 9$ or $9(48) = x$,

432 pairs of shoes **5.** $x - 2.6 = 11.7$ or
$11.7 + 2.6 = x$, 14.3 meters
7. $x + 2.40 = 42.35$ or $42.35 - 2.40 = x$,

$39.95 **9.** $12x = 156$ or $\frac{156}{12} = x$, 13 shelves

Pages 84–85 **1.** $r = 7$ **3.** $a = 11$
5. $t = 13.34$ **7.** $h = 6.33$ **9.** $u = 6$
11. $p = 14$ **13.** $f = 23.4$ **15.** $d = 9.3$
17. $x = 315$ **19.** 39 weeks **21.** 11 sales

Pages 86–87 **1.** 15 **3.** 10 **5.** 792 **7.** 640
9. 10 **11.** 150 **13.** 190 **15.** 360 **17.** 240
19. 0 **21.** 204 **23.** 4200 **25.** No. It is
true if $a = b$. For example, $4 \div 4 = 4 - 4$.
27. No. It is true if a and b are not zero and
if $a = b$. For example, $6 \div 6 = 6 \div 6$.

Pages 88–89 **1.** 204 **3.** 416 **5.** 1092
7. 90 **9.** 2000 **11.** 7300 **13.** 100
15. 7650 **17.** 162 **19.** 5600 **21.** 510
23. $6a + 42$ **25.** $4x + 20$ **27.** $12x + 36$
29. $7a + 7b$ **31.** $1.1x + 2.2$ **33.** $16a + 24$
35. $3(n + 5)$ **37.** $9(a + 8)$ **39.** $5(c + 5)$
41. $3(x + 32)$ **43.** $8(2x + 7)$ **45.** $9(8b + 5)$
47. Yes. Use the associative property of addition
twice. $a(b + c + d) = a([b + c] + d) =$
$a[b + c] + ad = ab + ac + ad$

Chapter 5

Pages 94–95 **1.** 146 meters below sea level
3. 16 kilometers east **5.** -6 **7.** 7 **9.** 0
11. -15 **13.** 12 **15.** 15 **17.** -60 **19.** 3

Pages 96–97 **1.** A, -1; B, -3; C, 2; D, -2;
E, 0; F, -4 **3.** $>$ **5.** $>$ **7** $<$ **9.** $>$ **11.** $<$
13. $<$ **15.** $<$ **17.** $>$ **19.** -8 -3 8
21. -8 -2 3 5 **23.** -16 -14 13 18
25. -12 -9 2 8 15 **27.** Asia **29.** -397
-156 -86 -40 -28 -16 2228 5642 5895
6194 6960 8848 **31.** Australia

Pages 98–99 **1.** -7 **3.** 13 **5.** -2 **7.** 8
9. 0 **11.** -8 **13.** -2 **15.** 9 **17.** 25
19. 0 **21.** -3 **23.** 7 **25.** -51 **27.** -52
29. -12 **31.** 12 **33.** -10 **35.** -15 **37.** 17
39. The price rose $7.

Pages 100–101 **1.** -7 **3.** -5 **5.** 4 **7.** 0
9. 13 **11.** -4 **13.** 33 **15.** -4 **17.** -45
19. 44 **21.** -50 **23.** -66 **25.** 21 **27.** -48
29. -23 **31.** 12 **33.** Subtraction is not
associative. **35.** $+$ $-$

Pages 102–103 **1.** 11 **3.** -4 **5.** -3 **7.** -9
9. -20 **11.** 13 **13.** 16 **15.** 2 **17.** -11
19. -2 **21.** -10 **23.** 9 **25.** -6 **27.** -3
29. 11 **31.** -9

Pages 104–105 **1.** 56 **3.** -32 **5.** 27 **7.** 24
9. -21 **11.** -16 **13.** 0 **15.** 96 **17.** 28
19. 19 **21.** 48 **23.** -51 **25.** -45 **27.** 216
29. 384 **31.** 9 **33.** 16 **35.** 90 **37.** -320
39. -180 **41.** 15,360 **43.** -64 **45.** -16
47. -20 **49.** 4 **51.** Positive

Pages 106–107 **1.** 6 **3.** -9 **5.** -7 **7.** 6
9. -8 **11.** 9 **13.** 8 **15.** -8 **17.** -9
19. 9 **21.** 0 **23.** -19 **25.** -6 **27.** 0
29. 6 **31.** -6 **33.** 9 **35.** -10 **37.** -8
39. -7 **41.** 3 **43.** -3 **45.** 3 **47.** -17
49. -63 **51.** -72 **53.** -2 **55.** -3

Pages 108–109 **1.** -30 **3.** 36 **5.** -2 **7.** 11
9. -4 **11.** -15 **13.** -9 **15.** 1 **17.** 3
19. -2 **21.** 2 **23.** -2 **25.** -16 **27.** 1
29. -15

Page 110 **1.** -15; Commutative property of
multiplication **3.** 1; Multiplication property
of one **5.** 7; Commutative property of addition
7. -3; Associative property of multiplication
9. -5; Commutative property of multiplication
11. 8 **13.** -300 **15.** 1800 **17.** -49

Chapter 6

Pages 112–113 **1.** Z E N I T H **3.** E L E V A
T I O N **5.** C H R O N O M E T E R
7. $(-4, -4)$ III **9.** $(-10, -1)$ III **11.** On the
x axis **13.** To the right of the y-axis
15. In quadrant II

Pages 114–115 **1.** About 75 **3.** About 110
5. About 33 **7.** About 125 **9.** About 500 m
11. About 700 m **13.** About 23 seconds

15. About 12 seconds **17.** About 125 m
19. About 0 m **21.** About 100 seconds

Pages 116–117 **1.** 100 **3.** 160 **5.** About
85 mm **7.** About 40 weeks **9.** About $3\frac{1}{3}$
weeks **11.** Amount saved in t weeks

13.

t	0	4	8	12	16	20
S	25	45	65	85	105	125

15. About 15 weeks **17.** Answers will vary.
19.

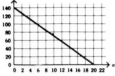

Pages 118–119 **1.** Graph is shown below.
3. −2, −1, 0, 1, 2 Graph is shown below.
5. −9, −8, −6, −4, −1, 0, 2 Graph is shown.

7. A line parallel to the line $y = x$ and 5 units
above it **9.** A line parallel to the line
$y = x$ and 7 units below it **11.** Graph is shown
below. **13.** −5, 0, 5, 10, 15 Graph is shown
below. **15.** 3, 2, 1, 0, −1, −2, −3 Graph is
shown below. **17.** 12, 8, 4, 0, −4, −8, −12
Graph is shown below.

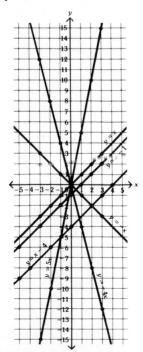

19. $y = -x$, $y = -2x$, $y = -4x$ **21.** Rising

Pages 120–121 **1.** d **3.** c **5.** $y = x + 1$
7. $y = x - 2$ **9.** $y = -x + 1$

11. $y = x + 1$

x	−3	−2	−1	0	1	2
y	−2	−1	0	1	2	3

13. $y = 2x$

x	−1	0	1
y	−2	0	2

15. $y = x - 2$

x	−1	0	1	2	3
y	−3	−2	−1	0	1

17. $y = -\frac{1}{2}x$

x	−2	0	2
y	1	0	−1

19. $y = -x + 2$

x	−1	0	1	2	3
y	3	2	1	0	−1

Pages 122–123 **1.** 41 **3.** 10 **5.** 14 **7.** 9
9. About 0.5 billion **11.** About 175 years
13. About 135 years
15.

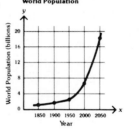

World Population

17. The graph should look something like the
one below.

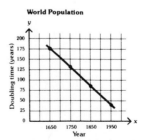

World Population

Pages 124–125 **1.** 330 km **3.** *Lilliput* will reach Lost Island about 3:45 A.M. See the graph below.

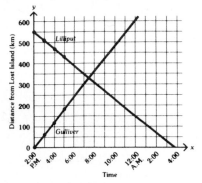

5. About 300 km

7.

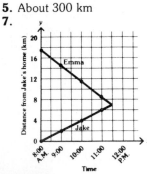

9. About 10.5 km

Chapter 7

Pages 134–135 **1.** 2, 3, 5, 7, 11, 13, 17, 19, 23, 29, 31, 37 **3.** 97 **5.** 2×7
7. Prime **9.** 2×6 or 3×4 **11.** 2×36 or 3×24 or 4×18 or 6×12 or 8×9
13. 3×19 **15.** 7×7 **17.** 3×21 or 7×9
19. 11×11 **21.** 2×72 or 3×48 or 4×36 or 6×24 or 8×18 or 9×16 or 12×12
23. 3×75 or 5×45 or 9×25 or 15×15
25. Prime **27.** 1, 2, 3, 6, 9, 18 **29.** 1, 2, 3, 6, 9, 18, 27, 54 **31.** 1, 2, 3, 5, 6, 9, 10, 15, 18, 30, 45, 90 **33.** 1, 2, 4, 5, 8, 10, 16, 20, 40, 80 **35.** 2 **37.** None **39.** None
41. None **43.** Answers will vary. An example is 3 and 5. **45.** Answers will vary. An example is 3 and 13. **47.** 2 and 3 **49.** 13 and 31, 17 and 71, 37 and 73, 79 and 97

Pages 136–137 **1.** 7128 is divisible by 2, 3, 4, 8, and 9. **3.** 4995 is divisible by 3, 5, and 9. **5.** 25,857 is divisible by 3 and 9.

7. 73,440 is divisible by 2, 3, 4, 5, 8, 9, and 10.
9. 854,850 is divisible by 2, 3, 5, and 10.
11. 770,770 is divisible by 2, 5, and 10.
13. 8,194,168 is divisible by 2, 4, and 8.
15. True **17.** Not divisible by 11
19. Divisible by 11

Pages 138–139 **1.** $2^3 \times 3$ **3.** $2 \times 3 \times 11$
5. $2^4 \times 3^2$ **7.** $2^3 \times 3^3$ **9.** $2 \times 3 \times 5 \times 7$
11. Factor trees will vary. $2^4 \times 3$
13. Factor trees will vary. $2 \times 3^4 \times 5$
15. Factor trees will vary. $2^3 \times 3^2 \times 7$
17. Factor trees will vary. $2 \times 3^2 \times 11$
19. Factor trees will vary. $2 \times 3^3 \times 11^2$
21. Factor trees will vary. $2^5 \times 5^3$
23. $2^2 \times 3^4 \times 5^4$ **25.** $3^3 \times 5^2$ **27.** $2^8 \times 3 \times 11 \times 13$ **29.** 3^3; 1, 3, 9, 27 **31.** $2^2 \times 11$; 1, 2, 4, 11, 22, 44 **33.** $2^2 \times 3 \times 7$; 1, 2, 3, 4, 6, 7, 12, 14, 21, 28, 42, 84
35. $3^2 \times 5^2 \times 7$; 1, 3, 5, 7, 9, 15, 21, 25, 35, 45, 63, 75, 105, 175, 225, 315, 525, 1575

Pages 140–141 **1.** 1, 2, 4 **3.** 1, 2, 3, 6
5. 1, 3, 9 **7.** 1, 3, 9 **9.** 1 **11.** 1, 3, 9
13. 6 **15.** 6 **17.** 17 **19.** 3 **21.** 4
23. 242 **25.** 1, 2, 3, 6, 9, 18; 18

Pages 142–143 **1.** 6, 12, 18, 24, 30 **3.** 13, 26, 39, 52, 65 **5.** 26, 52, 78, 104, 130
7. 36, 72, 108, 144, 180 **9.** 18, 36, 54; 18
11. 48, 96, 144; 48 **13.** 6, 12, 18; 6
15. 210, 420, 630; 210 **17.** 21, 42, 63; 21
19. 50, 100, 150; 50 **21.** 144 **23.** 1200
25. 3306 **27.** 1479 **29.** 210 **31.** 180
33. 540

Chapter 8

Pages 148–149 **1.** Answers will vary. Examples are $\frac{2}{4}, \frac{3}{6}, \frac{4}{8}, \frac{5}{10}$. **3.** Answers will vary. Examples are $\frac{2}{8}, \frac{3}{12}, \frac{4}{16}, \frac{5}{20}$.
5. Answers will vary. Examples are $\frac{8}{10}, \frac{12}{15}, \frac{16}{20}, \frac{20}{25}$. **7.** Answers will vary. Examples are $\frac{8}{18}, \frac{12}{27}, \frac{16}{36}, \frac{20}{45}$. **9.** Answers will vary. Examples are $\frac{9}{18}, \frac{3}{27}, \frac{4}{36}, \frac{5}{40}$ **11.** Answers will vary. Examples are $\frac{6}{8}, \frac{9}{12}, \frac{12}{16}, \frac{15}{20}$.
13. Answers will vary. Examples are $\frac{4}{10}, \frac{6}{15}, \frac{8}{20}, \frac{10}{25}$. **15.** Answers will vary. Examples

are $\frac{8}{14}, \frac{12}{21}, \frac{16}{28}, \frac{20}{35}$. **17.** 3 **19.** 10 **21.** 6
23. 30 **25.** 42 **27.** 108 **29.** 12 **31.** 63
33. 140 **35.** 0 **37.** 17, 36 **39.** 56, 224
41. 10

Pages 150–151 **1.** $\frac{3}{4}$ **3.** $\frac{3}{5}$ **5.** $\frac{6}{7}$ **7.** $\frac{4}{5}$
9. $\frac{11}{13}$ **11.** $\frac{9}{22}$ **13.** $\frac{2}{3}$ **15.** $\frac{1}{3}$ **17.** $\frac{3}{8}$ **19.** $\frac{1}{3}$
21. $\frac{79}{86}$ **23.** $\frac{29}{42}$ **25.** 2 **27.** 2 **29.** 4 **31.** 19
33. 5 **35.** 7 **37.** 39 **39.** 11 **41.** Yes, yes, yes

Pages 152–153 **1.** $3\frac{1}{2}$ **3.** 4 **5.** $4\frac{1}{3}$ **7.** $9\frac{2}{5}$
9. $16\frac{2}{7}$ **11.** $3\frac{1}{9}$ **13.** 16 **15.** $10\frac{7}{8}$ **17.** $28\frac{4}{7}$
19. $3\frac{1}{3}$ **21.** $2\frac{5}{9}$ **23.** $2\frac{1}{2}$ **25.** $\frac{7}{2}$ **27.** $\frac{41}{8}$
29. $\frac{25}{9}$ **31.** $\frac{56}{9}$ **33.** $\frac{43}{5}$ **35.** $\frac{39}{8}$ **37.** $\frac{17}{7}$
39. $\frac{77}{8}$ **41.** $\frac{13}{3}$ **43.** $\frac{53}{12}$ **45.** $\frac{64}{15}$ **47.** $\frac{99}{16}$
49. $\frac{43}{24}$ **51.** $\frac{79}{36}$ **53.** a and b are the same

nonzero number. **55.** a is less than b and b is nonzero. **57.** a is a multiple of b; a is not equal to b, and b is nonzero.

Page 154 **1.** 0.5 **3.** 0.125 **5.** 0.75 **7.** 0.9
9. 0.15 **11.** 0.16 **13.** 0.26 **15.** 0.04
17. 0.085 **19.** 0.066 **21.** 3.75 **23.** 6.5
25. 43.34375 **27.** 34.203125 **29.** 62.328
31. $\frac{3}{5}$ **33.** $\frac{17}{50}$ **35.** $\frac{1}{25}$ **37.** $\frac{89}{1000}$ **39.** $\frac{12,089}{500}$

Page 155 **1.** $0.\overline{3}$ **3.** $0.\overline{4}$ **5.** $0.\overline{45}$ **7.** $0.91\overline{6}$
9. $0.4\overline{6}$ **11.** $2.4\overline{6}$ **13.** $0.\overline{142857}$
15. $0.\overline{428571}$ **17.** $0.0\overline{675}$ **19.** $0.2\overline{16}$
21. $0.7\overline{227}$ **23.** $0.3\overline{60}$ **25.** $0.\overline{46341}$
27. $31.\overline{007017}$

Pages 156–157 **1.** $\frac{1}{6}$ **3.** $\frac{7}{24}$ **5.** $\frac{3}{8}$ **7.** $\frac{3}{8}$
9. $\frac{1}{2}$ **11.** $\frac{1}{4}$ **13.** $\frac{1}{16}$ **15.** $\frac{9}{16}$ **17.** $\frac{1}{5}$ **19.** $\frac{1}{3}$
21. 5 **23.** 10 **25.** $2\frac{1}{2}$ **27.** $3\frac{3}{4}$ **29.** $1\frac{1}{4}$
31. $\frac{6}{7}$ **33.** $3\frac{1}{3}$ **35.** $7\frac{1}{5}$ **37.** $\frac{1}{10}$ **39.** $\frac{1}{5}$
41. $4\frac{1}{12}$ **43.** $\frac{3}{10}$ **45.** $2\frac{1}{2}$ tons

Pages 158–159 **1.** 17 **3.** 34 **5.** 92 **7.** 65
9. $71\frac{1}{2}$ **11.** $4\frac{1}{3}$ **13.** $1\frac{4}{5}$ **15.** $2\frac{1}{4}$ **17.** $3\frac{4}{9}$
19. $\frac{7}{8}$ **21.** $18\frac{2}{3}$ **23.** 5 **25.** $6\frac{1}{4}$ **27.** 15

29. 36 **31.** $2\frac{1}{2}$ **33.** $4\frac{1}{8}$ **35.** 18
37. $\frac{5}{8}$ teaspoon **39.** $1\frac{2}{3}$ recipe

Page 161 **1.** $\frac{8}{5}$ **3.** $\frac{12}{7}$ **5.** $\frac{32}{23}$ **7.** 7 **9.** 16
11. $\frac{1}{5}$ **13.** $\frac{1}{12}$ **15.** $\frac{3}{8}$ **17.** $\frac{2}{11}$ **19.** $\frac{8}{19}$
21. $\frac{10}{71}$ **23.** $\frac{16}{67}$ **25.** $\frac{8}{7}$ **27.** $\frac{4}{21}$ **29.** $\frac{5}{19}$ **31.** 0

Pages 162–163 **1.** 14 **3.** $8\frac{1}{3}$ **5.** 12 **7.** 20
9. 45 **11.** $\frac{4}{5}$ **13.** $\frac{7}{16}$ **15.** $\frac{1}{2}$ **17.** $2\frac{1}{4}$ **19.** $\frac{2}{3}$
21. $\frac{2}{3}$ **23.** $1\frac{3}{4}$ **25.** 1 **27.** $1\frac{1}{6}$ **29.** $\frac{5}{8}$ **31.** $6\frac{1}{2}$
33. $8\frac{1}{2}$ **35.** 14 **37.** $33\frac{1}{3}$ **39.** 6 **41.** $8\frac{7}{16}$
43. $9\frac{1}{15}$ **45.** $14\frac{2}{5}$ **47.** $34\frac{1}{2}$ **49.** $11\frac{1}{3}$

51. 20 links **53.** Write the division as a fraction. Multiply the fraction by 1. Choose this multiplier so that the new divisor will be 1. Then multiply the numerator.

Pages 164–165 **1.** $3\frac{3}{5}$ **3.** 4 **5.** $1\frac{2}{5}$ **7.** $\frac{1}{4}$
9. $\frac{7}{20}$ **11.** 3 **13.** $\frac{1}{3}$ **15.** $4\frac{1}{2}$ **17.** $2\frac{2}{35}$
19. $\frac{34}{63}$ **21.** $\frac{6}{13}$ **23.** $2\frac{47}{99}$ **25.** 3 **27.** $1\frac{77}{128}$
29. 45 **31.** 5 **33.** 4

Pages 166–167 **1.** $s = 54$ **3.** $z = 32$
5. $w = \frac{15}{16}$ **7.** $u = \frac{6}{7}$ **9.** $x = 25\frac{2}{3}$
11. $r = 61\frac{1}{2}$ **13.** $a = 1\frac{4}{5}$ **15.** $c = \frac{23}{35}$
17. $r = 8\frac{24}{25}$ **19.** $y = 8\frac{8}{9}$ **21.** $t = 1$
23. $b = \frac{7}{10}$ **25.** $2\frac{2}{5}$ inches

Pages 168–169 **1.** $d = 12 \times 2\frac{1}{2}$; 30 nautical miles **3.** $12\frac{1}{2} = 3\frac{1}{3}r$; $3\frac{3}{4}$ nautical miles per hour **5.** $26 = 19\frac{1}{2}t$; $1\frac{1}{3}$ hours
7. $d = 5\frac{1}{4} \times 1\frac{1}{6}$; $6\frac{1}{8}$ nautical miles
9. $13 = 6\frac{1}{2}t$; 2 hours

Chapter 9

Pages 172–173 **1.** 4 **3.** 12 **5.** 20 **7.** 36
9. 18 **11.** 72 **13.** $\frac{10}{15}\frac{9}{15}$ **15.** $\frac{15}{24}\frac{16}{24}$
17. $\frac{20}{24}\frac{21}{24}$ **19.** $\frac{9}{12}\frac{2}{12}$ **21.** $\frac{9}{24}\frac{14}{24}$ **23.** $\frac{21}{30}\frac{25}{30}$

25. $\frac{18}{60}$ $\frac{25}{60}$ **27.** $\frac{28}{48}$ $\frac{9}{48}$ **29.** $\frac{27}{48}$ $\frac{22}{48}$ **31.** $\frac{6}{8}$ $\frac{5}{8}$ $\frac{4}{8}$

33. $\frac{20}{60}$ $\frac{36}{60}$ $\frac{45}{60}$ **35.** $\frac{100}{180}$ $\frac{135}{180}$ $\frac{162}{180}$ $\frac{144}{180}$ **37.** $\frac{9}{24}$ $\frac{20}{24}$ $\frac{6}{24}$ $\frac{16}{24}$

Pages 174–175 **1.** > **3.** > **5.** = **7.** >

9. = **11.** = **13.** $\frac{2}{3}$ $\frac{3}{4}$ $\frac{5}{6}$ **15.** $\frac{2}{5}$ $\frac{1}{2}$ $\frac{2}{3}$ **17.** $\frac{7}{12}$ $\frac{7}{8}$ $\frac{9}{10}$

19. $4\frac{7}{10}$ $4\frac{4}{5}$ $4\frac{5}{6}$ **21.** Spider **23.** Ladybug

25. Less than one **27.** Equal to one

Pages 176–177 **1.** $1\frac{1}{4}$ **3.** $1\frac{1}{10}$ **5.** $\frac{13}{15}$

7. $1\frac{1}{12}$ **9.** $1\frac{5}{12}$ **11.** $1\frac{3}{8}$ **13.** $1\frac{11}{40}$ **15.** $1\frac{1}{2}$

17. $1\frac{5}{8}$ **19.** $\frac{1}{6}$ **21.** $\frac{3}{20}$ **23.** $\frac{1}{6}$ **25.** $\frac{5}{24}$

27. $\frac{7}{12}$ **29.** $\frac{7}{18}$ **31.** $\frac{1}{4}$ **33.** $\frac{19}{24}$ **35.** $\frac{1}{6}$ hour

Pages 178–179 **1.** $7\frac{2}{3}$ **3.** 20 **5.** $21\frac{13}{16}$

7. $18\frac{11}{24}$ **9.** $23\frac{1}{2}$ **11.** $22\frac{1}{10}$ **13.** $28\frac{1}{2}$

15. $25\frac{1}{12}$ **17.** $19\frac{1}{24}$ **19.** $27\frac{2}{3}$ **21.** $33\frac{5}{21}$

23. 16 **25.** $17\frac{37}{60}$ **27.** $12\frac{1}{8}$ **29.** $17\frac{17}{18}$

31. $11\frac{161}{240}$ **33.** $14\frac{181}{240}$ **35.** $8\frac{23}{24}$ pounds

Pages 180–181 **1.** $7\frac{1}{2}$ **3.** $5\frac{5}{9}$ **5.** $6\frac{2}{3}$ **7.** $9\frac{11}{15}$

9. $11\frac{3}{4}$ **11.** $7\frac{5}{7}$ **13.** $23\frac{7}{18}$ **15.** $28\frac{14}{15}$ **17.** $19\frac{4}{7}$

19. $10\frac{9}{10}$ **21.** $40\frac{29}{36}$ **23.** $50\frac{4}{9}$ **25.** $\frac{1}{16}$ inch

27. $3\frac{5}{16}$ inches

Page 182 **1.** 2 **3.** $4\frac{1}{2}$ **5.** 3 **7.** $5\frac{9}{40}$ **9.** $7\frac{5}{12}$

11. $\frac{17}{20}$ **13.** $7\frac{1}{8}$ **15.** $1\frac{7}{24}$

Pages 184–185 **1.** $k = \frac{1}{2}$ **3.** $r = 7\frac{3}{5}$

5. $n = 1\frac{5}{8}$ **7.** $n = 6\frac{5}{12}$ **9.** $a = 2\frac{2}{5}$

11. $b = 5\frac{1}{3}$ **13.** $h = 1\frac{3}{10}$ **15.** $r = 3\frac{4}{7}$

17. $u = 13\frac{3}{20}$ **19.** $n = 1\frac{5}{8}$ **21.** $r = 3\frac{5}{6}$

23. $w = 42\frac{1}{2}$ **25.** $x = 8$ **27.** $n = 8\frac{1}{3}$

29. $16\frac{1}{12}$ pounds

Pages 186–187 **1.** $4\frac{19}{20} + x = 24$, $19\frac{1}{20}$ hours

3. $11\frac{3}{5} + x = 24$, $12\frac{2}{5}$ hours

5. $14\frac{1}{2} - 9\frac{1}{6} = x$, $5\frac{1}{3}$ hours

7. $3\frac{3}{8}(5\frac{1}{2}) = x$, $18\frac{9}{16}$ hours

Chapter 10

Pages 194–195 **1.** 10^2 **3.** 10^0 **5.** 10^6
  7. 10^3 **9.** 10^{-8} **11.** 1000 **13.** 0.01
  15. 1 **17.** 0.0000001 **19.** 1,000,000,000
  21. 1,000,000

Pages 196–197 **1.** 879.56 **3.** 9460
  5. 0.04384 **7.** 34,569 **9.** 89.523
  11. 0.0000023425 **13.** 17.8 **15.** 70.8
  17. 7870 **19.** 132 **21.** 15,000,000,000
  23. 10^2 cubic centimeters of wool

Pages 198–199 **1.** No **3.** No **5.** Yes **7.** No
  9. 2 **11.** 2 **13.** 1.5×10^2 **15.** 8.36×10^5
  17. 3.2×10^6 **19.** 8.752×10^2
  21. 7.06×10^4 **23.** 6×10^6 **25.** 9.25×10^2
  27. 4.82×10^1 **29.** 2.78×10^5 **31.** 1×10^1
  33. 3.5×10^7

Pages 200–201 **1.** No **3.** No **5.** No **7.** Yes
  9. -2 **11.** -2 **13.** -5 **15.** 3.69×10^{-1}
  17. 1.497×10^{-4} **19.** 4.7×10^{-2}
  21. 5×10^{-8} **23.** 6.1×10^{-5} **25.** 1×10^{-6}

Pages 202–203 **1.** 10^7 **3.** 10^{-8} **5.** 10^2
  7. 10^{-6} **9.** 10^0 **11.** 10^7 **13.** 10^{-1}
  15. 100,000 **17.** 10 **19.** 1 **21.** 10 **23.** 10
  25. $\frac{1}{10^1} \times \frac{1}{10^1} = \frac{1 \times 1}{10^1 \times 10^1} = \frac{1}{10^2} = 10^{-2}$
  27. $\frac{1}{10^4} \times \frac{1}{10^3} = \frac{1 \times 1}{10^4 \times 10^3} = \frac{1}{10^7} = 10^{-7}$

Pages 204–205 **1.** 94,500,000 **3.** 323,000
  5. 60,000,000 **7.** 0.00000013986 **9.** 0.2145
  11. 5.64672 **13.** 677,250,000 km
  15. 4,849,600,000 km **17.** 17,928,800,000 km
  19. 37,046,400,000 km

Pages 206–207 **1.** 10^3 **3.** 10^{-5} **5.** 10^5
  7. 10^{-3} **9.** 10^9 **11.** 10^{12} **13.** 10^{-1}
  15. 10^{-6} **17.** 10^0 **19.** 10 **21.** 0.01
  23. 0.1 **25.** 100 **27.** 1 **29.** 10 **31.** 10,000
  33. 10,000,000

Pages 208–209 **1.** 2300 **3.** 80,000
  5. 0.0027 **7.** 190,000,000 **9.** 3,500,000
  11. 17,000 **13.** 2 **15.** 600 **17.** 100
  19. 13,000 **21.** 500

Chapter 11

Pages 214–215 **1.** Answers will vary.
  Examples are $\frac{600}{3}$ and $\frac{200}{1}$ **3.** Answers will

vary. Examples are $\frac{540}{2}$ and $\frac{270}{1}$. **5.** Answers
will vary. Examples are $\frac{320}{1}$ and $\frac{640}{2}$.
7. Yes **9.** No **11.** No **13.** Yes **15.** No
17. Yes **19.** No **21.** Yes **23.** 100 million
liters **25.** (1.) No (2.) No (3.) No
(4.) Yes (5.) No

Pages 216–217 **1.** $r = 8$ **3.** $d = 1$
5. $m = 18$ **7.** $h = 3$ **9.** $y = 12$ **11.** $n = 35$
13. $z = 21$ **15.** $w = 36$ **17.** $a = 16$
19. $k = 9$ **21.** $h = 3$ **23.** $x = 0.9$
25. $4.95 **27.** 6 tennis balls

Pages 218–219 **1.** $\frac{2}{75} = \frac{75}{n}$, 2813 cm

3. $\frac{1}{20} = \frac{45.5}{n}$, 910 cm **5.** $\frac{3}{50} = \frac{33}{n}$, 550 cm

7. $\frac{5}{72} = \frac{4.9}{n}$, 71 m **9.** $\frac{5}{12} = \frac{n}{60}$, 25 m

11. $\frac{80}{4000} = \frac{1}{50}$, The scale is 1 to 50.

Pages 220–221 **1.** $\frac{9}{25} = \frac{x}{450}$, 162 votes

3. $\frac{5}{25} = \frac{x}{450}$, 90 votes **5.** $\frac{80}{300} = \frac{x}{10,000}$,

2667 people **7.** $\frac{75}{200} = \frac{x}{25,000}$, 9375

9. $\frac{85}{200} = \frac{x}{25,000}$, 10,625 **11.** $\frac{2}{500} = \frac{x}{100,000}$,

400 bulbs **13.** Worse than expected

Pages 222–223 **1.** 3 people per car
3. 2 people per car **5.** 17 people per car
7. 46 people per car **9.** 2 people per car
11. 765 people per car **13.** 82 people per car
15. 183 people per car **17.** 14 people per car

Pages 224–225 Answers will vary.

Chapter 12

Pages 230–231 **1.** 0.13 **3.** 0.3 **5.** 0.08
7. 0.126 **9.** 0.267 **11.** 0.038 **13.** 0.014
15. $0.12\frac{1}{2}$ **17.** $0.81\frac{2}{3}$ **19.** $0.06\frac{3}{4}$ **21.** 0.5675
23. 0 **25.** 72% **27.** 93% **29.** 9% **31.** 40%
33. 83.4% **35.** 30.9% **37.** $16\frac{1}{3}$% **39.** $45\frac{1}{2}$%
41. $3\frac{2}{3}$% **43.** 50% **45.** 6.3% **47.** 4.1%
49. 53 people **51.** 69%

Pages 232–233 **1.** 0.5 **3.** $\frac{1}{3}$ **5.** $0.66\frac{2}{3}$
7. $\frac{1}{4}$ **9.** $\frac{3}{4}$ **11.** 0.2 **13.** $\frac{2}{5}$ **15.** 0.6 **17.** $\frac{4}{5}$
19. $\frac{1}{6}$ **21.** $\frac{5}{6}$ **23.** 0.125 **25.** $\frac{3}{8}$ **27.** 0.625
29. $\frac{7}{8}$ **31.** $\frac{1}{10}$ **33.** $\frac{3}{10}$ **35.** 0.7 **37.** $\frac{9}{10}$
39. 1 **41.** $\frac{39}{100}$ **43.** $\frac{6}{25}$ **45.** $\frac{23}{40}$ **47.** 28%
49. 82.5% **51.** $57\frac{1}{7}$% **53.** 30% **55.** 12%
57. $\frac{1}{20}$ **59.** $\frac{99}{100}$; 99%

Pages 234–235 **1.** 1.2 **3.** 5 **5.** 3.08
7. 0.002 **9.** 0.001 **11.** 0.0023 **13.** $1\frac{2}{5}$
15. 4 **17.** 2 **19.** $\frac{1}{250}$ **21.** $\frac{3}{1000}$ **23.** $\frac{1}{625}$
25. 750% **27.** 300% **29.** 415% **31.** 860%
33. 0.4% **35.** 0.6% **37.** 0.7% **39.** 0.5%
41. 0.45% **43.** 80% **45.** 0.5%

Pages 236–237 **1.** 42 **3.** 68 **5.** 150 **7.** 55
9. 41.4 **11.** 60 **13.** 8.4 **15.** 54 **17.** 10
19. 54 **21.** 105 **23.** 1.6 **25.** 6.3 **27.** 4.8
29. 0.72 **31.** 0.02 **33.** $3.29 **35.** $0.44
37. $0.91

Pages 238–239 **1.** $12 **3.** $160 **5.** $180
7. $135 **9.** $837 **11.** $33.75 **13.** 3 years
15. $600 **17.** 6% **19.** 6 months **21.** $4000
23. $27,000

Pages 240–241 **1.** $6.30 **3.** $12.80
5. $15.64 **7.** $86 **9.** $60.48 **11.** $292.60
13. $335.75 **15.** $906.50 **17.** $37.40

Pages 242–243 **1.** 60% **3.** 56% **5.** 140%
7. 64% **9.** 8% **11.** $66\frac{2}{3}$% **13.** 300%
15. 12.5% **17.** 160% **19.** 0.8%
21. 178.3% **23.** 0.2% **25.** 12% **27.** 31%
29. 2%

Pages 244–245 **1.** 20% **3.** 25% **5.** 46%
7. 40% **9.** 2.5% **11.** Space heating, 57.2%;
Water heating, 15.0%; Cooking, 5.8%;
Refrigeration, 5.8%; Air conditioning, 3.8%;
Clothes drying, 1.5%; All others, 11.0%

Pages 246–247 **1.** 15 **3.** 320 **5.** 40 **7.** 450
9. 45 **11.** 75 **13.** 80 **15.** 160 **17.** 372
19. 56 **21.** 126 **23.** 3000 **25.** 770 **27.** 92
29. 175 students **31.** 740 seats

Pages 248–249 **1.** $187.50 **3.** $159.00
5. $14.50 **7.** $39.95 **9.** $6.25 **11.** $120
13. $14.40

Pages 250–251 **1.** 28% **3.** 18 **5.** 24 **7.** 42
9. 45 **11.** 80 **13.** 112 **15.** 200 **17.** 37.5%
19. 14 games **21.** $33\frac{1}{3}$% **23.** 35 games
25. 60%

Chapter 13

Pages 260–261 **1.** Plane $\mathcal{P}$ ∥ plane $\mathcal{S}$,
plane $\mathcal{N}$ ∥ plane $\mathcal{R}$ **3.** a ∥ b, a ∥ c, a ∥ d,
b ∥ c, b ∥ d, c ∥ d

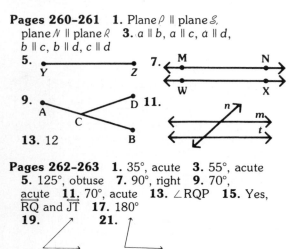

13. 12

Pages 262–263 **1.** 35°, acute **3.** 55°, acute
5. 125°, obtuse **7.** 90°, right **9.** 70°,
acute **11.** 70°, acute **13.** ∠RQP **15.** Yes,
$\overline{RQ}$ and $\overline{JT}$ **17.** 180°
19.   **21.**

23.
25. m∠6 = 105°, m∠7 = 105°, m∠8 = 75°

Pages 264–265 **1.** Angles 1, 4, 5, and 8
measure 130°. Angles 2, 3, 6, and 7
measure 50°. **3.** ∠3 and ∠6, ∠4 and ∠5;
yes **5.** ∠9 and ∠12, ∠10 and ∠11, ∠13
and ∠16, ∠14 and ∠15; yes **7.** No

Pages 266–267
1.

3. Art not actual size.

5.

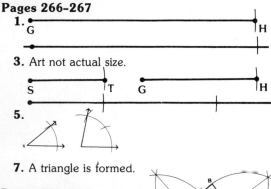

7. A triangle is formed.

Pages 268–269
1. Segment XW is
congruent to
segment YW.
3. Art is not actual
size.

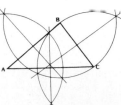

5. Art is not actual size.

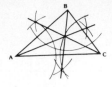

7. Construct a right angle and then bisect it.

Pages 270–271
1. Answers
will vary.
An example
is given.
3. Answers
will vary.
An example
is given.
5. Not possible **7.** Not possible
9. Answers
will vary.
An example
is given.
11. Answers
will vary.
An example
is given.
13. Not possible
15. Answers
will vary.
An example
is given.
17. Square **19.** Rhombus

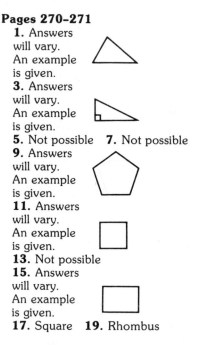

Pages 272–273 **1.** 1 **3.** 2 × 180°, or 360°
5. 3 **7.** 4 × 180°, or 720° **9.** 4
11. 5 × 180°, or 900° **13.** 5
15. 6 × 180°, or 1080° **17.** 6
19. 7 × 180°, or 1260° **21.** 7
23. 8 × 180°, or 1440° **25.** 9
27. 10 × 180°, or 1800° **29.** $(n - 2)180$;
18,000°

Pages 274–275 **1.** Yes **3.** Yes **5.** No
7. ∠X ≅ ∠R, ∠Y ≅ ∠S, ∠Z ≅ ∠T,
$\overline{XZ}$ ≅ $\overline{RT}$, $\overline{XY}$ ≅ $\overline{RS}$, $\overline{YZ}$ ≅ $\overline{ST}$ **9.** 3 cm
11. 3.6 cm **13.** 56° **15.** 2.8 cm **17.** 1.7 cm
19. 45° **21.** No. Answers will vary. The
triangles are similar but not necessarily
congruent.

Pages 276–277 **1.** and **3.** All triangles
constructed will be congruent to △ABC.

5. A correct construction is shown. Art is not actual size.

7. Not possible **9.** A correct construction is shown.

11. Not possible **13.** A correct construction is shown. Art is not actual size.

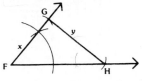

Pages 278–279 **1.** $\overline{AD}$ **3.** $\overline{AC}$, $\overline{AB}$, $\overline{BC}$, $\overline{BD}$
5. The diameter is twice as long as a radius.
7. 90° **9.** Answers will vary. **11.** Answers will vary. **13.** Answers will vary.
15. Answers will vary. **17.** The inscribed angle measures half as much as the central angle.
19. 80° **21.** 90°

Chapter 14

Pages 282–283 **1.** 14.9 cm **3.** 23.76 km
5. 246 dm **7.** 12.8 dm **9.** 2680 mm
11. 932 cm **13.** 9.2 m **15.** 43.2 cm
17. 2(22.4) + 2(18.1) = 44.8 + 36.2 = 81; 2(22.4 + 18.1) = 2(40.5) = 81

Pages 284–285 **1.** 750 mm² **3.** 5.04 cm²
5. 0.48 m² **7.** 28,900 cm² **9.** 29,768 cm²
11. 288 tiles **13.** About $8\frac{4}{7}$ m

Pages 286–287 **1.** 90 m² **3.** 7560 m²
5. 542.5 cm² **7.** 75 mm² **9.** 48 m

Pages 288–289 **1.** 31.4 cm **3.** 50.24 cm
5. 7.85 dm **7.** 26.376 km **9.** 3.14 m
11. 81.64 mm **13.** 345.4 m **15.** 94.2 cm
17. $\frac{355}{113}$

Pages 290–291 **1.** 28.26 cm² **3.** 314 m²
5. 3.14 km² **7.** 13.8474 km²
9. 0.053066 dm² **11.** 2826 m²
13. 9498.5 cm² **15.** 150.72 m²

Pages 292–293 **1.** 376 cm² **3.** 28,036 mm²
5. 360 cm² **7.** 300 m²

Pages 294–295 **1.** 150.7 mm² **3.** 650.0 dm²
5. 60.4 m² **7.** 427.0 cm²

Pages 298–299 **1.** 140 cm³ **3.** 84 mm³
5. 729 dm³ **7.** 3.5 m³

Pages 300–301 **1.** 452.2 mm³ **3.** 3617.3 dm³
5. 3.8 mm³ **7.** 254.3 cm³ **9.** 2388.0 m³

Chapter 15

Pages 304–305 **1.** 2 **3.** 3 **5.** 4 **7.** 6
9. Not a whole number **11.** Not a whole number **13.** 8 **15.** 9 **17.** Not a whole number **19.** 1-2 **21.** 2-3 **23.** 4-5 **25.** 5-6
27. 7-8 **29.** 9-10 **31.** Yes **33.** Yes
35. Yes **37.** Yes **39.** No

Page 307 **1.** 6 **3.** 4 **5.** 6 **7.** 9 **9.** 10
11. 3 **13.** 5 **15.** 23 **17.** 2 **19.** $\frac{1}{2}$ **21.** 5
23. 3 **25.** 5

Pages 308–309 **1.** $2\sqrt{2}$ **3.** $3\sqrt{2}$ **5.** $2\sqrt{6}$
7. $2\sqrt{7}$ **9.** $2\sqrt{10}$ **11.** $4\sqrt{3}$ **13.** $3\sqrt{6}$
15. $5\sqrt{3}$ **17.** $3\sqrt{10}$ **19.** $6\sqrt{5}$ **21.** $12\sqrt{2}$
23. 6 **25.** 24 **27.** $2\sqrt{5}$ **29.** 10 **31.** $2\sqrt{3}$
33. $3\sqrt{2}$ **35.** $4\sqrt{2}$ **37.** 14 **39.** 18 **41.** 26
43. 27 **45.** 45

Page 310 **1.** 1.7 **3.** 5.8 **5.** 11.4 **7.** 11.0
9. 28.0 **11.** 54.0 **13.** 12.8 **15.** 17.6
17. 24.5 **19.** 86.6 **21.** 36.5 **23.** 289.0
25. 274.3 km **27.** 419.1 km **29.** 792.0 km

Pages 312–313

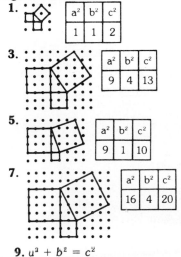

	a^2	b^2	c^2
1.	1	1	2

	a^2	b^2	c^2
3.	9	4	13

	a^2	b^2	c^2
5.	9	1	10

	a^2	b^2	c^2
7.	16	4	20

9. $a^2 + b^2 = c^2$

Pages 314–315 1. Yes **3.** Yes **5.** 3.606
7. 4.472 **9.** 13.892 **11.** 7.416 **13.** 9.798
15. 9 **17.** $b = 12.042$ **19.** $b = 5$ **21.** No

Pages 316–317 1. 7.21 km **3.** 3.61 m
5. Yes **7.** 24.19 m **9.** 97.98 m

Pages 318–319 1. $n = 6$ **3.** $n = 22$
5. $n = 35$ **7.** $n = 50$ **9.** 3.2 m

Pages 320–321 1. $\frac{3}{5} = 0.60$ **3.** $\frac{5}{13} \approx 0.38$
5. $\frac{8}{17} \approx 0.47$ **7.** $\frac{7}{25} = 0.28$ **9.** $\frac{10}{26} \approx 0.38$
11. $\frac{20}{29} \approx 0.69$ **13.** $\frac{12}{20} = 0.60$ **15.** $\frac{28}{53} \approx 0.53$
17. $\frac{4}{5} = 0.80$ **19.** $\frac{12}{13} \approx 0.92$ **21.** $\frac{15}{17} \approx 0.88$
23. $\frac{24}{25} = 0.96$ **25.** $\frac{24}{26} \approx 0.92$ **27.** $\frac{21}{29} \approx 0.72$
29. $\frac{16}{20} = 0.80$ **31.** $\frac{45}{53} \approx 0.85$ **33.** $\frac{3}{4} = 0.75$
35. $\frac{5}{12} \approx 0.42$ **37.** $\frac{8}{15} \approx 0.53$ **39.** $\frac{7}{24} \approx 0.29$
41. $\frac{10}{24} \approx 0.42$ **43.** $\frac{20}{21} \approx 0.95$ **45.** $\frac{12}{16} = 0.75$
47. $\frac{28}{45} \approx 0.62$ **49.** The ratios should be
about the same.

Pages 322–323 1. 0.956 **3.** 1.483 **5.** 0.500
7. 19.081 **9.** 2.246 **11.** $n \approx 5.74$
13. $n \approx 5.84$ **15.** $n = 10$ **17.** $n \approx 14.85$
19. $n \approx 26.22$ **21.** $n \approx 6.47$
23. About 3.43 m

Chapter 16

Pages 330–331 1. Census **3.** Sample
5. Sample **7.** (b) **9.** Answers will vary.
11.

Grade	Tally	Frequency
A	III	3
B	IIII	4
C	₩₩ ₩₩	10
D	III	3
F	II	2

13. $12\frac{1}{2}\%$ **15.** $21\frac{7}{8}\%$

Pages 332–333 1. Answers may vary. Reasons
2 and 4 are logical. **3.** Answers may vary.
Reasons 2 and 4 are logical. **5.** Answers may
vary. Reason 2 is logical. **7.** 528 loaves
9. 242 loaves **11.** 385 with, 55 without

Pages 334–335 1. $6\frac{1}{6}$ **3.** 7 **5.** $23\frac{1}{2}$
7. $250\frac{6}{13}$ **9.** 254 **11.** 58,700

Pages 336–337 1. 32 **3.** 6.6 **5.** 118 cm
7. 6.45 m

Pages 338–339 1. 173 days **3.** 130 days
5.

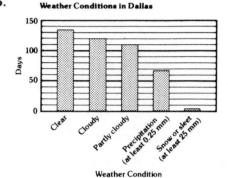

7. January 1 **9.** July 1

Pages 340–341 1. 546 million
3. 644 million **5.** 1976–1977 **7.** 210
9. 340 **11.** April **13.** January, 620;
February, 495; March, 470; April, 505;
May, 600; June, 610

Pages 342–343 1. 1.62 hours **3.** 2.16 hours
5. 15.84 hours **7.** $4,950,000
9. $12,600,000 **11.** 13% **13.** 30% **15.** 4%

Pages 344–345
1.

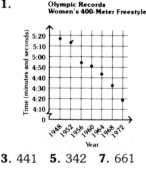

3. 441 **5.** 342 **7.** 661

Pages 346–347 1. Positive correlation
3. No correlation **5.** Negative correlation

7.

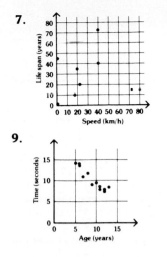

Life span (years) vs Speed (km/h)

9.

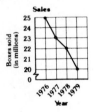

Time (seconds) vs Age (years)

Pages 348–349 **1.** Less fat than what?
3. Thicker than what? **5.** Mean, 451;
median, 40; mode, 30; Mean is the least
representative. **7.** Mean, 410; median, 270;
mode, 500; Median is the least representative.
9. Second **11.** Answers will vary. An example
is given below.

Sales — Boxes sold (in millions) vs Year (1976, 1977, 1978, 1979)

Chapter 17

Pages 352–353 **1.** 2 **3.** 1 **5.** 3 **7** BBB,
DDC, BBW, BCB, BWB, BWW, CBB, CBC,
CBW, WBB, WBC, WBW, WWB, WWW **9.** 2
11. 6 **13.** 12 **15.** 9 **17.** 81 **19.** 18

Pages 354–355 **1.** 6, 5, 4, 120 **3.** 360
5. 30 **7.** 343 **9.** 2401

Pages 356–357 **1.** $\frac{2}{12}$ or $\frac{1}{6}$ **3.** $\frac{3}{12}$ or $\frac{1}{4}$
5. $\frac{4}{12}$ or $\frac{1}{3}$ **7.** $\frac{9}{12}$ or $\frac{3}{4}$ **9.** $\frac{2}{12}$ or $\frac{1}{6}$
11. $\frac{1}{12}$ **13.** $\frac{6}{12}$ or $\frac{1}{2}$ **15.** $\frac{2}{7}$ **17.** $\frac{4}{7}$
19. $\frac{1}{7}$ **21.** $\frac{3}{7}$ **23.** $\frac{0}{7}$ or 0 **25.** $\frac{7}{7}$ or 1

Pages 358–359 **1.** 30 **3.** 14 **5.** $\frac{182}{870}$ or $\frac{91}{435}$
7. $\frac{16}{23}$ **9.** $\frac{380}{2352}$ or $\frac{95}{588}$ **11.** $\frac{650}{2352}$ or $\frac{325}{1176}$
13. $\frac{598}{2352}$ or $\frac{299}{1176}$ **15.** $\frac{570}{2352}$ or $\frac{95}{392}$

Pages 360–361 **1.** $\frac{10}{20}$ or $\frac{1}{2}$ **3.** $\frac{5}{20}$ or $\frac{1}{4}$ **5.** $\frac{11}{20}$
7. 27 times **9.** About 14 times **11.** 30 times
13. About 188 potatoes

Pages 364–365 **1.** $\frac{25}{144}$ **3.** $\frac{125}{1728}$ **5.** $\frac{12}{20}$ or $\frac{3}{5}$
7. $\frac{1}{4}$ **9.** $\frac{1}{36}$ **11.** $\frac{1}{216}$ **13.** $\frac{1}{36}$

Pages 366–367 **1.** $\frac{1}{42}$ **3.** $\frac{4}{63}$ **5.** $\frac{1}{119}$ **7.** $\frac{304}{3927}$
9. $\frac{1}{15}$ **11.** $\frac{1}{20}$ **13.** $\frac{1}{6}$

Chapter 18

Pages 370–371 **1.** -17 **3.** 0 **5.** $\frac{8}{1}$ **7.** $\frac{15}{1}$
9. $\frac{4}{100}$ **11.** $\frac{25}{100}$ **13.** $\frac{16}{5}$ **15.** $\frac{2}{3}$ **17.** Answers
may vary. Examples are $\frac{5}{1}$, $\frac{-5}{-1}$, and $\frac{10}{2}$.
19. Answers may vary. Examples are $\frac{1}{1}$, $\frac{-2}{-2}$,
and $\frac{3}{3}$. **21.** Answers may vary. Examples
are $\frac{10}{3}$, $\frac{20}{6}$, and $\frac{30}{9}$. **23.** Answers may vary.
Examples are $\frac{17}{4}$, $\frac{34}{8}$, and $\frac{51}{12}$. **25.** Whole
number, integer, rational number
27. Whole number, integer, rational
number **29.** Whole number, integer,
rational number **31.** Rational number
33. Whole number, integer, rational number

Pages 372–373 **1** $\frac{-6}{5}$ **3.** $\frac{-12}{5}$ **5.** $\frac{7}{9}$ **7.** $\frac{70}{35}$
9. < **11.** = **13.** < **15.** > **17.** < **19.** >
21. $\frac{-5}{6}$ $\frac{3}{-8}$ $\frac{-3}{4}$ **23.** $\frac{6}{-4}$ $\frac{-1}{2}$ $\frac{-7}{-8}$ **25.** $\frac{-5}{2}$ -2 $\frac{3}{-2}$
27. -1.7 -1.5 -1.4 **29.** $-8\frac{1}{5}$ -8 $-7\frac{1}{8}$

Pages 374–375 **1.** $-1\frac{2}{15}$ **3.** $-\frac{1}{8}$ **5.** $-\frac{23}{42}$
7. $\frac{1}{2}$ **9.** $\frac{1}{8}$ **11.** $-4\frac{1}{7}$ **13.** -3.8 **15.** -9.6
17. $-\frac{7}{12}$ **19.** $-2\frac{7}{8}$ **21.** $-\frac{11}{20}$ **23.** $-\frac{1}{12}$
25. $-1\frac{1}{4}$ **27.** $-3\frac{5}{12}$ **29.** $-\frac{5}{12}$ **31.** -1
33. 0.83

Pages 376–377 **1.** $x = -2$ **3.** $r = -3$
5. $b = 6$ **7.** $m = -9.5$ **9.** $c = 10$
11. $q = 10.6$ **13.** $y = -6$ **15.** $x = -5.1$
17. $d = -\frac{1}{6}$ **19.** $n = \frac{1}{8}$ **21.** $t = -\frac{3}{4}$
23. $b = -4\frac{3}{10}$ **25.** $z = -1\frac{7}{8}$ **27.** $t = -5\frac{3}{4}$

29. The water level dropped 251.26 cm the last half of the year.

Pages 378–379 **1.** $x = 5$ **3.** $n = 4$
5. $t = -2$ **7.** $y = 5$ **9.** $a = 10$
11. $d = -11$ **13.** $c = 5.6$ **15.** $k = 2.172$
17. $w = 2.95$ **19.** $x = \frac{7}{20}$ **21.** $a = -\frac{1}{8}$
23. $y = 1\frac{14}{15}$ **25.** $z = 5\frac{1}{10}$

Pages 380–381 **1.** $\frac{1}{3}$ **3.** $\frac{9}{28}$ **5.** $-2\frac{2}{3}$ **7.** $-2\frac{11}{12}$
9. $1\frac{1}{2}$ **11.** -2 **13.** $-\frac{3}{8}$ **15.** 9 **17.** $\frac{8}{15}$
19. -13.77 **21.** -0.189 **23.** -15
25. $-3.9°$ **27.** $-1.7°$

Pages 382–383 **1.** $\frac{3}{5}a$ **3.** $\frac{1}{3}c$ **5.** $-\frac{2}{9}y$
7. $-\frac{1}{12}v$ **9.** $-\frac{5}{11}s$ **11.** $-\frac{1}{5}r$ **13.** $-1n$
15. $-\frac{1}{4}k$ **17.** $-\frac{1}{10}x$ **19.** $-2\frac{1}{10}$ **21.** $-\frac{3}{10}$
23. $\frac{29}{30}$ **25.** $\frac{1}{5}$ **27.** $-\frac{2}{5}$ **29.** $-\frac{1}{12}$ **31.** $\frac{1}{12}$
33. -2.45 **35.** -8.54 **37.** 6.25

Pages 384–385 **1.** $n = -\frac{3}{10}$ **3.** $a = 10\frac{2}{3}$
5. $x = -1\frac{1}{2}$ **7.** $d = -33$ **9.** $s = -12$
11. $b = -2\frac{2}{5}$ **13.** $t = \frac{4}{7}$ **15.** $p = 9\frac{1}{3}$
17. $f = 1\frac{1}{5}$ **19.** $y = -21$ **21.** $x = -\frac{2}{21}$
23. $a = -\frac{2}{63}$ **25.** $n = \frac{3}{4}$ **27.** $t = -\frac{3}{4}$
29. $x = -14$ **31.** $a = \frac{4}{9}$ **33.** $n = -\frac{1}{4}$
35. $t = 3\frac{1}{2}$

Pages 386–387 **1.** $x = 2$ **3.** $t = -3$
5. $x = 5$ **7.** $d = -3\frac{1}{3}$ **9.** $y = 7$
11. $y = 3\frac{2}{3}$ **13.** $b = 0$ **15.** $e = -1$
17. $k = -2$ **19.** $x = -\frac{1}{5}$ **21.** $g = \frac{11}{12}$
23. $y = -3$ **25.** $m = -4\frac{1}{2}$ **27.** $n = -2$
29. $y = 20$ **31.** $62

Pages 388–389 **1.** $x > 100$ **3.** $x < 10$
5.

$\begin{array}{ccccccccc} -7 & -6 & -5 & -4 & -3 & -2 & -1 & 0 & 1 \end{array}$

7.

$\begin{array}{ccccccccc} 2 & 3 & 4 & 5 & 6 & 7 & 8 & 9 & 10 \end{array}$

9.

$\begin{array}{ccccccccc} -7 & -6 & -5 & -4 & -3 & -2 & -1 & 0 & 1 \end{array}$

11.

$\begin{array}{ccccccccc} -3 & -2 & -1 & 0 & 1 & 2 & 3 & 4 & 5 \end{array}$

13.

$\begin{array}{ccccccccc} 5 & 6 & 7 & 8 & 9 & 10 & 11 & 12 & 13 \end{array}$

15.

$\begin{array}{ccccccccc} -7 & -6 & -5 & -4 & -3 & -2 & -1 & 0 & 1 \end{array}$

17.

$\begin{array}{ccccccccc} -6 & -5 & -4 & -3 & -2 & -1 & 0 & 1 & 2 \end{array}$

19.

$\begin{array}{ccccccccc} -9 & -8 & -7 & -6 & -5 & -4 & -3 & -2 & -1 \end{array}$

Pages 390–391 **1.** $5 < 10$ **3.** $2 > -1$
5. $-2.9 < 5.1$ **7.** $0 < 15.4$ **9.** $4 > -1$
11. $-6.5 < -5.5$ **13.** $2.5 > -6$ **15.** $0 < 1.5$
17. $20 < 24$ **19.** $19.5 > -3$ **21.** $-32 < -28$
23. $0 > -4.2$ **25.** $-1.5 < 1$ **27.** No
29. $-4 > -9$ **31.** $27 > -3$ **33.** $-40 < 40$
35. $16 < 37$ **37.** $1 < 3$

Pages 392–393 **1.** $x < -2$ **3.** $z > 24$
5. $d \geq -4$ **7.** $16.1 < x$ **9.** $2.4 > r$
11. $2.7 \leq t$ **13.** $z \geq -0.4$ **15.** $x < -2.39$
17. $x \geq 6$ **19.** $e > 4$ **21.** $x < -13$
23. $x < -1.5$ **25.** $s \geq -12$ **27.** $t > 16$
29. $y > -4$ **31.** More than 7 sales

Trigonometric Ratios

Measure of angle	tan	sin	cos	Measure of angle	tan	sin	cos
1°	0.017	0.017	1.000	46°	1.036	0.719	0.695
2°	0.035	0.035	0.999	47°	1.072	0.731	0.682
3°	0.052	0.052	0.999	48°	1.111	0.743	0.669
4°	0.070	0.070	0.998	49°	1.150	0.755	0.656
5°	0.087	0.087	0.996	50°	1.192	0.766	0.643
6°	0.105	0.105	0.995	51°	1.235	0.777	0.629
7°	0.123	0.122	0.993	52°	1.280	0.788	0.616
8°	0.141	0.139	0.990	53°	1.327	0.799	0.602
9°	0.158	0.156	0.988	54°	1.376	0.809	0.588
10°	0.176	0.174	0.985	55°	1.428	0.819	0.574
11°	0.194	0.191	0.982	56°	1.483	0.829	0.559
12°	0.213	0.208	0.978	57°	1.540	0.839	0.545
13°	0.231	0.225	0.974	58°	1.600	0.848	0.530
14°	0.249	0.242	0.970	59°	1.664	0.857	0.515
15°	0.268	0.259	0.966	60°	1.732	0.866	0.500
16°	0.287	0.276	0.961	61°	1.804	0.875	0.485
17°	0.306	0.292	0.956	62°	1.881	0.883	0.469
18°	0.325	0.309	0.951	63°	1.963	0.891	0.454
19°	0.344	0.326	0.946	64°	2.050	0.899	0.438
20°	0.364	0.342	0.940	65°	2.145	0.906	0.423
21°	0.384	0.358	0.934	66°	2.246	0.914	0.407
22°	0.404	0.375	0.927	67°	2.356	0.921	0.391
23°	0.424	0.391	0.921	68°	2.475	0.927	0.375
24°	0.445	0.407	0.914	69°	2.605	0.934	0.358
25°	0.466	0.423	0.906	70°	2.748	0.940	0.342
26°	0.488	0.438	0.899	71°	2.904	0.946	0.326
27°	0.510	0.454	0.891	72°	3.078	0.951	0.309
28°	0.532	0.469	0.883	73°	3.271	0.956	0.292
29°	0.554	0.485	0.875	74°	3.487	0.961	0.276
30°	0.577	0.500	0.866	75°	3.732	0.966	0.259
31°	0.601	0.515	0.857	76°	4.011	0.970	0.242
32°	0.625	0.530	0.848	77°	4.332	0.974	0.225
33°	0.649	0.545	0.839	78°	4.705	0.978	0.208
34°	0.675	0.559	0.829	79°	5.145	0.982	0.191
35°	0.700	0.574	0.819	80°	5.671	0.985	0.174
36°	0.727	0.588	0.809	81°	6.314	0.988	0.156
37°	0.754	0.602	0.799	82°	7.115	0.990	0.139
38°	0.781	0.616	0.788	83°	8.144	0.993	0.122
39°	0.810	0.629	0.777	84°	9.514	0.995	0.105
40°	0.839	0.643	0.766	85°	11.430	0.996	0.087
41°	0.869	0.656	0.755	86°	14.301	0.998	0.070
42°	0.900	0.669	0.743	87°	19.081	0.999	0.052
43°	0.933	0.682	0.731	88°	28.636	0.999	0.035
44°	0.966	0.695	0.719	89°	57.290	1.000	0.017
45°	1.000	0.707	0.707				

Tangent

length of opposite side
length of adjacent side

Sine

length of opposite side
length of hypotenuse

Cosine

length of adjacent side
length of hypotenuse

Metric System

Length

The basic unit of length is the meter*. The distance from a door knob to the floor is about 1 meter.

Millimeter, centimeter, and kilometer are other commonly used units of length.

The thickness of a dime is about 1 millimeter.

The distance across a fingernail is about 1 centimeter.

The length of ten football fields placed end to end is about 1 kilometer.

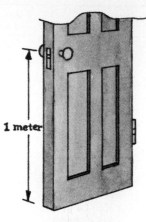

1 meter

Mass (weight)**

The basic unit of mass is the kilogram. The mass of this football is about 1 kilogram.

Gram is another commonly used unit of mass. The mass of a dollar bill is about 1 gram.

The mass of a grain of sand is about 1 milligram.

Capacity

The basic unit of capacity is the liter*. This milk carton holds about 1 liter.

Milliliter is another commonly used unit of capacity. An eyedropper holds about 1 milliliter of liquid.

*The word *meter* may also be spelled *metre,* and the word *liter* may be spelled *litre.* The -*er* spelling is in common usage in the United States and appears in this program.

**The units of mass are often referred to as units of weight. In common usage and in this program, the term *weight* is generally used to mean *mass* and the term *weigh* to mean *determine the mass of* or *have a mass of.*

Area

Square centimeter and square meter are commonly used units of area in the metric system.

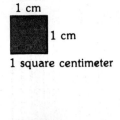

1 square centimeter

Volume

The cubic centimeter is a commonly used unit of volume. If the cube shown here were filled with water, the amount of water would be 1 milliliter. The mass of the water would be 1 gram.

A cube with a volume of 1 cubic decimeter measures 1 decimeter, or 10 centimeters, on each edge. If a cubic decimeter were filled with water, the amount of water would be 1 liter. The mass of the water would be 1 kilogram.

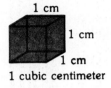

1 cubic centimeter

Temperature

The Celsius scale is commonly used in countries employing the metric system.

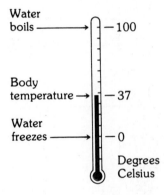

Water boils → — 100

Body temperature → — 37

Water freezes → — 0

Degrees Celsius

Prefixes and Symbols

This table shows the most common prefixes in the metric system, as well as their symbols and meanings.

Prefix	Symbol	Meaning
mega-	M	million
kilo-	k	thousand
hecto-	h	hundred
deka-	da	ten
deci-	d	tenth
centi-	c	hundredth
milli-	m	thousandth
micro-	μ	millionth

This display relates some of the prefixes in the metric system to the base-ten numeration system.

	kilo- thousands	hecto- hundreds	deka- tens	ones	deci- tenths	centi- hundredths	milli- thousandths

Here are official symbols for some common metric measures. They do not need periods. You need not add an -s for the plural form.

meter	m
kilometer	km
centimeter	cm
millimeter	mm
liter	L
milliliter	mL
kilogram	kg
gram	g
square meter	m^2
square centimeter	cm^2
cubic meter	m^3
cubic centimeter	cm^3

Tables

Metric System

Length

$$10 \text{ millimeters (mm)} = 1 \text{ centimeter (cm)}$$
$$\left.\begin{array}{l} 10 \text{ centimeters} \\ 100 \text{ millimeters} \end{array}\right\} = 1 \text{ decimeter (dm)}$$
$$\left.\begin{array}{l} 10 \text{ decimeters} \\ 100 \text{ centimeters} \end{array}\right\} = 1 \text{ meter (m)}$$
$$1000 \text{ meters} = 1 \text{ kilometer (km)}$$

Area

100 square millimeters (mm²) = 1 square centimeter (cm²)
10,000 square centimeters = 1 square meter (m²)
100 square meters = 1 are (a)
10,000 square meters = 1 hectare (ha)

Volume

1000 cubic millimeters (mm³) = 1 cubic centimeter (cm³)
1000 cubic centimeters = 1 cubic decimeter (dm³)
1,000,000 cubic centimeters = 1 cubic meter (m³)

Mass (weight)

1000 milligrams (mg) = 1 gram (g)
1000 grams = 1 kilogram (kg)
1000 kilograms = 1 metric ton (t)

Capacity

1000 milliliters (mL) = 1 liter (L)

Customary System

Length

12 inches (in.) = 1 foot (ft.)
$$\left.\begin{array}{l} 3 \text{ feet} \\ 36 \text{ inches} \end{array}\right\} = 1 \text{ yard (yd.)}$$
$$\left.\begin{array}{l} 1760 \text{ yards} \\ 5280 \text{ feet} \end{array}\right\} = 1 \text{ mile (mi.)}$$
6076 feet = 1 nautical mile

Area

144 square inches (sq. in.) = 1 square foot (sq. ft.)
9 square feet = 1 square yard (sq. yd.)
4840 square yards = 1 acre (A.)

Volume

1728 cubic inches (cu. in.) = 1 cubic foot (cu. ft.)
27 cubic feet = 1 cubic yard (cu. yd.)

Weight

16 ounces (oz.) = 1 pound (lb.)
2000 pounds = 1 ton (T.)

Capacity

8 fluid ounces (fl. oz.) = 1 cup (c.)
2 cups = 1 pint (pt.)
2 pints = 1 quart (qt.)
4 quarts = 1 gallon (gal.)

Time

60 seconds = 1 minute
60 minutes = 1 hour
24 hours = 1 day
7 days = 1 week
$$\left.\begin{array}{l} 365 \text{ days} \\ 52 \text{ weeks} \\ 12 \text{ months} \end{array}\right\} = 1 \text{ year}$$
366 days = 1 leap year

Geometric Formulas

Area

rectangle	$A = lw$
parallelogram	$A = bh$
triangle	$A = \frac{1}{2}bh$
circle	$A = \pi r^2$
trapezoid	$A = \frac{1}{2}h(a + b)$

Surface Area

cylinder	$A = 2\pi r^2 + 2\pi rh$
cone	$A = \pi r^2 + \pi rs$

Circumference

circle	$C = \pi d$ or
	$C = 2\pi r$

Perimeter

rectangle	$P = 2l + 2w$
rhombus	$P = 4s$
parallelogram	$P = 2a + 2b$

Volume

rectangular prism	$V = lwh$
prism	$V = Bh$
pyramid	$V = \frac{1}{3}Bh$
cylinder	$V = \pi r^2 h$
cone	$V = \frac{1}{3}\pi r^2 h$

Pythagorean Relation $a^2 + b^2 = c^2$

Glossary

Acute angle An angle that has a measure less than 90°.

Addition property of zero The sum of zero and a number is that number.

Adjacent angles Angles ABC and CBD are adjacent.

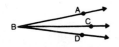

Alternate interior angles Angles 3 and 5 are alternate interior angles.

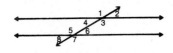

Altitude of a triangle A segment that extends from one vertex of the triangle to the opposite side and is perpendicular to that side.

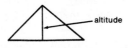

altitude

Angle ($\angle$) Two rays with the same endpoint.

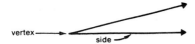

vertex

side

Arc Part of a circle.

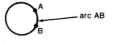

arc AB

Area A number indicating the size of the inside of a plane figure.

Associative property of addition The way in which addends are grouped does not affect the sum.
$$(7 + 2) + 5 = 7 + (2 + 5)$$

Associative property of multiplication The way in which factors are grouped does not affect the product.
$$(7 \times 2) \times 5 = 7 \times (2 \times 5)$$

Average A number obtained by dividing the sum of two or more addends by the number of addends.

Central angle An angle with its vertex at the center of a circle.

Chord A segment whose endpoints are on a circle. A diameter is a special chord.

Circle A plane figure with all of its points the same distance from a given point called the center.

Circumference The distance around a circle.

Common denominator A common multiple of two or more denominators. A common denominator for $\frac{1}{6}$ and $\frac{3}{8}$ is 48.

Common factor A number that is a factor of two or more numbers. A common factor of 6 and 12 is 3.

Common multiple A number that is a multiple of two or more numbers. A common multiple of 4 and 6 is 12.

Commutative property of addition The order in which numbers are added does not affect the sum.
$$4 + 6 = 6 + 4$$

Commutative property of multiplication The order in which numbers are multiplied does not affect the product.
$$4 \times 6 = 6 \times 4$$

Composite number A whole number, greater than 0, that has more than two factors.

Concentric circles Circles in the same plane that have the same center but different radii.

Cone A space figure shaped like this.

Congruent Having the same size and the same shape.

Consecutive angles In this quadrilateral, angles J and K are consecutive.

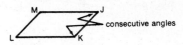

consecutive angles

Cosine For a given acute angle in a right triangle, the ratio:
$$\frac{\text{length of adjacent side}}{\text{length of hypotenuse}}$$

Cross-products For the ratios $\frac{3}{4}$ and $\frac{9}{12}$, the cross-products are 3×12 and 4×9.

Cube A prism with all square faces.

Cylinder A space figure shaped like this.

Degree (of an angle) A unit for measuring angles.

Diagonal   In a polygon, a segment that connects one vertex to another vertex but is not a side of the polygon.

Diameter   In a circle, a segment that passes through the center and has its endpoints on the circle.

Distributive property   A distributive property that relates multiplication and addition is used in this number sentence.
$$4 \times (7 + 3) =$$
$$(4 \times 7) + (4 \times 3)$$

Dividend   A number that is divided by another number. In $48 \div 6 = 8$, the dividend is 48.

Divisor   A number that divides another number. In $48 \div 6 = 8$, the divisor is 6.

Edge   In a space figure, a segment where two faces meet.

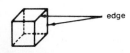

Endpoint   The point at the end of a segment or ray.

Equation   A mathematical sentence that uses the = symbol.
$$14 - 7 = 7$$

Equilateral triangle   A triangle with all three sides congruent.

Even number   A whole number with a factor of 2.

Exponent   In 4^3, the exponent is 3. It tells that 4 is to be used as a factor three times.
$$4^3 = 4 \times 4 \times 4$$

Face   A flat surface that is part of a polyhedron.

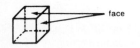

Factor   A number to be multiplied. In $3 \times 7 = 21$, the factors are 3 and 7.

Factorial   The product of a whole number and every whole number less than itself.
$$4! = 4 \times 3 \times 2 \times 1 = 24$$

Fraction   A number such as $\frac{2}{3}$. In $\frac{2}{3}$, the numerator 2 tells how many equal parts or items are being considered. The denominator 3 gives the total number of equal parts or items.

Frequency table   In statistics, a listing of the data and how many times each item of data occurred.

Greatest common factor   The greatest number that is a factor of two or more numbers. The greatest common factor of 8 and 12 is 4.

Hexagon   A six-sided polygon.

Hypotenuse   In a right triangle, the side opposite the right angle.

Improper fraction   A fraction that can be written as a mixed number or as a whole number greater than zero, such as $\frac{15}{2}$ or $\frac{2}{1}$.

Inscribed angle   An angle whose vertex is on a circle and whose sides cut off an arc of the circle.

Inscribed polygon   A polygon inside a circle with its vertices on the circle.

Integers   The whole numbers and their opposites. Some integers are $+2$, -2, $+75$, and -75.

Intersecting lines   Two lines that meet at exactly one point.

Isosceles triangle   A triangle with at least two sides congruent.

Least common multiple   The smallest number that is a common multiple of two given numbers. The least common multiple for 6 and 8 is 24.

Lowest terms   A fraction is in lowest terms if 1 is the only number that will divide both the numerator and the denominator.

Mean   Another name for "average." The mean of the set 2, 4, 5, 6, 6 is $23 \div 5$, or 4.6.

Median   The middle number in a set of numbers when the numbers are in order. The median of the set 2, 4, 5, 6, 6 is 5.

Midpoint   The point in a segment that divides it into two equal parts.

Mixed number   A number that has a whole number part and a fraction part, such as $3\frac{1}{4}$ and $6\frac{7}{8}$.

Mode   The number that occurs most often in a set of numbers. The mode of the set 2, 4, 5, 6, 6 is 6.

Multiple   A multiple of a number is the product of that number and a whole number. Some multiples of 3 are 3, 6, and 9.

Multiplication property of one   The product of a number and one is that number.

Negative integer   An integer less than 0, such as -1, -5, -7, or -10.

Obtuse angle   An angle that has a measure greater than 90°.

Octagon   An eight-sided polygon.

Odd number A whole number that does not have 2 as a factor.

Opposite angles In this quadrilateral, angles J and L are opposite angles.

Opposites Two numbers whose sum is 0. +5 and −5 are opposites because +5 + (−5) = 0.

Ordered pair A number pair, such as (3, 5), where 3 is the first number and 5 is the second number.

Origin On a coordinate grid, the point (0, 0) where the two number lines, or axes, intersect.

Parallel lines Lines in the same plane that do not meet.

Parallelogram A quadrilateral with opposite sides parallel.

Pentagon A five-sided polygon.

Percent (%) A word indicating "hundredths" or "out of 100." 45 percent (45%) means 0.45 or $\frac{45}{100}$.

Perimeter The distance around a polygon.

Permutations The ordered arrangements of a set of objects or numbers. The permutations of the set A, B, C are:

ABC BAC CAB
ACB BCA CBA

Perpendicular lines Two intersecting lines that form right angles.

Pi (π) The number obtained by dividing the circumference of any circle by its diameter. A common approximation for π is 3.14.

Polygon A plane figure made up of segments.

Polyhedron A space figure with all flat surfaces. The outline of each surface is a polygon.

Positive integer An integer greater than 0, such as +1, +2, +10, or +35.

Power 3^4 is read "3 to the fourth power."
$3^4 = 3 \times 3 \times 3 \times 3 = 81$
The fourth power of 3 is 81. 4^2 is read "4 to the second power" or "4 squared." *See* Exponent.

Precision A property of measurement that depends upon the size of the unit of measure. The smaller the unit, the more precise the measurement.

Prime factor A factor that is a prime number. The prime factors of 10 are 2 and 5.

Prime number A whole number, greater than 1, that has exactly two factors: itself and 1. 17 is a prime number.

Prism A polyhedron with two parallel faces, called *bases*, that are congruent.

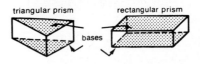

triangular prism   rectangular prism

bases

Probability A number that tells how likely it is that a certain event will happen.

Proportion A statement that two ratios are equal.
$$\frac{2}{5} = \frac{12}{30}$$

Pyramid Space figures shaped like these.

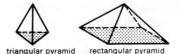

triangular pyramid   rectangular pyramid

Quadrant One of the four parts into which a plane is divided by two perpendicular lines.

Quadrilateral A four-sided polygon.

Quotient The answer to a division problem. In 48 ÷ 6 = 8, the quotient is 8.

Radius A segment with endpoints that are the center of a circle and a point on the circle.

Ratio A pair of numbers that expresses a rate or a comparison.

Rational number Any number that can be expressed as either a terminating decimal or a repeating decimal.
$4\frac{3}{4} = 4.75$ $\frac{1}{3} = 0.333\ldots$

Ray Part of a line that has one endpoint and goes on and on in one direction.

Reciprocals Two numbers whose product is 1. $\frac{3}{4}$ and $\frac{4}{3}$ are reciprocals because $\frac{3}{4} \times \frac{4}{3} = 1$.

Rectangle A parallelogram with four right angles.

Rectangular prism *See* Prism.

Rectangular pyramid *See* Pyramid.

Regular polygon A polygon with all sides congruent and all angles congruent.

Repeating decimal A decimal in which one or more digits keep repeating.
  0.5181818 . . .

Rhombus A parallelogram whose sides are congruent.

Right angle An angle that has a measure of 90°.

Right triangle A triangle with one right angle.

Scalene triangle A triangle with no two sides congruent.

Scientific notation A method of expressing a number as a product so that:

• the first factor is a number greater than or equal to 1, and less than 10, and

• the second factor is a power of 10.

Segment Part of a line, including the two endpoints.

Semicircle An arc that is one half of a circle.

Significant digits In a measurement, the digits needed to tell how many times the unit of measure is used. The measurement 7.60 meters has three significant digits, 7, 6, and 0.

Similar figures Figures with the same shape but not necessarily the same size.

Sine For a given acute angle in a right triangle, the ratio:
$$\frac{\text{length of opposite side}}{\text{length of hypotenuse}}$$

Sphere A space figure with all of its points the same distance from a given point called the *center*.

Square A rectangle with all four sides congruent.

Square root A number a is the square root of a number b if $a \times a = b$. 3 is the square root of 9.

Surface area The sum of the areas of all the surfaces of a space figure.

Tangent For a given acute angle in a right triangle, the ratio:
$$\frac{\text{length of opposite side}}{\text{length of adjacent side}}$$

Terminating decimal A decimal with a limited number of nonzero digits. Examples are 0.5 and 0.0082.

Transversal A line that intersects two or more lines in the same plane.

Trapezoid A quadrilateral with one pair of parallel sides.

Triangle A three-sided polygon.

Triangular prism *See* Prism.

Triangular pyramid *See* Pyramid.

Trigonometric ratios *See* Cosine, Sine, *and* Tangent.

Variable In an expression or an equation, a letter that represents a number.

Vertex (1) the common endpoint of two rays that form an angle. (2) The point of intersection of two sides of a polygon. (3) The point of intersection of the edges of a polyhedron.

Volume A number indicating the size of the inside of a space figure.

Index

surface area of, 292-293
volume of, 298-299
Positive correlation, 346
Positive integers, 94
Powers of ten, 2, 194-209,
305, 411-412
Precision in measurement,
60-61
Predictions, see Probability,
Statistics
Prime factor, 138-139
Prime factorization, 138-139,
241, 407
Prime number, 134-135
Prism, 292
surface area of, 292-293
volume of, 56-57, 59, 298-299
Probability
choices
counting by multiplication,
354-355
counting by tree diagram,
352-353
dependent, 366-367
independent, 364-365
computing, 358-359, 364-367
formula for, 356
meaning of, 356-357
outcomes
equally likely, 356-357
favorable, 356-357
possible, 352, 356-357
predictions, 360-361
tree diagrams, 352-354
Problems Around Us, 63, 129,
189, 255, 325, 395
Problem solving, 18-19, 34-35,
74-75, 82-83, 124-125,
168-169, 186-187,
218-219, 220-221,
222-223, 224-225,
240-241, 244-245,
248-249, 250-251,
316-317
adding decimals, 32-33
adding fractions and mixed
numbers, 176-179
adding whole numbers, 8-9
area, 54-55, 284-287,
290-291, 296-297
choosing the operation, 74-75,
82-83, 168-169, 186-187
circles, 288-291
dividing decimals, 40-43, 80-85

dividing fractions and mixed
numbers, 162-165,
168-169
dividing whole numbers,
16-19, 92
estimating, 6-7, 10, 30-31,
38-39
exponents, 22
graphs, 114-117, 122-125,
338-343
inequalities and, 392-393
integers, 98-99, 106-107
interest, 238-239, 252
interpreting remainders, 18-19
multiple-step problems, 240-241
multiplying decimals, 36-37
multiplying fractions and mixed
numbers, 156-160,
166-169
multiplying whole numbers,
12-13
percent, 230-233, 236-253,
342-343
perimeter, 282-283
powers of ten, 196-197
probability, 352-367
proportions, 214-223,
226-227, 318-319
Pythagorean relation, 314-317
rational numbers, 376-377,
380-381, 386-387
scale models, 218-219
scientific notation, 204-205,
208-209
similar triangles, 318-319
statistics, 330-337, 344-350
subtracting decimals, 32-35,
44, 72-75
subtracting fractions and mixed
numbers, 176-177,
180-181, 184-187
subtracting whole numbers, 8-9
surface area, 292-295, 302
too much or too little
information, 34-35, 63
trigonometric ratios, 320-323
volume, 56-57, 59, 298-301
write a problem, 224-225
Products, estimating, 10-11,
38-39
Proportions, 214-215
cross-products, 214-215
scale models, 218-219
similar triangles and, 318-319

solving, 216-223, 326, 333, 412
Protractor, 262
Pyramid, 292
surface area of, 292-293
volume of, 298-299
Pythagorean relation, 312-317

Quadrant, 112
Quadrilateral, 270-271
parallelogram, 271
rectangle, 271
rhombus, 271
square, 271
trapezoid, 271

Radius, 278
Random digits, 362-363
Range, see Statistics
Rational numbers, 370
adding, 374-375
comparing, 372-373
density of, 383
dividing, 380-381
equations involving, 376-379,
384-387
evaluating expressions with,
374-375, 380-383
inequalities involving, 390-393
meaning of, 370-371
multiplying, 380-381
ordering, 372-373
reciprocal of, 380
subtracting, 374-375
Ratios, 214-215
equal, 214-215
trigonometric, 320-323
Ray, 261
endpoint, 261
Reciprocal, 161, 380
using to solve equations,
166-167, 384-385
Rectangle, 271
area of, 54-55, 284-285
Regular polygon, 273
Repeating decimals, 155
Repetend, 155
Review, unit, 65, 131, 191, 257,
327, 397
Rhombus, 271
Right angle, 262-263
Right triangle, 270
hypotenuse, 314
Pythagorean relation, 314-317
trigonometric ratios, 320-323